Essentials of Psychologic...

Everything you need to know to administer, score, and interpret the major psy...

Essentials

of **Psychological Assessment** Series

ORDER FORM

Please send this order form with your payment (credit card or check) to:
John Wiley & Sons, Attn: J. Knott, 111 River Street, Hoboken, NJ 07030-5774

QUANTITY	TITLE	ISBN	PRICE
_____	_____	_____	_____
_____	_____	_____	_____
_____	_____	_____	_____
_____	_____	_____	_____
_____	_____	_____	_____

Shipping Charges:	Surface	2-Day	1-Day
First item	$5.00	$10.50	$17.50
Each additional item	$3.00	$3.00	$4.00

For orders greater than 15 items,
please contact Customer Care at 1-877-762-2974.

ORDER AMOUNT _____
SHIPPING CHARGES _____
SALES TAX _____
TOTAL ENCLOSED _____

NAME_____

AFFILIATION _____

ADDRESS_____

CITY/STATE/ZIP _____

TELEPHONE _____

EMAIL_____

❑ Please add me to your e-mailing list

PAYMENT METHOD:

❑ Check/Money Order   ❑ Visa   ❑ Mastercard   ❑ AmEx

Card Number _____ Exp. Date _____

Cardholder Name (Please print) _____

Signature _____

*Make checks payable to **John Wiley & Sons**. Credit card orders invalid if not signed.
All orders subject to credit approval. • Prices subject to change.*

**To order by phone, call toll free 1-877-762-2974
To order online: www.wiley.com/essentials**

Essentials of Psychological Testing

Essentials of Behavioral Science Series

Founding Editors, Alan S. Kaufman and Nadeen L. Kaufman

Essentials

of Psychological Testing

Susana Urbina

John Wiley & Sons, Inc.

Published by John Wiley & Sons, Inc., Hoboken, New Jersey.
Published simultaneously in Canada.

For general information on our other products and services please contact our Customer Care Department within the U.S. at (800) 762-2974, outside the United States at (317) 572-3993 or fax (317) 572-4002.

Wiley also publishes its books in a variety of electronic formats. Some content that appears in print may not be available in electronic books. For more information about Wiley products, visit our website at www.wiley.com.

Library of Congress Cataloging-in-Publication Data:

Urbina, Susana, 1946–
   Essentials of psychological testing / Susana Urbina.
      p. cm. — (Essentials of behavioral science series)
   Includes bibliographical references.
   ISBN 978-0-471-41978-5 (paper)
     1. Psychological tests. 2. Psychometrics. I. Title. II. Series.
BF176.U73 2004
150'.28'7—dc22
2004043537

10 9 8 7 6 5

*To all my teachers, in and out of schools, who taught me all I know
and to all my students, who taught me how to teach.*

CONTENTS

SERIES PREFACE

I
n the *Essentials of Behavioral Science* series, our goal is to provide readers with books that will deliver key practical information in an efficient, accessible style. The series features books on a variety of topics, such as statistics, psychological testing, and research design and methodology, to name just a few. For the experienced professional, books in the series offer a concise yet thorough review of a specific area of expertise, including numerous tips for best practices. Students can turn to series books for a clear and concise overview of the important topics in which they must become proficient to practice skillfully, efficiently, and ethically in their chosen fields.

Wherever feasible, visual cues highlighting key points are utilized alongside systematic, step-by-step guidelines. Chapters are focused and succinct. Topics are organized for an easy understanding of the essential material related to a particular topic. Theory and research are continually woven into the fabric of each book, but always to enhance the practical application of the material, rather than to sidetrack or overwhelm readers. With this series, we aim to challenge and assist readers in the behavioral sciences to aspire to the highest level of competency by arming them with the tools they need for knowledgeable, informed practice.

Essentials of Psychological Testing has three goals. The first is to survey the basic principles of psychometrics that test users need to use tests competently. The second goal is to supply, for each of these areas, the information required to understand and evaluate tests, and test use, at a basic level. The third goal is to provide readers who need or desire more comprehensive information on psychological testing with the major reference works in the field. It is important to emphasize that this volume is *not* intended to replace college courses in psychological testing, psychometrics, or tests and measurements. Rather, this book may serve as a review or refresher for those who have taken such courses, as well as a point of departure for further exploration of certain topics. For those who have not yet taken testing courses but are considering them, this volume may be useful as an orientation to the field and as a preview. Finally, for those who are curious about psychological tests but do not intend to pursue formal studies in psychometrics, this book will acquaint them with the essential concepts of this field.

Alan S. Kaufman, PhD, and Nadeen L. Kaufman, EdD, Founding Editors
Yale University School of Medicine

One

INTRODUCTION TO PSYCHOLOGICAL TESTS AND THEIR USES

The first and most general meaning of the term *test* listed in the dictionary is "a critical examination, observation, or evaluation." Its closest synonym is *trial.* The word *critical,* in turn, is defined as "relating to . . . a turning point or specially important juncture" (*Merriam-Webster's Collegiate Dictionary,* 1995). No wonder, then, that when the term *psychological* appears in front of the word *test,* the resulting phrase acquires a somewhat threatening connotation. Psychological tests are often used to evaluate individuals at some turning point or significant juncture in their lives. Yet, in the eyes of many people, tests seem to be trials on which too much depends and about which they know all too little. To a large extent, the purpose of this book is to give readers enough information about psychological tests and testing to remove their threatening connotations and to provide the means whereby consumers of psychological tests can gain more knowledge about their specific uses.

Thousands of instruments can accurately be called *psychological tests.* Many more usurp the label either explicitly or by suggestion. The first objective of this book is to explain how to separate the former from the latter. Therefore, we start with the defining features that legitimate psychological tests of all types share. These features not only define psychological tests but also differentiate them from other kinds of instruments.

PSYCHOLOGICAL TESTS

A *psychological test* is a systematic procedure for obtaining samples of behavior, relevant to cognitive or affective functioning, and for scoring and evaluating those samples according to standards. A clarification of each of the main terms in this definition is vital to an understanding of all future discussion of tests. Rapid Reference 1.1 explains the meaning and rationale of all the elements in the definition of a psychological test. Unless every condition mentioned in the definition is met, the procedure in question cannot accurately be called a psychological test. It is,

≡ *Rapid Reference 1.1*

Basic Elements of the Definition of Psychological Tests

Defining Element	Explanation	Rationale
Psychological tests are *systematic* procedures.	They are characterized by planning, uniformity, and thoroughness.	Tests *must be* demonstrably objective and fair to be of use.
Psychological tests are *samples of behavior.*	They are small subsets of a much larger whole.	Sampling behavior is efficient because the time available is usually limited.
The behaviors sampled by tests are *relevant to cognitive or affective functioning* or both.	The samples are selected for their empirical or practical psychological significance.	Tests, unlike mental games, exist to be of use; they are tools.
Test results are *evaluated* and *scored.*	Some numerical or category system is applied to test results, according to preestablished rules.	There should be no question about what the results of tests are.
To evaluate test results it is necessary to have *standards* based on empirical data.	There has to be a way of applying a common yardstick or criterion to test results.	The standards used to evaluate test results lend the only meaning those results have.

however, important to remember that in essence, psychological tests are simply behavior samples. Everything else is based on inferences.

Psychological tests are often described as *standardized* for two reasons, both of which address the need for objectivity in the testing process. The first has to do with uniformity of procedure in all important aspects of the administration, scoring, and interpretation of tests. Naturally, the time and place when a test is administered, as well as the circumstances under which it is administered and the examiner who administers it, affect test results. However, the purpose of standardizing test procedures is to make all the variables that are under the control of the examiner as uniform as possible, so that everyone who takes the test will be taking it in the same way.

The second meaning of standardization concerns the use of standards for evaluating test results. These standards are most often norms derived from a group of individuals—known as the *normative* or *standardization sample*—in the process of developing the test. The collective performance of the standardization group or groups, both in terms of averages and variability, is tabulated and becomes the standard against which the performance of other individuals who take the test after it is standardized will be gauged.

Strictly speaking, the term *test* should be used only for those procedures in which test takers' responses are evaluated based on their correctness or quality. Such instruments always involve the appraisal of some aspect of a person's cognitive functioning, knowledge, skills, or abilities. On the other hand, instruments whose responses are neither evaluated nor scored as right-wrong or pass-fail are called *inventories, questionnaires, surveys, checklists, schedules,* or *projective techniques,* and are usually grouped under the rubric of *personality tests.* These are tools designed to elicit information about a person's motivations, preferences, attitudes, interests, opinions, emotional make-up, and characteristic reactions to people, situations, and other stimuli. Typically, they use questions of the multiple-choice or true-false type, except for projective techniques, which are open ended. They can also involve making forced choices between statements representing contrasting alternatives, or rating the degree to which one agrees or disagrees with various statements. Most of the time personality inventories, questionnaires, and other such instruments are of the self-report variety but some are also designed to elicit reports from individuals other than the person being evaluated (e.g., a parent, spouse, or teacher). For the sake of expediency, and following common usage, the term *test* will be used throughout this book to refer to all instruments, regardless of type, that fit the definition of a psychological test. Tests that sample knowledge, skills, or cognitive functions will be designated as *ability tests,* whereas all others will be referred to as *personality tests.*

> **DON'T FORGET**
> ····································
> - The word *test* has multiple meanings.
> - The term *psychological test* has a very specific meaning.
> - In this book, *test* will be used to refer to all instruments that fit the definition of *psychological test.*
> - Tests designed to sample skills, knowledge, or any other cognitive function will be referred to as *ability tests;* all others will be labeled as *personality tests.*

Other Terms Used in Connection with Tests and Test Titles

Some other terms that are used, sometimes loosely, in connection with tests bear explaining. One of these is the word *scale,* which can refer to

- a whole test made up of several parts, for example, the *Stanford-Binet Intelligence Scale;*
- a subtest, or set of items within a test, that measures a distinct and spe-

cific characteristic, for example, the *Depression scale* of the Minnesota Multiphasic Personality Inventory (MMPI);

- an array of subtests that share some common characteristic, for example, the *Verbal scales* of the Wechsler intelligence tests;
- a separate instrument made up of items designed to evaluate a single characteristic, for example, the *Internal-External Locus of Control Scale* (Rotter, 1966); or
- the numerical system used to rate or to report value on some measured dimension, for example, a *scale* ranging from 1 to 5, with 1 meaning *strongly disagree* and 5 *strongly agree.*

Thus, when used in reference to psychological tests, the term *scale* has become ambiguous and lacking in precision. However, in the field of psychological measurement—also known as *psychometrics*—*scale* has a more precise meaning. It refers to a group of items that pertain to a single variable and are arranged in order of difficulty or intensity. The process of arriving at the sequencing of the items is called *scaling.*

Battery is another term often used in test titles. A battery is a group of several tests, or subtests, that are administered at one time to one person. When several tests are packaged together by a publisher to be used for a specific purpose, the word *battery* usually appears in the title and the entire group of tests is viewed as a single, whole instrument. Several examples of this usage occur in neuropsychological instruments (such as the Halstead-Reitan Neuropsychological Battery) where many cognitive functions need to be evaluated, by means of separate tests, in order to detect possible brain impairment. The term *battery* is also used to designate any group of individual tests specifically selected by a psychologist for use with a given client in an effort to answer a specific referral question, usually of a diagnostic nature.

PSYCHOLOGICAL TESTS AS TOOLS

The most basic fact about psychological tests is that they are tools. This means that they are always a means to an end and never an end in themselves. Like other tools, psychological tests can be exceedingly helpful—even irreplaceable—when used appropriately and skillfully. However, tests can also be misused in ways that may limit or thwart their usefulness and, at times, even result in harmful consequences.

A good way to illustrate the similarities between tests and other, simpler, tools is the analogy between a test and a hammer. Both are tools for specific purposes, but can be used in a variety of ways. A hammer is designed basically for pounding nails into various surfaces. When used appropriately, skillfully, and for its intended purpose a hammer can help build a house, assemble a piece of furniture, hang pictures in a gallery, and do many other things. Psychological tests are tools designed to help in drawing inferences about individuals or groups. When tests are used appropriately and skillfully they can be key components in the practice and science of psychology.

DON'T FORGET

Psychological tests are evaluated at *two* distinct points and in *two* different ways:

1. When they are being considered as potential tools by prospective users; at this point, their technical qualities are of primary concern.

2. Once they are placed in use for a specific purpose; at this point, the skill of the user and the way tests are used are the primary considerations.

Just as hammers may be used for good purposes other than those for which they were intended (e.g., as paperweights or doorstops), psychological tests may also serve purposes other than those for which they were designed originally, such as increasing self-knowledge and self-understanding. Furthermore, just as hammers can hurt people and destroy things when used incompetently or maliciously, psychological tests can also be used in ways that do damage. When test results are misinterpreted or misused, they can harm people by labeling them in unjustified ways, unfairly denying them opportunities, or simply discouraging them.

All tools, be they hammers or tests, can be evaluated based on how well they are designed and built. When looked at from this point of view, prior to being used, tests are evaluated only in a limited, technical sense and their appraisal is of interest mostly to potential users. Once they are placed into use, however, tests cannot be evaluated apart from the skills of their users, the ways they are used, and the purposes for which they are used. This in-use evaluation often involves issues of policy, societal values, and even political priorities. It is in this context that the evaluation of the use of tests acquires practical significance for a wider range of audiences.

Testing Standards

Because of the unique importance of tests to all the professionals who use them and to the general public, since the mid-1950s, three major professional organi-

≡ Rapid Reference 1.2
·····································

Testing Standards

- This designation will be used frequently throughout this book to refer to the *Standards for Educational and Psychological Testing,* published jointly in 1999 by the American Educational Research Association, American Psychological Association, and National Council on Measurement in Education.
- The *Testing Standards* are the single most important source of criteria for the evaluation of tests, testing practices, and the effects of test use.

zations have joined forces to promulgate standards that provide a basis for evaluating tests, testing practices, and the effects of test use. The most recent version of these is the *Standards for Educational and Psychological Testing,* published in 1999 by the American Educational Research Association (AERA) and prepared jointly by AERA, the American Psychological Association (APA), and the National Council on Measurement in Education (NCME). As Rapid Reference 1.2 indicates, these standards are cited throughout this book and hereafter will be referred to as the *Testing Standards.*

PSYCHOLOGICAL TESTS AS PRODUCTS

The second most basic fact about psychological tests is that they are products. Although this is an obvious fact, most people are not mindful of it. Tests are products primarily marketed to and used by professional psychologists and educators, just as the tools of dentistry are marketed and sold to dentists. The public at large remains unaware of the commercial nature of psychological tests because they are advertised through publications and catalogs targeted to the professionals who use them. Nevertheless, the fact remains that many, if not most, psychological tests are conceived, developed, marketed, and sold for applied purposes in education, business, or mental health settings. They also must make a profit for those who produce them, just like any other commercial product.

As we will see, from the very beginning, the psychological testing enterprise was fueled principally by the need to make practical decisions about people. Since tests are professional tools that can be used both to benefit people *and* as commercial products, some clarification of the various parties in the testing enterprise and their roles is justified. Rapid Reference 1.3 shows a list of the major participants in the testing process and their roles.

As the *Testing Standards* stipulate, "the interests of the various parties involved in the testing process are usually, but not always, congruent" (AERA, APA, NCME, 1999, p. 1). For example, test *authors* are usually, though not always, aca-

Rapid Reference 1.3

Participants in the Testing Process and Their Roles

Participants	Their Roles in the Testing Process
Test authors and developers	They conceive, prepare, and develop tests. They also find a way to disseminate their tests, by publishing them either commercially or through professional publications such as books or periodicals.
Test publishers	They publish, market, and sell tests, thus controlling their distribution.
Test reviewers	They prepare evaluative critiques of tests based on their technical and practical merits.
Test users	They select or decide to take a specific test off the shelf and use it for some purpose. They may also participate in other roles, e.g., as examiners or scorers.
Test administrators or examiners	They administer the test either to one individual at a time or to groups.
Test takers	They take the test by choice or necessity.
Test scorers	They tally the raw responses of the test taker and transform them into test scores through objective or mechanical scoring or through the application of evaluative judgments.
Test score interpreters	They interpret test results to their ultimate consumers, who may be individual test takers or their relatives, other professionals, or organizations of various kinds.

demicians or investigators who are mainly interested in psychological theorizing or research, rather than in practical applications or profits. Test *users* are most interested in the appropriateness and utility of the tests they use for their own purposes, whereas test *publishers* are naturally inclined to consider the profit to be made from selling tests foremost. Furthermore, participants in the testing process may perform one or more of all the various roles described in Rapid Reference 1.3. Test users may administer, score, and interpret the results of tests they have selected or may delegate one or more of these functions to others under their supervision. Similarly, test publishers can, and often do, hire test developers to create instruments for which they think a market exists. Nevertheless, of all participants in the testing process, the *Testing Standards* assign "the ultimate responsibility for appropriate test use and interpretation" predominantly to the test user (p. 112).

HISTORY OF PSYCHOLOGICAL TESTING

Even though psychological tests can be used to explore and investigate a wide range of psychological variables, their most basic and typical use is as tools in making decisions about people. It is no coincidence that psychological tests as we know them today came into being in the early part of the 20th century. Prior to the rise of urban, industrial, democratic societies, there was little need for most people to make decisions about others, outside of those in their immediate families or close circle of acquaintances. In rural, agrarian, autocratic societies, major life decisions about individuals were largely made for them by parents, mentors, rulers and, above all, by the gender, class, place, and circumstances into which people were born. Nonetheless, well before the 20th century, there are several interesting precursors of modern psychological testing within a variety of cultures and contexts.

Antecedents of Modern Testing in the Occupational Realm

A perennial problem in any field of employment is the question of how to select the best possible people for a given job. The oldest known precursors of psychological testing are found precisely in this area, within the system of competitive examinations developed in the ancient Chinese empire to select meritorious individuals for government positions. This forerunner of modern personnel selection procedures dates back to approximately 200 B.C.E. and went through a number of transformations in its long history (Bowman, 1989). The Chinese civil service examinations encompassed demonstrations of proficiency in music, archery, and horsemanship, among other things, as well as written exams in subjects such as law, agriculture, and geography. Apparently, the impetus for the development of this enlightened system of human resource utilization—open to any individual who was recommended to the emperor by local authorities throughout the empire—was the fact that China did not have the sort of hereditary ruling classes that were common in Europe until the 20th century. The Chinese imperial examination system ended in 1905 and was replaced with selection based on university studies. In the meantime, however, that system served as an inspiration for the civil service exams developed in Britain in the 1850s, which, in turn, stimulated the creation of the U.S. Civil Service Examination in the 1860s (DuBois, 1970).

Antecedents of Modern Testing in the Field of Education

One of the most basic questions in any educational setting is how to ascertain that students have acquired the knowledge or expertise their teachers try to instill in them. Thus, it is not surprising that the earliest use of testing within the realm of education occurred during the Middle Ages with the rise of the first universities in Europe in the 13th century. At about that time, university degrees came to be used as a means of certifying eligibility to teach, and formal oral examinations were devised to give candidates for degrees an opportunity to demonstrate their competence (DuBois, 1970). Little by little, the use of examinations spread to the secondary level of education and, as paper became cheaper and more available, written examinations replaced the oral exams in most educational settings. By the late 19th century, in both Europe and the United States, examinations were a well-established method of ascertaining who should be awarded university degrees as well as who would be able to exercise a profession, such as medicine or law.

Antecedents of Modern Testing in Clinical Psychology

Another fundamental human question that can be and has been addressed by means of psychological testing is the problem of differentiating the "normal" from the "abnormal" within the intellectual, emotional, and behavioral arenas. However, in contrast to the occupational or educational contexts where the bases on which decisions are made have traditionally been fairly clear, the realm of psychopathology remained shrouded in mystery and mysticism for a much longer period.

Several antecedents of psychological tests stem from the field of psychiatry (Bondy, 1974). Many of these early tests were developed in Germany in the second half of the 19th century, although some of them date from the early part of that century and stemmed from France. Almost invariably these instruments were devised for the express purpose of assessing the level of cognitive functioning of patients with various kinds of disorders such as mental retardation or brain damage. Among the behavior samples used in these early tests were questions concerning the meaning of proverbs and the differences or similarities between pairs of words, as well as memory tasks such as the repetition of digit series presented orally. Many of the techniques developed in the 19th century were ingenious and survived to be incorporated into modern tests that are still in wide use (see McReynolds, 1986).

In spite of their cleverness, developers of the early forerunners of clinical tests were handicapped by at least two factors. One was the dearth of knowledge—and the abundance of superstitions and misconceptions—concerning psychopathology. In this regard, for instance, the distinction between psychosis and mental retardation was not even clearly formulated until 1838, when the French psychiatrist Esquirol suggested that the ability to use language is the most dependable criterion for establishing a person's level of mental functioning. A second factor preventing the widespread dissemination and use of the early psychiatric tests was their lack of standardization in terms of procedures or of a uniform frame of reference against which to interpret results. To a large extent, the techniques developed by 19th-century neurologists and psychiatrists like Guislain, Snell, von Grashey, Rieger, and others were devised for the purpose of examining a specific patient or patient population. These behavior samples were collected in an unsystematic fashion and were interpreted by clinicians on the basis of their professional judgment rather than with reference to normative data (Bondy, 1974).

A significant breakthrough was achieved in psychiatry during the 1890s, when Emil Kraepelin set out to classify mental disorders according to their causes, symptoms, and courses. Kraepelin wanted to bring the scientific method to bear on psychiatry and was instrumental in delineating the clinical picture of schizophrenia and bipolar disorder, which—at the time—were known respectively as *dementia praecox* and *manic-depressive psychosis*. He proposed a system for comparing sane and insane individuals on the basis of characteristics such as distractibility, sensitivity, and memory capacity and even pioneered the use of the free-association technique with psychiatric patients. Although some of Kraepelin's students devised a battery of tests and continued to pursue the goals he had set out, the results of their work were not as fruitful as they had hoped (DuBois, 1970).

Antecedents of Modern Testing in Scientific Psychology

The investigations of the German psychophysicists Weber and Fechner in the mid-19th century initiated a series of developments that culminated in Wilhelm Wundt's creation of the first laboratory dedicated to research of a purely psychological nature in Leipzig, Germany, in 1879. This event is considered by many as the beginning of psychology as a separate, formal discipline, apart from philosophy. With the rise of the new discipline of experimental psychology, there also arose much interest in developing apparatus and standardized procedures for mapping out the range of human capabilities in the realm of sensation and perception. The first experimental psychologists were interested in discovering general laws governing the relationship between the physical and psychological worlds. They had little or no interest in individual differences—the main item of interest in differential psychology and psychological testing—which they, in fact, tended to view as a source of error. Nevertheless, their emphases on the need for accuracy in their measurements and for standardized conditions in the lab would prove to be important contributions to the forthcoming field of psychological testing.

Wundt's German lab flourished in the last decades of the 19th century and trained many psychologists from the United States and elsewhere who would go back to their countries to establish their own similar labs. At about the same time, an Englishman named Francis Galton became interested in the measurement of psychological functions from an entirely different perspective. Galton was a man of great intellectual curiosity and many accomplishments, whose privileged social and financial position allowed him to pursue a wide range of interests. He was also a cousin and a great admirer of Charles Darwin, whose theory of evolution of species by natural selection had revolutionized the life sciences in the mid-19th century. After reading his cousin's treatise on the origin of species, Galton decided to pursue his interest in the notion that intellectual gifts tend to run in families. To this end he set up an anthropometric lab in London, where for several years he collected data on a number of physical and physiological characteristics—such as arm span, height, weight, vital capacity, strength of grip, and sensory acuity of various kinds—on thousands of individuals and families. Galton was convinced that intellectual ability was a function of the keenness of one's senses in perceiving and discriminating stimuli, which he in turn believed was hereditary in nature. Through the accumulation and cross-tabulation of his anthropometric data, Galton hoped to establish both the range of variation in these characteristics, as well as their interrelationships and concordance across individuals with different degrees of familial ties (Fancher, 1996).

Galton did not succeed in his ultimate objective, which was to promote *eugenics,* a field of endeavor he had originated that aimed at improving the human race through selective breeding of its ablest specimens. To this end, he wanted to devise a way of assessing the intellectual capacity of children and adolescents through tests so as to identify the most gifted individuals early and encourage them to produce many offspring. Nevertheless, Galton's work was continued and considerably extended in the United States by James McKeen Cattell, who also tried, fruitlessly, to link various measures of simple discriminative, perceptive, and associative power (which he labeled "mental" tests) to independent estimates of intellectual level, such as school grades.

In light of some events of the 20th century, such as those in Nazi Germany, Galton's aim seems morally offensive to most contemporary sensibilities. However, at the time he coined the term *eugenics* and enunciated its aims, the genocidal potential of this endeavor was not generally perceived, and many illustrious individuals of that era were enthusiastic eugenicists. In the process of his pursuit, however misguided it may seem to us today, Galton did make significant contributions to the fields of statistics and psychological measurements. While charting data comparing parents and their offspring, for instance, he discovered the phenomena of regression and correlation, which provided the groundwork for much subsequent psychological research and data analyses. He also invented devices for the measurement of hearing acuity and weight discrimination, and initiated the use of questionnaires and word association in psychological research. As if these accomplishments were not enough, Galton also pioneered the twin-study method that, once refined, would become a primary research tool in behavior genetics.

One additional contribution to the nascent field of psychological testing in the late 1800s deserves mention because it would lead directly to the first successful instrument of the modern era of testing. While studying the effects of fatigue on children's mental ability, the German psychologist Hermann Ebbinghaus—best known for his groundbreaking research in the field of memory—devised a technique known as the Ebbinghaus Completion Test. This technique called for children to fill in the blanks in text passages from which words or word-fragments had been omitted. The significance of this method, which would later be adapted for a variety of different purposes, is twofold. First, because it was given to whole classes of children simultaneously, it foreshadowed the development of group tests. What is more important, however, is that the technique proved to be an effective gauge of intellectual ability, as the scores derived from it corresponded well with the students' mental ability as determined by rank in class. As a result of this, Alfred Binet was inspired to use the completion technique and other complex mental tasks in developing the scale that would become the first successful intelligence test (DuBois, 1970).

The Rise of Modern Psychological Testing

By the early 1900s everything necessary for the rise of the first truly modern and successful psychological tests was in place:

- Laboratory tests and tools generated by the early experimental psychologists in Germany,
- Measurement instruments and statistical techniques developed by Galton and his students for the collection and analysis of data on individual differences, and
- An accretion of significant findings in the budding sciences of psychology, psychiatry, and neurology.

All of these developments provided the foundation for the rise of modern testing. The actual impetus for it, however, came from the practical need to make decisions in educational placement.

In 1904, the French psychologist Alfred Binet was appointed to a commission charged with devising a method for evaluating children who, due to mental retardation or other developmental delays, could not profit from regular classes in the public school system and would require special education. Binet was particularly well prepared for this task, as he had been engaged in investigating individual differences by means of a variety of physical and physiological measures, as well as tests of more complex mental processes, such as memory and verbal comprehension. In 1905, Binet and his collaborator, Theodore Simon, published the first useful instrument for the measurement of general cognitive abilities or global intelligence. The 1905 Binet-Simon scale, as it came to be known, was a series of 30 tests or tasks varied in content and difficulty, designed mostly to assess judgment and reasoning ability irrespective of school learning. It included questions dealing with vocabulary, comprehension, differences between pairs of concepts, and so on, as well as tasks that included repeating series of numbers, following directions, completing fragmentary text passages, and drawing.

The Binet-Simon scale was successful because it combined features of earlier instruments in a novel and systematic fashion. It was more comprehensive in its coverage than earlier instruments devoted to evaluating narrower abilities. It was, in fact, a small battery of carefully selected tests arranged in order of difficulty and accompanied by precise instructions on how to administer and interpret it. Binet and Simon administered the scale to 50 normal children ranging in age from 3 to 11 years, as well as to children with various degrees of mental retardation. The results of these studies proved that they had devised a procedure for sampling cognitive functioning whereby a child's general level of intellectual ability could be described quantitatively, in terms of the age level to which her or his performance on the scale corresponded. The need for such a tool was so acute that the 1905 scale would be quickly translated into other languages and adapted for use outside France.

The Birth of the IQ

Binet himself revised, expanded, and refined his first scale in 1908 and 1911. Its scoring developed into a system in which credit for items passed was given in terms of years and months so that a *mental level* could be calculated to represent quality of performance. In 1911 a German psychologist named William Stern proposed that the mental level attained on the Binet-Simon scale, relabeled as a *mental age score,* be divided by the chronological age of the subject to obtain a mental quotient that would more accurately represent ability at different ages. To eliminate the decimal, the mental quotient was multiplied by 100, and soon became known as the *intelligence quotient,* or *IQ.* This now-familiar score, a *true ratio*

IQ, was popularized through its use in the most famous revision of the Binet-Simon scales—the Stanford-Binet Intelligence Scale—published in 1916 by Lewis Terman. In spite of several problems with the ratio IQ, its use would last for several decades, until a better way of integrating age into the scoring of intelligence tests (described in Chapter 3) was devised by David Wechsler (Kaufman, 2000; Wechsler, 1939). Binet's basic idea—namely, that to be average, below average, or above average in intelligence means that one performs at, below, or above the level typical for one's age group on intelligence tests—has survived and become one of the primary ways in which intelligence is assessed.

While Binet was developing his scales in France, in England, Charles Spearman (a former student of Wundt's and follower of Galton) had been trying to prove empirically Galton's hypothesis concerning the link between intelligence and sensory acuity. In the process he had developed and expanded the use of correlational methods pioneered by Galton and Karl Pearson, and provided the conceptual foundation for *factor analysis,* a technique for reducing a large number of variables to a smaller set of factors that would become central to the advancement of testing and trait theory.

Spearman also devised a theory of intelligence that emphasized a general intelligence factor (or *g*) present in all intellectual activities (Spearman, 1904a, 1904b). He had been able to gather moderate support for Galton's notions by correlating teachers' ratings and grades with measures of sensory acuity, but soon realized that the tasks assembled in the Binet-Simon scale provided a far more useful and reliable way of assessing intelligence than the tools he had been using. Even though Spearman and Binet differed widely in their views about the nature of intelligence, their combined contributions are unsurpassed in propelling the development of psychological testing in the 20th century.

Group Testing

At the time Binet died, in 1911, he had already considered the possibility of adapting his scale to other uses and developing group tests that could be administered by one examiner to large groups for use in the military and other settings. The fulfillment of that idea, however, would not take place in France but in the United States, where the Binet-Simon scale had been rapidly translated and revised for use primarily with schoolchildren and for the same purpose as it had been developed in France.

Upon the entry of the United States into World War I in 1917, the APA president, Robert Yerkes, organized a committee of psychologists to help in the war effort. It was decided that the most practical contribution would be to develop a group test of intelligence that could be efficiently administered to all recruits into the U.S. Army, to help in making personnel assignments. The committee, made up of leading test experts of the day, including Lewis Terman, hastily assembled and tried out a test that came to be known as the *Army Alpha*. It consisted of eight subtests measuring verbal, numerical, and reasoning abilities, as well as practical judgment and general information. The test, which would eventually be administered to more than a million recruits, made use of materials from various other instruments, including the Binet scales. In constructing it, the committee relied heavily on an unpublished prototype group test developed by Arthur Otis, who had devised multiple-choice items that could be scored objectively and rapidly.

The Army Alpha proved to be extremely useful. It was followed rapidly by the Army Beta, a supposedly equivalent test that did not require reading and could thus be used with recruits who were illiterate or non–English speaking. Unfortunately, the haste with which these tests were developed and put into use resulted in a number of inappropriate testing practices. In addition, unwarranted conclusions were made on the basis of the massive amounts of data that quickly accumulated (Fancher, 1985). Some of the negative consequences of the ways in which the Army testing program, and other massive testing efforts from that era, were implemented damaged the reputation of psychological testing in ways that have been difficult to surmount. Nevertheless, through the mistakes that were made early in the history of modern testing, a great deal was learned that later served to correct and improve the practices in this field. Furthermore, with the Army tests the field of psychology decisively stepped out of the lab and academic settings and demonstrated its enormous potential to contribute to real-world applications.

After World War I, psychological testing came into its own in the United States. Otis published his Group Intelligence Scale, the test that had served as a model for the Army Alpha, in 1918. E. L. Thorndike, another important American pioneer working at Teachers College at Columbia, produced an intelligence test for high school graduates, standardized on a more select sample (namely, college freshmen) in 1919. From then on, the number of published tests grew rapidly. Procedural refinements were also swiftly instituted in test administration and scoring. For example, test items of different types began to be presented in a mixed order rather than as separate subtests so that an overall time limit could be used for a test, eliminating the need for separate timing of subtests. Issues of standardization, such as eliminating words that could be read with different pronunciations in spelling tests, came to the fore, as did tests' *trustworthiness*—a term that, at that time, encompassed what is currently meant by *reliability* and *validity* (DuBois, 1970).

OTHER DEVELOPMENTS IN PSYCHOLOGICAL TESTING

The successes achieved with the Binet and Army tests proved their worth in helping to make decisions about people. This soon led to efforts to devise instruments to help in different kinds of decisions. Naturally, the settings where antecedents of psychological tests had arisen—schools, clinics, and psychology labs—also gave rise to the new forms and types of modern psychological tests.

A thorough review of the history of testing in the first half of the 20th century is beyond the scope of this work. Nevertheless, a brief summary of the most salient developments is instructive both for its own sake and to illustrate the diversity of the field, even in its early phase.

Standardized Testing in Educational Settings

As the number of people availing themselves of educational opportunities at all levels grew, so did the need for fair, equitable, and uniform measures with which to evaluate students at the beginning, middle, and final stages of the educational process. Two major developments in standardized educational testing in the early part of the 20th century are highlighted in the ensuing paragraphs.

Standardized Achievement Tests

Pioneered by E. L. Thorndike, these measures had been under development since the 1880s, when Joseph Rice began his attempts to study the efficiency of learning in schools. Thorndike's handwriting scale, published in 1910, broke new ground in creating a series of handwriting specimens, ranging from very poor to excellent, against which subjects' performance could be compared. Soon after, standardized tests designed to evaluate arithmetic, reading, and spelling skills would follow, until measures of these and other subjects became a staple of elementary and secondary education. Today, standardized achievement tests are used not only in educational settings, but also in the licensing and certification of professionals who have completed their training. They are also used in other situations, including personnel selection, that require the assessment of mastery of a given field of knowledge.

Scholastic Aptitude Tests

In the 1920s objective examinations, based loosely on the Army Alpha test, began to be used in addition to high school grades for the purpose of making admissions decisions in colleges and universities. This momentous development, which culminated in the creation of the Scholastic Aptitude Test (SAT) in 1926, foreshadowed the arrival of many more instruments that are used to select can-

≡ *Rapid Reference 1.4*

The Big Test

Nicholas Lemann's (1999) book *The Big Test: The Secret History of the American Meritocracy* uses college admissions testing programs, specifically the SAT, to illustrate the intended and unintended consequences that such testing programs can have for society. The large-scale use of standardized test scores for deciding on admissions into leading institutions of higher education was pioneered by James Bryant Conant, president of Harvard University, and Henry Chauncey, the first president of the Educational Testing Service (ETS), in the 1940s and 1950s. Their goal was to change the process whereby access to these institutions—and to the positions of power that usually accrue to those who attend them—is gained from one based on wealth and social class to one based mainly on ability as demonstrated through test scores. Lemann maintains that although this use of testing did open up the doors of higher education to children of the middle and lower socioeconomic classes, it also generated a new meritocratic elite that perpetuates itself across generations and largely excludes the children of underprivileged racial minorities who lack the early educational opportunities needed to succeed on the tests.

didates for graduate and professional schools. Among the best known examples of tests of this type are the Graduate Record Exam (GRE), Medical College Admission Test (MCAT), and Law School Admission Test (LSAT), used by doctoral programs, medical schools, and law schools, respectively. Although each of these tests contains portions specific to the subject matter of its field, they also typically share a common core that emphasizes the verbal, quantitative, and reasoning abilities needed for success in most academic endeavors. Interestingly, although their purpose is different from that of the standardized achievement tests, their content is often similar. Rapid Reference 1.4 presents information about a fascinating account of the history of higher education admissions testing in the United States.

Personnel Testing and Vocational Guidance

The optimal utilization of people's talents is a major goal of society to which psychological testing has been able to contribute in important ways almost from its beginnings. Decisions concerning vocational choice need to be made by individuals at different points in their lives, usually during adolescence and young adulthood but also increasingly at midlife. Decisions concerning the selection and placement of personnel within business, industry, and military organizations need to be made on an ongoing basis. Some of the main instruments that came into being early and have proved to be particularly helpful in making both of these kinds of decisions are described in the following sections.

Tests of Special Skills and Aptitudes

The success of the Army Alpha test stimulated interest in developing tests to select workers for different occupations. At the same time, applied psychologists had been working out and using a basic set of procedures that would justify the use of tests in occupational selection. Basically, the procedures involved (a) identifying the skills needed for a given occupational role by means of a *job analysis,* (b) administering tests designed to assess those skills, and (c) correlating the test results with measures of job performance. Using variations of this procedure, from the 1920s on, psychologists were able to develop instruments for selecting trainees in fields as diverse as mechanical work and music. Tests of clerical, spatial, and motor abilities soon followed. The field of personnel selection in industry and the military grew up around these instruments, along with the use of job samples, biographical data, and general intelligence tests of the individual and group types. Many of the same instruments have also been used profitably in identifying the talents of young people seeking vocational guidance.

Multiple Aptitude Batteries

The use of tests of separate abilities in vocational counseling would largely give way in the 1940s to multiple aptitude batteries, developed through the factor analytic techniques pioneered by Spearman and expanded in England and the United States through the 1920s and 1930s. These batteries are groups of tests, linked by a common format and scoring basis, that typically profile the strengths and weaknesses of an individual by providing separate scores on various factors such as verbal, numerical, spatial, logical reasoning, and mechanical abilities, rather than the single global score provided by the Binet and Army test IQs. Multiple aptitude batteries came into being following the widespread realization, through factor analyses of ability test data, that intelligence is not a unitary concept and that human abilities comprise a broad range of separate and relatively independent components or factors.

Measures of Interests

Just as tests of special skills and aptitudes arose in industry and later found some use in vocational counseling, measures of interests originated for the purpose of vocational guidance and later found some use in personnel selection. Truman L. Kelley, in 1914, produced a simple Interest Test, possibly the first interest inventory ever, with items concerning preferences for reading materials and leisure activities as well as some involving knowledge of words and general information. However, the breakthrough in this particular area of testing took place in 1924, when M. J. Ream developed an empirical key that differentiated the responses of successful and unsuccessful salesmen on the Carnegie Interest Inventory developed by Yoakum and his students at the Carnegie Institute of Technology in 1921 (DuBois, 1970). This event marked the beginning of a technique known as *empirical criterion keying*, which, after refinements such as cross-validation procedures and extensions to other occupations, would be used in the Strong Vocational Interest Blank (SVIB), first published in 1927, and in other types of inventories as well. The current version of the SVIB—called the Strong Interest Inventory® (SII)—is one of the most widely used interest inventories and has been joined by many more instruments of this type.

Clinical Testing

By the start of the 20th century the field of psychiatry had embarked on more systematic ways of classifying and studying psychopathology. These advances provided the impetus for the development of instruments that would help diagnose psychiatric problems. The main examples of this type of tools are discussed here.

Personality Inventories   subjective

The first device of this kind was the Woodworth Personal Data Sheet (P-D Sheet), a questionnaire developed during World War I to screen recruits who might suffer from mental illnesses. It consisted of 116 statements regarding feelings, attitudes, and behaviors obviously indicative of psychopathology to which the respondent answered simply yes or no. Although the P-D Sheet showed some promise, World War I ended before it was placed into operational use. After the war there was a period of experimentation with other, less obvious, kinds of items and with scales designed to assess neuroticism, personality traits—such as introversion and extraversion—and values. Innovations in the presentation of items aimed at reducing the influence of social desirability, like the forced-choice technique introduced in the Allport-Vernon Study of Values in 1931, came into being. However, the most successful personality inventory of that era, and one which still survives today, was the Minnesota Multiphasic Personality Inventory (MMPI; Hathaway & McKinley, 1940). The MMPI combined items from the P-D Sheet and other inventories, but used the empirical criterion keying technique pioneered with the SVIB. This technique resulted in a less transparent instrument on which respondents could not dissemble as easily because many of the items had no obvious reference to psychopathological tendencies.

Since the 1940s, personality inventories have flourished. Many refinements have been introduced in their construction, including the use of theoretical perspectives—such as Henry Murray's (1938) system of needs—and internal consistency methods of selecting items. Furthermore, factor analysis, which had been so crucial to the study and differentiation of abilities, also began to be used in personality inventory development. In the 1930s, J. P. Guilford pioneered the use of factor analysis to group items into homogeneous scales while, in the 1940s, R. B. Cattell applied the technique to try to identify the personality traits that are most pivotal and, therefore, worthy of investigation and assessment. Currently, factor analysis plays an integral role in most facets of test theory and test construction.

Projective Techniques finger drawings

Although personality inventories had some success, mental health professionals working with psychiatric populations felt a need for additional help in diagnosing and treating mental illness. In the 1920s, a new genre of tools for the assessment of personality and psychopathology emerged. These instruments, known as *projective techniques,* had their roots in the free association methods pioneered by Galton and used clinically by Kraepelin, Jung, and Freud. In 1921, a Swiss psychiatrist named Hermann Rorschach published a test consisting of ten inkblots to be presented for interpretation, one at a time, to the examinee. The key to the success of this first formal projective technique was that it provided a standardized method for obtaining and interpreting subjects' responses to the inkblot cards, responses that—by and large—reflect the subject's unique modes of perceiving and relating to the world. Rorschach's test was taken up by several American psychologists and propagated in various universities and clinics in the United States after his untimely death in 1922. The Rorschach technique, along with other pictorial, verbal, and drawing instruments, like the Thematic Apperception Test, sentence completion tests, and human figure drawings provided a whole new repertoire of tools—more subtle and incisive than the questionnaires—with which clinicians could investigate aspects of personality that test takers themselves may have been unable or unwilling to reveal. Though there is much controversy about their validity, primarily because they often rely on qualitative interpretations as much as or more than on numerical scores, projective techniques are still a significant part of the toolkit of many clinicians (Viglione & Rivera, 2003).

Neuropsychological Tests

The role of brain dysfunction in emotional, cognitive, and behavioral disorders has been increasingly recognized throughout the past century. However, the major impetus for the scientific and clinical study of brain-behavior relationships, which is the subject of *neuropsychology*, came from Kurt Goldstein's investigations of the difficulties he observed in soldiers who had sustained brain injuries during World War I. Often these soldiers showed a pattern of deficits involving problems with abstract thinking, memory, as well as the planning and execution of relatively simple tasks, all of which came to be known under the rubric of *organicity*, which was used as a synonym for brain damage. Over several decades, a number of instruments meant to detect organicity, and distinguish it from other psychiatric disorders, came into being. Many of these were variations of the performance—as opposed to verbal—tests that had been developed to assess general intellectual ability in individuals who could not be examined in English or who had hearing or speech impairments. These tests involved materials like form boards, jigsaw puzzles, and blocks as well as paper-and-pencil tasks such as mazes and drawings. A great deal has been learned about the brain and its functioning in the past few decades and much of the initial thinking in neuropsychological assessment has had to be revised based on new information. Brain damage is no longer viewed as an all-or-none condition of organicity with a common set of symptoms, but rather as a huge range of possible disorders resulting from the interaction of specific genetic and environmental factors in each individual case. Nevertheless, the field of neuropsychological assessment has continued to grow in the number and types of instruments available and has contributed both to the clinical and scientific understanding of the many and varied relationships between brain functioning and cognition, emotions, and behaviors (Lezak, 1995).

CURRENT USES OF PSYCHOLOGICAL TESTS

Present-day testing is, on the whole, more methodologically sophisticated and better informed than at any time in the past. The current uses of tests, which take place in a wide variety of contexts, may be classified into three categories: (a) decision-making, (b) psychological research, and (c) self-understanding and personal development. As can be gleaned from this list, presented in Rapid Reference 1.5, the

Rapid Reference 1.5

Current Uses of Psychological Tests

- The first and foremost use of tests is in the pragmatic process of *making decisions about people*, either as individuals or as groups.

- The second use of tests in terms of frequency and longevity is in scientific *research on psychological phenomena* and individual differences.

- The most recent, and least developed, use of tests is in the therapeutic process of *promoting self-understanding and psychological adjustment.*

three kinds of uses differ vastly in their impact and in many other respects, and the first one of them is by far the most visible to the public.

Decision Making

The primary use of psychological tests is as decision-making tools. This particular application of testing invariably involves value judgments on the part of one or more decision makers who need to determine the bases upon which to select, place, classify, diagnose, or otherwise deal with individuals, groups, organizations, or programs. Naturally, this use of testing is often fraught with controversy since it often results in consequences that are unfavorable for one or more parties. In many situations in which tests are used to make decisions and people disagree with the decisions made, the use of tests itself is attacked regardless of whether or not it was appropriate.

When tests are used for making significant decisions about individuals or programs, testing should be merely a part of a thorough and well-planned decision-making strategy that takes into account the particular context in which the decisions are made, the limitations of the tests, and other sources of data in addition to tests. Unfortunately, very often—for reasons of expediency, carelessness, or lack of information—tests are made to bear the responsibility for flawed decision-making processes that place too much weight on test results and neglect other pertinent information. A number of decisions made by educational, governmental, or corporate institutions on a routine basis, usually involving the simultaneous evaluation of several people at once, have been and still are made in this fashion. Although they carry important consequences—such as employment, admission to colleges or professional schools, graduation, or licensure to practice a profession—for the individuals involved, decisions are based almost exclusively on test scores. This practice, a legacy of the way in which testing originated, is one that testing professionals, as well as some government agencies, are trying to change. One of several important steps in this direction is the publication of a resource guide for educators and policymakers on the use of tests as part of high-stakes decision making for students (U.S. Department of Education, Office for Civil Rights, 2000).

Psychological Research

Tests are often used in research in the fields of differential, developmental, abnormal, educational, social, and vocational psychology, among others. They provide a well-recognized method of studying the nature, development, and interrelationships of cognitive, affective, and behavioral traits. In fact, although a number of tests that originated in the course of psychological investigations have become commercially available, many more instruments remain archived in dissertations, journals, and various compendiums of experimental measures discussed in Sources of Information about Tests at the end of this chapter. Because there are seldom any immediate practical consequences attendant to the use of tests in research, their use in this context is less contentious than when they are used in decision making about individuals, groups, organizations, or programs.

Self-Understanding and Personal Development

Most humanistic psychologists and counselors have traditionally perceived the field of testing, often justifiably, as overemphasizing the labeling and categorization of individuals in terms of rigid numerical criteria. Starting in the 1970s, a few of them, notably Constance Fischer (1985/1994), began to use tests and other assessment tools in an individualized manner, consonant with humanistic and existential-phenomenological principles. This practice, which views testing as a way to provide clients with information to promote self-understanding and positive growth, has evolved into the *therapeutic model of assessment* espoused by Finn and Tonsager (1997). Obviously, the most pertinent application of this model is in counseling and psychotherapeutic settings in which the client is the main and only user of test results.

PSYCHOLOGICAL ASSESSMENT VERSUS PSYCHOLOGICAL TESTING

For reasons that are mostly related to the marketing of tests, some test authors and publishers have begun to use the word *assessment* in the titles of their tests. Thus, in the mind of the general public the terms *assessment* and *testing* are often seen as synonymous. This is an unfortunate development. The distinction between these terms is one that many people in the field believe is worth preserving, and one that the general public, as potential assessment clients or consumers of tests, should be aware of as well.

The use of tests for making decisions about a person, a group, or a program should always take place within the context of *psychological assessment*. This process can occur in

> ## DON'T FORGET
>
> - Tests and *assessments* are NOT synonymous.
> - Tests are among the tools used in the process of assessment.

health care, counseling, or forensic settings, as well as in educational and employment settings. Psychological assessment is a flexible, not standardized, *process* aimed at reaching a defensible determination concerning one or more psychological issues or questions, through the collection, evaluation, and analysis of data appropriate to the purpose at hand (Maloney & Ward, 1976).

Steps in the Assessment Process

The first and most important step in psychological assessment is to identify its goals as clearly and realistically as possible. Without clearly defined objectives that are agreed upon by the assessor and the person requesting the assessment, the process is not likely to be satisfactory. In most instances, the process of assessment ends with a verbal or written report, communicating the conclusions that have been reached to the persons who requested the assessment, in a comprehensible and useful manner. In between these two points, the professional conducting the assessment, usually a psychologist or a counselor, will need to employ her or his expertise at every step. These steps involve the appropriate selection of instruments to be used in gathering data, their careful administration, scoring, interpretation, and—most important of all—the judicious use of the data collected to make inferences about the question at hand. This last step goes beyond psychometric expertise and requires a knowledge of the field to which the question refers, such as health care, educational placement, psychopathology, organizational behavior, or criminology, among others. Examples of issues amenable to investigation through psychological assessment include

- *diagnostic questions,* such as differentiating between depression and dementia;
- *making predictions,* such as estimating the likelihood of suicidal or homicidal behaviors; and
- *evaluative judgments,* such as those involved in child custody decisions or in assessing the effectiveness of programs or interventions.

None of these complex issues can be resolved by means of test scores alone because the same test score can have different meanings depending on the examinee and the context in which it was obtained. Furthermore, no single test score or set of scores can capture all the aspects that need to be considered in resolving such issues.

Psychological tests may be key components in psychological assessment, but the two differ fundamentally in important ways. Rapid Reference 1.6 lists several dimensions that differentiate psychological testing and assessment. Even though

≡ Rapid Reference 1.6

Typical Differences between Psychological Testing and Assessment

Basis	Psychological Testing	Psychological Assessment
Degree of complexity	Simpler; involves one uniform procedure, frequently unidimensional.	More complex; each assessment involves various procedures (interviewing, observation, testing, etc.) and dimensions.
Duration	Shorter, lasting from a few minutes to a few hours.	Longer, lasting from a few hours to a few days or more.
Sources of data	One person, the test taker.	Often collateral sources, such as relatives or teachers, are used in addition to the subject of the assessment.
Focus	How one person or group compares with others (*nomothetic*).	The uniqueness of a given individual, group, or situation (*idiographic*).
Qualifications for use	Knowledge of tests and testing procedures.	Knowledge of testing and other assessment methods as well as of the area assessed (e.g., psychiatric disorders, job requirements).
Procedural basis	Objectivity required; quantification is critical.	Subjectivity, in the form of clinical judgment, required; quantification rarely possible.
Cost	Inexpensive, especially when testing is done in groups.	Very expensive; requires intensive use of highly qualified professionals.
Purpose	Obtaining data for use in making decisions.	Arriving at a decision concerning the referral question or problem.
Degree of structure	Highly structured.	Entails both structured and unstructured aspects.
Evaluation of results	Relatively simple investigation of reliability and validity based on group results.	Very difficult due to variability of methods, assessors, nature of presenting questions, etc.

there is little question about the general superiority of assessment over testing with regard to comprehensiveness and utility, the greater complexity of the assessment process makes its results far more difficult to evaluate than those of testing. Nevertheless, in recent years, evidence of the efficacy of assessment, at least in the realm of health care delivery, has begun to be assembled (Eisman et al., 2000; Kubiszyn et al., 2000; Meyer et al., 2001).

TEST USER QUALIFICATIONS

As the number of tests has continued to grow and their uses have expanded, not only in the United States but around the world, the question of test misuse has become of increasing concern for the public, the government, and various professions. Psychology, which is the profession from which tests arose and the one with which they are most distinctly associated, has taken the lead in trying to combat their misuse. The *Testing Standards* promulgated by the APA and other professional organizations (AERA, APA, & NCME, 1999) are a major vehicle to this end. The APA also addresses issues related to testing and assessment in its ethical principles and code of conduct (APA, 2002), as do other professional associations (e.g., American Counseling Association, 1995; National Association of School Psychologists, 2000).

Although the technical qualities of a number of tests are far from ideal and can contribute to problems in their use, it is generally conceded that the primary reason for test misuse lies in the insufficient knowledge or competence on the part of many test users. Tests may appear relatively simple and straightforward to potential users who are unaware of the cautions that must be exercised in their application. Because of this, in the past few decades, professional associations in the United States and elsewhere have been developing documents that outline more clearly and specifically than ever before the skills and knowledge base required for competent test use (American Association for Counseling and Development, 1988; Eyde, Moreland, Robertson, Primoff, & Most, 1988; International Test Commission, 2000; Joint Committee on Testing Practices, 1988).

One of the clearest expositions of these requirements is in a report prepared over the course of five years by the APA Task Force on Test User Qualifications (APA, 2000). This report outlines (a) the core knowledge and skills essential to those who use tests to make decisions or formulate policies that affect the lives of test takers, and (b) the expertise that test users in the specific contexts of employment, education, career counseling, health care, and forensic work must possess. Core or generic knowledge and skills in psychometrics, statistics, test selection, administration, scoring, reporting, and safeguarding are considered relevant to all test users. Additional knowledge and supervised experience required for the use of tests in the various contexts and with diverse groups of test takers are also outlined in the report, as are the variety of uses of tests in classification, description, prediction, intervention planning, and tracking in each context.

Another aspect of testing that has contributed to test misuse over the decades is the relative ease with which test instruments can be obtained by people who are not qualified to use them. To some extent, the availability of tests is a function of the freedom with which information flows in democratic societies like the United States, especially in the era of the World Wide Web. Another reason for this problem—alluded to earlier in this chapter—is the fact that many tests are commercial products. As a result, some test publishers have been willing to sell tests to persons or institutions without using adequate safeguards to ascertain whether they possess the proper credentials. At one point, during the 1950s and 1960s, the *Testing Standards* included a three-tiered system for classifying tests in terms of the qualifications needed for their use (APA, 1966, pp. 10–11). This system, which labeled tests as Level A, B, or C depending on the training required to use them, was easily circumvented by individuals in schools, government agencies, and businesses. Although many test publishers still use the system, the *Testing Standards* no longer do. Rapid Reference 1.7 outlines the elements typically included in a three-tiered classification system of test user qualifications.

In 1992, a number of the publishers of tests and providers of assessment services established the Association of Test Publishers (ATP). This nonprofit organization tries to uphold a high level of professionalism and ethics in the testing enterprise. One way in which they monitor the distribution of tests is by requiring some documentation attesting to a minimum level of training from those who would purchase their products.

Qualification forms for test purchase are now included in the catalogs of all reputable test publishers. No matter how sincere publishers may be in their efforts to preserve the security of test materials and to prevent their misuse, the effectiveness of these efforts is by necessity limited. Not only is it not feasible to verify the qualifications that purchasers claim on the forms they submit, but in addition no formal set of qualifications—whether by education or by licensure—can ensure that an individual is competent to use a particular test properly in a given situation (see Chapter 7).

SOURCES OF INFORMATION ABOUT TESTS

In psychological testing, as in every other human endeavor, the Internet has created an inexhaustible supply of information. Thus, alongside the print references

Rapid Reference 1.7

Test User Qualification Levels

All reputable test publishers require test purchasers to complete a form specifying the credentials that qualify them to use the testing materials they wish to buy and certifying that the materials will be used in accordance with all applicable ethical and legal guidelines. Although the number of levels and the specific credentials required at each level differ among publishers, their qualification criteria are typically organized into at least three tiers, based roughly on a categorization of tests and training requirements originally outlined by the American Psychological Association (APA; 1953, 1954).

	Lowest Tier (Level A)	Intermediate Tier (Level B)	Highest Tier (Level C)
Type of instruments to which this level applies	A limited range of instruments, such as educational achievement tests, that can be administered, scored, and interpreted without specialized training, by following the instructions in their manuals.	Tools that call for some specialized training in test construction and use and in the area in which the instruments will be applied, such as aptitude tests and personality inventories applicable to normal populations.	Instruments that require extensive familiarity with testing and assessment principles, as well as with the psychological fields to which the instruments pertain, such as individual intelligence tests and projective techniques.
Kinds of credentials or requirements necessary to purchase materials at this level	Some publishers do not require any credentials to purchase tests at this level. Others may require a bachelor's degree in an appropriate field or that orders for materials be placed through an agency or institution, or both.	Test purchasers usually must have either a Master's-level degree in psychology (or in a related field) or course work in testing and assessment commensurate with the requirements for using the instruments in question.	Test purchasers must have the kind of advanced training and supervised experience that is acquired in the course of obtaining a doctoral degree, or professional licensure in a field pertinent to the intended use of the instruments, or both.

that the field has traditionally had, there now is a large number of on-line and electronic media resources that are easily accessible.

Internet Resources

For the person who seeks information about psychological tests, a good starting point is the Testing and Assessment section of the APA's Web site (http://www.apa.org). Within this section, among other things, there is an excellent article on "FAQ/Finding Information About Psychological Tests" (APA, 2003) that provides guidance on how to locate published and unpublished tests as well as important documents relevant to psychological testing. *Published tests* are commercially available through a test publisher, although they sometimes go out of print as books do. *Unpublished tests* have to be obtained directly from the individual investigator who created them, unless they appear in the periodical literature or in specialized directories (discussed shortly). directly from author

Two other great entry points on the Internet, for those who seek information about a specific test, are (a) the Buros Institute of Mental Measurements (BI) Test Reviews Online Web page (http://www.unl.edu/buros), which offers free information on nearly 4,000 commercially available tests as well as more than 2,000 test reviews that can be purchased and displayed online; and (b) the Educational Testing Service (ETS) Test Collection database (at http://www.ets.org/testcoll/index.html), which is the largest of its kind in the world. In addition, the Educational Resources Information Center (ERIC) system Web site (http://eric.ed.gov)—funded by the U.S. Department of Education—contains a wealth of materials related to psychological testing.

Another way to obtain information about both published and unpublished tests online is through the electronic indexes of the periodical literature in psychology, education, or business. The PsycINFO database of the APA, available through many libraries or by subscription, provides an entry point at which to use the name of a test to find bibliographic references, abstracts, and even full text of articles about it. In addition to exact titles, PsycINFO and other

DON'T FORGET
....

One of the most basic distinctions among tests concerns whether they are published.

- *Published tests* are commercially available through test publishers.
- *Unpublished tests* must be obtained from the individual investigator who developed them, from special directories of unpublished measures, or from the periodical literature.

DON'T FORGET

....

Appendix A lists all of the commercially available, published tests and psychological assessment instruments mentioned throughout this book, along with codes identifying their publishers.

Appendix B provides current Internet addresses for the publishers listed in Appendix A. More detailed information on test publishers, including street addresses and telephone numbers, is available in the latest edition of *Tests in Print* (Murphy, Plake, Impara, & Spies, 2002).

databases also can be searched by subjects, keywords, and authors, which makes them especially useful when only partial information is available.

Once a test is located through any of these resources, one can usually also determine whether it is published and how it can be obtained. If the test is published, it may be ordered from the company that publishes it by those who meet the qualifications to use it. Ordering information is available in the publishers' catalogs, many of which are now available online as well as in printed form. The ATP Web site (http://www.testpublishers.org) has links to many test publishers and providers of assessment services. Internet addresses for all of the organizations mentioned in this section, and other important sources of information on tests, can be found in Rapid Reference 1.8.

≡*Rapid Reference 1.8*

....

Internet Sources of Information on Psychological Tests

Organization (Acronym)	Website
American Educational Research Association (AERA)	http://www.aera.net
American Psychological Association (APA)	http://www.apa.org
Association of Test Publishers (ATP)	http://www.testpublishers.org
Buros Institute of Mental Measurements (BI)	http://www.unl.edu/buros
Educational Resources Information Center (ERIC)	http://eric.ed.gov
Educational Testing Service (ETS)	http://www.ets.org/testcoll/index.html
International Test Commission (ITC)	http://www.intestcom.org
National Council on Measurement in Education (NCME)	http://www.ncme.org

Print Resources

Published Tests

As far as commercially available, published tests are concerned, the most important sources of information stem from the Buros Institute of Mental Measurements (BI) in Lincoln, Nebraska. In particular, the BI (http://www.unl.edu/buros) produces two series of volumes that can guide users to almost every published test available in the United States. One of these is the *Tests in Print (TIP)* series and the other is the *Mental Measurements Yearbook (MMY)* series. *Tests in Print* is a comprehensive bibliography of all tests that are commercially available at the time a given volume of the series is published. Each entry has the test title, acronym, author, publisher, publication date, and other basic information about the test as well as cross-references to the reviews of the test in all the *MMY*s available at that point. In addition, the *TIP* series contains an extremely useful classified index of tests that are in print, as well as indexes of test scores, publishers, acronyms, and names of authors and reviewers. The *MMY* series, in turn, goes back to 1938, when the late Oscar Buros published the first yearbook to assist test users by providing evaluative test reviews written by qualified and independent professionals. Although the *MMY*s are still published in book form, their entries and reviews are also available online and in other electronic media. The Buros Institute also publishes many other test-related materials.

PRO-ED (http://www.proedinc.com) is the publisher of *Tests,* a series of encyclopedic volumes listing short descriptions of instruments in psychology, education, and business. The *Test Critiques* series, dating back to 1984, is the companion to *Tests.* Each volume in this series contains test reviews and cumulative indexes to all its previous volumes.

Unpublished Tests

The goal of behavioral scientists who use psychological tests is to investigate psychological constructs as well as individual and group differences. Many existing tests are used exclusively for scientific research and are not commercially available. These tests are referred to as *unpublished* measures because they cannot be purchased; conditions for their use are typically established by the authors of each instrument and most often require a letter requesting permission to use them. Information about unpublished tests—and often the instruments themselves—is available in the periodical literature in psychology (e.g., through PsycINFO online) and in various directories (e.g., Goldman, Mitchell, & Egelson, 1997; Robinson, Shaver, & Wrightsman, 1991). The previously mentioned article "FAQ/Finding Information About Psychological Tests" (APA, 2003) lists several print and electronic resources for information on unpublished tests.

🐚 TEST YOURSELF 🐚

1. **Which of the following is *not* an essential element of psychological testing?**
   (a) Systematic procedures
   (b) The use of empirically derived standards
   (c) Preestablished rules for scoring
   (d) Sampling behavior from affective domains

2. **The single most important source of criteria for evaluating tests, testing practices, and the effects of test use can be found in the**
   (a) *Ethical Principles of Psychologists and Code of Conduct.*
   (b) *Standards for Educational and Psychological Testing.*
   (c) *Diagnostic and Statistical Manual of Mental Disorders.*
   (d) *Report of the Task Force on Test User Qualifications.*

3. **The earliest antecedents of modern testing for personnel selection date back to**
   (a) China, B.C.E.
   (b) ancient Greece.
   (c) the Inca empire.
   (d) Medieval Europe.

4. **Evaluating psychological tests is *least* problematic**
   (a) prior to their being placed into use.
   (b) once they have been placed into use.

5. **Compared to the other areas listed, the development of criteria or bases for decision making has been substantially slower in the context of**
   (a) educational assessment.
   (b) occupational assessment.
   (c) clinical assessment.

6. **Credit for devising the first successful psychological test in the modern era is usually given to**
   (a) Francis Galton.
   (b) Alfred Binet.
   (c) James McKeen Cattell.
   (d) Wilhelm Wundt.

7. **The true ratio IQ or intelligence quotient was derived by**
   (a) adding the mental age (MA) and the chronological age (CA) of the test taker.
   (b) subtracting the CA from the MA and multiplying the result by 100.
   (c) dividing the CA by the MA and multiplying the result by 100.
   (d) dividing the MA by the CA and multiplying the result by 100.

8. **The primary purpose for which psychological tests are currently used is**
   (a) psychological research.
   (b) educational research.
   (c) decision making.
   (d) self-understanding and personal development.

9. **Compared to psychological testing, psychological assessment is generally**
   (a) simpler.
   (b) more structured.
   (c) more expensive.
   (d) more objective.

10. **Which of the following would be the best source of information on a test that is *not* commercially available?**
    (a) *Mental Measurements Yearbooks*
    (b) *Test Critiques*
    (c) *Tests in Print*
    (d) PsycINFO

Answers: 1. d; 2. b; 3. a; 4. a; 5. c; 6. b; 7. d; 8. c; 9. c; 10. d.

Two

ESSENTIAL STATISTICS FOR TESTING

By and large, the progress of science dovetails with the invention of measuring tools and advances in measurement procedures and techniques. The science of astronomy, for example, really took off in the 17th and 18th centuries following the invention of a telescope suitable for observing the cosmos and Descartes's invention of analytic geometry, which led to a more precise calculation of distances between celestial bodies, among other things. Similarly, the enormous current strides in the field of neuroscience owe much to the development of techniques such as positron emission tomography (PET) and functional magnetic resonance imaging (fMRI), which allow scientists to visualize and measure small biochemical changes and events in the brain.

As we saw in Chapter 1, the modern field of psychological testing also had its start with the invention of successful tools. The Binet-Simon intelligence scales provided for the measurement of important cognitive processes—such as comprehension, judgment, and memory—through behavior samples calibrated according to age. Arthur Otis's invention of objective multiple choice items led to the first group tests of general intelligence. Statistical techniques developed at approximately the same time as the first tests allowed for the analysis of data collected by means of those tests.

MEASUREMENT

The concept of measurement is at the heart of psychological testing as a scientific enterprise for the study of human behavior. *Measurement* involves the use of certain devices or rules for assigning numbers to objects or events (Stevens, 1946). If we apply this process systematically, then to a large extent, a phenomenon that is measured is made more easily subject to confirmation and analysis, and thus is made more objective as well. In other words, by systematically analyzing, categorizing, and quantifying observable phenomena we place them in the scientific arena.

Central to the definition of psychological tests is the fact that they consist of carefully chosen samples of behavior to which a numerical or category system is applied according to some preestablished standards. Psychological testing is largely coextensive with the field of *psychometrics,* or psychological measurement, and is one of the primary tools for the science and practice of psychology.

The use of numbers in testing requires us to delve into statistics. For many students of psychology the use of statistics and quantitative data in general poses a problem that may seem insurmountable: namely, that dealing with numbers tends to cause some anxiety. This anxiety is connected with the distress that classes in mathematics and statistics often induce for reasons that may be related as much to emotional or attitudinal factors as to those subjects themselves or to the way they have been taught traditionally. This chapter presents the statistical concepts needed to understand the basic principles of psychological testing. Those who have mastered basic statistics may be able to skip all or most of the chapter. As for the rest, any motivated reader of this book can achieve a serviceable grasp of the concepts described here. It is important, however, to realize that these concepts follow a logical progression; in order to proceed to each new topic it is essential to master the preceding ones. Additional help in understanding basic statistical methods is readily available in many excellent textbooks, such as the ones listed in Rapid Reference 2.1.

VARIABLES AND CONSTANTS

One of the most basic distinctions we can make in any science is that between variables and constants. As the terms themselves imply, a *variable* is anything that varies whereas a *constant* is anything that does not. Our world has many variables and few constants. One example of a constant is π (pi), the ratio of the circumference of a circle to its diameter, a number that is usually rounded to 3.1416. Variables, on the other hand, are everywhere and they can be classified in a multitude of ways. For example, some variables are visible (e.g., sex, color of eyes) and others invisible (e.g., personality, intelligence); some are defined so as to pertain to very small sets and others to very large sets (e.g., the number of children in a family or the average income of individuals in a country); and some are continuous, others discrete.

This last distinction is important for our purposes and bears some explaining. Technically, *discrete* variables are those with a finite range of values—or a potentially infinite, but countable, range of values. *Dichotomous* variables, for instance, are discrete variables that can assume only two values, such as sex or the outcome of coin tosses. *Polytomous* variables are discrete variables that can assume more than two values, such as marital status, race, and so on. Other discrete variables

≡ *Rapid Reference 2.1*

Advice on Statistics

Basic Premises

1. To understand psychological tests, one needs to deal with numbers and statistics.
2. Understanding statistics is possible for anyone who reads this book.
3. The best way to increase one's grasp of statistical concepts is to apply them.

Recommended Sources of Help with Statistics

Books

- Howell, D. C. (2002). *Statistical methods for psychology* (5th ed.). Pacific Grove, CA: Duxbury.
- Kirk, R. E. (1999). *Statistics: An introduction* (4th ed.). Fort Worth, TX: Harcourt Brace.
- Urdan, T. C. (2001). *Statistics in plain English*. Mahwah, NJ: Erlbaum.
- Vogt, W. P. (1998). *Dictionary of statistics and methodology: A nontechnical guide for the social sciences* (2nd ed.). Thousand Oaks, CA: Sage.

Video

- Blatt, J. (Producer/Writer/Director). (1989). *Against all odds: Inside statistics* [VHS videocassette]. (Available from The Annenberg/CPB Project, 901 E St., NW, Washington, DC 20004-2006)

can assume a wider range of values but can still be counted as separate units; examples of these are family size, vehicular traffic counts, and baseball scores. Although in practice it is possible to make errors in counting, in principle, discrete variables can be tallied precisely and without error.

Continuous variables such as time, distance, and temperature, on the other hand, have infinite ranges and really cannot be counted. They are measured with scales that could be theoretically subdivided into infinity and have no breaks in between their points, such as the scales in analog clocks, yardsticks, and glass thermometers. Since our measuring instruments (even atomic clocks!) can never be calibrated with enough precision to measure continuous variables exactly, the measurements we take of such variables are more or less accurate approximations.

Before we start dealing with numbers, another word of caution is in order. In psychological testing, we are almost always interested in variables that are continuous (e.g., degrees of integrity, extraversion, or anxiety), yet we measure with tools, such as tests or inventories, that are not nearly as precise as those in the physical and biological sciences. Even in those sciences the discrete measurement of continuous variables poses some limitations on the accuracy measurements. It therefore stands to reason that in the behavioral sciences we must be particularly aware of potential sources of error and look for pertinent estimates of error whenever we are presented with the results of any measurement process. For example, if polls taken from samples of potential voters are used to estimate the outcome of an election, the estimated margins of error have to be displayed alongside the results of the polls.

In summary, when we look at the results of any measurement process, we need to hold clearly in mind the fact that they are *inexact*. With regard to psychological testing in particular, whenever scores on a test are reported, the fact that they are estimates should be made clear; furthermore, the limits within which the scores might range as well as the confidence levels for those limits need to be given, along with interpretive information (see Chapter 4).

DON'T FORGET

- Although numbers may seem precise, all measurements are prone to error.
- When we are measuring discrete variables, errors arise only from inaccurate counting. Good practice requires the prevention, detection, and correction of inaccurate counting.
- When we are measuring continuous variables, on the other hand, measurement error is inevitable, as a consequence of the limitations of measurement tools.
- As measurement tools, psychological tests are subject to many limitations. Hence, margins of error must always be estimated and communicated along with test results.

THE MEANING OF NUMBERS

Because numbers can be used in a multitude of ways, S. S. Stevens (1946) devised a system for classifying different levels of measurement on the basis of the relationships between numbers and the objects or events to which the numbers are applied. These levels of measurement or scales—outlined in Table 2.1—specify some of the major differences in the ways numbers may be used as well as the types of statistical operations that are logically feasible depending on how numbers are used.

Nominal Scales

At the simplest level of his classification, Stevens placed what he called *nominal* scales. The word *nominal* is derived from the Latin root *nomen*, meaning *name*. As

Table 2.1 Levels of Measurement

Scale Type	Defining Characteristic	Properties of Numbers	Examples
Nominal	Numbers are used instead of words.	Identity or equality	SS#s; football players' jersey numbers; numerical codes for nonquantitative variables, such as sex or psychiatric diagnoses
Ordinal	Numbers are used to order a hierarchical series.	Identity + rank order	Ranking of athletes or teams; percentile scores
Interval	Equal intervals between units but no true zero.	Identity + rank order + equality of units	Fahrenheit and Celsius temperature scales; calendar time
Ratio	Zero means "none of" whatever is measured; all arithmetical operations possible *and* meaningful.	Identity + rank order + equality of units + additivity	Measures of length; periods of time

this implies, in such scales, numbers are used solely as labels to identify an individual or a class. The nominal use of numbers to label individuals is exemplified by the Social Security numbers (SS#s) that identify most people who live in the United States; these numbers are useful because each is assigned to only one person and can therefore serve to identify persons more specifically than their first and last names, which can be shared by many people. Numbers can also be used to label *categorical data,* which are data related to variables such as gender, political affiliation, color, and so forth—that is, data that derive from assigning people, objects, or events to particular categories or classes. When entering demographic data into a computer for analysis, for instance, investigators typically create a nominal scale that uses numbers to indicate the levels of a categorical variable. For example, the number 1 (one) may be assigned to all females and 2 (two) to all males. The only requirement for this use of numbers is that all the members of a set designated by a given number should be equal with regard to the category assigned to that number. Naturally, while the numbers used in nominal scales can certainly be added, subtracted, multiplied, or divided, the results of such operations are not meaningful. When we use numbers to identify categories, such as pass-fail or psychiatric diagnoses, the only property of such numbers is *identity;* this means that all members of a category must be assigned the same number and that no two categories may share the same number. The only permissible arithmetic operation is counting the frequencies within each category. One can then, of course, manipulate those frequencies further by calculating proportions and doing further analyses based on them.

Ordinal Scales

The numbers used in *ordinal* scales convey one more bit of meaning than those in nominal scales, albeit a significant one. In these scales, in addition to identity, there is the property of *rank order,* which means that the elements in a set can be lined up in a series—from lowest to highest or vice versa—arranged on the basis of a single variable, such as birth order or level of academic performance within a given graduating class. Although rank order numbers convey a precise meaning in terms of position, they carry no information with regard to the distance between positions. Thus, the students in a class can be ranked in terms of their performance, but this ranking will not reflect the amount of difference between them, which could be great or small. Similarly, in any hierarchical organization, say, the U.S. Navy, ranks (e.g., ensign, lieutenant, commander, captain, admiral) denote different positions, from lowest to highest, but the differences between them in terms of accomplishments or prestige are not the same. If those ranks were assigned numbers, such as 1, 3, 7, 14, and 35, the order of precedence would be maintained, but no further meaning would be added.

In psychological testing, the use of ordinal numbers to convey test results is pervasive. Rank ordered test scores are reported as *percentile rank (PR) scores*—not to be confused with the familiar percentage scores widely used in school grading. Percentile scores are simply ordinal numbers set on a scale of 100, so that the rank indicates the percentage of individuals in a group who fall at or below a given level of performance. For example, the percentile rank score of 70 indicates a level of performance that equals or exceeds that of 70% of the people in the group in question. Percentile rank scores, often referred to simply as *percentiles,* are the main vehicle whereby test users convey normative information derived from tests, and thus they will be discussed again, at greater length, in the next chapter.

Numerical data from ordinal scales can be manipulated statistically in the same way as nominal data. In addition, there are a few statistical techniques, such as Spearman's rho (r_s) correlation coefficient for rank differences, that are specifically appropriate for use with ordinal data.

Interval Scales

In interval scales, also known as *equal-unit* scales, numbers acquire yet one more important property. In these scales, the difference between any two consecutive numbers reflects an equal empirical or demonstrable difference between the objects or events that the numbers represent. An example of this is the use of days to mark the passage of calendar time. One day consists of 24 hours, each hour of 60 minutes, and each minute of 60 seconds; if two dates are 12 days apart, they are exactly three times as far apart as two dates that are only 4 days apart. Note, however, that calendar time in months is not an equal-unit scale because some months are longer than others. Furthermore, calendar time also typifies a characteristic of interval scales that limits the meaning of the numbers used in them, namely, that there is no true zero point. In the case of calendar time, there is no agreed upon starting point for the beginning of time. Different cultures have devised arbitrary starting points, such as the year Christ was presumed to have been born, to mark the passage of years. For instance, the much anticipated arrival of the new millennium at the end of the year 2000 of the Christian or Common Era came in the year 5761 of the Jewish calendar and in the year 4699 of the Chinese calendar, both of which start many years before the beginning of the Common Era.

In interval scales, the distances between numbers are meaningful. Thus, we can apply most arithmetical operations to those numbers and get results that make sense. However, because of the arbitrariness of the zero points, the numbers in an interval scale cannot be interpreted in terms of ratios.

Ratio Scales

Within *ratio* scales, numbers achieve the property of *additivity*, which means they can be added—as well as subtracted, multiplied, and divided—and the result expressed as a ratio, all with meaningful results. Ratio scales have a true or absolute zero point that stands for "none of" whatever is being measured. In the physical sciences, the use of this type of measurement scale is common; times, distances, weights, and volumes can be expressed as ratios in a meaningful and logically consistent way. For instance, an object that weighs 16 pounds is twice as heavy as one that weighs 8 pounds (16/8 = 2), just as an 80-pound object is twice as heavy as a 40-pound object (80/40 = 2). In addition, the zero point in the scale of weights indicates absolute weightlessness. In psychology, ratio scales are used primarily when we measure in terms of frequency counts or of time intervals, both of which allow for the possibility of true zeros.

Categorical or discrete data can be measured—or accounted for—only with nominal scales, or with ordinal scales if the data fall in a sequence of some kind. Continuous, or metric, data can be measured with interval scales, or ratio scales if there is a true zero point. In addition, continuous data can be converted into classes or categories and handled with nominal or ordinal scales. For instance, we could separate people into just three categories—tall, medium, and short—by establishing a couple of arbitrary cut-off points in the continuous variable of height.

When we move from nominal to ratio scales, we go from numbers that carry less information to numbers that carry more. As a consequence of this, going from one level of measurement to another requires us to be aware of whether the information that the numbers entail is preserved through whatever transformations or manipulations we apply to them.

Why Is the Meaning of Numbers Relevant to Psychological Testing?

Though it is not universally favored, Stevens's system for classifying scales

DON'T FORGET

- In measurement there has to be a demonstrable link between the numbers applied to objects, events, or people and the reality the numbers represent.
- When the rules used to create this link are not understood, the results of the measurement process are easily misinterpreted.
- As we shift from one level of measurement to another, we must be aware of whether the information the numbers entail is preserved in the transformations or manipulations we apply.
- Scores are numbers with specific meanings. Unless the limitations in the meaning of scores are understood, inaccurate inferences are likely to be made from the scores.

of measurement helps to keep the *relativity* in the meaning of numbers in proper perspective. The results of most psychological tests are expressed in scores, which are numbers that have specific meanings. Unless the limitations in the meaning of scores are understood, inaccurate inferences are likely to be made on the basis of those scores. Unfortunately, this is too often the case, as can be seen in the following examples.

Example 1: Specific limitations of ordinal scales. As mentioned earlier, many scores are reported in the form of percentile ranks, which are ordinal-level numbers that do not imply equality of units. If two scores are separated by 5 percentile rank units—e.g., the 45th and 50th percentiles—the difference between them and what the difference represents in terms of what is being measured cannot be equated with the difference separating any other scores that are 5 percentile units apart—for example, the 90th and 95th percentiles. In a distribution of scores that approximates the normal curve, discussed later in this chapter and portrayed in Figure 2.2, the majority of test scores cluster around the center of the distribution. This means that in such distributions differences between rank scores are always greater at the extremes or tails of the distribution than they are in the middle.

Example 2: The problem of ratio IQs. The original intelligence quotients devised for use with the Stanford-Binet Intelligence Scale (S-B) were *ratio IQs*. That is to say, they were real *quotients*, derived by dividing the mental age (MA) score a child had obtained on the S-B test by the child's chronological age (CA) and multiplying the result by 100 to eliminate the decimals. The idea was that average children would have similar mental and chronological ages and IQs of approximately 100. Children functioning below the average would have lower mental than chronological ages and IQs below 100, while those functioning above the average would have higher mental than chronological ages and IQs above 100. This notion worked fairly well for children in the early and middle school ages during which there tends to be a somewhat steady pace of intellectual growth from year to year. However, the MA/CA ratio simply did not work for adolescents and adults because their intellectual development is far less uniform—and changes are often imperceptible—from year to year. The fact that the maximum chronological age used in calculating the ratio IQ of the original S-B was 16 years, regardless of the actual age of the person tested, created additional problems of interpretation. Furthermore, the mental age and chronological age scales are not at the same level of measurement. Mental age, as assessed through the first intelligence tests, was basically an ordinal-level measurement, whereas chronological age can be measured on a ratio scale. For these reasons, dividing one number by the other to obtain a quotient simply did not lead to logically consistent and meaningful results. Rapid Reference 2.2 shows numerical examples highlighting some of the problems that have caused ratio IQs to be abandoned.

≡ Rapid Reference 2.2

....

Examples of Ratio IQ Computation With Attendant Problems

Subject	Mental Age (MA)	Chronological Age (CA)	Difference (MA – CA)	Ratio IQ[a]
Ally	6 years	5 years	1 year	$6/5 \times 100 = 120$
Ben	12 years	10 years	2 years	$12/10 \times 100 = 120$
Carol	18 years	15 years	3 years	$18/15 \times 100 = 120$

[a]In the actual computation of ratio IQs, both mental ages and chronological ages were expressed in months instead of years.

Problem 1: The mental age score required to obtain any given IQ keeps rising for each successive chronological age, so that the ratio IQs at different chronological ages are not equivalent.

Problem 2: Whereas chronological age rises steadily, mental age does not. Since the highest mental age achievable on a given intelligence test cannot be limitless, even when a limit is placed on the maximum chronological age used to compute IQs—as was done in the S-B scale for a long time—the IQs that most adults can attain are artificially constrained compared to those of children and adolescents.

Solution: Because of this and other problems with ratio IQs, as well as with the concept of mental ages, the use of the ratio IQ has been abandoned. The term *IQ* is now used for a score that is not a ratio IQ and is not even a quotient. This score, known as the *deviation IQ*, was pioneered by David Wechsler and is explained in Chapter 3.

What Can We Conclude About the Meaning of Numbers in Psychological Measurements?

In psychology, it is essential to keep in mind that most of our measurement scales are of an ordinal nature. Equality of units is approximated by the scales used in many types of test scores, but such equality is never as permanent or as complete as it is in the physical sciences, because the units themselves are relative to the performance of the samples from which they are derived. The use of ratio scales in psychology is limited to measures of frequencies, reaction times, or variables that can be meaningfully expressed in physical units. For example, if we were using assembly-line output per hour as a measure of speed of performance in an assembly line job, we could say that Worker A, who produces 15 units per hour, is 3 times as fast as Worker B, who produces only 5 units per hour. Note, however, that we could not say that Worker A is 3 times as good an employee as Worker B, because speed is probably not the only index of job performance even in an assembly line operation. Overall level of performance is a more complex variable that most likely can be assessed only with a qualitative, ordinal scale.

TYPES OF STATISTICS

Since the use of numbers to represent objects and events is so pervasive in psychological testing, the field involves substantial application of *statistics,* a branch of mathematics dedicated to organizing, depicting, summarizing, analyzing, and otherwise dealing with numerical data. Numbers and graphs used to describe, condense, or represent data belong in the realm of *descriptive statistics.* On the other hand, when data are used to estimate population values based on sample values or to test hypotheses, *inferential statistics*—a more ample set of procedures based on probability theory—are applied. Fortunately, although both descriptive and inferential statistics are used extensively in the development of tests, most of the quantitative aspects of test score interpretation require only a good grasp of descriptive statistics and a relatively small number of techniques of the inferential type. Moreover, even though a background in higher level math is desirable in order to understand thoroughly the statistics involved in testing, it is possible to understand them at a basic level with a good dose of logic and a relatively limited knowledge of math.

The words *statistic* and *statistics* are also used to refer to measures derived from sample data—as opposed to those derived from populations, which are called *parameters.* Means, standard deviations, correlation coefficients, and other such numbers calculated from sample data are all statistics derived in order to estimate what is of real interest, namely, the respective population parameters. *Parameters* are mathematically exact numbers (or constants, such as π) that are not usually attainable unless a population is so fixed and circumscribed that all of its members can be accounted for, such as all the members of a college class in a given semester. In fact, one of the main purposes of inferential statistics is to estimate population parameters on the bases of sample data and probability theory.

DON'T FORGET

The Two Meanings of *Statistics*

1. The study and application of methods for organizing, depicting, summarizing, analyzing, and otherwise dealing with numerical data.

2. Numbers (e.g., means, correlation coefficients) that describe the characteristics of variables or of sets of data derived from samples, as opposed to those derived from populations, which are called *parameters.*

Descriptive Statistics

Raw data are unwieldy. They usually consist of a bunch of numbers that do not convey much meaning, even

Table 2.2 Raw Data: 60 Test Scores

41	50	39	40	40	31	42	29	37	36
35	45	44	49	38	34	35	32	41	41
39	47	30	45	43	47	35	46	42	41
34	37	38	40	39	39	36	32	48	39
33	42	44	48	47	40	33	46	46	40
44	37	45	43	39	42	37	45	43	38

after close examination, such as the 60 numbers listed in Table 2.2. These numbers are the scores of 60 college students on the first test given in a psychological testing course; the test consists of 50 multiple-choice items. Simply looking at the numbers in the table yields some information, such as the fact that most scores seem to be somewhere between 30 and 50. With descriptive statistics, we can summarize the data so they are easier to understand. One way to summarize data is to represent them graphically; another way is to condense them into statistics that represent the information in a data set numerically.

Frequency Distributions

Before applying any statistical formulas, it is always a good idea to organize raw data in some sensible way so they can be inspected. Normally, this is accomplished by means of a *frequency distribution*. Table 2.3 presents a distribution of the test scores in Table 2.2, listing the number of times or frequencies with which each score occurred and the percentage of times that it occurred. The Cumulative Percent column shows the consecutive addition of the numbers in the Percent column from the lowest to the highest scores. This last set of figures allows us to see the percentage of the 60 cases that fell at or below each score and can thus be easily read as percentile rank scores for the individuals who obtained each score.

When the range of scores is very great, *grouped frequency distributions* help to organize scores into a still more compact form. In these distributions, scores are grouped into intervals of a convenient size to accommodate the data, and the frequencies are listed for each interval instead of for each of the scores. Naturally, what is gained in compactness is lost in terms of the detail of information.

Graphs

Once the data have been organized into a frequency distribution, they can be transposed into any one of several graphic formats, such as pie charts or bar graphs (for discrete or categorical data) and histograms or frequency polygons (for continuous or metric data). The data from Table 2.3 are graphically displayed in the form

Table 2.3 Frequency Distribution of 60 Test Scores

Scores	Frequency (f)	Percent[a] (P)	Cumulative Percent[a] (CP)
50	1	1.7	100.0
49	1	1.7	98.3
48	2	3.3	96.7
47	3	5.0	93.3
46	3	5.0	88.3
45	4	6.7	83.3
44	3	5.0	76.7
43	3	5.0	71.7
42	4	6.7	66.7
41	4	6.7	60.0
40	5	8.3	53.3
39	6	10.0	45.0
38	3	5.0	35.0
37	4	6.7	30.0
36	2	3.3	23.3
35	3	5.0	20.0
34	2	3.3	15.0
33	2	3.3	11.7
32	2	3.3	8.3
31	1	1.7	5.0
30	1	1.7	3.3
29	1	1.7	1.7

[a]Rounded to the nearest tenth.

of a frequency polygon in Figure 2.1. It is customary to use the horizontal axis (also called the *abscissa*, the *baseline*, or the *X-axis*) to represent the range of values of the variable in question and the vertical axis (called the *ordinate* or *Y-axis*) to depict the frequencies with which each of the values occur in the distribution. The rules and procedures for transforming frequency distributions of various types into graphs are presented in most textbooks on basic statistics (see, e.g., Kirk, 1999).

Numerical Description of Data

In addition to helping us visualize data through graphs, descriptive statistics also provides tools that allow for the properties of data to be summarized numeri-

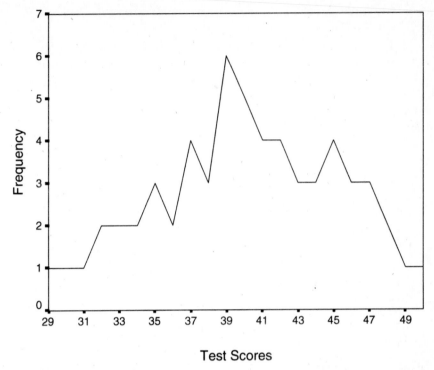

Figure 2.1 Frequency polygon for test scores in Table 2.3 (*n* = 60)

cally. These tools describe the central tendency and the variability of numerical data.

Measures of Central Tendency

One of the first things one wants to know when inspecting a data set is where the bulk of the data can be located, as well as the data's most representative or central value. The principal measures of central tendency—the mode, median, and mean—tell us these things. As with any other statistics, each of these measures has particular advantages and disadvantages depending on the types of data and distributions one wishes to describe. Their relative merits and disadvantages, which are beyond the scope of this work, are also discussed in most statistics textbooks (see, e.g., Howell, 2002).

- The *mode,* or most frequently occurring value in a distribution, is useful primarily when dealing with qualitative or categorical variables. Strictly speaking, there can be only one mode or—if there is no variability in a distribution—no mode at all. However, if two or more values in a distribution are tied with the same maximum frequency, the distribution is said to be *bimodal* or *multimodal*.

- The *median* (*Mdn*) is the value that divides a distribution that has been arranged in order of magnitude into two halves. If the number of values (*n*) in the distribution is odd, the median is simply the middle value; if *n* is even, the median is the midpoint between the two middle values.
- The *mean* or arithmetic average (μ for a population mean, and *M* for a sample mean) is obtained by summing all the values in a distribution and dividing the total by the number of cases in the distribution. Thus, its actual value may or may not be represented in the data set. In spite of this, and of the fact that it is the measure of central tendency most influenced by extreme scores, the mean has many desirable properties that make it the most widely used central tendency indicator for quantitative variables.

C A U T I O N

In the pages to come you will encounter a few statistical formulas. If you are tempted to skip them, DON'T. Remember, this is a book on the *Essentials of Psychological Testing*. The only formulas you will encounter in the book are those that convey concepts *essential* for understanding testing and the meaning of test scores.

Measures of Variability

These statistics describe how much dispersion, or *scatter,* there is in a set of data. When added to information about central tendency, measures of variability help us to place any given value within a distribution and enhance the description of a data set. Although there are many measures of variability, the main indexes used in psychological testing are the range, the semi-interquartile range, the variance, and the standard deviation.

- The *range* is the distance between two extreme points—the highest and lowest values—in a distribution. Even though the range is easily computed, it is a very unstable measure as it can change drastically due to the presence of one or two extreme scores.
- The *semi-interquartile range* is one half of the *interquartile range* (IQR), which, in turn, is the distance between the points that demarcate the tops of the first and third quarters of a distribution. The first quartile point (Q_1), or 25th percentile, marks the top of the lowest quarter (quartile) of the distribution. The third quartile point (Q_3), or 75th percentile, is at the top of the third quarter of the distribution and marks the beginning of the top quartile. The interquartile range is the range

between Q_1 and Q_3; therefore, it encompasses the middle 50% of a distribution. In the example presented in Table 2.3, the 25th percentile is at the score of 37 and the 75th percentile is at 44. The interquartile range is $44 - 37 = 7$ and the semi-interquartile range is $7 \div 2 = 3.5$. Note that whereas 53% of the scores fall within a narrow 8-point range, the other 47% of the scores are spread over all the remaining range of 14 score points.

- The *variance* is the sum of the squared differences or deviations between each value (X) in a distribution and the mean of that distribution (M), divided by N. More succinctly, the variance is the average of the *sum of squares* (SS). The sum of squares is an abbreviation for the sum of the squared deviation values or deviation scores, $\Sigma(X - M)^2$. Deviation scores have to be squared before being added, in order to eliminate negative numbers. If these numbers were not squared, the positive and negative deviation scores around the mean would cancel each other out and their sum would be zero. The sum of squares represents the total amount of variability in a score distribution and the variance (SS/N) represents its average variability. Due to the squaring of the deviation scores, however, the variance is not in the same units as the original distribution.

- The *standard deviation* is the square root of the variance. Along with the variance, it provides a single value that is representative of the individual differences or deviations in a data set—computed from a common reference point, namely, the mean. The standard deviation is a gauge of the average variability in a set of scores, expressed in the same units as the scores. It is the quintessential measure of variability for testing as well as many other purposes and is useful in a variety of statistical manipulations.

Rapid Reference 2.3 lists some of the basic notation symbols that will be used in this book, along with the formulas for the mean, interquartile range, standard deviation, and variance. The measures of central tendency and variability for the 60 test scores from Table 2.3 are listed in Table 2.4. Although the detailed information about the 60 scores is lost, the statistics in Table 2.4 concisely describe where the scores cluster as well as the average amount of dispersion in the data set.

The Importance of Variability

Whereas it may be true that variety is the spice of life, it is the very meat of testing. The psychological testing enterprise depends on variability across individuals.

≡Rapid Reference 2.3

Basic Notation and Formulas

X = A single data point or value in a distribution; in psychological testing, X almost always stands for a raw score.

Σ = Sum of.

n = Sample size, that is, the total number of cases in a distribution; in psychological testing, n almost always represents number of people or number of scores.

N = Population size.

M_X or $\overline{X}$ = Mean of $X = \dfrac{\Sigma X}{n}$

μ = Population mean

Mdn = Median = 50th percentile.

Q_1 = 1st quartile point = 25th percentile.

Q_3 = 3rd quartile point = 75th percentile.

$Q_1 - Q_3$ = Interquartile range (IQR).

$IQR \div 2$ = Semi-interquartile range.

s^2 = Sample variance = $\dfrac{\Sigma(X - M)^2}{n - 1}$

σ^2 = Population variance = $\dfrac{\Sigma(X - \mu)^2}{N}$

s or SD = Sample standard deviation = $\sqrt{s^2}$

σ = Population standard deviation = $\sqrt{\sigma^2}$

Table 2.4   Descriptive Statistics for the 60 Test Scores from Table 2.3

Measures of Central Tendency		Measures of Variability	
Mean	= 40.13	Range = 50 – 29	= 21
Median	= 40.00	Variance	= 25.745
Mode	= 39	Standard deviation	= 5.074
Q_1 or 25th percentile = 37		Interquartile range = $Q_3 - Q_1$ = 44 – 37 =	7
Q_3 or 75th percentile = 44		Semi-interquartile range = 7 ÷ 2	= 3.5

Without individual differences there would be no variability and tests would be useless in helping us to make determinations or decisions about people. All other things being equal, the greater the amount of variability there is among individuals, in whatever characteristic we are attempting to assess, the more accurately we can make the distinctions that need to be made among them. Knowing the shapes of score distributions as well as their central tendencies and variabilities provides the basis for a good portion of the essentials of test score interpretation discussed in Chapter 3.

Putting It Into Practice

- Go to Table 2.3 and count how many scores are within ± 1 SD of the mean—that is, between 40 ± 5.
- It turns out that 41 out of the 60 scores, roughly 2/3 of them, are between 35 and 45.
- This proportion is typical for distributions that approximate the shape of the normal curve like the distribution in Figure 2.1.

THE NORMAL CURVE MODEL

Definition

The normal curve, also known as the *bell curve,* is a distribution that in some ways is similar to the one in Figure 2.1. Its baseline, equivalent to the X-axis of the distribution in Figure 2.1, shows the standard deviation (σ) units; its vertical axis, or ordinate, usually does not need to be shown because the normal curve is not a frequency distribution of data but a mathematical model of an ideal or theoretical distribution. The height to which the curve rises at every single point along the baseline is determined by a mathematical formula that describes the specific relationships within the model and establishes the exact shape and proportions of the curve. Like all ideal models, the normal curve does not exist; it is based on probability theory. Fortunately, for our purposes, one can understand the basic facts about the normal curve without knowing much about its mathematical bases.

Although the normal curve model is an ideal, it is often approximated by the distributions of real data, such as the data from Table 2.3, presented in Figure 2.1. The similarity between the model and the distributions of many variables in the natural world has made it useful in descriptive statistics. Even more important is the fact that many chance events, if repeated a sufficiently large number of times, generate distributions that approximate the normal curve. It is this connection to probability theory that makes the normal curve serve an important role in inferential statistics. As we shall see, the usefulness of the normal curve model derives from its properties to which we now turn.

Properties of the Normal Curve Model

Many of the properties of the normal curve model are clearly evident upon visual inspection (see Figure 2.2). For instance, it can be seen that the normal distribution has each of the following properties:

- It is *bell shaped,* as its nickname indicates.
- It is *bilaterally symmetrical,* which means its two halves are identical (if we split the curve into two, each half contains 50% of the area under the curve).
- It has tails that approach but never touch the baseline, and thus its *limits extend to ± infinity* (±∞), a property that underscores the theoretical and mathematical nature of the curve.
- It is *unimodal;* that is, it has a single point of maximum frequency or maximum height.
- It has a *mean, median,* and *mode* that coincide at the center of the distribution because the point where the curve is in perfect balance, which is the mean, is also the point that divides the curve into two equal halves, which is the median, and the most frequent value, which is the mode.

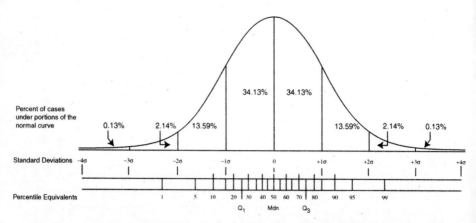

Figure 2.2 The normal curve with percentages of cases in each unit σ segment from –4 to +4, cumulative percentages, and percentile equivalents

In addition to these properties, the normal curve has other, less obvious characteristics that are linked to its mathematical function rule. This formula—which is not essential—is available in most statistics textbooks and in some of the normal curve Web sites mentioned in Rapid Reference 2.4. It involves two constant elements (π and e) and two values that can vary. Each particular normal curve is just one instance of a family of normal curve distributions that differ as a function of the two values of each specific curve that can vary. The two values that can vary are the mean, designated as μ, and the standard deviation, designated as σ. Once the μ and σ parameters for a normal distribution are set, one can calculate the height of the ordinate (Y-axis), at every single point along the baseline (X-axis), with the formula that defines the curve. When the normal curve has a mean of zero and a standard deviation of 1, it is called the *standard normal distribution*. Since the total area under the normal curve equals unity (1.00), knowledge of the height of the curve (the Y-ordinate) at any point along the baseline or X-axis allows us to calculate the proportion (p) or percentage ($p \times 100$) of the area under curve that is above and below any X value as well as between any two values of X. The statistical table resulting from these calculations, which shows the areas and ordinates of the standard normal curve, is available in Appendix C, along with a basic explanation of how the table is used.

In a normal curve, the standard deviation or σ units are positioned at equal distances along the X-axis, at points that mark the inflections of the curve itself (i.e., the points where the curve changes direction). Figure 2.2 shows the normal curve

Rapid Reference 2.4

Normal Curve Web Sites

These are just three of the many Web sites that can be found by entering "the normal curve" in a good online search engine:

- http://www.ms.uky.edu/~mai/java/stat/GaltonMachine.html

This site has a simple and visually appealing demonstration of the process that results in the bell curve.

- http://stat-www.berkeley.edu/~stark/Java/NormHiLite.htm

This Web page has an interactive tool that lets you highlight any segment of the normal curve and see immediately what percentage of the area is in the highlighted segment.

- http://www.psychstat.smsu.edu/introbook/sbk11.htm

This is one of several sites that explains basic facts about the normal curve clearly and succinctly.

divided at every σ unit from -4 to $+4$ as well as the percentages of the area comprised in each segment. Note that if you add all the percentages in the areas above the mean, the result equals 50%, as does the sum of all the areas below the mean. Furthermore, the area between $+1\sigma$ and -1σ is 68.26% (34.13% $\times$ 2)—roughly 2/3 of the curve—and the area between $+2\sigma$ and -2σ is 95.44%, almost the entire curve. Knowledge of these basic facts about the normal curve is exceedingly useful in statistics.

USES OF THE NORMAL CURVE MODEL

Descriptive Uses

Since the proportions of the area under the standard normal curve that lie above and below any point of the baseline or between any two points of the baseline are preestablished—and easy to find in the tables of areas of the normal curve such as the one in Appendix C—we can readily apply these proportions to any other distribution that has a similar shape. In testing, this particular application of the normal distribution is used repeatedly in generating the standard scores described in the next chapter.

Under some circumstances, even when a distribution approximates but does not exactly match the normal curve, we can still use the proportions within the normal curve model to normalize scores. *Normalizing* scores involves transforming them so that they have the same meaning, in terms of their position, as if they came from a normal distribution. This procedure, which is not as complicated as it may appear, makes use of the cumulative percentages computed from a frequency distribution (see Table 2.3). It will be discussed in more detail, with examples, in the next chapter.

Inferential Uses of the Normal Curve Model

In inferential statistics the normal curve model is useful for (a) estimating population parameters and (b) testing hypotheses about differences. Applications of the normal curve model to the estimation of population parameters and to hypothesis testing make use of two interrelated notions, namely, sampling distributions and standard errors.

Sampling distributions are hypothetical, as opposed to real, distributions of values predicated on the assumption that an infinite number of samples of a given size could be drawn from a population. If this were done, and if the statistics for those samples were recorded, many (but not all) of the resulting distributions of statistics or sampling distributions would be normal. The mean of each hypo-

Table 2.5   Standard Error of the Mean for the Data from Tables 2.3 and 2.4

Mean $(M) = 40.13$ Standard deviation $(s) = 5.074$ Sample size $(n) = 60$

$$\text{Standard error of the mean } (SE_M) = \frac{s}{\sqrt{n}} = \frac{5.074}{\sqrt{60}} = \frac{5.074}{7.7459} = .655$$

thetical sampling distribution would equal the population parameter and the standard deviation of the sampling distribution would be the standard error of the statistic in question.

The *standard error* (*SE*) of an obtained sample statistic is thus conceived of as the standard deviation of the sampling distribution that would result if we obtained the same statistic from a large number of randomly drawn samples of equal size. It can easily be calculated using sample statistics (see, e.g., Table 2.5). Once we have obtained a given statistic and its standard error from a sample, the assumption of a normal sampling distribution allows us to use the areas of the normal curve to estimate the population parameter based on the obtained statistic.

> **DON'T FORGET**
>
> Appendix C contains the Table of Areas and Ordinates of the Normal Curve, along with an explanation of how it is used. As is true of all the formulas in this book, the information in Appendix C is presented only because familiarity with it is an *essential* requirement for understanding test scores.

Estimating Population Parameters

A Hypothetical Example

In order to estimate a population parameter, such as the average height of all adult women in the United States, we might obtain a randomly drawn sample of 50 adult women, one from each state. Suppose that the mean height for that sample, which would be an *estimate* of the population mean, is 64 inches and suppose that the standard deviation is 4 inches. If we were to repeat this procedure over and over, drawing an infinite number of samples of 50 women each and recording the means of those samples each time, the sampling distribution of means that would result would fit the normal curve model. The mean of that theoretical sampling distribution could be construed as the population mean (i.e., the average height of all adult women in the United States).

Obviously, such a course of action is not only impractical, but also impossible. Therefore, we use inferential statistics to estimate the population mean. We find the *standard error of the mean* (SE_M) with the formula $s/\sqrt{n}$, where s is the standard deviation of the sample (4) and n is the number of cases in the sample (50). In this case, dividing 4 by the square root of 50 equals 7.07, which makes the $SE_M = 0.565$. Thus, based on our obtained sample statistics, we could say that the actual average height of adult women in the United States is within the range of our obtained mean of 64 in. ±0.565 in., or between 63.435 and 64.565 in. Adding and subtracting 1 SE_M from the sample mean gives us a 68% confidence interval for the population mean, because 68% of the area under the normal curve is within ±1σ (or in this case ±1 SE_M). If we wanted to make a statement with a higher level of confidence, we could choose a larger confidence interval by selecting a larger number of σ units and multiplying it times the SE_M. As we see in Figure 2.2, the segment between ±2σ encompasses 95.44% of the area under the normal curve; therefore, in our example, the interval between 64 ±2 SE_M or 64 ±2 (0.565 in.) = 64 ±1.13 in. and encompasses the range of 62.87 to 65.13 in. within which we could be 95.44% confident that the average height of adult women in the United States lies.

Example with data from Table 2.3: If we calculate the standard error of the mean (SE_M) for the data in Table 2.3, using the formula $s/\sqrt{n}$, where s is the standard deviation (5.074) and n is the number of cases in the sample (60), the $SE_M = .655$ (see Table 2.5). If the sample of 60 students had been drawn at random from all the students who ever took that particular test, we could then assume that there is approximately a 68% probability that the mean for the population of *all* the students who took that test is within ±.655 points, or ±1 SE_M, of the obtained mean

DON'T FORGET

Two Essential Concepts of Inferential Statistics: Sampling Distributions and Standard Errors

- *Sampling distributions* are theoretical distributions of the values of a variable, or of a statistic, that would result if one were to collect and record values (e.g., scores) or statistics (e.g., means, standard deviations, correlation coefficients, etc.) for an infinite number of samples of a given size from a particular population. Sampling distributions do not actually exist; they are hypothetical contrivances that are used for assigning probability estimates to obtained values or statistics through a device known as the *standard error.*

- *Standard errors* are statistical entities that *can* be computed, by various formulas, on the basis of sample data; they provide the means by which obtained values or sample statistics are compared to their theoretical sampling distributions. A standard error is the estimated standard deviation of the theoretical sampling distribution of an obtained value or statistic.

of 40.13, or somewhere in the range of 39.475 and 40.785. Similarly, we can say with 95.44% confidence—meaning that our chances of being wrong are less than 5%—that the interval between the mean of 40.13 $\pm 2\ SE_M$, that is, the range from 38.82 to 41.44, includes the population mean.

The Significance of Standard Errors

Standard errors are extremely important in inferential statistics. In both of the examples just presented, we could estimate ranges within which population parameters are likely to be found based on the assumptions that (a) the obtained sample mean is the best estimate we have of the population mean, and (b) the standard error of the mean is the equivalent of the standard deviation of the hypothetical sampling distribution of means, assumed to be normal. Similar assumptions, along with the estimates afforded by the areas under the standard normal curve and other theoretical distributions that appear in statistics textbook tables—such as the Student's *t* distribution—can be used not only to generate probability statements about population parameters derived from other sample statistics, but also to generate probability statements about obtained differences between sample statistics themselves.

When differences between sample means or proportions are tested for significance, the obtained differences are divided by the standard errors of those differences, calculated by formulas appropriate to the specific type of difference to be tested. The resulting ratios, called *critical ratios,* along with the appropriate distributions for the statistics in question, can then be used to ascertain the probability that an obtained difference could have resulted by chance. Although most of the techniques of inferential statistics are well beyond the scope of this book, we shall encounter standard errors again in connection with the reliability and validity of test scores, in Chapters 4 and 5. Rapid Reference 2.5 summarizes the main reasons why the normal curve model is so important in the field of psychological testing.

Non-normal Distributions

Creating graphic representations of obtained distributions permits a comparison of the obtained frequency distributions to the normal distribution. This matters a great deal because, to the extent that a frequency polygon or histogram differs in shape from the normal curve, the proportions of area under the curve no longer apply. Furthermore, the particular way in which distributions differ from the normal curve may carry significant implications concerning the data.

There are many ways in which distributions can differ from the normal curve

⟾ Rapid Reference 2.5

Why Is the Normal Curve So Important in Psychological Testing?

In testing, the normal curve model is used in ways that parallel the distinction between descriptive and inferential statistics:

1. The normal curve model is used *descriptively* to locate the position of scores that come from distributions that are normal. In a process known as *normalization*, described in Chapter 3, the normal curve is also used to make distributions that are not normal—but approximate the normal—conform to the model, in terms of the relative positions of scores.

2. The normal curve model is applied *inferentially* in the areas of (a) *reliability*, to derive confidence intervals to evaluate obtained scores and differences between obtained scores (see Chapter 4), and (b) *validity*, to derive confidence intervals for predictions or estimates based on test scores (see Chapter 5).

model. The manner and extent to which they deviate from it has implications with regard to the amount of information the distributions convey. An extreme case can be illustrated by the distribution that would result if all values in a set of data occurred with the same frequency. Such a distribution, which would be rectangular in shape, would imply no difference in the likelihood of occurrence of any given value and thus would not be useful in making decisions on the basis of whatever is being measured.

A different, and more plausible, type of deviation from the normal curve model happens when distributions have two or more modes. If a distribution is bimodal, or multimodal, one needs to consider the possibility of sampling problems or special features of the sample. For example, a distribution of class grades in which the peak frequencies occur in the grades of A and D, with very few B or C grades, could mean that the students in the class are atypical in some way or that they belong to groups that differ significantly in preparation, motivation, or ability level. Naturally, information of this nature would almost invariably have important implications; in the case of this example, it might lead a teacher to divide the class into sections and use different pedagogical approaches with each.

Two other ways in which distributions may deviate from the normal curve model carry significant implications that are relevant to test data. These deviations pertain to the properties of the kurtosis and skewness of frequency distributions.

Kurtosis

This rather odd term, which stems from the Greek word for *convexity,* simply refers to the flatness or peakedness of a distribution. Kurtosis is directly related to the amount of dispersion in a distribution. *Platykurtic* distributions have the greatest amount of dispersion, manifested in tails that are more extended, and *leptokurtic* distributions have the least. The normal distribution is *mesokurtic,* meaning that it has an intermediate degree of dispersion.

Kurtosis Applied: The Hypothesis of Greater Male Variability. In the field of differential psychology, a long-standing hypothesis has held that the range of intelligence is greater among males than it is among females. The hypothesis arose from observations concerning the overrepresentation of males in the ranks of people of extraordinary accomplishments as well as in institutions for the mentally retarded. Although there has been much debate about this hypothesis and some support for it (see, e.g., Halpern, 1997; Hedges & Nowell, 1995), for a variety of reasons—including the nature of intelligence tests themselves—the issue is not settled. If the hypothesis of greater male variability proved to be accurate, it would mean that more males than females are at the extreme high and low ends of the distribution of intelligence test scores. In such a case, the distributions of intelligence test scores for females and males would differ in kurtosis. Their graphic representations, if superimposed, might look like the hypothetical distributions in Figure 2.3, which shows a leptokurtic distribution for females and

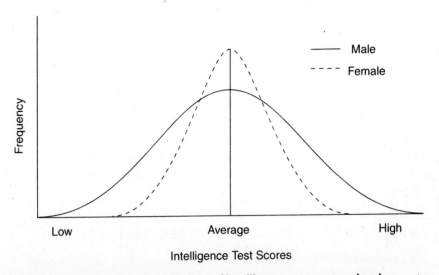

Figure 2.3 Hypothetical distributions of intelligence test scores, showing greater male than female variability (platykurtic vs. leptokurtic curve)

a platykurtic one for males, with no difference in the average scores of males and females.

Skewness

The *skewness* (*Sk*) of a distribution refers to a lack of symmetry. As we have seen, the normal distribution is perfectly symmetrical, with $Sk = 0$; its bulk is in the middle and its two halves are identical. A skewed distribution is asymmetrical. If most of the values are at the top end of the scale and the longer tail extends toward the bottom, the distribution is *negatively* skewed ($Sk < 0$); on the other hand, if most of the values are at the bottom and the longer tail extends toward the top of the scale, the distribution is *positively* skewed ($Sk > 0$).

Skewness Applied. The meaning of skewness with regard to test score distributions is easy to see. If a distribution is negatively skewed, it means that most people obtained high scores; if it is positively skewed, it means that most scored in the low end. Figure 2.4 displays examples of negatively and positively skewed distributions. Panel A of the figure shows a positively skewed distribution of scores on a test in which most of the students scored low; Panel B shows a negatively skewed distribution of scores on a test in which most test takers scored high.

Why Is the Shape of Distributions Relevant to Psychological Testing?

When a test is under development, the shape and characteristics of the score distributions obtained with its preliminary versions help to determine what adjustments, if any, need to be made to the test. The shape of the score distributions that are obtained during the process of test development should conform to expectations based on what the test is measuring and on the type of test takers who make up the preliminary or standardization samples. For example, if an achievement test is aimed at college-level students and the distribution of scores from a representative sample of college students is negatively skewed, it means that the test may be too easy and the test developer may need to add more difficult items to the test in order to bring the bulk of the scores more toward the center of the distribution. Conversely, if the same test is given to a representative sample of elementary school students and the distribution of their scores is positively skewed, the result conforms to expectations and does not suggest a need for readjustment.

ESSENTIALS OF CORRELATION AND REGRESSION

So far, our discussion has dealt primarily with the description and treatment of statistics derived from measures of a single variable, or *univariate* statistics. If we were interested only in test scores themselves (an unlikely possibility), those sta-

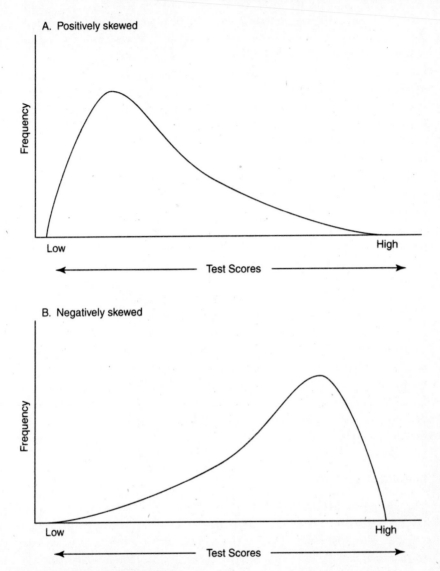

Figure 2.4 Skewed distributions

tistics would suffice. However, in order for test scores to have some meaning in
the practical arena, they need to provide information about other variables that
are significant in the real world. Correlational methods are the techniques used to
obtain indexes of the extent to which two or more variables are related to each
other, indexes that are called *correlation coefficients*. Correlational methods are the

major tools we have to demonstrate linkages (a) between scores on different tests, (b) between test scores and nontest variables, (c) between scores on parts of tests or test items and scores on whole tests, (d) between part scores or item scores and nontest variables, and (e) between scores on different parts of a test or different items from a single test. Because of these multiple applications, the notion of correlation plays an important part in the forthcoming discussions of reliability, validity, and test development in later chapters.

With correlation we enter the realm of *bivariate* or *multivariate* statistics. Instead of having a single frequency distribution of measures on one variable we need at least two sets of measurements or observations on the same group of people (e.g., scores on two different tests) or matched pairs of observations for two sets of individuals (e.g., the scores of twin pairs on the same test). When we compute a correlation coefficient to describe the relationship between two variables, data are organized in the form of bivariate distributions, like the ones presented in Table 2.6 for two sets of fictitious data.

In order to compute a correlation coefficient all we need is the data (i.e., observations) on two variables. The variables might be annual income and years of education for a set of people, the amount of rain and the size crops for a period of several years, the average length of women's skirts and the performance of the stock market over a period of time, the position of the sun in the sky and the amount of daylight in a given location, the scores on a test and an index of job performance for a group of employees, or any others. Two variables (usually labeled X and Y) can be correlated using any one of several correlational methods that differ with regard to the kinds of data and the kinds of relationships for which they are appropriate.

Linear Correlation

The relationship between two variables is said to be *linear* when the direction and rate of change in one variable are constant with regard to the changes in the other variable. When plotted on a graph, the data points for this type of relationship form an elliptical pattern that is straight or nearly so. If there is a correlation between two variables and the relationship between them is linear, there are only two possible outcomes: (a) a positive correlation or (b) a negative correlation. If there is no correlation, the data points do not align themselves into any definite pattern or trend and we may assume that the two sets of data do not share a common source of variance. If there is either a positive or a negative correlation of any magnitude, we can evaluate the possibility that the correlation could have resulted from chance, using the size of the sample on which the correlation was

Table 2.6   Two Sets of Bivariate Data

Individual	Score on Test X	Score on Test Y
	A. Data for a perfect positive correlation	
1	3	5
2	4	6
3	6	8
4	7	9
5	8	10
6	9	11
7	10	12
8	11	13
9	13	15
10	14	16
	B. Data for a perfect negative correlation	
1	140	5
2	130	6
3	110	8
4	100	9
5	90	10
6	80	11
7	70	12
8	60	13
9	40	15
10	30	16

computed and statistical tables that show the probability that a coefficient of a given magnitude could have occurred by chance. Naturally, the larger the coefficient, the less likely it is that it could be the result of chance. If the probability that the obtained coefficient resulted from chance is very small, we can be confident that the correlation between X and Y is greater than zero. In such cases, we assume that the two variables share a certain amount of common variance. The larger and the more statistically significant a correlation coefficient is, the larger the amount of variance we can assume is shared by X and Y. The proportion of variance shared by two variables is often estimated by squaring the correlation coefficient (r_{xy}) and obtaining the *coefficient of determination*, or r_{xy}^2. Although coefficients of determination tell us how much of the variance in Y can be explained by the variance in X, or vice versa, they do not necessarily indicate that there is a causal relationship between X and Y.

Scatterplots

The graphic depiction of bivariate data in the form of scatter diagrams or scatterplots is essential in order for us to visualize the kind of relationship at hand. The scatterplots in Figure 2.5 present the patterns of points that result from plotting the bivariate distributions from Table 2.6. These figures let us literally see the strength and direction of the relationship between the two variables in each set. We can see that in both parts of the figure, the patterns fall in a straight diagonal line, indicating that both of the plotted relationships are linear and strong; in fact, the correlations are perfect, something that is rarely seen with real data. A strong correlation means that as the values of one variable increase or decrease, there is a corresponding amount of change in the values of the other variable. The direction of the pattern of points in a scatterplot tells us whether the corresponding changes are in the same or opposite directions. In the perfect pattern depicted in Figure 2.5, Panel A, the relationship is invariant: For every unit increase in the scores of Test X, there is a corresponding increase of one unit in the scores of Test Y. In Figure 2.5, Panel B, we see another perfect, invariant pattern: For every decrease of 10 units in Test X, there is a corresponding increase of one unit in Test Y. The relationships are in opposite directions but both of them maintain a perfect correspondence relative to their respective scales.

The Discovery of Regression

The reader may recall from Chapter 1 that Francis Galton made significant contributions to the development of psychometrics. One of the most important of these was Galton's discovery of the phenomenon he called *regression,* a discovery that resulted from his attempts to chart the resemblance between parents and offspring on a number of variables and to produce evidence of their hereditary nature. In terms of the variable of height, for instance, Galton discovered that parents who were taller than average tended to have children who, as adults, were also taller than the average height of the parents in his sample, but closer to that average than the parents themselves. The reverse was true for parents who were shorter than the average; their children, as adults, also tended to be shorter than the average height of parents in Galton's sample, but closer to that average than the parents themselves. When he plotted these bivariate data of matched sets of heights of parents and children, as well as other sets of variables, Galton

A. Perfect positive correlation, $r = +1.00$

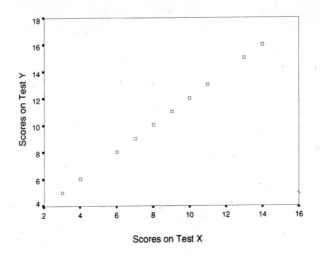

B. Perfect negative correlation $r = -1.00$

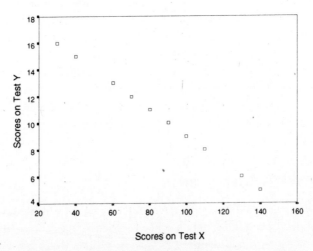

Figure 2.5 Scatterplots of bivariate data from Table 2.6

discerned that this pattern of *regression toward the mean* kept repeating itself: Extreme scores of parents on one variable tended to be associated with scores that were closer to the mean in the offspring. Furthermore, Galton found that if he plotted the heights of offspring at various ranges, relative to the average heights of parents within those intervals, he obtained a linear pattern he called the *regression line*. Galton understood that the slope of the regression line represented the strength or magnitude of the relationship between the heights of parents and children: The greater the slope of the line, the stronger the relationship between the two variables.

In spite of the significance of his discovery, Galton's conclusions about the phenomenon of regression were not quite accurate (see Cowles, 2001). This was partly a result of restrictions in the data he used in his analyses and partly due to his misinterpretation of the causes of correlations between variables. Given that the genetic bases of heredity were unclear at the time when Galton was working on these problems, his misinterpretation of regression is understandable. Nevertheless, the procedures he developed to portray the relationship between variables have proved to be extremely useful in assessing the amount of variance shared by variables. More importantly, regression analyses have given us a basis for making *predictions* about the value of Variable Y, based on knowledge of the corresponding value of Variable X, with which Variable X has a known and significant degree of correlation. After all, it is true that if a set of parents is taller than the average, we can also expect their children to be taller than average. Galton himself devised a way to quantify the relationship between variables by transforming the values of each into a common scale and computing a numerical index or coefficient that summarized the strength of their relationship. However, it was Karl Pearson, a mathematician and disciple of Galton, who refined the method and developed the most widely used formula for computing correlation coefficients.

CORRELATION COEFFICIENTS

As we have seen, *correlation* simply refers to the extent to which variables are related. The degree and the direction of the correlation between variables is measured by means of various types of *correlation coefficients*, which are numbers that can fluctuate anywhere from −1.00 to +1.00. Rapid Reference 2.6 lists some other basic but often misunderstood facts concerning correlation coefficients in general.

Unlike the so-called hard sciences, where experimentation is the typical way to

≡ *Rapid Reference 2.6*

....

Three Essential Facts About Correlation in General

1. *The degree of relationship between two variables is indicated by the number in the coefficient, whereas the direction of the relationship is indicated by the sign.*
   A correlation coefficient of –0.80, for example, indicates exactly the same degree of relationship as a coefficient of +0.80. Whether positive or negative, a correlation is low to the extent that its coefficient approaches zero. Although these facts may seem obvious, the apparently compelling nature of negative signs often causes people to forget them.

2. *Correlation, even if high, does not imply causation.*
   If two variables, X and Y, are correlated, it may be because X causes Y, because Y causes X, or because a third variable, Z, causes both X and Y. This truism is also frequently ignored; moderate to high correlation coefficients are often cited as though they were proof of a causal relationship between the correlated variables.

3. *High correlations allow us to make predictions.*
   While correlation does not imply causation, it does imply a certain amount of common or shared variance. Knowledge of the extent to which things vary in relation to one another is extremely useful. Through regression analyses we can use correlational data on two or more variables to derive equations that allow us to predict the expected values of a dependent variable (Y), within a certain margin of error, based on the known values of one or more independent variables ($X_1, X_2, \ldots X_k$), with which the dependent variable is correlated.

proceed, in the behavioral sciences the ability to manipulate variables is often restricted. Thus, research in psychology relies on correlational methods to a great extent. Fortunately, the array of research designs and methods of analysis that can be applied to data has grown immensely with the power and availability of modern computers. Some of the currently commonplace techniques for the simultaneous analysis of data from multiple variables, such as multiple regression and path analysis, are so sophisticated that they allow psychologists and other social scientists to make some inferences about causal relationships with a high degree of confidence.

Which statistical technique is used to compute a coefficient of correlation depends on the nature of the variables to be correlated, the types of scales used in measuring them, and the pattern of their relationship. Once again, a full review of methods is beyond the scope of this book. However, the most widely used index of the amount of correlation between two variables bears some discussion.

Pearson Product-Moment Correlation Coefficient

The basic formula that Karl Pearson devised for computing the correlation coefficient of bivariate data from a sample is formally known as the *Pearson product-moment correlation coefficient*. The definitional formula of this coefficient, more commonly referred to as the Pearson *r*, is

$$r_{xy} = \frac{\Sigma\, xy}{N s_x s_y} \tag{2.1}$$

where

r_{xy} = the correlation between X and Y;
x = the deviation of a score X from the mean of X scores;
y = the deviation of a corresponding Y score from the mean of Y scores;
$\Sigma\, xy$ = the sum of all the cross-products of the deviations (i.e., the sum of the products of each x deviation times its corresponding y deviation);
N = the number of pairs in the bivariate data set;
s_x = the standard deviation of the X scores; and
s_y = the standard deviation of the Y scores

Although the computational raw-score formula for the Pearson *r* is more complicated than the definitional formula, the easy availability of computer software to compute correlation coefficients makes the computational formula practically unnecessary. On the other hand, Formula (2.1) and the even shorter Formula (2.2) are of considerable help in understanding the numerical meaning of the correlation coefficient. Rapid Reference 2.7 lists the basic notation for correlation along with two versions of the formula for the Pearson *r*.

The Pearson *r* is actually the mean of the cross-products of the standard scores of the two correlated variables. The formula that embodies this definition is

$$r_{xy} = \frac{\Sigma\, z_x z_y}{N} \tag{2.2}$$

where

r_{xy} = the correlation between X and Y;
z_x = the standard scores of variable X, obtained by dividing each deviation score on X by the standard deviation of X; and
z_y = the standard scores of variable Y, obtained by dividing each deviation score on Y by the standard deviation of Y

≡ Rapid Reference 2.7

Basic Notation for Correlation

Variable X	Variable Y
X = A score on variable X	Y = A score on variable Y
$x = X - \bar{X}$ = Deviation score on X	$y = Y - \bar{Y}$ = Deviation score on Y
S_x = Standard deviation of X	S_y = Standard deviation of Y
z_x = Standard score on variable X	z_y = Standard score on variable Y
$z_x = \dfrac{X - \bar{X}}{S_x}$	$z_y = \dfrac{Y - \bar{Y}}{S_y}$

Formulas for the Pearson r:

$$r_{xy} = \frac{\Sigma\, xy}{N S_x S_y} \quad \text{Formula (2.1), definitional formula}$$

$$r_{xy} = \frac{\Sigma\, z_x z_y}{N} \quad \text{Formula (2.2), standard score formula}$$

where N = number of paired observations of X and Y used to compute r.

Coefficient of determination $= r_{xy}^2$

Summing the cross-products of the z scores of the X and Y variables and dividing by the number of pairs in a data set produces an average that reflects the amount of relationship between X and Y, namely, the Pearson r.

Formula (2.2) is of interest in the context of psychological testing, not just because of its brevity and conceptual basis, but also because it serves to introduce the notion of *standard scores,* or *z scores,* with which we shall deal again in the next chapter. The reader may have noticed that the values along the baseline of the normal curve in the Table of Areas of the Normal Curve presented in Appendix C are given in terms of z scores. The reason for this is that a z score represents the distance between each value in a distribution and the mean of that distribution, expressed in terms of the standard deviation unit for that distribution. The standard score formula (2.2) for the Pearson r simply provides a more compact way of expressing the relationship between two variables.

Conditions Necessary for the Use of the Pearson r

Although it is, by far, the most widely used correlation coefficient, the Pearson r is appropriate only for data that meet certain conditions. Since Pearson developed his formula, many different methods have been developed to obtain correlation coefficients for various types of bivariate data. The derivation of the Pearson product-moment correlation coefficient rests on the following assumptions:

1. The pairs of observations are independent of one another.
2. The variables to be correlated are continuous and measured on interval or ratio scales.
3. The relationship between the variables is linear; that is, it approximates a straight-line pattern, as described earlier.

Whether the first and second of these assumptions or conditions have been met is easily ascertained from knowledge of the manner in which the data were collected and of the type of data at hand. If the pairs of scores or observations to be correlated are obtained independently of one another, the first assumption has been satisfied. If the data for both variables represent continuous quantities, the second assumption has been met.

Satisfying the third, and most critical, assumption of the Pearson r requires inspection of the scatterplot of the bivariate data to see whether the distribution of cases falls into the elliptical shape that is indicative of a linear relationship portrayed in Figure 2.6, Panel A. When this assumption is violated, the Pearson r is not an accurate index of correlation.

Deviations from Linearity

For purposes of determining the applicability of the Pearson r to a set of bivariate data, there are two ways in which a scatterplot can deviate from the elliptical shape that indicates a linear positive relationship. The first and most obvious way is if there is a significant bending of the elliptical shape, as in Figure 2.6, Panels B and C. Such deviations indicate that there is no longer a linear relationship and, therefore, that the relationship between X and Y is not the same throughout the range of their values. The second way in which scatterplots can deviate from the ellipse that indicates a linear relationship is a condition called *heteroscedasticity*. This simply means that the dispersion or variability in the scatterplot is not uniform throughout the range of values of the two variables. In order to use the Pearson r correlation coefficient, the scatterplot needs to show a fairly uniform amount of dispersion, or *homoscedasticity*, throughout the range. The scatterplot in Figure 2.6, Panel A, is homoscedastic, whereas the ones in Figure 2.6, Panels D and E, are heteroscedastic.

One of the ways to avoid the inappropriate application of the Pearson r is by

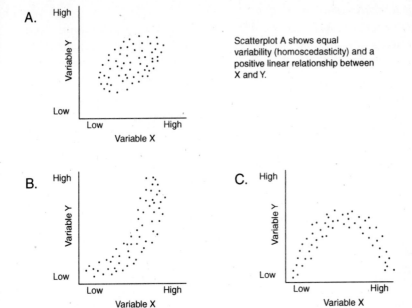

A.

Scatterplot A shows equal variability (homoscedasticity) and a positive linear relationship between X and Y.

Scatterplots in B and C show nonlinear relationships between X and Y.

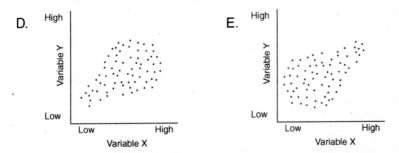

Scatterplots D and E show unequal variabity (heteroscedasticity); D shows greater variability at the high end of the range where as E shows greater variability at the low end.

Figure 2.6 Scatterplots illustrating various characteristics of bivariate data

Note. Each point marks the location of one pair of observations, or scores on X and Y.

producing a scatterplot of the bivariate data and inspecting its shape for possible deviations from linearity. If the Pearson *r* formula is applied to data that deviate from a straight linear relationship, either in terms of a bending in the shape of the scatterplot or due to heteroscedasticity, the resulting correlation coefficient will be an incorrect index of the relationship between X and Y.

Range Restriction and Correlation

An important and often overlooked feature of the Pearson r concerns the way it is affected by the variability of the correlated variables. Stated simply, the effect of a restriction in the range of either one of the variables is to reduce the size of r.

Example 1: An extreme case. The most extreme, though not very realistic, case of range restriction would be a situation in which there is no variability at all in one of the correlated variables. If we refer to the definitional formula for the Pearson r presented in Rapid Reference 2.7, we can easily see that if there were no variability in the scores on either X or Y (i.e., if all the values of either X or Y were the same), all the deviation scores of the respective variable and the numerator of the Pearson r coefficient formula would be zero, thereby resulting in a correlation coefficient of zero. This is just one instance of the singular importance of variability highlighted earlier in this chapter.

Example 2: The effect of range restriction in employment testing. If all the people who applied for a large number of available positions in a new corporation were hired, regardless of their scores on a preemployment aptitude test, chances are that we would find a fairly high correlation between their scores and measures of job productivity obtained a few months after they were hired. Since we can assume that a large group of applicants would exhibit fairly broad ranges both in aptitude test scores and in job productivity, the relationship between aptitude and productivity would most likely be reflected by the correlation coefficient. If, after a while, the personnel selection process gets more restrictive—so that only those applicants who obtain high scores on the aptitude test are hired—the net effect of this change would be to constrict the range of ability among newly hired employees. Thus, if a new coefficient were computed only with data for the newly hired, the degree of correlation between aptitude test scores and productivity would be reduced. The scatter diagram in Figure 2.7 represents the high positive correlation between aptitude test scores and job productivity there might be among the large heterogeneous group of people initially hired. The small segment in the upper right-hand portion of the diagram represents the low, almost nonexistent, correlation there would probably be in the much more restricted group of top applicants hired later on.

Just as a restriction in the range of correlated variables will lower the correlation between them, a wide range of variability in the correlated variables will tend to augment the size of the obtained correlation coefficient and possibly overestimate the relationship between the two variables. The fact that correlation coefficients depend on the variability of the samples within which they are found emphasizes the importance of examining the composition of samples from the point of view of their appropriateness. Although some statistical corrections for range

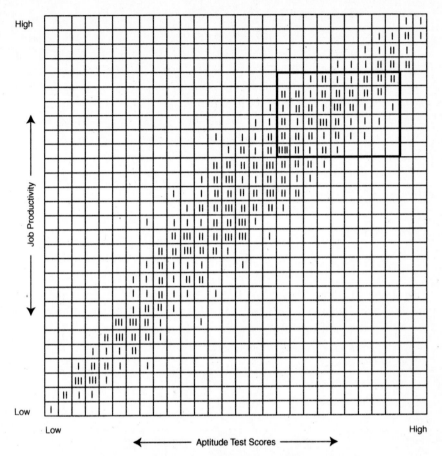

Figure 2.7 The effect of restricted range on correlation

restrictions can be used when the variability in a sample is reduced, there is no substitute for making sure that the variability of the samples within which coefficients are computed corresponds to the variability of the group or groups to which the obtained correlations will be applied.

Other Correlational Methods

The Pearson r can be used in a wide range of cases, as long as the necessary conditions are met. When they are not met, other procedures can be applied to obtain correlations for bivariate data. For example, when the variables to be correlated are in ordinal form, the correlation method of choice—already mentioned in connection with ordinal scales—is Spearman's rank-difference coefficient of correlation, commonly known as *Spearman's rho* (r_S). If the relationship between two variables is curvilinear, the correlation ratio—commonly known as *eta* (η)—may be used. When one of the variables to be correlated is dichotomous, the *point biserial correlation,* or r_{pb}, is used, whereas if both variables are dichotomous, the *phi* or *fourfold coefficient* (ϕ) is employed. Dichotomous variables often come into play in analyzing test item data recorded in terms of pass-fail or true-false responding.

There are many other types of correlation coefficients that are suited to specific types of data. They can be found in statistics textbooks when the need arises. One particularly important variant is the *multiple correlation coefficient* (R), which is used when a single dependent variable (Y) is correlated with two or more combined predictors ($X_1, X_2, \ldots, X_k$).

CONCLUSION

This chapter has presented the basic statistical concepts needed to understand test scores and their meaning. Statistics exist to help us make sense of data, but they do not answer questions. In order to do that we have to use our judgment along with the statistics. We will encounter these concepts again in the context of the various technical aspects of tests—such as normative information, reliability, and validity—that allow us to evaluate their quality as instruments of psychological measurement.

🐾 TEST YOURSELF 🐾

1. **Which of the following scales of measurement is the only one that has a meaningful zero point?**
   (a) Nominal
   (b) Ratio
   (c) Ordinal
   (d) Interval

2. **Tom and Jerry scored at the 60th and 65th percentiles, respectively, on a language skills test. Mary and Martha scored at the 90th and 95th percentiles, respectively, on the same test. We can conclude that the difference between Tom and Jerry in terms of their language skills is the same as the difference between Mary and Martha. The preceding statement is**
   (a) true.
   (b) false.

3. **On a test of general cognitive ability, a 5-year-old child obtains a mental age score of 4 years and a 10-year-old child obtains a mental age score of 9 years. If one were to compute their IQs according to the original ratio IQ formula, the result would be as follows:**

   (a) Both children would obtain the same ratio IQ.

   (b) The 5-year-old would obtain a higher ratio IQ.

   (c) The 10-year-old would obtain a higher ratio IQ.

4. **In the distribution 2, 2, 2, 2, 3, 3, 3, 8, 11, the mean, median, and mode are, respectively,**

   (a) 4, 3, and 2.

   (b) 2, 4, and 3.

   (c) 3, 4, and 2.

   (d) 2, 3, and 4.

5. **For testing and many other purposes, the quintessential index of the variability in a distribution of scores is the**

   (a) sum of the squared deviation scores.

   (b) the square root of the variance.

   (c) the semi-interquartile range.

6. **Which of the following statements about the normal curve model is *not* true?**

   (a) It is bilaterally symmetrical.

   (b) Its limits extend to infinity.

   (c) Its mean, median, and mode coincide.

   (d) It is multimodal.

7. **The area of a normal distribution between $+1\sigma$ and -1σ encompasses approximately _____ of the curve.**

   (a) 50%

   (b) 68%

   (c) 95%

   (d) 99%

8. **If the shape of the distribution of scores obtained from a test is significantly skewed, it means that the test is probably _____ for the test takers in question.**

   (a) too easy

   (b) too hard

   (c) either too easy or too hard

   (d) just right

(continued)

9. **Which of the following coefficients represents the strongest degree of correlation between two variables?**

   (a) −.80

   (b) −.20

   (c) +.20

   (d) +.60

10. **If the range of values of either one of two variables that are correlated using the Pearson product-moment coefficient of correlation (Pearson _r_) is restricted, the size of the obtained coefficient will be**

    (a) reduced.

    (b) increased.

    (c) unaffected.

Answers: 1. b; 2. b; 3. c; 4. a; 5. b; 6. d; 7. b; 8. c; 9. a; 10. a

Three

ESSENTIALS OF TEST SCORE INTERPRETATION

No matter how many statistics are used in psychological testing, in the final analysis the meaning of test scores derives from the frames of reference we use to interpret them and from the context in which the scores are obtained. To be sure, test scores also need to be reliable and test items need to be carefully developed and evaluated so that they contribute to the meaning of scores; these are matters with which we deal in Chapters 4 and 6. Presently, we turn to the frames of reference for interpreting test scores, a topic that is closely connected to the validity of inferences we can make on the basis of tests, discussed at length in Chapter 5. The context in which testing takes place, an issue of paramount importance that is related to the process of test selection and test administration, is discussed in the final chapter. Rapid Reference 3.1 lists three excellent sources of information where many of the topics discussed in this chapter are covered in greater detail.

RAW SCORES

A *raw score* is a number (X) that summarizes or captures some aspect of a person's performance in the carefully selected and observed behavior samples that make up psychological tests. By itself, a raw score does not convey any meaning. High scores may be a favorable result on tests of ability, but not favorable on tests that evaluate some aspect of psychopathology. In the Minnesota Multiphasic Personality Inventory (MMPI) for instance, elevated scores usually indicate some kind of maladjustment yet low scores do not necessarily indicate good adjustment. Even if we know the type of test from which a score was obtained, we can be misled. Some tests of cognitive ability—in particular, many neuropsychological instruments—are scored in terms of number of errors or speed of performance, so that the higher the score, the less favorable the result. Moreover, we cannot even know how high "high" is without some kind of frame of reference. A score that sounds high—such as an IQ of 130, for example—may have quite different

≡*Rapid Reference 3.1*

For more extensive information on technical aspects of many of the topics discussed in this chapter, see any one of the following sources:

- Angoff, W. H. (1984). *Scales, norms, and equivalent scores.* Princeton, NJ: Educational Testing Service.
- Petersen, N. S., Kolen, M. J., & Hoover, H. D. (1989). Scaling, norming, and equating. In R. L. Linn (Ed.), *Educational measurement* (3rd ed., pp. 221–262). New York: American Council on Education/Macmillan.
- Thissen, D., & Wainer, H. (Eds.). (2001). *Test scoring.* Mahwah, NJ: Erlbaum.

meanings depending on the test from which it was derived, the areas the test covers, and how recent its norms are, as well as specific aspects of the situation in which the score was obtained and the characteristics of the test taker.

FRAMES OF REFERENCE FOR TEST-SCORE INTERPRETATION

Underlying all other issues regarding score interpretation, in one way or another, is the matter of the frames of reference used to interpret a given score. Depending on their purpose, tests rely on one or both of the following sources of information to derive frames of reference for their meaning:

1. *Norms. Norm-referenced test interpretation* uses standards based on the performance of specific groups of people to provide information for interpreting scores. This type of test interpretation is useful primarily when we need to compare individuals with one another or with a reference group in order to evaluate differences between them on whatever characteristic the test measures. The term *norms* refers to the test performance or typical behavior of one or more reference groups. Norms are usually presented in the form of tables with descriptive statistics— such as means, standard deviations, and frequency distributions—that summarize the performance of the group or groups in question. When norms are collected from the test performance of groups of people, these reference groups are labeled *normative* or *standardization samples.* Gathering norms is a central aspect of the process of standardizing a norm-referenced test.

2. *Performance criteria.* When the relationship between the items or tasks of a test and standards of performance is demonstrable and well defined, test scores may be evaluated via *criterion-referenced interpretation.* This type of interpretation makes use of procedures, such as sampling from content domains or work-related behaviors, designed to assess

whether and to what extent the desired levels of mastery or performance criteria have been met.

NORM-REFERENCED TEST INTERPRETATION

Norms are, by far, the most widely used frame of reference for interpreting test
scores. The performance of defined groups of people is used as a basis for score
interpretation in both ability and personality testing. When norms are the frame
of reference, the question they typically answer is "How does the performance of
this test taker compare to that of others?" The score itself is used to place the test
taker's performance within a preexisting distribution of scores or data obtained
from the performance of a suitable comparison group.

Developmental Norms

Ordinal Scales Based on Behavioral Sequences
Human development is characterized by sequential processes in a number of behavioral realms. A classic example is the sequence that normal motor development follows during infancy. In the first year of life, most babies progress from
the fetal posture at birth, through sitting and standing, to finally walking alone.
Whenever a universal sequence of development involves an orderly progression
from one behavioral stage to another—more advanced—stage, the sequence itself can be converted into an *ordinal* scale and used normatively. In such cases, the
frame of reference for test score interpretation is derived from observing and
noting certain uniformities in the order and timing of behavioral attainments
across many individuals. The pioneer in the development of this type of scales
was Arnold Gesell, a psychologist and pediatrician who published the Gesell Developmental Schedules in 1940 based on a series of longitudinal studies conducted by him and his associates at Yale over a span of several decades (Ames,
1989).

    The Provence Birth-to-Three Developmental Profile. A current example of an instru-
ment that uses ordinal scaling is the Provence Birth-to-Three Developmental
Profile ("Provence Profile"), which is part of the Infant-Toddler Developmental
Assessment (IDA; Provence, Erikson, Vater, & Palmieri, 1995). The IDA is an integrated system designed to help in the early identification of children who are
developmentally at risk and possibly in need of monitoring or intervention.
Through naturalistic observation and parental reports, the Provence Profile provides information about the timeliness with which a child attains developmental
milestones in eight domains, in relation to the child's chronological age. The de-

velopmental domains are Gross Motor Behavior, Fine Motor Behavior, Relationship to Inanimate Objects, Language/Communication, Self-Help, Relationship to Persons, Emotions and Feeling States (Affects), and Coping Behavior. For each of these domains, the profile groups items into age brackets ranging from 0 to 42 months. The age brackets are as small as 2 months at earlier ages and as wide as 18 months in some domains at later ages. Most span between 3 and 6 months. The number of items in each age group differs as well, as does the number of items that need to be present or competently performed to meet the criterion for each age bracket. Table 3.1 lists four sample items from each of three developmental domains of the IDA's Provence Profile. The scores on items at each age range and in each domain are added to arrive at a *performance age* that can then be evaluated in comparison to the child's *chronological age*. Discrepancies between performance and chronological age levels, if any, may then be used to determine the possible presence and extent of developmental delays in the child.

Theory-Based Ordinal Scales

Ordinal scales may be based on factors other than chronological age. Several theories, such as Jean Piaget's proposed stages of cognitive development from in-

Table 3.1 Sample Items From the Provence Profile of the Infant-Toddler Developmental Assessment

Domain	Age Range (in months)	Item
Gross Motor Behavior	4 to 7	Sits alone briefly
	7 to 10	Pulls to stand
	13 to 18	Walks well alone
	30 to 36	Walks up and down stairs
Language/Communication	4 to 7	Laughs aloud
	7 to 10	Responds to "no"
	13 to 18	Shows shoe when asked
	30 to 36	Knows rhymes or songs
Self-Help	4 to 7	Retrieves lost pacifier or bottle
	7 to 10	Pushes adult hand away
	13 to 18	Partially feeds self with spoon or fingers
	30 to 36	Puts shoes on

Source: Adapted from the *Infant-Toddler Developmental Assessment (IDA). Administration Manual* by Sally Provence, Joanna Erikson, Susan Vater, and Saro Palmeri and reproduced with permission of the publisher. Copyright © 1995 by The Riverside Publishing Company. All rights reserved.

fancy to adolescence or Lawrence Kohlberg's theory of moral development, posit an orderly and invariant sequence or progression derived at least partly from behavioral observations. Some of these theories have generated ordinal scales designed to evaluate the level that an individual has attained within the proposed sequence; these tools are used primarily for purposes of research rather than for individual assessment. Examples of this type of instrument include standardized scales based on Piaget's delineation of the order in which cognitive competencies are acquired during infancy and childhood, such as the Ordinal Scales of Psychological Development, also known as the Infant Psychological Development Scales (Užgiris & Hunt, 1975).

Mental Age Scores

The notion of mental age scores was discussed in Chapter 2 in connection with the ratio IQs of the early Stanford-Binet intelligence scales. The mental age scores derived from those scales were computed on the basis of the child's performance, which earned credits in terms of years and months, depending on the number of chronologically arranged tests that were passed. In light of the difficulties presented by this procedure, described in Chapter 2, this particular way of arriving at mental age scores has been abandoned. However, several current tests still provide norms that are presented as *age equivalent scores* and are based on the average raw score performance of children of different age groups in the standardization sample.

Age equivalent scores, also known as *test ages,* simply represent a way of equating the test taker's performance on a test with the average performance of the normative age group with which it corresponds. For example, if a child's raw score equals the mean raw score of 9-year-olds in the normative sample, her or his test age equivalent score is 9 years. In spite of this change in the procedures used to obtain age equivalent scores, inequalities in the rate of development at different ages remain a problem when this kind of age norm is used, because the differences in behavioral attainments that can be expected with each passing year diminish greatly from infancy and early childhood to adolescence and adulthood. If this is not understood, or if the meaning of a *test age* is extended to realms other than the specific behavior sampled by the test—as it is, for example, when an adolescent who gets a test age score of 8 years is described as having "the mind of an 8-year-old"—the use of such scores can be quite misleading.

Grade Equivalent Scores

The sequential progression and relative uniformity of school curricula, especially in the elementary grades, provide additional bases for interpreting scores in terms of developmental norms. Thus, performance on achievement tests within school settings is often described by grade levels. These *grade equivalent* scores are derived by locating the performance of test takers within the norms of the students at each grade level—and fractions of grade levels—in the standardization sample. If we say, for instance, that a child has scored at the seventh grade in reading and the fifth grade in arithmetic, it means that her or his performance on the reading test matches the average performance of the seventh-graders in the standardization sample and that, on the arithmetic test, her or his performance equals that of fifth-graders.

In spite of their appeal, grade equivalent scores also can be misleading for a number of reasons. To begin with, the content of curricula and quality of instruction vary across schools, school districts, states, and so forth; therefore, grade equivalent scores do not provide a uniform standard. In addition, the advance expected in the early elementary school grades, in terms of academic achievement, is much greater than it is in middle school or high school; thus, just as with mental age units, a difference of one year in retardation or acceleration is far more meaningful in the early grades than it is by the last years of high school. Moreover, if a child who is in the fourth grade scores at the seventh grade in arithmetic, it does not mean the child has mastered seventh-grade arithmetic; rather, it means that the child's score is significantly above the average for fourth-graders in arithmetic. Furthermore, grade equivalent scores are sometimes erroneously viewed as standards of performance that all children in a given grade must meet, whereas they simply represent average levels of performance that—due to the inevitable variability across individuals—some students will meet, others will not, and still others will exceed.

DON'T FORGET

All developmental norms are relative, except as they reflect a behavioral sequence or progression that is *universal* in humans.

- *Theory-based ordinal scales* are more or less useful depending on whether the theories on which they are based are sound and applicable to a given segment of a population or to the population as a whole.

- *Mental age norms or age equivalent score scales* reflect nothing more than the *average performance of certain groups of test takers of specific age levels*, at a given time and place, on a specific test. They are subject to change over time, as well as across cultures and subcultures.

- *Grade-based norms or age equivalent score scales* also reflect the average performance of certain groups of students in specific grades, at a given time and place. They too are subject to variation over time, as well as across curricula in different schools, school districts, and nations.

Within-Group Norms

Most standardized tests use some type of *within-group norms*. These norms essentially provide a way of evaluating a person's performance in comparison to the performance of one or more appropriate reference groups. For proper interpretation of norm-referenced test scores it is necessary to understand the numerical procedures whereby raw scores are transformed into the large variety of *derived scores* that are used to express within-group norms. Nevertheless, it is good to keep in mind that all of the various types of scores reviewed in this section serve the simple purpose of placing a test taker's performance within a normative distribution. Therefore, the single most important question with regard to this frame of reference concerns the exact make-up of the group or groups from which the norms are derived. The composition of the normative or standardization sample is of utmost importance in this kind of test score interpretation because the people in that sample set the standard against which all other test takers are measured.

The Normative Sample

In light of the important role played by the normative sample's performance, the foremost requirement of such samples is that they should be representative of the kinds of individuals for whom the tests are intended. For example, if a test is to be used to assess the reading skills of elementary school students in Grades 3 to 5 from across the whole nation, the normative sample for the test should represent the national population of third-, fourth-, and fifth-graders in all pertinent respects. The demographic make-up of the nation's population on variables like gender, ethnicity, language, socioeconomic status, urban or rural residency, geographic distribution, and public- or private-school enrollment must be reflected in the normative sample for such a test. In addition, the sample needs to be sufficiently large as to ensure the stability of the values obtained from their performance.

The sizes of normative samples vary tremendously depending on the type of test that is standardized and on the ease with which samples can be gathered. For example, group ability tests used in school settings may have normative samples numbering in the tens or even hundreds of thousands, whereas individual intelligence tests, administered to a single person at a time by a highly trained examiner, are normed on much smaller samples—typically consisting of 1,000 to 3,000 individuals—gathered from the general population. Tests that require specialized samples, such as members of a certain occupational group, may have even smaller normative samples. The recency of the normative information is also important if test takers are to be compared with contemporary standards, as is usually the case.

CAUTION

Although the three terms are often used interchangeably—here and elsewhere—and may actually refer to the same group, strictly speaking, the precise meanings of *standardization sample, normative sample,* and *reference group* are somewhat different:

- The *standardization sample* is the group of individuals on whom the test is originally standardized in terms of administration and scoring procedures, as well as in developing the test's norms. Data for this group are usually presented in the manual that accompanies a test upon publication.

- The *normative sample* is often used as synonymous with the standardization sample, but can refer to any group from which norms are gathered. Additional norms collected on a test after it is published, for use with a distinct subgroup, may appear in the periodical literature or in technical manuals published at a later date. See, for example, the study of older Americans by Ivnik and his associates (1992) at the Mayo Clinic wherein data were collected to provide norms for people beyond the highest age group in the standardization sample of the Wechsler Adult Intelligence Scale–Revised (WAIS-R).

- *Reference group,* in contrast, is a term that is used more loosely to identify any group of people against which test scores are compared. It may be applied to the standardization group, to a subsequently developed normative sample, to a group tested for the purpose of developing local norms, or to any other designated group, such as the students in a single class or the participants in a research study.

Relevant factors to consider in the make-up of the normative sample vary depending on the purpose of the test as well as the population on which it will be used. In the case of a test designed to detect cognitive impairment in older adults, for instance, variables like health status, independent versus institutional living situation, and medication intake would be pertinent, in addition to the demographic variables of gender, age, ethnicity, and such. Rapid Reference 3.2 lists some of the most common questions that test users should ask concerning the normative sample when they are in the process of evaluating the suitability of a test for their purposes.

Reference groups can be defined on a continuum of breadth or specificity depending upon the kinds of comparisons that test users need to make to evaluate test scores. At one extreme, the reference group might be the general population of an entire nation or even a multinational population. At the other end, reference groups may be drawn from populations that are narrowly defined in terms of status or settings.

Subgroup norms. When large samples are gathered to represent broadly defined populations, norms can be reported in the aggregate or can be separated into *sub-*

≡Rapid Reference 3.2

Information Needed to Evaluate the Applicability of a Normative Sample

In order to evaluate the suitability of a norm-referenced test for a specific purpose, test users need to have as much information as possible regarding the normative sample, including answers to questions such as these:

- How large is the normative sample?
- When was the sample gathered?
- Where was the sample gathered?
- How were individuals identified and selected for the sample?
- Who tested the sample?
- How did the examiner or examiners qualify to do the testing?
- What was the composition of the normative sample, in terms of
  —age?
  —sex?
  —ethnicity, race, or linguistic background?
  —education?
  —socioeconomic status?
  —geographic distribution?
  —any other pertinent variables, such as physical and mental health status or membership in an atypical group, that may influence test performance?

Test users can evaluate the suitability of a norm-referenced test for their specific purposes only when answers to these questions are provided in the test manual or related documents.

group norms. Provided that they are of sufficient size—and fairly representative of their categories—subgroups can be formed in terms of age, sex, occupation, ethnicity, educational level, or any other variable that may have a significant impact on test scores or yield comparisons of interest. Subgroup norms may also be collected after a test has been standardized and published to supplement and expand the applicability of the test. For instance, before the MMPI was revised to create the MMPI-2 and a separate form for adolescents (the MMPI-A), users of the original test—which had been normed exclusively on adults—developed special subgroup norms for adolescents at various age levels (see, e.g., Archer, 1987).

Local norms. On the other hand, there are some situations in which test users may wish to evaluate scores on the basis of reference groups drawn from a specific geographic or institutional setting. In such cases, test users may choose to develop a set of *local norms*, for members of a more narrowly defined population such as the employees of a particular company or the students of a certain university. Local norms can be used for evaluating the performance of students or employees within a given setting, or for making decisions about school or job applicants in relation to the standards of a certain place or institution.

Convenience norms. Occasionally, for reasons of expediency or financial constraints, test developers use norms based on a group of people who simply happen to be available at the time the test is being constructed. These *convenience norms* are of limited use because they are not representative of any defined population; they are often composed of individuals who are easily accessible to the test developers, such as the students in a college class or the residents of a particular retirement home. In cases like these, the nature of the normative sample should be made clear to potential users of the test.

Scores Used for Expressing Within-Group Norms

Percentiles

Percentile rank scores, already discussed in Chapter 2, are the most direct and ubiquitous method used to convey norm-referenced test results. Their chief advantages are that they are readily understood by test takers and applicable to most sorts of tests and test populations. A *percentile score* indicates the relative position of an individual test taker compared to a reference group, such as the standardization sample; specifically, it represents the percentage of persons in the reference group who scored at or below a given raw score. Thus, higher percentile scores indicate higher raw scores in whatever the test measures; the 50th per-

CAUTION

Due to the similarity of the two terms, percentile scores are often confused with percentage scores. These two types of scores are, in fact, quite different and use entirely different frames of reference:

- *Percentiles* are scores that reflect the rank or position of an individual's performance on a test in comparison to a reference group; their frame of reference is other people.
- *Percentage scores* reflect the number of correct responses that an individual obtains out of the total possible number of correct responses on a test; their frame of reference is the content of the entire test.

One way to avoid confusion is to make it a practice to use the percent symbol (%) strictly for percentage scores and use a different abbreviation, such as *PR* or *%ile*, to designate percentile scores.

centile (P_{50}) or median, corresponds to the raw score point that separates the top and bottom halves of the score distribution of the reference group. In a normal distribution the 50th percentile is also the group's mean level of performance.

An additional advantage of percentile rank scores comes into play when there is more than one normative group for the same test or when normative groups are subdivided by categories, such as gender, age, or ethnicity. When additional norms are available, a raw score can be located within the distributions of two or more different groups or subgroups and easily converted into percentile ranks. For example, interest inventory scores for various occupational groups are often reported for men and women as separate sex group norms, so that test takers can see their rankings on a given interest and occupational scale compared to both groups. This information is particularly useful for those who are considering an occupation that is significantly segregated along sex lines, such as engineering or nursing. The separation of norms allows individuals to gauge the relative strengths of their expressed interests in comparison to members of both sex groups.

If test scores were evenly distributed throughout their range, resulting in a rectangular frequency polygon, percentiles would probably be the scores of choice in nearly all situations. However, as seen in Figure 2.2 and in Figure 3.1 later in this chapter, in a normal distribution the majority of scores tend to cluster around a central value and scatter more widely at the extremes. This fact, which is also true of many non-normal distributions, means that percentile score units are usually markedly unequal at different points of the range. In a normal or nearly normal distribution, such as those obtained from most tests, the percentage of the people who score near the middle is much greater than at the extremes. Therefore, any given difference in percentile rank score units magnifies the apparent discrepancy in the relative performance of individuals whose scores are in the middle range and compresses the apparent extent of the difference in the relative performance of individuals at the high and low ends of the distributions.

Another disadvantage of percentile rank scores pertains to the most extreme scores in a distribution. To be sure, for any given normative group there is always a score that is the highest and one that is the lowest. As long as scores are interpreted strictly in reference to a specific normative sample, the highest score can be said to be at the 100th percentile because all the cases are at or below that score; technically, we could even describe the score below the lowest one obtained by everyone in a specific sample as the zero percentile score, although this is not done ordinarily. In terms of the larger population that the normative sample represents, however, the interpretation of such scores is problematic.

Test ceiling and test floor. The issue of how to accommodate individuals at the highest and lowest ends of the spectrum of ability for which a test is designed is

Putting It Into Practice

Using Percentile Rank Scores: The Disadvantage of Unequal Units

The Vocabulary subtest of the Wechsler Adult Intelligence Scale–Third Edition (WAIS-III), a test for individuals aged 16 to 89 years, consists of 33 vocabulary words. Each word definition may accrue a score of 0, 1, or 2 points. Thus, the subtest raw scores can range between 0 and 66, depending on the quality of the responses.

The WAIS-III manual (Wechsler, 1997) displays the performance of the standardization samples in tables for various age ranges. For individuals between the ages of 45 and 54, the table shows that raw scores ranging from 45 to 48 points are ranked at the 50th percentile and raw scores from 49 to 51 points are at the 63rd percentile. In contrast, raw scores between 15 and 19 points rank at the 2nd percentile and those between 20 and 24 points rank at the 5th percentile.

This clearly highlights the problem of inequality of percentile score units: For people in the 45- to 54-year-old age group, a difference of only 6 points (45 to 51) in the middle of the raw score distribution results in a difference of 13 percentile rank units (50th to 63rd percentiles), whereas a raw score difference of 9 points (15 to 24) at the low end of the range results in a difference of only 3 percentile rank units (2nd to 5th percentiles).

---

most relevant in the context of test development, discussed in Chapter 6. Nevertheless, at this point, it is worth noting that the individuals employed in standardizing a test do set the upper and lower limits of performance on that test. If a test taker reaches the highest score attainable on an already standardized test, it means that the *test ceiling,* or maximum difficulty level of the test, is insufficient: one cannot know how much higher the test taker might have scored if there were additional items or items of greater difficulty in the test. Similarly, if a person fails all the items presented in a test or scores lower than any of the people in the normative sample, the problem is one of insufficient *test floor.* In cases like these, the individuals in question have not been adequately tested.

Standard Scores

One way to surmount the problem of the inequality of percentile units and still convey the meaning of test scores relative to a normative or reference group is to transform raw scores into scales that express the position of scores, relative to the mean, in standard deviation units. This can be accomplished by means of simple linear transformations. A *linear transformation* changes the units in which scores are expressed while leaving the interrelationships among them unaltered. In other words, the shape of a linearly derived scale score distribution for a given group of test takers is the same as that of the original raw score distribution. A great advantage of this procedure is that the normally distributed scores of tests with different means, standard deviations, and score ranges can be meaningfully compared—and averaged—once they have been linearly transformed into a common scale, as long as the same reference group is used.

The first linear transformation performed on raw scores is to con-

CAUTION

As was true of the previous chapter, the statistical formulas and procedures presented here are the *essential* ones needed for a basic understanding of score transformations. Although the statistical operations described in this book can be and are routinely carried out with computer software programs, such as SPSS and SAS, the formulas and steps involved must be understood in order to achieve a basic grasp of the meaning of various scores.

vert them into standard-score deviates, or *z scores*. A *z* score (see Appendix C) expresses the distance between a raw score and the mean of the reference group in terms of the standard deviation of the reference group. It will be recalled that the mean and standard deviation of *z* scores are zero and 1, respectively, and that the distribution of *z* scores is bilaterally symmetrical, with one half of the cases on each side of the mean. The position of *z* scores relative to the mean is indicated by the use of a positive sign (or no sign) for the *z* scores that are above the mean and a negative sign for those below it. Thus, the sign of a *z* score indicates the direction in which a score deviates from the mean of a group, whereas its numerical value reflects the score's distance from the mean in standard-deviation units. For example, a *z* score of +1.25 indicates that the original raw score is 1¼ *SD* units *above* the mean of the group, whereas a raw score that falls ¾ *SD* units *below* the mean converts into a *z* score of –0.75. If the distribution of scores for the reference sample is normal, *z* scores can be readily transformed into percentiles by referring to the Table of Areas of the Normal Curve presented and explained in Appendix C.

Rapid Reference 3.3 shows the linear transformation formulas used for deriving *z* scores from raw scores and for transforming *z* scores into the other types of standard scores. Because the transformation of raw scores into *z* scores is usually the first one in the process of score transformations, *z* scores are considered to be the most basic type of standard score and are often identified simply as standard scores. This also distinguishes them from other familiar types of derived or standard scores, such as IQs, that have become associated with specific tests and to which we turn next.

Additional systems for deriving standard scores. Although *z* scores allow us to know immediately the magnitude and direction of the difference between any given

≡ Rapid Reference 3.3

Formula for transforming raw scores into z scores:

$$z = \frac{X - \bar{X}}{SD_X}$$

where X = Raw score
$\bar{X}$ = Reference group mean
SD_X = Standard deviation (SD) of the reference group

Formula for transforming z scores into other derived standard scores:

New standard score = (z score) (New SD) + New mean

Example: To transform a z score of +1.00 to an IQ score with $M = 100$ and $SD = 15$,

IQ score = (+1.00) (15) + 100 = 115

score and the mean of its distribution, they involve negative values and decimals. Because of this, z scores usually undergo additional linear transformations. The goal of the standard score systems that result from these subsequent transformations is simply to express test results in more convenient form.

The numbers chosen as the means and standard deviations in transforming z scores into various other standard score formats are arbitrary. However, through their frequent use in the contexts in which they are employed, these score formats have become familiar and have acquired certain commonly understood meanings—which may not always be warranted—for those who use them. Figure 3.1 displays the normal curve with the baselines for percentiles, z scores, and the following widely used standard score systems:

- *T-scores* ($M = 50$, $SD = 10$), used in many personality inventories, such as the Minnesota Multiphasic Personality Inventory (MMPI) and the California Psychological Inventory (CPI).
- *College Entrance Examination Board (CEEB) scores* ($M = 500$, $SD = 100$), used by the College Board's SAT as well as by the Educational Testing Service for many of their graduate and professional school admission testing programs, such as the Graduate Record Exam (GRE).
- *Wechsler scale subtest scores* ($M = 10$, $SD = 3$), used for all the subtests of

Putting It Into Practice

Transforming Raw Scores Into z Scores

1. Assume that all the students in a large eighth-grade class took achievement tests in social science, grammar, and math. The scores of the class on all three tests were *normally distributed*, but the tests were different in the following ways:

	Total Number of Items	Mean	SD
Social science test	50	35	5
Grammar test	20	15	3
Math test	100	70	10

2. Further assume that you had a reason to want to compare the scores of three of the students in the class in relation to each other and in relation to the entire class. The three students in question—Alfred, Beth, and Carmen—scored as follows:

	Raw Scores		
	Alfred	**Beth**	**Carmen**
Social science test	49	38	48
Grammar test	15	12	18
Math test	68	95	75

3. These scores cannot be compared or averaged across tests, because they are on different scales. To compare the scores, even on a single test, we must refer to the means, standard deviations (SDs), and numbers of items of each test. An easier way to compare them is to convert each of the raw scores into z scores—by subtracting the respective test mean from each raw score and dividing by the corresponding standard deviations, as shown in the formula in Rapid Reference 3.3—with the following results:

	z Scores		
	Alfred	**Beth**	**Carmen**
Social science test	+2.80	+0.60	+2.60
Grammar test	0.00	−1.00	+1.00
Math test	−0.20	+2.50	+0.50
Average grade	+0.87	+0.70	+1.37

4. The linear transformations of raw scores into z scores lets us average the three grades for each student and compare the students' performance on all the tests to each other and to their whole class. *Furthermore, since we assumed normal distributions for all the tests, we can use the table in Appendix C to translate each z score into a percentile rank score.*

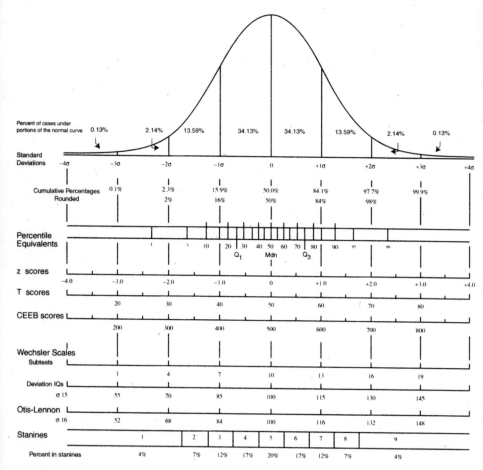

Figure 3.1 The normal curve, percentiles, and selected standard scores

·Note: Adapted from *Test Service Notebook #148* of The Psychological Corporation.

the Wechsler scales, as well as for the subtests of several other instruments.

- *Wechsler scale deviation IQs* (*M* = 100, *SD* = 15), used for the summary scores of all the Wechsler scales and other tests, including many that do not label their scores as "IQs."
- *Otis-Lennon School Ability Indices* (*M* = 100, *SD* = 16), used in the Otis-Lennon School Ability Test (OLSAT), which is the current title of the series of group tests that started with the Otis Group Intelligence Scale.

OLSAT indexes are included in Figure 3.1, as an example of a standard score system with a mean of 100 and standard deviation other than 15, to illustrate the arbitrariness of the choice of units in standard score systems. Although most standard score systems that use a mean of 100 select 15 as their standard deviation, there are some that use other standard deviations, such as 12 or 18. These alternative choices can make a significant difference in the interpretation of scores. For example, if two normally distributed tests—both with means of 100—have standard deviations of 12 and 15, respectively, a standard score of 112 on the first test will transform into a z score of $+1.00$, and rank at the 84th percentile, whereas on the second test a standard score of 112 will transform into a z score of $+0.80$ and rank at only the 79th percentile.

A note about deviation IQs. The scores known as *deviation IQs* were introduced by David Wechsler in 1939 for use in his first intelligence scale, the Wechsler-Bellevue I, which later became the Wechsler Adult Intelligence Scale (WAIS). These scores came into wider use after the first edition of the Wechsler Intelligence Scale for Children (WISC) was published in 1949. They are called *deviation* IQs to differentiate them from the original *ratio* IQs used in the Stanford-Binet and other scales. Deviation IQs are obtained by adding the scale scores the test taker obtains on various subtests and locating this sum in the appropriate normative table, rather than by the MA/CA × 100 formula.

The Wechsler IQ–type score scale has been adopted by numerous other test developers to express the summary scores of various tests, including the Stanford-Binet's most recent edition, which uses 15 as its standard deviation unit rather than its original standard deviation of 16. Among the multitude of tests that employ standard scores with a mean of 100 and standard deviation of 15 are all of the major instruments designed to assess general cognitive functioning, such as the Kaufman series of tests (e.g., Kaufman-Assessment Battery for Children, Kaufman Adolescent and Adult Intelligence Test, etc.), the Differential Ability Scales, the Das-Naglieri Cognitive Assessment System, and many others. Although they share the same type of units as the Wechsler tests for their global or summary scores, all of these newer tests have discarded the use of the term *IQ* to designate their scores. This is a sensible move because the so-called deviation IQs are *not* quotients. Furthermore, as can be seen from the titles of some of the more recently developed instruments, test authors are increasingly abandoning the use of the word *intelligence* to designate the construct assessed by their tests in favor of other, more neutral, terms.

Nonlinear Transformations

Not all score transformations are linear. *Nonlinear transformations* are those that convert a raw score distribution into a distribution that has a different shape than the original. This can be done through methods that afford test developers greater flexibility in dealing with raw score distributions than linear conversions

Putting It Into Practice

Transforming z Scores Into Different Standard Scores

1. To illustrate the conversion of z scores into different types of standard score systems, we return to the previous example of the three students from an eighth-grade class whose z scores on three normally distributed achievement tests were as follows:

	z Scores		
	Alfred	**Beth**	**Carmen**
Social science test	+2.80	+0.60	+2.60
Grammar test	0.00	−1.00	+1.00
Math test	−0.20	+2.50	+0.50

2. To transform these z scores into a more convenient scale, we apply the formula for converting them into other standard scores, presented earlier in Rapid Reference 3.3:

> New standard score = (z score) (New SD) + New mean

3. Using the appropriate means and standard deviations for each system, we obtain the following scores:

	Alfred	**Beth**	**Carmen**
T scores ($M = 50$, $SD = 10$)			
Social science test	78	56	76
Grammar test	50	40	60
Math test	48	75	55
CEEB-type scores ($M = 500$, $SD = 100$)			
Social science test	780	560	760
Grammar test	500	400	600
Math test	480	750	550
Wechsler scale IQs ($M = 100$, $SD = 15$)			
Social science test	142	109	139
Grammar test	100	85	115
Math test	97	138	108

4. Note that because these were all linear transformations, *the scores stand in exactly the same positions relative to one another regardless of the differences in units.* This can be seen most clearly in the relationship between T scores and CEEB scores, wherein the CEEB mean and standard deviation equal the T score mean and standard deviation times 10; therefore, in our example, each CEEB score equals the corresponding T score times 10.

do. Although some nonlinear score transformations involve complex operations that are well beyond our scope in this book, others do not. For instance, the transformation of normally distributed raw scores into percentile rank scores, which we have already considered, is a nonlinear conversion. It is accomplished by transforming each raw score into a z score and locating the z score in the Table of Areas of the Normal Curve to derive the proportion or percentage of the area of the normal curve that is below that point. In this section, we discuss two additional and widely used types of nonlinearly derived standard scores.

Normalized standard scores are used when a score distribution approximates but does not quite match the normal distribution. To normalize scores one first finds the percentage of persons in the reference sample who fall at or below each raw score (see, e.g., the Cumulative Percent (CP) column for the distribution of 60 test scores in Table 2.3). Next, the percentages are converted into proportions. These proportions are then located in the Table of Areas of the Normal Curve to obtain the z scores corresponding to those areas (see Appendix C). Standard scores derived in this fashion are indistinguishable in form from those obtained by the linear transformation formula, but should always be identified as normalized standard scores to alert the test user to the fact that they come from a distribution that was not normal. Once normalized standard scores are obtained, they can be transformed into any of the other convenient standard score systems we have discussed, such as T scores, deviation IQs, or CEEB scores, using the same procedure employed with linearly derived z scores that is described in Rapid Reference 3.3.

Stanines were originally devised by the U.S. Air Force during World War II. The "*stan*dard *nine*," or *stanine*, scale transforms all the scores in a distribution into single-digit numbers from 1 to 9. This device has the distinct advantage of reducing the time and effort needed to enter scores on a computer for storage and further processing. Stanine transformations also make use of cumulative frequency and cumulative percentage distributions, such as the ones in Table 2.3; stanine scores are allocated on the basis of the percentage of cases at given score ranges. Table 3.2, Part A, shows the normal curve percentages within each stanine unit and the cumulative percentages used in converting raw scores to stanines. Part B contains a few examples of stanine transformations, using some of the scores from Table 2.3. Figure 3.1 displays the position of stanine scores within the normal curve. As can be seen in the figure, stanine 5 comprises the middle 20% of the scores. The mean of the stanine scale is 5 and its standard deviation is approximately 2. Even though the stanine scale is economical and simple, its brevity and simplicity also result in a certain loss of precision.

Putting It Into Practice

Normalized Standard Scores

To demonstrate the process of normalizing the scores of a distribution that does not conform to the normal curve but approximates it, we can use five of the raw scores from the distribution of 60 test scores presented in Table 2.3 in Chapter 2. The raw scores selected arbitrarily for this exercise are 49, 40, 39, 36, and 29. Steps involved in this conversion are as follows:

> Raw score → Cumulative percent (CP) → Cumulative proportion (cp) → Normalized z score

1. The raw score and cumulative percent are located in the distribution.
2. The cumulative proportion is the cumulative percent divided by 100.
3. A *normalized z score* is obtained from the Table of Areas of the Normal Curve in Appendix C by finding the proportion of the area of the curve that comes closest to the cumulative proportion for a given score. For scores with cumulative proportions above 0.50, the areas in the larger portion—from column (3) of the table—must be used to obtain the normalized z scores, which will bear a positive sign. For scores with cumulative proportions below 0.50, the areas in the smaller portion—from column (4) of the table—must be used, and the resulting normalized z scores will have negative signs.
4. These procedures yield the following results:

Raw Score	Cumulative %	cp	Normalized z Score[a]
49	98.3	0.983	+2.12
40	53.3	0.533	+0.08
39	45.0	0.450	−0.13
36	23.3	0.233	−0.73
29	1.7	0.017	−2.12

[a]Normalized standard scores have the same meaning as linearly derived standard scores in terms of the position of the original raw scores they represent, relative to their distributions. They can be transformed into various other standard score systems, but must always be identified as having been derived nonlinearly from a normalization procedure.

Table 3.2 Converting Raw Scores to Stanine Scores

A. Normal Curve Percentages for Use in Stanine Conversion

	Stanine								
	1	2	3	4	5	6	7	8	9
Percentage of cases within each stanine	4	7	12	17	20	17	12	7	4
Cumulative % at each stanine	4	11	23	40	60	77	89	96	100

B. Selected Test Scores from Table 2.3 Converted to Stanines

Selected Scores[a]	Cumulative %	Stanine Scores
49	98.3	9
47	93.3	8
45	83.3	7
43	71.7	6
41	60.0	5
39	45.0	5
37	30.0	4
35	20.0	3
33	11.7	3
31	5.0	2
29	1.7	1

[a]See Table 2.3 in Chapter 2 for the complete distribution of 60 test scores.

INTERTEST COMPARISONS

In most circumstances, norm-referenced test scores cannot be compared unless they are obtained from the same test, using the same normative distribution. An additional reason for lack of comparability of test scores stems from differences in scale units, like the various sizes of SD units discussed earlier in connection with deviation IQs. Furthermore, even when the tests, the norms, and the scale units employed are the same, test scores do not necessarily have the same meaning. When test scores are used in the context of individual assessment, it must be kept in mind that many other factors extraneous to the test may also enter into test results (e.g., the test taker's background and motivation, the influence of the examiners, and the circumstances under which the tests were taken).

DON'T FORGET

1. Test scores cannot be meaningfully compared if
   - the tests or test versions are different,
   - the reference groups are different, or
   - the score scales differ,

   except when the tests, groups, or scales have been purposefully equated. Angoff's (1984) monograph on *Scales, norms, and equivalent scores* is one of the best sources of information on equating procedures.

2. Even when test scores have been made comparable, the context in which testing takes place, as well as the backgrounds of test takers, need to be taken into account in test score interpretation.

Equating Procedures

Notwithstanding the cautions outlined in the preceding section, there are a number of situations in which it is necessary or desirable to compare scores of individuals or groups across time, or in various psychological functions, against a uniform norm. For such situations, test developers and publishers have devised several ways of achieving *some* comparability of scores across tests. Essentially, these are all designed in order to place test scores in a common frame of reference. An additional benefit of equating techniques is that they may reduce the considerable cost and time involved in standardizing tests. Most equating procedures involve highly technical details, described in Angoff's (1984) monograph and other sources (e.g., Petersen et al., 1989). The following brief descriptions of some of the more frequently used approaches may provide the reader with basic explanations of what they entail.

- *Alternate forms* consist of two or more versions of a test meant to be used interchangeably, intended for the same purpose, and administered in identical fashion. Creating alternate forms that are alike in the content they cover but vary in the specific items they contain is one of the simplest ways of producing comparable tests. A stricter form of comparability can be achieved with the type of alternate versions of tests known as *parallel forms*. These forms are equated not only in content coverage and procedures, but also in some of their statistical characteristics such as raw score means and standard deviations, as well as indexes of their reliability and validity. Alternate forms are especially useful when a person has to take the same test on more than one occasion. *Practice effects* (i.e., score increases attributable to prior exposure to test items or to items similar to those in a test) do enter into play when an alternate form of a previously taken test is given, but they are not quite as great as when the same version of the test is taken more than once.

- *Anchor tests* consist of common sets of items administered to different groups of examinees in the context of two or more tests and provide a different solution to the problem of test score comparability. Having the responses of more than one normative group to common sets of items, within a given time frame, allows for the use of score equating procedures—based on statistics derived from the common items—that permit extrapolating and comparing the scores on one test to those of another, for both individuals and groups. This technique may be used when test developers wish to provide for comparisons of levels of performance in different skill areas—such as reading comprehension and written expression—from two different tests, on a uniform scale. In recent years, however, this sort of comparability is more likely to be achieved either through simultaneous norming or item response theory techniques, to be discussed shortly.

- *Fixed reference groups* provide a way of achieving some comparability and continuity of test scores over time. This method makes use of anchor tests embedded in each successive form of a test to provide a linkage to one or more earlier forms of the same test. In this fashion a test series becomes linked through a chain of common items to the scores of the group selected as a fixed reference for the purpose of maintaining the continuity of the score scale over time. The College Board's SAT is the best known example of a test that has made use of fixed reference groups. Until April of 1995, all SAT scores were expressed in terms of the mean and standard deviation of the 11,000 college applicants who took the test in 1941; on that scale, a score of 500 corresponded to the mean of the 1941 fixed reference group, a score of 400 fell 1 *SD* below that mean, and so on. After April of 1995, reported SAT scores reflect a *recentering* of the score scale on contemporary college applicants, so that a score of 500 represents a current average level of performance on the test. The use of a fixed reference group on the SAT over several decades allowed for the evaluation of increases or declines in the caliber of performance of college applicants of different eras, as can be seen in Rapid Reference 3.4. In addition to the recentered standard scores, the percentile rank scores of college applicants on the SAT still can be, and still are, reported using the most recent group of college-bound seniors as a reference group.

- *Simultaneous norming* of two or more tests on the same standardization sample, often referred to as *co-norming,* is yet another method used to achieve comparability of scores. By norming tests at the same time and on the same group of people, one can readily compare the performance of individuals or subgroups on more than one test, using the same standard.

≡≡*Rapid Reference 3.4*

Changing Reference Group Standards by Recentering the SAT

From the 1940s to the 1990s, the scores of college applicants on both the Verbal and Math portions of the SAT had shown significant declines. Thus, after recentering took place in the 1990s, the recentered Verbal score of 500 turned out to be the equivalent of a score of 420 when compared to the 1941 reference group. This shift represents a decline of almost 1 SD unit. The recentered Math score of 500 was found to be the equivalent of a score of 470 for the 1941 reference group.

Various reasons have been adduced for these changes. Among those reasons, the most plausible ones center on the increased socioeconomic and ethnic diversity of college applicants and on changes in the quality of secondary school curricula from the early 1940s to the early 1990s.

This capability is particularly helpful when one wishes to contrast relative levels of performance on two or more psychological functions, such as expressive and receptive vocabulary levels or short- and long-term memory, for the same individual or subgroup. The Woodcock-Johnson III (WJ III) provides an outstanding example of co-norming of two test batteries. The WJ III Tests of Cognitive Abilities (WJ III COG) is a battery designed to measure both general and specific cognitive functions, whereas the WJ III Tests of Achievement (WJ III ACH) battery is meant to assess a person's academic strengths and weaknesses. These two batteries were normed on the same large sample of individuals, ranging from preschoolers to older adults, representative of the population of the United States, and thus provide ample opportunity for comparing intraindividual levels of performance in a number of indexes of cognitive functioning and academic skills.

Item Response Theory (IRT)

A variety of sophisticated procedures based on mathematical models are increasingly replacing the traditional equating techniques that have just been described. These procedures, which date back to the 1960s and are also known as *latent trait models,* are most often grouped under the label of *item response theory* (*IRT*). The term *latent trait* reflects the fact that these models seek to estimate the levels of various—unobservable—abilities, traits, or psychological constructs that underlie the observable behavior of individuals, as demonstrated by their responses to test items. Unlike the previously discussed techniques for equating tests and test scores, IRT methods apply mathematical models to test *item* data from large and diverse samples, hence the name *item response theory*. These data are used to calibrate test items along one or more parameters and derive probability estimates of the amount of ability, or trait level, needed to respond to each item in a certain way. Essentially, these models place both persons and test items on a common scale (Embretson & Reise, 2000).

Additional elements and basic procedures of IRT will be discussed at greater length in Chapter 6. In the present context, however, the point worth noting about IRT models is that if they meet certain conditions they can produce item parameter estimates that are *invariant* across populations. This means that these estimates are not necessarily tied to the performance of any specific reference group. Instead, item response data can be interpreted in terms of an ability or trait dimension. Thus, when IRT models are applied to the arrays of item response and test score data from various samples and the assumptions of the models are met, they can be used in two reciprocal ways: (a) to estimate the probability that persons with specified levels of the ability or trait in question will answer an item correctly or respond to it in a certain way, and (b) to estimate the trait levels needed in order to have a specified probability of responding to an item in a certain way.

Computerized Adaptive Testing

One of the main advantages of IRT methodology is that it is ideally suited for use in computerized adaptive testing (CAT). When individuals take computerized adaptive tests (CATs), their ability levels can be estimated based on their responses to test items during the testing process; these estimates are used to select subsequent sets of test items that are appropriate to the test takers' ability levels. Although many CATs have a fixed number of items, others are designed so that testing can stop whenever a specified stopping rule is satisfied and trait or ability levels have been established with sufficient precision. In any case, CAT procedures shorten test length and testing time significantly; they can also reduce the frustration that many paper-and-pencil test takers may experience when they are exposed to test booklets that contain items considerably above, or below, their levels of ability. Large-scale testing programs, such as those of the Educational Testing Service and the U.S. Department of Defense, have been trying out and using CAT methodology for several years (see, e.g., Campbell & Knapp, 2001; Drasgow & Olson-Buchanan, 1999). Although this methodology has clear advantages over paper-and-pencil tests of fixed length—and its range of applications is bound to expand—it does present some new problems related to test security, test costs, and the inability of examinees to review and amend their responses (Wainer, 2000).

Test Revisions

Test names can easily present a possible source of confusion for potential test users who are not sufficiently informed. Taking test titles at face value is rarely justified. Some of the discrepancies between the titles of tests and what the tests actually assess are fairly obvious: personality inventories do not actually inventory personality. Others are not as readily apparent: Aptitude tests may or may not test aptitudes, and so forth.

Even if tests share the same name, they may not be equivalent. Many tests undergo revisions from time to time and retain the same title, except for the addition of a number or letter that identifies a specific version (e.g., WISC, WISC-R, WISC-III, WISC-IV). In general, the more successful and widely used tests are more likely to be revised than other tests. The objectives and extent of test revisions may range from small changes in the wording of items to major reorganizations in content, scoring, or administrative procedures.

A test that has been modified in any way cannot be considered comparable to a previous version, unless the similarity is established empirically. When a test revision is minor and not expected to affect scores, the comparability of the old and revised versions can be established relatively easily. This is usually accomplished by giving both versions of the test to the same group of people. If the two versions are highly correlated and have similar means, standard deviations, and score distributions, for most practical purposes it is assumed that both versions are interchangeable. A typical instance of this practice is when paper-and-pencil tests, like the MMPI-2, are transferred to a computer-based administration format without any changes in test content or scoring.

Major test revisions of norm-referenced tests, on the other hand, require restandardization of the test with a new normative sample. Thus, when the changes are significant enough to justify differences in the test's scale or scoring, one is actually dealing with a new and different test, albeit a test that may bear some resemblance to and share the same title as previous versions. A preeminent example is the Stanford-Binet Intelligence Scale (S-B), which was first published in 1916. The fourth and fifth editions of the S-B, published in 1986 and 2003, respectively, are altogether different from its earlier versions in almost every respect and over time they have become more similar in form and content to the Wechsler scales than to the original S-B.

Longitudinal Changes in Test Norms

When a test is revised and standardized on a new sample after a period of several years, even if revisions in its content are minor, score norms tend to drift in one direction or another due to changes in the population at different time periods. One such change, discussed in Rapid Reference 3.4, is the decline in average SAT scores from the fixed reference group tested in 1941 to the college applicants of the 1990s. A puzzling longitudinal trend in the opposite direction, known as the *Flynn effect,* has been well documented in successive revisions of major intelligence tests (like the S-B and the Wechsler scales) that invariably involve the administration of both the old and new versions to a segment of the newer standardization sample, for comparative purposes. Data from revisions of various intelligence tests in the United States as well as in other countries— extensively analyzed by J. R. Flynn (1984, 1987)—show a pronounced, long-term upward trend in the level of performance required to obtain any given IQ score. The Flynn effect presumably reflects population gains over time in the kinds of cognitive performance that intelligence tests sample. A variety of factors—such as improved nutrition, better prenatal care, and greater environmental complexity—have been proposed as reasons for this finding. Still, the extent to which the Flynn effect generalizes to populations throughout the world—as well as its possible causes where it does appear—remain a subject of considerable controversy (Neisser, 1998).

A pertinent example of longitudinal changes in personality test performance was seen in the renorming of the MMPI (originally published in the 1940s), which took place in the 1980s as part of the development of the MMPI-2 (Butcher, Dahlstrom, Graham, Tellegen, & Kaemmer, 1989). Alterations in the content of the inventory were relatively minor. Nevertheless, the shift from the original MMPI norms to those of the MMPI-2 resulted in modifications of the score levels considered clinically significant on various scales due to substantial changes in the ways people from the two different time periods responded to the items.

The kinds of changes just described are commonplace when normative samples are updated. They underscore the need for such updating in order to maintain the currency of within-group norms. Such changes also explain the reason why the documentation that accompanies any type of norm-referenced test should provide a complete and accurate description of the composition of the samples used to standardize and norm it, including the dates when the samples were gathered. Test documents should incorporate answers to all the questions listed in Rapid Reference 3.2, including a clear exposition of the steps taken in the development of the test and of the administration and scoring procedures used during its standardization. Test users, in turn, need to be aware of this information and take it into account when selecting tests and interpreting test scores.

Putting It Into Practice

How the "Flynn Effect" May Affect Apparent Changes in Intelligence Test Scores: An Example Using the Wechsler Intelligence Scale for Children (WISC)

John obtained a Wechsler IQ score of 117 on the WISC-R at the age of 9 and a Wechsler IQ of 107 on the WISC-III at age 13. This seemingly significant decline in his performance cannot be taken at face value.

One factor that may partly explain the apparent decline is the Flynn effect. This effect refers to the higher level of performance typically seen in the normative groups of newer versions of general intelligence tests compared to their older counterparts—for example, the WISC-III, published in 1991, compared to the WISC-R, published in 1974. According to the WISC-III manual, a sample of 206 children aged 6 to 16 were given the WISC-R and WISC-III in counterbalanced order, with intervals ranging from 12 to 70 days between the two tests. Their average Full Scale IQs were 108.2 on the WISC-R and 102.9 on the WISC-III (Wechsler, 1991).

Although the correlation between the two versions of the WISC for this sample was high (.89), the children's scores on the WISC-III were on average lower—by slightly more than 5 points—than those on the WISC-R. The difference in the mean IQ scores of this group indicates that the norms of the two tests are such that, on the whole, any given IQ score represents a higher level of performance on the newer test than on the older one.

Naturally, many factors besides the Flynn effect could have contributed to the obtained difference between John's two IQs. Chief among them are the measurement error in each score (see Chapter 4) and the possibility that John might have undergone an actual decline in general intellectual functioning due to some illness or life event.

CRITERION-REFERENCED TEST INTERPRETATION

In the realm of educational and occupational assessment, tests are often used to help ascertain whether a person has reached a certain level of competence in a field of knowledge or skill in performing a task. For such cases, the frame of reference for test score interpretation must change. Instead of comparing a person's performance to that of others, the performance of an individual, or a group, is compared to a predetermined criterion or standard. When used in this context, *criterion* may refer either to knowledge of a specific content domain or to competence in some kind of endeavor. Standards by which criterion-referenced tests are evaluated are typically defined in terms of specified levels of knowledge or expertise necessary to pass a course, obtain a degree, or get a professional license; they may also involve a demonstration of sufficient competence to do a job or to create a product. Often, but not always, the application of criterion-referenced tests involves the use of cutoff scores, or score ranges, that separate competence from incompetence or demarcate different levels of performance. In such cases, the validity of the inferences made on the basis of scores needs to be established through empirical links between test scores and performance on the criterion.

Varieties of Criterion-Referenced Test Interpretation

The term *criterion-referenced testing*, popularized by Glaser (1963), is sometimes used as synonymous with *domain-referenced, content-referenced, objective-referenced,* or *competency* testing. This rather confusing state of affairs is due, in part, to the fact that criterion-referenced test interpretation makes use of at least two underlying sets of standards: (a) those that are based on the *amount of knowledge* of a content domain as demonstrated in standardized objective tests, and (b) those that are based on the *level of competence* in a skill area as displayed in the quality of the performance itself or of the product that results from exercising the skill. Occasionally, the term *criterion-referenced testing* is also used to refer to interpretations based on the preestablished relationship between the scores on a test and expected levels of performance on a criterion, such as a future endeavor or even another test. In this particular usage, the "criterion" is a specific outcome and may or may not be related to the tasks sampled by the test. The latter is in sharp contrast to content-referenced or performance-based tests, in which the test tasks are essentially samples of behavior directly related to the criterion. Rapid Reference 3.5 lists some of the major points on which norm-referenced testing differs from criterion-referenced testing, as well as some of the differences among types of criterion-referenced testing.

In addition to the foregoing distinctions, the particular manner in which criterion-referenced tests are used also varies. Sometimes the criteria are strictly quantitative, as when certain percentages (e.g., 80% or 90%) of correct responses needed to establish adequate mastery are set. At other times, the criteria are more qualitative and subjective in nature. Furthermore, sometimes performance on these tests is evaluated on an all-or-none basis with regard to whether a certain level of competence has been achieved, and sometimes there may be allowances for intermediate levels of competence.

In spite of the differences in emphases and nomenclature among criterion-referenced tests, these instruments do share some common characteristics. Typically, criterion-referenced tests (a) are meant to assess the extent to which test takers are proficient in certain skills or knowledge domains, and (b) are scored in such a way that one person's performance does not influence the relative stand-

≡ *Rapid Reference 3.5*

Norm- Versus Criterion-Referenced Test Interpretation

- *Norm-referenced* tests seek to locate the performance of one or more individuals, with regard to the construct the tests assess, on a continuum created by the performance of a reference group.
- *Criterion-referenced* tests seek to evaluate the performance of individuals in relation to standards related to the construct itself.
- Whereas in norm-referenced test interpretation the frame of reference is always people, in criterion-referenced test interpretation the frame of reference may be

  —knowledge of a content domain as demonstrated in standardized, objective tests; or

  —level of competence displayed in the quality of a performance or of a product.
- The term *criterion-referenced testing* is sometimes also applied to describe test interpretations that use the relationship between the scores and expected levels of performance or standing on a criterion as a frame of reference.

ing of others. Whereas norm-referenced tests seek to rank or place one or more individuals in relation to others with regard to the construct they assess, criterion-referenced tests seek to evaluate the performance of individuals in relation to the actual construct itself.

In the present context, only those aspects of criterion-referenced test interpretation necessary for a basic understanding of its premises and terminology will be discussed. Several of these concepts are revisited in greater detail in Chapter 5 in connection to the topic of validity, with which they are inextricably related. Rapid Reference 3.6 lists a few sources of information from the extensive literature that is available on various kinds of criterion-referenced testing.

Testing Knowledge of Content Domains

In order to use knowledge of content domains as a frame of reference for test score interpretation, there needs to be a carefully defined and clearly demarcated field or subject from which to derive samples (i.e., test items or tasks) to gauge the test taker's knowledge. Moreover, the objectives to be assessed both in terms of knowledge of a content domain and application of that knowledge, as well as the standards to be used in assessing those objectives, should stem from a consensus of people who are experts in the field. Such a situation is encountered primarily

≡ *Rapid Reference 3.6*

Selected Readings on Criterion-Referenced Testing

The literature on criterion-referenced testing, dating back to the 1960s, is abundant. To pursue the topic at greater length, readers may want to consult one or more of the following sources:

- Cizek's (2001) book on *Setting Performance Standards*, which focuses on both theoretical and practical aspects of standard setting and its many ramifications;
- Popham and Husek's (1969) classic article on the implications of criterion-referenced measurement;
- Hambleton and Rogers' (1991) book chapter on "Advances in Criterion-Referenced Measurement," which provides a useful introduction to the field and a description of technical developments from the 1960s to the 1980s;
- Wigdor and Green's (1991) edited volume on various aspects of performance assessment in the workplace; and
- Linn's (1994) brief but enlightening clarification of some of the confusion in various interpretations of the meaning of criterion-referenced testing.

Full references on these works are listed in the reference section at the end of this book.

---

in educational or training settings, where subjects and disciplines tend to be partitioned into lessons, courses, programs of study, and other curricular units to which students are exposed and from which content areas and learning outcomes can be sampled. These tests are usually described as measures of "achievement." They tend to have items—such as multiple-choice questions—that call for test takers to select a response or to complete a highly structured task (such as writing a short paragraph on a topic or solving a mathematical problem).

When knowledge domains are the frame of reference for test interpretation, the question to be answered is "How much of the specified domain has the test taker mastered?" and scores are most often presented in the form of percentages of correct answers. This sort of criterion-referenced test interpretation is often described as *content-* or *domain-referenced testing*. In fact, some consider these two terms as synonymous with criterion-referenced testing. Planning for such tests requires the development of a *table of specifications* with cells that specify the number of items or tasks to be included in the test for each of the learning objectives and content areas the test is designed to evaluate. The proportion of test items allocated to each cell reflects the weight or importance assigned to each objective and area. Rapid Reference 3.7 shows examples of various objectives and items in two content areas typical of domain-referenced tests. Examples of tables of spec-

≡Rapid Reference 3.7

Examples of Domain-Referenced Test Objectives and Items

I. *Domain:* Arithmetic

   A. *Content area to be assessed:* Multiplication of fractions

   B. *Objectives to be assessed:*

      1. Knowledge of the steps involved in multiplying fractions

      2. Understanding of the basic principles involved in multiplying fractions

      3. Application of principles in solving fraction multiplication problems

   C. *Sample test items for each objective:*

      Item 1. List the steps involved in multiplying fractions.

      Item 2. Draw a diagram to show 1/4 of 1/2 of a pie.

      Item 3. How much is $3/4 \times 1/2$?

II. *Domain:* Vocabulary

   A. *Content area to be assessed:* Word knowledge

   B. *Objectives to be assessed:*

      1. Word definition

      2. Comprehension of word meaning

      3. Application of word knowledge in written expression

   C. *Sample test items for each objective:*

      Item 1. What does "mariner" mean? _____

      Item 2. Which word is closest in meaning to "mariner"?

         a. marinate

         b. marimba

         c. sailor

         d. pirate

         e. wanderer

      Item 3. Make up a sentence using "mariner" in a meaningful context.

ifications for content-referenced tests and guidance in how they are prepared can be found in Gronlund (2003) and Linn and Gronlund (1995, pp. 119–125).

Performance Assessment

For purposes of decision-making in the workplace, and in the realm of education as well, there is often a need to ascertain or certify competence in the performance of tasks that are more realistic, more complex, more time consuming, or more difficult to evaluate than those typical of content- or domain-referenced testing. This kind of assessment calls for evaluating performance through work samples, work products, or some other behavioral display of competence and skill in situations that simulate real-life settings.

When the purpose of an assessment is to ascertain levels of competence in the kinds of contexts in which skills are applied in real life, the criterion in "criterion-referenced" test interpretation is the quality either of the performance itself or of the product that results from applying a skill. In this frame of reference, the typical questions to be answered are: "Does this test taker display mastery of the skill in question?" or "How proficient is this test taker, or group of test takers, in the continuum of competence relevant to this particular endeavor?"

Evaluation and Scoring in the Assessment of Performance

In light of the questions that the evaluation of proficiency is designed to answer, the assessment of performance entails a different set of procedures than those used when testing for knowledge in content domains. In general, the assessment of performance tends to rely more heavily on subjective judgment. An exception to this rule occurs when criteria can be quantified in terms of speed of performance, number of errors, units produced, or some other objective standard. A classic and simple example of an objective type of performance assessment is the typing test given to those who apply for clerical jobs that require a good deal of typing. Even in this type of test, however, the actual numerical criterion that is used as a cutoff score for acceptable performance—for example, 65 words per minute with no more than 5 errors—is likely to be set arbitrarily. Most other kinds of performance assessments involve (a) identifying and describing qualitative criteria for evaluating a performance or product, and (b) developing a method for applying the criteria. The usual methods for evaluating qualitative criteria involve *rating scales* or *scoring rubrics* (i.e., scoring guides) that describe and illustrate the rules and principles to be applied in scoring the quality of a performance or product. A well known example of this type of procedure is the scoring of athletic performances by designated expert judges in events such as figure skating on ice or diving competitions.

Mastery testing. Procedures that evaluate test performance on the basis of whether the individual test taker does or does not demonstrate a preestablished level of mastery are known as *mastery tests.* Many of these tests yield all-or-none scores, such as *pass* or *fail,* based on some criterion level that separates mastery from nonmastery. A typical example with which most readers will be familiar is provided by the driving tests many states require for the issuance of a driver's license. In these tests, what matters is whether individuals can demonstrate that they know the rules of driving and are able to handle an automobile in various traffic situations. Moreover, it is expected that the vast majority of people who take the driving test will be able to pass it, even if it takes more than one trial, and no distinctions need to be made among test takers in terms of their levels of performance, other than whether they pass it or fail it.

There are some situations and skills—such as landing an airplane on an aircraft carrier or performing brain surgery—when anything short of ascertaining that complete mastery has been achieved may not be an option. On the other hand, in educational circles the notion of testing for mastery can be interpreted in different ways. Some educators and other concerned parties have argued that all able students should achieve complete mastery of the prescribed instructional objectives at one level before graduating or moving on to the next, regardless of how long it takes. However, most people are willing to concede that when testing is designed to evaluate mastery of the basic skills that are taught in schools—such as reading, writing, and arithmetic—there clearly is room for various levels of achievement between mastery and nonmastery. In such cases, the problem becomes one of designating appropriate targets that students are expected to achieve, within a continuum of performance, in order to be promoted or graduate.

Predicting Performance

Sometimes the term *criterion-referenced test interpretation* is used to describe the application of empirical data concerning the link between test scores and levels of performance, to a criterion such as job performance or success in a program of study. In this context, the term *criterion* is used in a different sense, and more in accord with traditional psychometric practice, than in the preceding examples. Here, the criterion is an outcome to be estimated or predicted by means of a test. This type of information constitutes the basis for establishing the predictive validity of tests to be discussed more fully in Chapter 5. Nevertheless, it is mentioned at this point because, when the relationship between test scores and criteria is used for selection or placement of individuals in educational, training, or employment settings, that relationship can also be construed as a frame of reference for score interpretation. In this framework, the questions to be answered with the help of the test scores are "What level of criterion performance can one expect from a person who obtains this score?" or "Is the test taker's performance on the test sufficient to assure the desired level of criterion performance in a given endeavor?"

Information on the relationship between test scores and criteria can be presented in a variety of ways, including correlation coefficients and regression equations, which are described more extensively in the context of validity in Chapter 5. For the present purposes, however, two procedures that are especially relevant to the sort of criterion-referenced test interpretation discussed in the preceding paragraph—namely, expectancy tables and expectancy charts—will serve to clarify this approach.

Expectancy tables show the distribution of test scores for one or more groups of individuals, cross-tabulated against their criterion performance. Assuming that there is a substantial degree of correlation between test scores and criterion measures, this information can be used to gauge the probable criterion standing of individuals who scored at different levels. For example, using information from previous classes, a teacher might cross-tabulate the test scores at midterm as the predictor and final grade on the course as the criterion, as shown in Table 3.3. The resulting table can inform future students about what their final grades are likely to be based on their test scores at midterm.

Expectancy charts are used when criterion performance in a job, training program, or program of study can be classified as either successful or unsuccessful. These charts present the distribution of scores for a group of individuals along with the percentage of people at each score interval who succeeded (or failed) in terms of the criterion. When the trend is such that the percentage of successful individuals is much greater among high scorers than among low scorers, charts of this type can be extremely useful in making selection decisions.

Relationship Among the Frames of Reference

One cannot distinguish between norm- and criterion-referenced tests simply by looking at exemplars of each type. In fact, to a great extent, the distinctions be-

Table 3.3 Expectancy Table: Relationship Between Midterm Test Scores and Final Grades

Midterm Test Score	Number of Cases	Percentage Receiving Each Final Grade			
		D or F	C	B	A
90 and above	9		11	22	67
80 to 89	12	8	25	50	17
70 to 79	13	23	46	31	
60 to 69	3	33	67		
59 and below	3	67	33		

tween both frames of reference for test interpretation—as well as among the varieties within each frame—are matters of emphasis. Even though scores can be expressed in a variety of ways, fundamentally, all of testing relies on a normative framework.

The standards used in criterion-referenced test score interpretations must be based on expectations that are realistic or feasible for the population of test takers for whom the test is meant. Depending on the goals for which a test is used, it may be that too few or too many people are able to satisfy the criterion, in which case the test may prove to be impractical. In other words, criteria are based both on the testing purpose and also, to some extent, on what people can accomplish in a given situation.

The use of cutoff scores or other standards of performance in criterion-referenced interpretation does not mean that differences in the test performance of individuals will be eliminated or go unnoticed, nor does it preclude score comparisons across individuals. For instance, even if two applicants for a secretarial job meet the 65-words-per-minute criterion on a typing test, all other things being equal, the one who can type 90 words per minute is more likely to be chosen over the one who can type only 65.

Similarly, the use of norms does not prevent an examination of test performance from the point of view of content or behavioral criteria. In scoring classroom tests, for example, teachers who have carefully sampled from the material assigned for a test may choose to assign letter grades on the basis of the norms for the class (on the curve grading) or on the basis of performance criteria tied to the percentage of items answered correctly. Some standardized tests used in educational settings—such as the Iowa Tests of Basic Skills (ITBS), the Stanford Diagnostic Mathematics Test (SDMT), and the Stanford Diagnostic Reading Test (SDRT)—also try to provide for both norm-referenced and criterion-referenced interpretations. However, reviews of these tests suggest that this attempt meets with success only with regard to one type of interpretation or the other, but not both, because norm-referenced and criterion-referenced tests require somewhat different emphases in the way they are constructed. For more information on this issue, consult the reviews of the ITBS, SDMT, and SDRT in the 13th *Mental Measurements Yearbook,* edited by Impara and Plake (1998).

How, then, does norm-referenced test interpretation differ from criterion-referenced interpretation? The fundamental difference between the two is in their primary objectives:

- In norm-referenced testing, the primary objective is to make distinctions among individuals in terms of the ability or trait assessed by a test;

- In criterion-referenced testing, the primary objective is to evaluate a person's degree of competence or mastery of a skill or knowledge domain in terms of a preestablished standard of performance.

As we have seen, these two objectives are not always or necessarily mutually exclusive and, in some situations, the same instrument can be used for both objectives. Which of the two objectives is the primary one is determined by the specific purpose of the test user. That purpose, in turn, should help the test user determine which test development approach is the most suitable.

With regard to the varieties of criterion-referenced test interpretation, it should be fairly clear that the distinction between domain-based and performance-based assessment is also arbitrary to some extent. Knowledge of content domains must be demonstrated through observable behavior or performance in which one or more skills play a part. By the same token, every kind of performance requires some type of knowledge. Moreover, whereas in subjects that are elementary and fairly structured content domains can be mapped out, when it comes to more advanced and less structured areas—such as knowledge that cuts across various disciplines—this kind of parceling becomes difficult or impossible. Similarly, thresholds for mastery can be preestablished easily with regard to basic skills, but in fields that involve higher level skills, such standard setting may not be applicable because achievements are far more wide ranging.

Criterion-Referenced Test Interpretation in Clinical Assessment

Criteria such as mastery of a skill or knowledge in a given field are clearly not applicable in connection with instruments designed to assess personality. Therefore, the term *criterion-referenced interpretation* is not ordinarily used for tests of this type. Nevertheless, some tests relevant to both emotional and cognitive functioning are used by clinicians to help establish whether certain diagnostic criteria have been met. These tests use cutoff scores—established on the basis of normative data—to screen for the presence of certain disorders based on established links with clinical criteria. This particular application constitutes criterion-referenced interpretation, in the same sense as when the relationship between test scores and criteria is used to select or place individuals in educational or employment settings. Both of these practices involve the estimation or prediction of certain outcomes. Likewise, this sort of interpretation of clinical tests depends on validity evidence relevant to the diagnostic criteria (see Chapter 5). Examples of tests that are used in this fashion include instruments such as the Beck Depression Inventory, which can help to evaluate the intensity of depressive disorders, and the Mini-Mental State Examination, which helps in screening for cognitive impairment. These tests and other clinical tools—such as behavioral checklists and rating scales—that involve the use of cutoffs and score ranges to evaluate behavior symptomatic of mental disorders can also be said to be criterion-referenced.

Item Response Theory As a Basis for Combining Frames of Reference

Because their goal is to estimate a test taker's position on a latent trait or ability dimension, IRT methods are well suited to the development of tests whose scores can be interpreted in terms of both normative and criterion-referenced bases. Although the data used in IRT modeling are derived from the performance of reference samples, they can be combined with other kinds of item analyses to create scales that provide information of both a comparative (i.e., norm-referenced) and substantive (i.e., criterion-referenced) nature. One recent example of how this can be accomplished is found in the work Primi (2002) has done, which integrates cognitive theory and IRT in the construction of a measure of the type of ability needed to solve geometric matrix problems. Another is a hierarchical IRT model proposed by Janssen, Tuerlinckx, Meulders, and De Boeck (2000), which is applied to a test measuring mastery targets in reading comprehension at the elementary school level.

Social Considerations in Norm- and Criterion-Referenced Testing

The prevailing pressures to use criterion-referenced testing to certify competencies and make consequential decisions in educational and occupational settings has grown out of a dissatisfaction with the perceived weaknesses of norm-referenced testing. Some of this dissatisfaction arises from the view that the use of norm-referencing in education is a major cause of declining standards, given that no matter how poorly a student population might perform as a whole, relative to their own norms, at least half of them will always be above average.

Another source of dissatisfaction with norm-referenced testing stems from the fact that, when used as a basis for decisions in the educational and occupational realms, it often places members of underprivileged minority groups at a disadvantage compared to individuals who may have had more educational opportunities. However, in an ironic twist, during the past few decades the use of criterion-referenced testing to certify competencies has become a subject of as much or more heated debate than norm-referenced testing in the professional and political arenas. Undoubtedly, much of the debate about both types of testing hinges on misunderstandings of the proper role of tests as tools—rather than as arbiters—as well as on policies that seem to alternate between the two extremes of overemphasis on and opposition to standardized testing in what have come to be known as "high stakes" decisions (see, e.g., Jaeger, 1989; Mehrens, 1992; U.S. Department of Education, Office for Civil Rights, 2000; Wigdor & Green, 1991).

🐟 TEST YOURSELF 🐟

1. **If not accompanied by further information, a high raw score is**
    (a) meaningless.
    (b) still always better than a low score.

2. _____ **constitute the most widely used frame of reference for test score interpretation.**
    (a) Content domains
    (b) Work samples
    (c) Criteria
    (d) Norms

3. **Of all the following developmental norms, which ones are the most universally applicable?**
    (a) Theory-based ordinal scales
    (b) Mental age norms
    (c) Natural sequences
    (d) Grade-based norms

4. **With regard to the samples used to establish within-group norms, the single most important requirement is that they should be**
    (a) gathered locally by the institution or organization that will use them.
    (b) very large, numbering in the thousands.
    (c) representative of the group for which they will be used.
    (d) convenient to obtain in the process of standardization.

5. **The concepts of test ceiling and test floor are most closely related to the issue of**
    (a) test validity.
    (b) test difficulty.
    (c) the type of standard scores used in a test.
    (d) the type of items used in a test.

(continued)

6. **When transformed into the Wechsler-scale type of deviation IQs, a z score of –1.00 would become a Wechsler IQ of**
   (a) 85.
   (b) 95.
   (c) 105.
   (d) 115.

7. **Which of the following score transformation procedures is the only one that qualifies as a linear transformation?**
   (a) Normalized standard scores
   (b) Percentiles to stanines
   (c) Raw scores to percentile scores
   (d) z scores to T scores

8. **If a group of present-day individuals were to take both the original Wechsler Adult Intelligence Scale (WAIS) and its latest revision, the WAIS-III, chances are that their IQ scores would be**
   (a) the same on both tests.
   (b) higher on the WAIS-III than on the WAIS.
   (c) higher on the WAIS than on the WAIS-III.

9. **The essential characteristic of item response theory models is that they place _____ on a common scale.**
   (a) items and tests
   (b) items and persons
   (c) persons and tests

10. **One of the main advantages of IRT methodology is that it is ideally suited for use in _____ testing.**
    (a) computer adaptive
    (b) paper-and-pencil
    (c) personality

Answers: 1. a; 2. d; 3. c; 4. c; 5. b; 6. a; 7. d; 8. c; 9. b; 10. a.

Four

ESSENTIALS OF RELIABILITY

The term _reliability_ suggests trustworthiness. To the extent that decisions of any kind are to be made, wholly or in part, on the basis of test scores, test users need to make sure that the scores are reasonably trustworthy. When used in connection with tests and measurements, reliability is based on the consistency and precision of the results of the measurement process. In order to have some degree of confidence or trust in scores, test users require evidence to the effect that the scores obtained from tests would be consistent if the tests were repeated on the same individuals or groups and that the scores are reasonably precise.

Whereas reliability in measurement implies consistency and precision, lack of reliability implies inconsistency and imprecision, both of which are equated with measurement error. In the context of testing, _measurement error_ may be defined as any fluctuation in scores that results from factors related to the measurement process that are irrelevant to what is being measured. _Reliability,_ then, is a quality of test scores that suggests they are sufficiently consistent and free from measurement error to be useful.

Note that, in order to be useful, test scores do not need to be either totally consistent or error free. As we saw in Chapter 1, even in the physical sciences—some of which can boast of incredibly reliable instrumentation—measurements are always subject to some degree error and fluctuation. In the social and behavioral sciences, measurements are much more prone to error due to the elusive nature of the constructs that are assessed and to the fact the behavioral data through which they are assessed can be affected by many more intractable factors than other types of data (see Rapid Reference 5.2 on Deconstructing Constructs in Chapter 5). Psychological test scores, in particular, are especially susceptible to influences from a variety of sources—including the test taker, the examiner, and the context in which testing takes place—all of which may result in variability that is extraneous to the purpose of the test.

TRUTH AND ERROR IN PSYCHOLOGICAL MEASUREMENT

One of the most enduring approaches to the topic of reliability is the classical test theory notion of the *true score* (see, e.g., Gulliksen, 1950). In a way, this notion could be said to represent the object of the quest, or Holy Grail, of the psychometric enterprise. Although true scores do not really exist, it is nevertheless possible to imagine their existence: True scores are the hypothetical entities that would result from error-free measurement. Methods for estimating the reliability of scores provide a way of estimating true scores, or at least the boundaries within which true scores might lie. The concepts of reliability and error in test scores—which must obviously enter into consideration with regard to any score—are applied in parallel yet somewhat different ways when dealing with one or more scores of a single individual than when dealing with the scores of groups.

The Concept of the True Score in Individual Data

In classical test theory, an individual's *true score* is conceptualized as the average score in a hypothetical distribution of scores that would be obtained if the individual took the same test an infinite number of times. In practice, it is obviously impossible to obtain such a score for even one individual, let alone for many. Instead of true scores, what one derives from tests are *observed scores* (i.e., the scores that individuals actually obtain).

With regard to a single score, the ideas presented so far can be stated succinctly by means of the following equation:

$$X_o = X_{true} + X_{error} \tag{4.1}$$

which expresses the concept that any observed score (X_o) is made up of two components: a true score component (X_{true}) and an error score component (X_{error}). From a realistic point of view, the magnitudes of both of these components will always remain unknown in any given instance. Nevertheless, in theory, the true score component is construed to be that portion of the observed score which reflects whatever ability, trait, or characteristic the test assesses. Conversely, the error component, which is defined as the difference between the observed score and the true score, represents any other factors that may enter into the observed score as a consequence of the measurement process.

True Scores in Group Data

The singular importance of interindividual variability was already discussed in Chapter 2, where it was pointed out that the usefulness of psychological testing hinges on obtaining some variability across individuals. Without score variability, tests could not help us to make comparative decisions about people. It may also be recalled that, in the same chapter, the sample variance (s^2) was defined as the average amount of variability in a group of scores. Based on this information, Formula (4.1)—which pertains to a single test score—can be extrapolated and applied to the distribution of test scores obtained from a sample, or a population, in the following fashion:

$$\text{Sample variance} = s^2 = s_t^2 + s_e^2 \tag{4.2}$$

or

$$\text{Population variance} = \sigma^2 = \sigma_t^2 + \sigma_e^2 \tag{4.3}$$

Both of these formulas express the same idea, namely, that the variance in a set of observed scores for a sample (s^2) or a population (σ^2) consists of a portion that is true variance (s_t^2 or σ_t^2) and a portion that is error variance (s_e^2 or σ_e^2). True variance consists of those differences among the scores of individuals within a group that reflect their standing or position in whatever characteristic the test assesses. Error variance is made up of the differences among test scores that reflect factors irrelevant to what the test assesses. Formulas (4.2) and (4.3) also imply that the reliability of scores increases as the error component decreases. In fact, a *reliability coefficient* (r_{xx})—about which more will be said later in this chapter—may be defined as the ratio of true score variance (s_t^2) to total test score variance (s^2), or,

$$r_{xx} = \frac{s_t^2}{s^2} \tag{4.4}$$

In other words, if all the test score variance were true variance, score reliability would be perfect (1.00). A reliability coefficient may be viewed as a number that estimates the proportion of the variance in a group of test scores that is accounted for by error stemming from one or more sources. From this perspective, the evaluation of score reliability involves a two-step process that consists of (a) determining what possible sources of error may enter into test scores and (b) estimating the magnitude of those errors.

THE RELATIVITY OF RELIABILITY

Although the practice of describing *tests* as reliable is common, the fact is that the quality of reliability is one that, if present, belongs not to tests but to test *scores*. This distinction is emphasized consistently by most of the contributors to the contemporary literature on reliability (see, e.g., Rapid Reference 4.1). Even

≡ Rapid Reference 4.1

An excellent collection of readings on reliability, with more detailed and extensive explanations of many topics covered in this chapter, can be found in *Score Reliability: Contemporary Thinking on Reliability Issues*, edited by Bruce Thompson (2003b).

though it may seem subtle at first glance, the distinction is fundamental to an understanding of the implications of the concept of reliability with regard to the use of tests and the interpretation of test scores. If a test is described as reliable, the implication is that its reliability has been established permanently, in all respects, for all uses, and with all users. This would be akin to saying that a fine piano that is well tuned will always be in tune and will sound just as good regardless of the kind of music that is played on it or of who plays it. In fact, the quality of the sound a piano makes is a function not only of the instrument itself, but also of variables related to the music, the piano player, and the setting (e.g., the acoustics of the room) where the piano is played. Similarly, although reliability in testing hinges to a significant extent on characteristics of the test itself, the reliability of test scores—which is what results from the use of the instrument and, like the music a piano makes, is what really matters—can also be affected by many other variables.

Even as applied to test scores, moreover, the quality of reliability is relative. The score a person obtains on a test is not reliable or unreliable in any absolute sense. Rather, an obtained score may be more or less reliable due to factors uniquely pertinent to the test taker (e.g., fatigue, lack of motivation, the influence of drugs, etc.) or to the conditions of the testing situation (e.g., the presence of distracting noises, the personality of the examiner, the strictness with which time limits are enforced, etc.). All of these factors may singly or jointly affect the obtained score to a greater or lesser extent, including up to the point where the score becomes so unreliable that it should be discarded. Even though they are unrelated to the test itself, all such matters need to be taken into account in the assessment process.

In contrast, when reliability (r_{xx}) is considered from the point of view of test score data obtained *from a large sample, under standardized conditions,* the measurement errors that may impinge on the individual scores of members of the sample, while still present, are assumed to be distributed at random. Since random errors are equally likely to influence scores in a positive or a negative direction, the errors can also be assumed to cancel each other out. Even then, however, reliability estimates will vary from sample to sample depending on their composition and the circumstances in which the testing occurs. For instance, if a test is aimed at adults ranging in age from 18 to 90 years, the estimated reliability of its scores will be susceptible to the influence of different factors depending on whether the estimate is based on data obtained from the older age groups, from the younger age groups, or from a group that is representative of the entire age range for which the test is intended.

A Note About Truth and Error

The need to identify and investigate the true components and the error components of scores is considered in more detail in the next section. At

this point, however, it is important to emphasize that these judgments always have to be made in relation to what a test attempts to assess and to the circumstances under which it is administered. For example, test scores that denote the speed with which individuals can place 100 pegs in a pegboard, if given under standardized conditions, would by and large reflect the test takers' typical levels of manual dexterity quite reliably. If the same test were given (a) under conditions meant to distract the test takers or (b) under conditions that unintentionally distracted the test takers, both sets of scores would reflect levels of manual dexterity under distracting conditions. However, the influence of the distractions would be seen as a source of error variance, or as reducing the reliability of what the scores are intended to indicate only in the second instance.

SOURCES OF ERROR IN PSYCHOLOGICAL TESTING

As we have seen, error can enter into the scores of psychological tests due to an enormous number of reasons, many of which are outside the purview of psychometric estimates of reliability. Generally speaking, however, the errors that enter into test scores may be categorized as stemming from one or more of the following three sources: (a) the context in which the testing takes place (including factors related to the test administrator, the test scorer, and the test environment, as well as the reasons the testing is undertaken), (b) the test taker, and (c) the test itself. Some of the errors stemming from these sources can be minimized or eliminated provided that proper testing practices are followed by the parties who are involved in the process of developing, selecting, administering, and scoring tests.

add test administrator

Still others, such as test takers' carelessness or attempts at impression management in responding to test items, cannot be eliminated but may be detected by various types of checks built into the test. At any rate, practices related to the appropriate use of tests—practices most of which are aimed at reducing the error in scores—are discussed at greater length in Chapter 7, which deals with issues relevant to test selection, administration, and scoring, among others.

For the purpose of this discussion of reliability, it will be assumed that test users, test administrators, and test scorers carefully select the appropriate instruments, prepare suitable test environments, establish good rapport with the test takers, and both administer and score tests in accordance with well established standardized procedures. Furthermore, it will also be assumed that test takers are properly prepared and well motivated to take tests. Whether these assumptions are or are not justified in specific instances, the fact remains that the behaviors that they entail are subject to the control of one or more of the individuals involved in the testing process and are not pertinent to the tests themselves in a direct way. To the extent that these assumptions are justified, the error in test scores that stems from sources unrelated to the tests can obviously be eliminated or at least minimized.

In considering reliability for the remainder of this chapter, the sources of error to be discussed pertain primarily to factors outside the conscious control of the parties in the testing process, namely, random or chance factors. Before we proceed, however, it should be noted that measurement error can be systematic and consistent as well as random. Just as a balance may be off by a few pounds, a test may have an intrinsic characteristic of some sort that affects all test takers. Traditional estimates of reliability may fail to detect this sort of consistent error, depending on its source, because they are based on methods meant to detect inconsistencies in the results of a test. Systematic and consistent errors in measurement affect not only the reliability but also the validity of test results. In order to detect them, one must be able to compare the results of one instrument with those of other tools that assess the same construct but do not share the factor that causes the consistent error. To detect the error in the case of the balance that is off by a few pounds, for instance, one would have to weigh the same person or object on one or more additional and well calibrated scales.

Rapid Reference 4.2 lists some of the possible sources of error that may render test scores inconsistent. This list categorizes the sources of error assessed by traditional estimates of reliability, along with the types of tests to which those error sources pertain most directly, and the reliability coefficients typically used to estimate them. A conceptual explanation of each of the sources of error and reliability estimates is presented next, in the same order as they are listed in Rapid

≡ *Rapid Reference 4.2* [content reliability = .7]

Sources of Measurement Error With Typical Reliability Coefficients Used to Estimate Them

[Interrelator reliability = .9] [retest / time reliability = .7]

Source of Error	Type of Tests Prone to Each Error Source	Appropriate Measures Used to Estimate Error
Interscorer differences [2 dif administrators]	Tests scored with a degree of subjectivity	Scorer reliability
Time sampling error [2 dif occasions -practice effect]	Tests of relatively stable traits or behaviors [4-6 weeks] [state vs trait]	Test-retest reliability (r_{tt}) a.k.a. stability coefficient
Content sampling error [do measure content well]	Tests for which consistency of results, as a whole, is desired	Alternate-form reliability (r_{II}) or split-half reliability [same test, same people] [split test in half]
Interitem inconsistency [2 test, 2 test occasions]	Tests that require interitem consistency	Split-half reliability or more stringent internal consistency measures, such as Kuder-Richardson 20 (K-R 20) or coefficient alpha (α) [odd/even] [1st half] [2nd half]
Interitem inconsistency and content heterogeneity combined	Tests that require interitem consistency *and* homogeneity	Internal consistency measures *and* additional evidence of homogeneity
Time and content sampling error combined	Tests that require stability *and* consistency of results, as a whole	Delayed alternate-form reliability

[Item relates to total IS Cronbach Alpha Exploratory Factor Analysis]

Reference 4.2. Considerations regarding when and how these concepts and procedures are applied in the process of test use are discussed in a subsequent section of this chapter.

Interscorer Differences

Interscorer (or *interrater*) *differences* is the label assigned to the errors that may enter into scores whenever the element of subjectivity plays a part in scoring a test. It is assumed that different judges will not always assign the same exact scores or ratings to a given test performance even if (a) the scoring directions specified in the test manual are explicit and detailed and (b) the scorers are conscientious in applying those directions. In other words, score variability that is due to interscorer differences does not imply carelessness either in preparing the directions for scoring or in the actual scoring of a test. It refers to variations in scores that stem from differences in the subjective judgment of the scorers.

Scorer Reliability

The basic method for estimating error due to interscorer differences consists of having at least two different individuals score the same set of tests, so that for each test taker's performance two or more independent scores are generated. The correlations between the sets of scores generated in this fashion are indexes of *scorer reliability*. Very high and positive correlations, in the order of .90 or higher, suggest that the proportion of error that is accounted for by interscorer differences is 10% or less, since $1 - (\geq .90) = \leq .10$.

Time Sampling Error

Time sampling error refers to the variability inherent in test scores as a function of the fact that they are obtained at one point in time rather than at another. This concept hinges on two related notions, namely, (a) that whatever construct or behavior a test evaluates is liable to fluctuate in time, and (b) that some of the constructs and behaviors assessed through tests are either less subject to change, or change at a much slower pace, than others. For example, psychological constructs related to abilities, such as verbal comprehension or mechanical aptitude, usually are seen as being less prone to fluctuation over time than constructs related to personality, such as agreeableness or warmth. Within the realm of personality and emotional functioning the difference between more and less stable constructs has been codified in the traditional distinction of _traits_—which are construed to be relatively enduring characteristics—versus _states,_ which are by definition temporary conditions. To some extent, this distinction may also be applied to cognitive characteristics. Verbal ability, for instance, is assumed to be far more stable within an individual than attention and memory capacities, both of which are more susceptible to the influence of transient conditions or emotional states. At any rate, it is clear that whereas a certain amount of time sampling error is assumed to enter into all test scores, as a rule, one should expect less of it in the scores of tests that assess relatively stable traits.

Test-Retest Reliability

To generate estimates of the amount of time sampling error liable to affect the scores of a given test, it is customary to administer the same test on two different occasions, separated by a certain time interval, to one or more groups of individuals. The correlation between the scores obtained from the two administrations is a *test-retest reliability* (or *stability*) *coefficient* (r_{tt}) and may be viewed as an index of the extent to which scores are likely to fluctuate as a result of time sampling error. When this procedure is used, the time interval between the two test administrations always has to be specified, as it will obviously affect the stability of the scores. Realistically speaking, however, there are many factors that can differentially affect the test scores derived from a group of people across two occasions. Because of this, there is no fixed time interval that can be recommended for all tests. If the interval is very short, for instance, test takers may remember their responses from the first occasion and this could affect their scores on the second one. On the other hand, if the interval is very long, there is always the possibility that intervening experiences—including steps that the test takers may have taken in reaction to the first administration—may affect the scores on the second occasion. In addition to these considerations, test users must also evaluate stability coefficients from the point of view of theoretical expectations pertinent to the traits and behaviors assessed by the test. One example would be the differences in the rate of change that may be expected as a function of the age of the test takers. Reading comprehension, for instance, can change fairly rapidly in young children but should remain stable through adulthood, unless some unusual circumstance—such as special training or brain injury—affects it.

Content Sampling Error

Content sampling error is the term used to label the trait-irrelevant variability that can enter into test scores as a result of fortuitous factors related to the content of the specific items included in a test. A simple example of how content sampling error might enter into test scores is presented in Rapid Reference 4.3. This illustration of content sampling error is rather contrived because it pertains to error introduced into test scores as a result of faulty test construction, and thus could have been avoided easily. In the example, the teacher's selection of items results in inadequate coverage of the content knowledge the test is supposed to evaluate. Consequently, a good portion of score variability is unrelated to the students' level of mastery of the specified material, rendering their scores not only less reliable but also less valid than they would be otherwise. A more typical example is posed by cases in which—for reasons outside of the control of the test developer—the specific content of a test either favors or disadvantages some of the test takers, based on their different experiential histories. For instance, a test designed to evaluate reading comprehension may fortuitously include several passages that are familiar to some test takers and not familiar to others. Obviously, those test takers who are familiar with the passages would be able to answer ques-

$$\equiv Rapid\ Reference\ 4.3$$

A Simple Illustration of Content Sampling Error Resulting From Faulty Test Construction

Take the case of a content-referenced classroom test that is intended to evaluate knowledge of *all* the material contained in five textbook chapters. Suppose that the teacher preparing the test develops most of the items from the content of just three of the chapters, neglecting to include items from the remaining two chapters. Suppose further that several of the students have also concentrated on only three chapters in studying for the test.

Content sampling error in the scores on such a test would result primarily from the teacher's uneven sampling from the material that the test was intended to cover. *All other things being equal*, the consequences of the teacher's inadequate content sampling would be as follows: (a) Those students who studied the same three chapters from which the test content was drawn would score close to 100%, (b) those who concentrated on two of those chapters and one other would get grades of about 67%, and (c) those who were unfortunate enough to concentrate on only one of the "right" chapters, and the two chapters not included in the test, would score at approximately 33%.

If we assumed that all the students who studied only three out of the five chapters had actually mastered 60% of the material the test was supposed to cover, their true scores should have approximated that percentage. The discrepancies between their obtained scores and their true level of mastery of the material is content sampling error. In this particular case, the error in the scores would lower not only the reliability of the scores but also their validity.

tions based on them more easily and expediently than the rest, on account of their greater familiarity with the material rather than because of a higher level of achievement in reading comprehension.

Alternate-Form Reliability

Alternate-form reliability procedures are intended to estimate the amount of error in test scores that is attributable to content sampling error. To investigate this kind of reliability, two or more different forms of the test—identical in purpose but differing in specific content—need to be prepared and administered to the same group of subjects. The test takers' scores on each of the versions are then correlated to obtain *alternate-form reliability* (r_{11}) *coefficients*. Since it is unlikely that the same chance factors, favoring some test takers and not others, will affect the different forms, high and positive correlations (e.g., .90 or higher) between scores on the various forms may be taken as an indication that content sampling error is not a major influence on test scores (e.g., 10% or less). Delayed alternate-form reliability, a variation of this procedure used to assess the combined effects of time and content sampling, is discussed later in this section.

Split-Half Reliability

Developing alternate forms of a test, or administering the same test twice, often involves theoretical or practical problems that make these courses of action difficult. One solution is simply to administer a test to a group of individuals and to create two scores for each person by splitting the test into halves.

How to split a test in half. The best way to split tests into halves for the purpose of computing split-half reliability coefficients depends on how tests were designed. In particular, it is im-

perative to consider two possibilities: (a) whether some test items differ systematically from other items across the length of the test, and (b) whether speed plays a significant role in test performance. Both of these conditions can have profound effects on the magnitude of split-half reliability coefficients.

1. *Systematic differences across test items* can occur due to a variety of reasons. For example, many ability tests start with the easiest items and get progressively more difficult, or are divided into parts or subtests that cover different content. Still others, like the Wonderlic Personnel Test, are structured in a *spiral-omnibus format* so that items dealing with verbal, numerical, spatial, and analytic tasks are rotated systematically. Many personality inventories are also arranged so that items from different scales are rotated throughout the test.

2. *When test performance depends primarily on speed,* items are usually pegged at a low enough difficulty level for all test takers to complete correctly, but time limits are set so that most test takers will not be able to finish the test. For example, tests of clerical aptitude often include tasks that require test takers to scan a long list of pairs of numbers, letters, or symbols within a brief time period and to indicate whether each pair is or is not identical. In this kind of highly speeded test, scores depend

primarily on the number of items completed, rather than on the number of correct responses. Since most test takers will produce perfect or nearly perfect performance on all the items they attempt, any division of such a test into half-scores in terms of items—as well as any measure of internal consistency—will yield nearly perfect coefficients.

Rapid Reference 4.4 presents possible solutions to the problem of how tests of various types may be split into halves. Once this has been accomplished, the correlation between the scores on one half of the test and those on the other half (r_{hh}) is used to derive a *split-half reliability coefficient*. Since r_{hh} actually estimates the consistency of scores on the two half-tests, the *Spearman-Brown (S-B) formula* is applied to r_{hh} to obtain the estimate for the full test. This formula is based on the classical test theory notion that a larger number of observations will produce a more reliable result than a smaller number of observations. In other words, all other things being equal, a score that is based on a longer test will be closer to the true score than one based on a shorter test. The general version of the S-B formula is

$$r_{S\text{-}B} = \frac{nr_{xx}}{1 + (n-1)r_{xx}} \tag{4.5}$$

≡Rapid Reference 4.4

Some Solutions to the Problem of How to Split a Test in Half

- A rule of thumb for splitting tests of various types to compute split-half reliability coefficients is to *divide the test into the two most nearly comparable halves*. Although this can be accomplished in many ways, it is often done by means of an odd-even split, with the odd items (1, 3, 5, etc.) and even items (2, 4, 6, etc.) making up the two halves.

- To the extent that speed plays a role in test performance, any single-trial reliability estimate—such as the split-half method—will produce spuriously high results. This occurs because, for tests that are significantly speeded, score reliability is primarily a function of the consistency of the speed with which test takers perform on the test, as opposed to the consistency of the caliber of their responses. Thus, for speeded tests, one possible solution is to use *two-trial reliability methods*, such as test-retest or alternate forms. Another is to split the test in terms of separately timed halves and then compute the reliability coefficient in the same fashion as the usual split-half.

- *Why is this important to a potential test user?* If the method used to compute estimates of the internal consistency of test scores is not appropriate to the way a test was designed, the resulting reliability coefficients will be misleading. Potential test users who are considering the issue of reliability in the process of selecting a test need to attend to these matters.

where

r_{S-B} = Spearman-Brown estimate of a reliability coefficient,

n = the multiplier by which test length is to be increased or decreased, and

r_{xx} = the reliability coefficient obtained with the original test length.

This formula can be used to estimate the effect that lengthening a test by any amount, or shortening a test to any fraction of its original size, will have on the obtained coefficient. For example, if the obtained r_{xx} for a 30-item test is 0.80 and one wishes to estimate what the reliability coefficient would be if the length of the test were increased to 90 items, by adding 60 *comparable* items, one would find n to be 3 and r_{S-B} to be 0.92. If one wanted to shorten the same test to 15 items, n would be ½ and r_{S-B} would go down to 0.67. When applied to a split-half reliability coefficient (r_{hh}), which involves estimating the reliability of the whole test based on the correlation between its two halves, the S-B formula can be simplified as follows:

$$r_{S-B} = \frac{2r_{hh}}{1 + r_{hh}} \tag{4.6}$$

Interitem Inconsistency

Interitem inconsistency refers to error in scores that results from fluctuations in *items* across an entire test, as opposed to the content sampling error emanating from the particular configuration of items included in the test as a whole. Although interitem inconsistencies may be apparent upon careful examination of item content—and of the cognitive processes that may enter into play in responding to different items in a test—from the statistical point of view, they manifest themselves in low correlations among test items. Such inconsistencies can be due to a variety of factors, including content sampling error, many of which are fortuitous and unpredictable. They can also result from content heterogeneity.

Content Heterogeneity

Content heterogeneity results from the inclusion of items or sets of items that tap content knowledge or psychological functions that differ from those tapped by other items in the same test. This factor is largely within the control of the test developers, who should determine the degree of heterogeneity of test content based on the purpose of the test and on the kind of population for which the test is intended. To the extent that a test is purposefully designed to sample heterogeneous content, content heterogeneity cannot be considered to be a source of error. Heterogeneity in test content, or in the cognitive functions tapped by

DON'T FORGET

Deconstructing Heterogeneity and Homogeneity

In psychological testing, the concepts of homogeneity and heterogeneity are used in reference to the composition of (a) the behavior samples or items that make up a test, and (b) groups of test takers, such as standardization samples or populations. Since both of these aspects can affect *all* the statistics used to evaluate tests (see, e.g., the section on range restriction and correlation as well as Fig. 2.7 in Chapter 2), it is important to remember the following:

* *Heterogeneity and homogeneity are always relative terms.* Any entity that is composed of separate elements is heterogeneous to the extent that its elements are dissimilar in some respect. Thus, any group made up of multidimensional constituents, such as people or test items, is heterogeneous in some respects. By the same token, no such group is homogeneous in *all* respects.
* *In order to characterize a group as heterogeneous or homogeneous,* it is necessary to decide which variable or variables will serve as the bases for evaluating similarity or dissimilarity. For instance:
* *The items in a test* may be heterogeneous with regard to content and format—if some consist of words while others consist of numbers or if some are presented orally, others in writing—but homogeneous with regard to cognitive function if they all involve memory (e.g., remembering words and numbers).
* *A group of people* may be heterogeneous with regard to sex and age, if it includes males and females ranging in age from 17 to 45, but homogeneous with regard to educational status, if it includes only college freshmen.

different test items, is a source of error only when a test is supposed to be homogeneous in one or more ways across all of its items. Rapid Reference 4.5 shows some item sets that vary in terms of their heterogeneity.

Internal Consistency Measures

Internal consistency measures are statistical procedures designed to assess the extent of inconsistency across test items. Split-half reliability coefficients accomplish this to some extent. However, even a very short test can be split in half in several different ways—for example, a four-item test can be split into halves in 3 different ways, a six-item test in 10 ways, and so on—and each split may yield a somewhat different correlation between the halves. One way to overcome this logistical problem is do an odd-even split—with one half of the test consisting of odd items and the other half of even items—or any other split that will result in the two most nearly comparable halves (see Rapid Reference 4.4).

Another solution is provided by formulas that take into account interitem correlation (i.e., the correlation between performance on *all the items* within a test).

≡Rapid Reference 4.5

Examples of Sets of Test Items From Most to Least Heterogeneous Content

Set (A)

Item 1: What number should come next in the following series?
 3   6   12   24   _____

Item 2: Which of the five items listed is least like the other four?
 Pork   Beef.   Chicken   Tuna .   Veal

Item 3: A train travels 40 feet in 1/2 of a second. At this same speed, how far will it travel in 4 seconds?

Set (B)

Item 1: 4 + 10 = _____

Item 2: If a dozen eggs cost $1.03, how much will three dozen eggs cost?

Item 3: The price of an item is reduced by 60% during a sale. By what percent should the price be increased to go back to the original price?
 60%   80%   100%   120%   150%

Set (C)

Item 1: 4 × 5 = _____

Item 2: 7 × 11 = _____

Item 3: 15 × 15 = _____

• *Set A is the most heterogeneous:* The items differ in terms of content domains, formats, and skills required.

• *Set B is next:* The items share the same content domain (Math), but differ in format and skills required (i.e., addition, multiplication, and fractions in Math *plus* basic reading skills).

• *Set C is the most homogeneous:* Its items share a common domain, format, and skill required (understanding the operation of multiplication and its symbols).

The two most frequently used formulas used to calculate interitem consistency are the *Kuder-Richardson formula 20 (K-R 20)* and *coefficient alpha* (α), also known as *Cronbach's alpha* (Cronbach, 1951), which is simply a more general case of the K-R 20 postulation. Both the K-R 20 and coefficient alpha require a single (one-trial) administration of a test to a group of individuals. The magnitude of the K-R 20 and alpha coefficients is a function of two factors: (a) the number of items in the test, and (b) the ratio of variability in test takers' performance across all the items in the test to total test score variance. All other things being equal, the magnitude of K-R 20 and coefficient alpha will be higher (a) as the number of items increases and (b) as the ratio of item score variance to total test score variance decreases. Conceptually, both K-R 20 and coefficient alpha produce estimates of reliability that are equivalent to the average of all the possible split-half coefficients that would result from all the possible different ways of splitting the test in half. As such, they represent a combined estimate of content sampling error as well as content heterogeneity. Therefore, unless a test is highly homogeneous, K-R 20 and coefficient alpha reliabilities will be lower than any single split-half coefficient. Rapid Reference 4.6 contains the K-R 20 formula and one version of the

Rapid Reference 4.6

Formulas for Calculating Internal Consistency

Kuder-Richardson formula 20 (K-R 20)

$$r_{\text{K-R 20}} = \left(\frac{n}{n-1}\right) \frac{s_t^2 - \Sigma\, pq}{s_t^2}$$

where

n = number of items in the test

s_t^2 = variance of total scores on the test

$\Sigma\, pq$ = sum of p times q for each item on the test

p = proportion of persons who pass each item or answer it in a specific direction

q = proportion of persons who fail each item or answer it in the opposite direction

The $r_{\text{K-R 20}}$ formula is applied to tests whose items are scored as right or wrong, or in any other dichotomous fashion, such as true or false, if all the items are phrased so that the meaning of each alternative is uniform throughout the test.

Coefficient alpha (α) or Cronbach's alpha

$$\alpha = \left(\frac{n}{n-1}\right) \frac{s_t^2 - \Sigma(s_i^2)}{s_t^2}$$

where

n = number of items in the test

s_t^2 = variance of total scores on the test

$\Sigma(s_i^2)$ = sum of the variances of item scores

This coefficient alpha formula and a variation known as *standardized item alpha*, which uses the average interitem correlation instead of item score and total score variances, are used for tests whose items have multiple possible responses (e.g., *strongly agree, agree, disagree,* and *strongly disagree*). Cortina (1993) provides an extensive discussion of the meaning of coefficient alpha formulas and the various factors that can affect their results.

coefficient alpha formula, along with a basic explanation of their components and applicability.

Since both K-R 20 and coefficient alpha are heavily dependent on the amount of interitem variability within a test, it stands to reason that any lack of uniformity in the content of test items, such as content heterogeneity, will lower these coefficients. For instance, suppose internal consistency coefficients for three tests of equal length—made up of items like those presented in Sets A, B, and C of Rapid Reference 4.5—were calculated. If this were done, the test resembling the mix of items in Set A in terms of heterogeneity would have the lowest internal consistency because the differences in test takers' mastery of the various skills and content domains tapped by the test items would be reflected in their performances. The test with the most homogeneous items, namely, items such as those in Set C, would have the highest coefficient.

Why is this important? When a test is purposefully designed to include items that are diverse in terms of one or more dimensions, K-R 20 and coefficient alpha will overestimate content sampling error, and thus are inappropriate. Depending on the design of the test, and based on an examination of its content, homogeneous items may be placed into subtests or otherwise segregated in order to compute separate measures of interitem consistency among groups of similar items. On the other hand, when homogeneity across all test items is desired, the magnitude of K-R 20 or coefficient alpha is an index of the extent to which this aim has been realized. In fact, the difference between the magnitude of the most appropriate split-half reliability coefficient and either the K-R 20 or α coefficients can be taken as an indication of the amount of heterogeneity in the items of a test. The closer the two estimates are, the more homogeneous the test content is.

Factor analytic techniques can also be used to investigate the heterogeneity and possible multidimensionality of test items. These techniques, discussed at greater length in Chapter 5, are used to detect similarities among a set of variables—such as responses to test items—based on the interrelatedness of their patterns of variability among one or more groups of test takers.

Time and Content Sampling Error Combined

Time sampling and content sampling error can be estimated in a combined fashion for tests that require both stability and consistency of results. As we shall see shortly, it is also possible to estimate the combined effects of other sources of error on test scores through other means. However, the delayed alternate-form design provides a good method for estimating time and content sampling error with a single coefficient.

Delayed Alternate-Form Reliability

Delayed alternate-form reliability coefficients can be calculated when two or more alternate forms of the same test are administered on two different occasions, separated by a certain time interval, to one or more groups of individuals. Just as with test-retest reliability, the interval between the two administrations needs to be clearly specified, along with the make-up of the samples and other conditions that might affect the magnitude of the obtained coefficients. If the two forms of a test are administered in immediate or close succession, the resulting alternate-form coefficient will be primarily a function of the reliability across forms. With longer intervals between the administrations of the two forms, the error variance in scores will reflect time fluctuations as well as content sampling error in the test.

A note about practice effects. One inevitable consequence of using the same test, or alternate forms of a test, repeatedly with the same subjects is that this introduces an additional source of unwanted variability in scores due to *practice effects*. Naturally, the length of the interval between the administrations affects the extent to which scores on the second or subsequent administrations of the test will be subject to practice effects. With short intervals, practice effects can be quite significant, especially when test items involve novel tasks that require test takers to grasp certain problem-solving strategies likely to be remembered. One-trial methods for estimating score reliability, such as the split-half technique and coefficient alpha, are not prone to practice effects, whereas two-trial procedures, such as test-retest and alternate-form reliability, usually are. To the extent that individuals differ in the amount of improvement shown upon retesting due to practice, the obtained correlations across two trials are likely to be reduced. Even more importantly, however, when tests are administered repeatedly for the purpose of assessing change over time, as they are in longitudinal studies, practice effects can be a significant confounding variable that must be taken into account (see, e.g., Kaufman & Lichtenberger, 2002, pp. 163–165).

RELIABILITY IN TEST USE

Score reliability is a perennial consideration in psychological testing because of the ever present possibility that errors from various sources will enter into test results. However, the manner in which the reliability of scores is considered differs at various points in the process of test development as well as in the actual application of tests. From the perspective of a test user, which is most pertinent for our purposes, reliability estimates must be carefully considered and applied in the stages of (a) test selection and (b) test score interpretation. Chapter 7 deals with these matters in greater detail; nevertheless, since the uses of statistical estimates of reliability are presented in this chapter, the different ways in which reliability is considered at each stage will be introduced at this point to provide a context for the ensuing discussion.

Reliability Considerations in Test Selection

When test users are deciding which test to use for a given purpose, they must look at the data that have already been gathered concerning the reliability of the scores from specific tests. These data usually can be found in test manuals, handbooks, and articles prepared by the authors or developers of tests, but they may also appear in the psychological literature as a result of the work of independent investigators who have used the tests. Typically, reliability data are presented in the form of correlation coefficients. Because of the pervasive use of the Pearson r coefficient in evaluating the reliability and validity of test scores, the essential aspects of this correlational method, including its limitations (discussed in Chapter 2), must be thoroughly understood before delving into these topics. One particularly relevant fact to keep in mind is that the magnitude of correlation coefficients depends to some extent on the variability of the samples for which they were calculated (see the section on Range Restriction and Correlation in Chapter 2).

The various types of coefficients that can be computed to estimate measurement error, along with the most pertinent sources of error, have already been described, albeit in the abstract. At the point of selecting a test, potential test users need to apply these notions to the particular situations for which they wish to employ a test. Rapid Reference 4.7 lists the basic steps involved in test selection from the point of view of reliability; a more extensive discussion of these considera-

⟨Rapid Reference 4.7

Reliability Considerations in Test Selection

Step 1 Determine the potential sources of error that may enter into the scores of the prospective instruments that are under review.

Step 2 Examine the reliability data available on those instruments, including the types of samples on which the data were obtained.

Step 3 Evaluate the data on reliability in light of all the other attributes of the tests in question, such as normative and validity data, cost and time constraints, and so forth.

Step 4 All other things being equal, select the test that promises to produce the most reliable scores for the purpose and population at hand.

tions is presented in the next few paragraphs. As a preliminary caveat, it must be noted that in evaluating the psychometric characteristics of a test—whether it be in relation to reliability, validity, normative data, or any other technical aspect of an instrument—there are no fixed rules that apply to all tests or all test uses.

Evaluating Potential Sources of Error in Test Scores

The foremost precaution for minimizing error in test scores is to adhere strictly to standardized procedures for the administration and scoring of tests (see Chapter 7). Beyond that, test users need to evaluate the possible relevance of each of the sources of error listed in Rapid Reference 4.2, in view of the choice of instruments available and of the purposes for which they might be employed. For example:

- If the scoring of a test involves subjective judgment, scorer reliability has to be taken into account.
- If a test is going to be used to evaluate change over time, such as possible improvement through a therapeutic intervention, an estimate of time sampling error—as well as of possible practice effects—in the scores of the instruments under consideration is essential.
- If there is a possibility that a person will have to be retested at a later date to confirm or ratify previous findings, the availability of an alternate form of the test, with high delayed alternate-form score reliability, would be highly desirable.
- If homogeneity and consistency across the entire test are desired, one would look for a high K-R 20 or alpha coefficient.

Evaluating Reliability Data

Reliability coefficients provide test users with some information concerning the magnitude of error that is likely to enter into scores from various sources. However, in evaluating reliability data, one must keep in mind the fact that these estimates are affected by the characteristics of the sample for which they were computed and may or may not generalize to other groups of test takers. Among other things, this means that small differences in the magnitude of coefficients of different tests are not likely to be of as much significance as other considerations. Furthermore, in light of the variety of factors that can impinge on the reliability of test scores, there is a growing recognition that investigators must routinely include score reliability data for their own samples in reporting the results of their research studies (see, e.g., Baugh, 2003; Onwuegbuzie & Daniel, 2002).

When a test is to be used in individual assessment, as opposed to research involving group data, the importance of critically examining the published information on score reliability prior to selecting a test cannot be overemphasized. In addition to evaluating the samples on which the data were obtained with regard to size, representativeness, and variability, test users should ponder whether the available coefficients are the most appropriate for the type of instrument at hand and for the intended uses of the test. Furthermore, if a test is made up of subtests or other parts whose scores are to be interpreted singly or in combination, estimates of reliability for each of the part scores should be available in addition to the estimates for the total test score.

In a manner of speaking, a reliability coefficient might be described as the correlation of the test with itself. Though not totally accurate, this description is a reminder that reliability coefficients are based on data—such as two administrations of the same test, two versions of the same test, interitem correlations, and so on—that *ought to be* highly consistent. Low reliability estimates (below .70) suggest that the scores one derives from a test may not be very trustworthy. Thus, although there is no minimum threshold for a reliability coefficient to be considered as adequate for all purposes, it is understood that, all other things being equal, the higher the coefficient, the better. Most test users look for coefficients to be at least in the range of .80 or higher.

Evaluating Score Reliability Data in Light of Other Test Attributes

Test selection decisions must be made on a case-by-case basis, taking into account all the characteristics of the available instruments and of the constructs they purport to assess, as well as the requirements of the specific situation in which test scores will be used. As fundamental as score reliability is, it is by no means the only consideration in test selection. In addition to the issue of reliability, validity data (Chapter 5) and the availability of normative or criterion-referenced information for test score interpretation (Chapter 3) are of paramount importance. Although practical considerations—such as cost, ease of administration and scoring, time constraints, and the like—necessarily play a role in test selection, to the extent that test use is likely to have a significant impact on test takers, such considerations should not be the determining factors in test choice.

Evaluation of Error From Multiple Sources

Most test scores are susceptible to measurement error stemming from more than one source. In classical test theory, this realistic possibility is accommodated by (a) methods that estimate the combined influence of two sources, such as delayed alternate-form reliability, which estimates both time and content sampling error; or (b) adding up the amounts of error variance estimated by all pertinent reliability coefficients to arrive at an estimate of total error variance. Both of these strategies hinge on the fact that reliability coefficients may be interpreted as estimates of the proportion of score variance attributable to error from various sources (see Formula [4.4]). For example, if the delayed alternate-form reliability coefficient of a test is .75, 75% of score variance can be interpreted as true variance and 25% $(1 - .75 = .25)$ of the variance can be attributed to the combined influence of time and content sampling error. If test scores are likely to be affected by several sources of error, the reliability estimates that assess error from different sources may be combined. Rapid Reference 4.8 describes such an analysis of sources of error variance for scores from the WAIS-III Vocabulary subtest (Psychological Corporation, 1997).

Generalizability Theory

An alternative approach to reliability that attempts to be more comprehensive than the one we have been discussing is what has come to be known as *generalizability theory,* or simply *G theory* (Cronbach, Gleser, Nanda, & Rajaratnam, 1972; Shavelson & Webb, 1991). Generalizability theory is an extension of classical test theory that uses analysis of variance (ANOVA) methods to evaluate the combined effects of multiple sources of error variance on test scores simultaneously.

A distinct advantage that G theory has—compared to the method for combining reliability estimates illustrated in Rapid Reference 4.8—is that it also allows for the evaluation of the interaction effects from different types of error sources. Thus, it is a more thorough procedure for identifying the error variance component that may enter into scores. On the other hand, in order to apply the experimental designs that G theory requires, it is necessary to obtain multiple observations for the same group of individuals on all the independent variables that might contribute to error variance on a given test (e.g., scores across occasions, across scorers, across alternate forms, etc.). On the whole, however, when this is feasible, the results provide a better estimate of score reliability than the approaches described earlier. In spite of the fact that G theory was originally introduced in the early 1960s, relatively few test authors have applied it in developing new instruments. However, as familiarity with this technique becomes more widespread, it is likely to gain in popularity. Readers who wish to become acquainted with the basic procedures of G theory might consult a brief introduction provided by Thompson (2003a), which includes a simple computational example. A more comprehensive and detailed treatment of the conceptual framework and statistical aspects of generalizability theory can be found in Robert Brennan's volume on this topic (2001).

≡ Rapid Reference 4.8

Analysis of Multiple Sources of Error Variance in Scores From a Single Test

The Wechsler Adult Intelligence Scale–Third Edition (WAIS-III) Vocabulary subtest consists of a series of increasingly difficult words that are read to the test taker by the examiner and simultaneously presented visually in a stimulus booklet. The test taker's definitions, given orally, are recorded verbatim and immediately scored by the examiner, using a scale of 2, 1, or 0 points, depending on the quality of the examinee's responses. In scoring the answers, examiners are guided by a thorough familiarity with samples of responses provided in the manual for each of the words—at the three score levels—as well as by the dictionary definitions of each word (Psychological Corporation, 1997).

The total score for the Vocabulary subtest is the sum of the points earned by the examinee on all the attempted items (words). A score of this nature is susceptible to time and content sampling error, as well as to the possibility of interscorer differences. Average reliability estimates provided in the WAIS-III manual (which might be consulted by those who want more detailed information) for the Vocabulary subtest are as follows:

Error Source/ Type of Reliability	Average Coefficient	Proportion and Percent (%) of Error Variance
Time sampling/stability (test-retest)	.91	$1 - .91 = .09$ (9%)
Content sampling/internal consistency	.93	$1 - .93 = .07$ (7%)
Interscorer differences/ interrater (scorer)	.95	$1 - .95 = .05$ (5%)
Total measured error variance		$.09 + .07 + .05 = .21$ (21%)
Estimated true variance		$1 - .21 = .79$ (79%)

From the preceding calculations, it should be quite evident that to rely on a *single-source* estimate of reliability for a test of the kind exemplified by the Vocabulary subtest of the WAIS-III would give a highly misleading impression of the possible amount of error in its scores. Furthermore, this example points out that in order for scores that are subject to multiple sources of error to be sufficiently trustworthy the reliability estimates for each single source needs to be quite high, in the range of .90 or higher.

See Example I: Applying the SEM in the text for a specific application of this analysis of multiple sources of error and its effect on the reliability of a score from the WAIS-III Vocabulary subtest.

The Item Response Theory Approach to Reliability

More sophisticated methods of estimating reliability are available through item response theory (IRT) (introduced in Chapter 3 and discussed further in Chapter 6). A full explanation of the technical aspects of IRT models is beyond the scope of this text, but the advantages that these models provide, especially for large scale and computer adaptive testing, have been rapidly spurring their development and application in the past few decades. With IRT methods, reliability and measurement error are approached from the point of view of the information function of individual test items, as opposed to the test as a whole. Because the difficulty level and discriminative power of individual items—relative to the trait assessed by the test—can be more carefully calibrated through IRT methods, the information that each test taker's response provides is more precise and thus more reliable. In the type of computer adaptive testing that these methods allow, the selection of the most appropriate items to present to test takers is determined by their previous responses. Using IRT methodology and adaptive testing, adequate reliability with minimal measurement error can be obtained with tests that are shorter than the traditional tests (which provide the same fixed content to all test takers), provided that a sufficiently extensive and inclusive item bank is available. This is just one of the many fundamental ways in which the model-based version of measurement known as IRT differs from the rules and assumptions of classical test theory (see, e.g., Embretson & Reise, 2000, pp. 13–39).

RELIABILITY CONSIDERATIONS IN TEST INTERPRETATION

Once a test has been chosen, administered, and scored, reliability data are applied in the process of test interpretation for two distinct but related purposes. The first is to acknowledge and quantify the margin of error in obtained test scores. The second purpose is to evaluate the statistical significance of the difference between obtained scores to help determine the import of those differences in terms of what the scores represent.

Quantifying Error in Test Scores: The Standard Error of Measurement

In the interpretation of any single score—or score average—from a test, reliability data are used to derive the upper and lower limits of the range within which test takers' true scores are likely to fall. A confidence interval is calculated for an obtained score on the basis of the estimated reliability of scores from the test in question. The size of the interval depends on the level of probability that is chosen.

Example 1: Applying the SEM

The estimated score reliability of the Vocabulary subtest of the WAIS-III described in Rapid Reference 4.8—after subtracting the estimated error variance from three relevant sources—is .79. As is true of all Wechsler subtest scores, Vocabulary has scaled scores that can range from 1 to 19, with $M = 10$ and $SD = 3$. To illustrate the most basic application of reliability data, let us assume that an individual named Maria obtains a score of 15 on the WAIS-III Vocabulary subtest.

Step 1. In order to obtain a confidence interval for Maria's obtained score (X_o) of 15, we need the *standard error of measurement (SEM)* for Vocabulary. The *SEM* is a statistic that represents the standard deviation of the hypothetical distribution we would have if Maria were to take this subtest an infinite number of times. As mentioned earlier in this chapter, the mean of such a hypothetical distribution would be Maria's *true score* on the Vocabulary subtest. Inspection of the formula in Rapid Reference 4.9 reveals that the *SEM* is a function of the reliability coeffi-

≡ Rapid Reference 4.9

....

Standard Error of Measurement (*SEM*) Formula

$$SEM = SD_t \sqrt{1 - r_{xx}}$$

where

SD_t = the standard deviation of the test

r_{xx} = the reliability coefficient

Standard Error of the Difference Between Two Scores (SE_{diff}) Formulas

SE_{diff} Formula 1:

$$SE_{diff} = SD\sqrt{2 - r_{11} - r_{22}}$$

where

SD = the standard deviation of Test 1 and Test 2

r_{11} = the reliability estimate for scores on Test 1

r_{22} = the reliability estimate for scores on Test 2

SE_{diff} Formula 2:

$$SE_{diff} = \sqrt{(SEM_1)^2 + (SEM_2)^2}$$

where

SEM_1 = the standard error of measurement of Test 1

SEM_2 = the standard error of measurement of Test 2

SE_{diff} Formula 1 is used if the two test scores being compared are expressed in the same scale, and SE_{diff} Formula 2 is used when they are not.

cient of the scores of the test in question and that it is expressed in terms of the test's standard deviation unit. Because of this, the size of the *SEM* cannot be taken by itself as an index of reliability. Tests that have large standard deviation units, such as the SAT with $SD = 100$, will have much larger *SEM*s than tests with small standard deviation units, such as the Wechsler scale subtests with $SD = 3$, even if their reliability coefficients are equal in magnitude.

Step 2. Since we cannot ever obtain multiple Vocabulary subtest scores for Maria, nor average them to find an estimate of her true score, we must choose an available score that can be placed at the center of the interval to be created by the *SEM*. Here, two possibilities arise: (a) we can either use the obtained score, X_o, as an estimate of Maria's true score, or (b) we can estimate her true score (T') with the following formula, based on Dudek (1979):

$$T' = r_{xx} (X_o - M) + M \qquad (4.7)$$

where

T' = the individual's estimated true score
r_{xx} = estimated reliability of test scores
X_o = the individual's obtained score
M = the mean of the test score distribution

In Maria's case, since $X_o = 15$, $r_{xx} = .79$, and $M = 10$ for the Vocabulary subtest, as for all Wechsler subtest scores, her estimated true score is 14 ($T' = (.79) (15 - 10) + 10 = 13.95$, or 14). Note that since her score is above the mean, *her estimated true score is lower than her obtained score.* In contrast, an obtained score of 5 on the same subtest—which deviates from the mean by an equal amount as Maria's, but in the opposite direction—would result in an estimated true score of 6, which is *higher* than X_o (if $X_o = 5$, $T' = (.79) (5 - 10) + 10 = 6.05$, or 6). The reason for this difference in the true score estimates of obtained scores that are above the mean and those that are below the mean is that the estimation procedure takes into account the effect of regression toward the mean. By the same token, if $X_o = M$, the best estimate of the true score would be the mean itself.

Step 3. Whether it is necessary to calculate T' in order to create a confidence interval depends on how much an obtained score deviates from the mean. If an obtained score is close to the mean, the estimated true score will not differ from it by much; on the other hand, as obtained scores get more extreme, calculating estimated true scores that are closer to the mean becomes more advisable. Be that as it may, Step 3 involves calculating the *SEM*. Using the formula in Rapid Reference 4.9, we find that $SEM = 3\sqrt{1 - .79} = 1.37$. Since this *SEM*, like the other standard errors described in Chapter 2, represents the standard deviation of a hypothetical distribution of scores that is assumed to be normal, we can interpret it in terms of the normal curve frequencies. It may be recalled, from Chapter 3, that approximately 68% of the area under the normal curve is comprised within ±1 SD from the mean, 95% is within ±1.96 SDs, and so on. Applying these percentages to Maria's estimated true score (T') of 14 and applying the obtained SEM of 1.37, we can say that (a) chances are 68/100, or $p = .32$, that Maria's true score is somewhere within the interval of 14 ± 1.37, that is between 13 and 15; and (b) chances are 95/100, or $p = .05$, that her true score is within 14 ± (1.37) (1.96), that is, between 11 and 17.

Interpreting the Significance of Differences Between Scores

Assessment goals often entail comparisons (a) between two or more scores obtained by the same individual on different parts of a test battery, as when levels of performance in different domains are compared, or (b) between the scores of two or more persons on the same test, for the purpose of evaluating their relative merits or characteristics. In both of these cases, reliability data may be used to derive probability statements concerning the likelihood that the obtained differences between scores—and what the scores represent—could have been due to chance. The statistic used for this purpose is the *standard error of the difference between scores,* or SE_{diff}. It can be calculated using either one of the two formulas listed in Rapid Reference 4.9, depending on whether the scores to be compared are expressed on the same scale (Formula 1) or not (Formula 2). Regardless of which of the two formulas is used the SE_{diff} will be larger than the SEM of either one of the scores involved in the comparison because the evaluation of differences between scores has to take into account the error present in both scores.

Example 2: Applying the SE$_{diff}$

To illustrate the use of the standard error of the difference between scores, let us suppose we wish to estimate the statistical significance of the difference between Maria's obtained scores on two subtests of the WAIS-III: her Vocabulary subtest score of 15 and her Information subtest score of 10. The Vocabulary subtest is described in Rapid Reference 4.8; the Information subtest assesses knowledge of common events, objects, places, and people.

Step 1. Since we want to estimate the significance of a difference between two obtained scores, the first step is to calculate that difference. In this case, $15 - 10 = 5$. There is a 5-point difference between Maria's Vocabulary subtest score and her Information subtest score. Knowing this, we can proceed to evaluate whether the obtained difference is statistically significant (i.e., unlikely to have occurred by chance).

Step 2. We need to calculate the standard error of the difference between scores on the Vocabulary and Information subtests of the WAIS-III. Since the two subtests are expressed on the same score scale ($M = 10$ and $SD = 3$), we may use Formula 1 from Rapid Reference 4.9. This requires knowledge of the reliability coefficients for the subtest scores. The combined coefficient for Vocabulary is .79, as estimated in Rapid Reference 4.8. For the Information subtest, the coefficient is estimated to be .85, based on the combined internal consistency and stability coefficients of .91 and .94, respectively, available in the *WAIS-III/WMS-III Technical Manual* (Psychological Corporation, 1997). Thus, the standard error of the difference between Vocabulary and Information subtest scores is

$$SE_{diff} = 3\sqrt{2 - .79 - .85} = 1.80$$

Step 3. To determine the statistical significance of the obtained score difference of 5 points, we divide that difference by the SE_{diff} and obtain a critical value of $5/1.80 = 2.78$.

Step 4. Consulting the Table of Areas of the Normal Curve in Appendix C, for a z value of 2.78, we find that the area in the smaller portion that is cut off by that z value is .0027. Since there was no reason to presuppose that either one of the subtest scores (Vocabulary or Information) would be higher than the other, a two-tailed significance test for the null hypothesis of no difference between the scores is appropriate. Therefore, we multiply .0027 by 2 and obtain .0054, which indicates that the probability that Maria's Vocabulary and Information subtest scores would differ by 5 points due to chance is 5.4 in 1,000. Given this high level of significance for the difference, all other things being equal, we can safely infer that there *really is* a difference: Maria's knowledge of vocabulary, as measured by the Vocabulary subtest of the WAIS-III, most likely exceeds her knowledge of general information concerning common events, places, objects, and people, as measured by the Information subtest.

Why is it important to create confidence intervals for obtained scores and for differences between obtained scores? Two basic reasons can be adduced in answer to this question. The first is that confidence intervals for obtained scores remind us that test scores are not as precise as their numerical nature would seem to suggest. Thus, whenever important decisions are to be made with the help of test scores, especially when cutoff scores are used, serious consideration has to be given to measurement error as quantified by the *SEM*. The second reason, which is related to the first, is that confidence intervals prevent us from attaching undue meaning to score differences that may be insignificant in light of measurement error. In recognition of the importance of these facts, many test manuals include tables listing the standard errors of measurement for scores as well as the numerical ranges for each possible score that can be derived from a test, along with the levels of confidence for each score range. For instance, for an obtained Full Scale IQ of 110 on the WAIS-III, the 90% confidence level interval is between 96 and 113 (Wechsler, 1997, p. 198). The availability of this information in test manuals encourages test users to apply confidence intervals in interpreting scores without having to calculate them. However, the determination of whether or not the published figures are applicable and meaningful in each instance of test use still rests with the user.

Table 4.1 and Figure 4.1 illustrate how the score reliability and *SEM* data might be used in the analysis of 4—out of a total of 14—subtest scores one can obtain from the WAIS-III. In addition to Maria's Vocabulary and Information subtest scores, already encountered in the previous examples, two other fictitious WAIS-III subtest scores, namely, Arithmetic and Digit Span, have been added to her profile. These subtests were selected because the primary abilities they assess—quantitative ability and short-term auditory memory, respectively—are sufficiently unique to make a comparison among them and the other two scores both interesting and plausible. The error bands calculated at the 90% confidence level, based on the *SEM*s for the respective subtests, are presented in Table 4.1. The *SEM*s, in turn, have been calculated based on combinations of *all* the pertinent reliability figures presented in the *WAIS-III/WMS-III Technical Manual* for each of the four subtests (Psychological Corporation, 1997). This more rigorous practice is in contradistinction to the use of the (smaller) *SEM*s, based on only one estimate of reliability estimate, which are provided in the tables of the test manual for IQ and index scores of the WAIS-III (see Wechsler, 1997, pp. 195–202). Figure 4.1 displays the data from Table 4.1 in graphic form. Inspection of this figure quickly reveals that once the *SEM* is taken into account the probable ranges of Maria's scores overlap considerably, which means that some of the score differences obtained may be due to measurement error. At the same time, this sort of profile analysis allows the test user to explore *hypotheses* about the possible meaning of the differences in Maria's performance on the abilities tapped by the subtests whose error bands do not overlap (i.e., Vocabulary and Information, Arithmetic and Digit Span, and Digit Span and Information). It appears, for example, that Maria may have relative strengths in short-term memory capacity and vocabulary, whereas her store of general information may be a relative weakness. Naturally, any conclusions based on such differences are subject to confirmation or revision in light of additional data. Nevertheless, when a psychological assessment calls for an evaluation of an individual's possible strengths and weaknesses either in the intellectual area or in some other respect—vocational interests, for example—this type of exploratory analysis, while not definitive, can be quite helpful.

Table 4.1 Profile of Maria's Obtained Scores on Four WAIS-III Subtests With SEMs and Error Bands at 90% Confidence Level

WAIS-III Subtest	Maria's Obtained Score (X_o)	Estimated Reliability Coefficient[a]	SEM[b] (1.64)[c] = Error Band	Maria's X_o ± Error Band at 90% Confidence Level
Vocabulary	15	.79	1.37 (1.64) = 2.25	15 ± 2.25 = 12.75 to 17.25
Arithmetic	12	.74	1.53 (1.64) = 2.51	12 ± 2.51 = 9.49 to 14.51
Digit Span	17	.83	1.24 (1.64) = 2.03	17 ± 2.03 = 14.97 to 19.03
Information	10	.85	1.16 (1.64) = 1.90	10 ± 1.90 = 8.10 to 11.90

Note: WAIS-III = Wechsler Adult Intelligence Scale–Third Edition; SEM = standard error of measurement; X_o = observed score; SD = standard deviation.

[a] Estimated reliability after subtracting all pertinent estimates of error variance as seen in the example of Rapid Reference 4.8.

[b] $SEM = SD \sqrt{1 - r_{xx}}$

[c] 1.64 is the z value for $p = .10$ (90% confidence level).

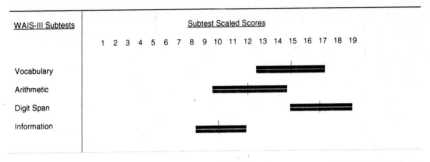

Figure 4.1 Graphic profile of Maria's WAIS-III subtest scores, illustrating the use of error bands in Table 4.1

The standard error of the difference between scores (SE_{diff}), discussed earlier, serves a similar purpose as the profile analysis displayed in Figure 4.1. It provides data regarding score discrepancies that may have practical or psychological significance. Typically, the SE_{diff} values—also found in many test manuals—are used to evaluate the statistical significance of the obtained differences between scores that are of special interest. The manuals of the recent editions of the Wechsler scales, for instance, routinely include tables showing the point differences in IQs (Verbal versus Performance IQs) and index scores needed for statistical significance at the 90% and 95% confidence levels. Recognizing that a *statistically* significant difference may not necessarily be *psychologically* significant, the authors of these test manuals—and those of other tests as well—also provide tables showing the frequencies with which score differences of various magnitudes were found among the standardization samples of the tests in question. This information addresses the question of how common or how rare any given difference is among the normative sample. Its importance derives from the assumption (not always justified but worth pondering) that if differences of a certain magnitude occur frequently, they probably have less interpretive significance than those that occur rarely.

> # DON'T FORGET
> ....
> The use of standard errors of measurement (*SEM*s) for test scores, and standard errors for test score differences (*SE$_{diffs}$*), both of which are derived from estimates of score reliability, are essential pieces of information because
>
> 1. *SEM*s provide confidence intervals for obtained test scores that alert test users to the fact that scores are subject to fluctuation due to measurement error, and
>
> 2. the confidence intervals obtained with the use of *SE$_{diff}$* statistics forestall the overvaluation of score differences that may be insignificant in light of measurement error.

The SE_{diff} can, of course, also be used to calculate the probability that an obtained difference between the scores of two individuals on the same test may be due to measurement error. For instance, in educational- or employment-selection decisions made with the help of tests, differences between the scores of candidates may be evaluated for significance in light of the SE_{diff}, in addition to other relevant factors. Once again, as with profile analysis, this process calls attention to the fact that obtained score differences cannot be taken at face value.

The Relationship Between Reliability and Validity

From the psychometric perspective, evidence of score reliability is considered to be a necessary, but not sufficient, condition for validity (see, e.g., Sawilowsky, 2003). In fact, as we shall see in the next chapter, the two concepts are intrinsically related in that score reliability can in itself be seen as minimal evidence that a valid measure of a sample of behavior has been attained.

Assessment professionals generally agree that evidence of score reliability is not a sufficient basis on which to make valid inferences about the meaning of scores. However, some room for disagreement exists with regard to the extent to which reliability evidence is seen as *essential* for the valid appraisal of all the types behavior samples that can be gathered through tests. For instance, when test scores are derived from behavior samples that are unique or idiosyncratic, they may not be repeatable or consistent. Tests that call forth an individual's optimal level of performance, such as work samples or portfolios, may produce results that are valid and reliable in terms of accuracy and precision but not in terms of consistency or stability (see, e.g., Moss, 1994). Similarly, instruments that are individually administered, like many intelligence scales or projective techniques, are highly susceptible to influences stemming from the quality of rapport between the examiner and the test taker, as well as other motivational and situational factors. In the context of individual assessment, such instruments may provide valid glimpses into aspects of a person's psychological make-up that might not be reproduced with a different examiner or in a different circumstance, even if standardized procedures are rigidly observed (Masling, 1960; McClelland, 1958; Smith, 1992).

CONCLUSION

The use of psychological tests would be greatly simplified if reliability coefficients and SEMs could be taken at face value in evaluating test scores. As this chapter attests, however, the reliability of scores is a relative judgment based both on psychometric data and on the context within which tests are administered. We shall see in Chapter 5 that the same is true of the validity of test score data. Thus, although availability of appropriate psychometric data on score reliability is a basic prerequisite for any use of test scores, the context within which psychological testing takes place is also a fundamental consideration in the interpretation of obtained scores of individuals or groups. As the potential impact of decisions to be made with the help of test scores increases, both of these factors assume greater importance.

 TEST YOURSELF

1. **A true score is**
   (a) a hypothetical entity.
   (b) a real entity.
   (c) equal to the observed score.
   (d) equal to the observed score plus error.

2. **If the reliability of a test is well established, test users can assume that the scores obtained from that test will be reliable.** True or False?

3. **Which of the following sources of error in test scores is *not* assessed by traditional estimates of reliability?**
   (a) Interscorer differences
   (b) Time sampling
   (c) Content sampling
   (d) Deviations from standardized procedures

4. **_____ reliability coefficients are used to estimate time sampling error in test scores.**
   (a) Test-retest
   (b) Alternate form
   (c) Scorer
   (d) Split-half

5. **Which of the following types of reliability coefficients results in a combined estimate of error stemming from two different sources?**
   (a) Scorer
   (b) Test-retest
   (c) Alternate form
   (d) Delayed alternate form

(continued)

6. **All other things being equal, scores obtained from longer tests are _____ those obtained from comparable tests that are shorter.**

   (a) less reliable than

   (b) more reliable than

   (c) just as reliable as

7. **The magnitude of a reliability coefficient is more likely to be affected by the _____ than by the _____ of the sample for which it is computed.**

   (a) size/heterogeneity

   (b) heterogeneity/size

8. **One of the distinct advantages of generalizability theory over traditional approaches to score reliability is that generalizability theory**

   (a) requires a smaller number of observations.

   (b) results in smaller error components.

   (c) allows for the evaluation of interaction effects.

   (d) uses less complicated statistical methods.

9. **Suppose that a student obtains a score of 110 on a test with $M = 100$, $SD = 20$, and an estimated reliability of .96. Chances are 68 out of 100 that the student's true score falls somewhere between**

   (a) 100 and 110.

   (b) 102 and 112.

   (c) 106 and 114.

   (d) 110 and 120.

10. **The standard error of measurement of Test A is 5 and the standard error of measurement of Test B is 8. The standard error of the difference for comparing scores from the two tests will be**

    (a) less than 8.

    (b) less than 5.

    (c) between 5 and 8.

    (d) greater than 8.

Answers: 1. a; 2. b; 3. d; 4. a; 5. d; 6. b; 7. b; 8. c; 9. c; 10. d.

Five

ESSENTIALS OF VALIDITY

Psychological tests exist in order to help us draw inferences about people and their behavior. Validity—which is, by far, the most fundamental issue regarding test scores and their uses—hinges on the evidence we can bring to bear to support any inference that is to be made on the basis of test results. The primacy of validity considerations is recognized in the current *Testing Standards* by the placement of this topic in the first chapter, which defines *validity* as "the degree to which all the accumulated evidence supports the intended interpretation of test scores for the proposed purpose" (AERA, APA, NCME, 1999, p. 11). Implicit in this definition are three interrelated ideas that reflect the testing profession's current views about this central and multifaceted concept:

1. The validity of test scores stems from all the accumulated evidence to support their interpretation and uses. Thus, validity is always a matter of degree rather than an all-or-none determination. *Validation*—which is the process whereby validity evidence is gathered—begins with an explicit statement by the test developer of the conceptual framework and rationale for a test, but is in its very nature open-ended because it includes all the information that adds to our understanding of test results.

2. As the theoretical understanding of and empirical evidence for test score interpretations accumulates, the validity of inferences (i.e., hypotheses) made on the bases of test scores for various proposed purposes may be enhanced or diminished. A corollary to this notion, explicitly stated in the *Testing Standards* (AERA, APA, NCME, 1999), is that "validation is the joint responsibility of the test developer [who provides evidence and a rationale for the intended use of the test] and the test user [who evaluates the available evidence within the context in which the test is to be used]" (p. 11).

3. Because of the many different purposes to which test scores may be

DON'T FORGET

Perhaps no other theorist has been more influential in reshaping the concept of validity than Samuel Messick. According to Messick (1989, p. 13), "validity is an integrated evaluative judgment of the degree to which empirical evidence and theoretical rationales support the *adequacy* and *appropriateness* of *inferences* and *actions* based on test scores or other modes of assessment."

applied, the evidentiary bases for test score interpretations can be derived through a variety of methods. Contributions to the validity evidence of test scores can be made by any systematic research that supports or adds to their meaning, regardless of who conducts it or when it occurs. As long as sound scientific evidence for a proposed use of test scores exists, qualified test users are free to employ scores for their purposes, regardless of whether these were foreseen by the developers of the test. This proposition helps to explain the multifaceted nature of validation research, as well as its often redundant and sometimes conflicting findings. It also accounts for the longevity of some instruments, such as the MMPI and the Wechsler scales, for which a vast literature—encompassing numerous applications in a variety of contexts—has been accumulated over decades of basic and applied research.

The alert reader may have gathered at this point that validity, just as reliability, is not a quality that characterizes tests in the abstract or any specific test or test data. Rather, validity is a matter of *judgments* that pertain to test scores as they are employed for a given purpose and in a given context. Hence, the process of validation is akin to hypothesis testing: It subsumes the notions of test score meaning, and test score reliability, discussed in the two previous chapters, as well as the ways in which the applications of test data to psychological research and practice can be justified, the topic covered in the present chapter. Rapid Reference 5.1 lists some of the most significant contributions to the topic of validity from the 1950s to the 1990s.

HISTORICAL PERSPECTIVES ON VALIDITY

The rise of modern psychological testing took place at about the same time that psychology was becoming an established scientific discipline. Both fields date their beginnings to the late part of the 19th and early years of the 20th centuries.

≋ Rapid Reference 5.1

Basic References on Validity

Samuel Messick articulated his views on validity most explicitly in a chapter that appeared in *Educational Measurement* (3rd ed., pp. 13–103), a notable volume edited by Robert L. Linn and published jointly by the American Council on Education and Macmillan in 1989. Messick's Validity chapter, and his other works on the topic (e.g., Messick, 1988, 1995), have directly influenced its treatment in the current version of the *Testing Standards* (AERA, APA, NCME, 1999). Other key contributions that are widely acknowledged as having shaped the evolution of theoretical concepts of validity include the following:

- Cronbach, L. J., & Meehl, P. E. (1955). Construct validity in psychological tests. *Psychological Bulletin, 52,* 281–302.
- Loevinger, J. (1957). Objective tests as instruments of psychological theory [Monograph Supplement]. *Psychological Reports, 3,* 635–694.
- Embretson, S. (1983). Construct validity: Construct representation versus nomothetic span. *Psychological Bulletin, 93,* 179–197.
- Cronbach, L. J. (1988). Five perspectives on validity argument. In H. Wainer & H. I. Braun (Eds.), *Test validity* (pp. 3–17). Hillsdale, NJ: Erlbaum.

As a result of this historical coincidence, our understanding of the nature, functions, and methodology of psychological tests and measurements has evolved over the past century in tandem with the development and growing sophistication of psychological science.

At the beginning, scientific psychology was primarily concerned with establishing psychophysical laws, through the experimental investigation of the functional relationship between physical stimuli and the sensory and perceptual responses they arouse in humans. Theoretical psychology consisted primarily of armchair speculation of a philosophical nature, until well into the first quarter of the 20th century. Neither of these statements implies that the contributions of the pioneers of psychology were not of value (see, e.g., Boring, 1950; James, 1890). Nevertheless, arising against this backdrop, the first psychological tests came to be seen, somewhat naively, as scientific tools that measured an ever-expanding catalog of mental abilities and personality traits in much the same way as the psychophysicists were measuring auditory, visual, and other sensory and perceptual responses to stimuli such as sounds, light, and colors of various types and intensities. Furthermore, as we saw in Chapter 1, the success that the Stanford-Binet and the Army Alpha had in helping to make practical decisions about individuals in education and employment settings led to a rapid proliferation of tests in the first two decades of the 20th century. The wide range of applications for which these instruments were used soon overtook the theoretical and scientific rationales for them that were available at the time. In short, many early psychological tests were developed and used without the benefit of the psychometric theory, ethical principles, and practical guidelines that would begin to accumulate in later decades (von Mayrhauser, 1992).

The Classic Definition of Validity

Recognition of this state of affairs within the profession resulted in the first attempts to delineate the characteristics that would distinguish a good test from a bad one. Thus, the first definition of *validity* as "the extent to which a test measures what it purports to measure" was formulated in 1921 by the National Association of the Directors of Educational Research (T. B. Rogers, 1995, p. 25). It was ratified by many testing experts—including Anne Anastasi in all the editions of her influential textbook on *Psychological Testing* (1954–1988) as well as Anastasi and Urbina (1997, p. 8). The view that "test validity concerns *what* the test measures and *how well* it does so" (Anastasi & Urbina, p. 113) is still regarded by many as the heart of the issue of validity. In spite of its apparent simplicity, this view poses a number of problems, especially when it is seen from the perspective of the current *Testing Standards* (AERA, APA, NCME, 1999) and of the flux that still exists with regard to defining some of the most basic constructs within the field of psychology.

Problematic Aspects of the Traditional View of Validity

The issues that the classic definition of validity raises revolve around its unstated but clear assumptions that

1. validity is a property of tests, rather than of test score interpretations;
2. in order to be valid, tests scores should measure some purported construct directly; and
3. score validity is, at least to some extent, a function of the test author's or developer's understanding of whatever construct she or he intends to measure.

While these assumptions may be justified in certain cases, they definitely are not justified in every case. The first assumption, for instance, is tenable only as long as validation data support the stated purpose of the test *and* as long as the test is used specifically for that purpose and with the kinds of populations for which validity data have been gathered. The second and third assumptions are justified only for tests that measure behavior which can be linked to psychological constructs in fairly unequivocal ways, such as certain memory functions, speed and accuracy in the performance of various cognitive processing tasks, or extent of knowledge of a well-defined content universe. They are not necessarily tenable for (a) tests designed to assess multidimensional or complex theoretical constructs about which there is still much debate, such as intelligence or self-concept; (b) tests developed on the basis of strictly empirical—as opposed to theoretical or logical—relationships between scores and external criteria, such as the original MMPI; or (c) techniques whose purpose is to reveal covert or un-conscious aspects of personality, such as projective devices. For instruments of this nature, what is being measured is behavior that can be linked more or less di-rectly to the constructs that are of real interest, primarily through a network of correlational evidence. Rapid Reference 5.2 defines the various meanings of the word *construct* and may help to clarify the distinctions just made, as well as those to come later in this chapter.

The idea that test score validity is a function of the degree to which tests mea-sure what they purport to measure also leads to some confusion between the con-sistency or precision of measurements (i.e., their reliability) and their validity. As we saw in Chapter 4, if a test measures whatever it measures *well,* its scores may be deemed to be reliable (consistent, precise, or trustworthy), but they are not necessarily valid in the contemporary, fuller sense of the term. In other words, test scores may be relatively free of measurement error, and yet may not be very use-ful as bases for making the inferences we need to make.

Moreover, the implication that a test score reflects what the test author intends it to reflect has been as a source of additional misunderstandings. One of them concerns the titles of tests, which should never be—but often are—taken at face value. Test titles range from those that are quite accurate and empirically defen-sible to those that merely reflect test authors' (unfulfilled) intentions or test pub-lishers' marketing concerns. A second, and even more important, problem with the notion that valid test scores reflect their expressed purpose is that it can lead to superficial or glib empirical definitions of psychological constructs. Possibly the most famous example of this is E. G. Boring's 1923 definition of *intelligence* as "whatever it is that intelligence tests measure" (cited by Sternberg, 1986, p. 2).

As a result of these misunderstandings, the field of psychological testing has been saddled with instruments—purporting to measure ill-defined or faddish constructs—whose promises vastly overstate what they can deliver, whose use in psychological research impedes or delays progress in the discipline, and whose existence, by association, diminishes the image of the field as a whole. Early mea-sures of masculinity-femininity are a prime example of this sort of problem (Con-stantinople, 1973; Lenney, 1991; Spence, 1993), although there are many others.

≡ Rapid Reference 5.2

Deconstructing Constructs

Because the term *construct* is used so frequently in this chapter, a clarification of its meaning is necessary at this point. Generally speaking, a *construct* is anything that is devised by the human mind but not directly observable. Constructs are abstractions that may refer to concepts, ideas, theoretical entities, hypotheses, or inventions of many sorts.

In psychology, the word *construct* is applied to concepts, such as traits, and to the theoretical relationships among concepts that are inferred from consistent empirical observations of behavioral data. Psychological constructs differ widely in terms of

- their breadth and complexity,
- their potential applicability, and
- the degree of abstraction required to infer them from the available data.

As a rule, narrowly defined constructs require less abstraction but have a smaller range of application. Moreover, since it is easier to obtain consensual agreement about constructs that are narrow, simple, and less abstract, these are also more easily assessed than broader and multifaceted constructs that may have acquired different meanings across diverse contexts, cultures, and historical periods.

Examples:

- Whereas *manual dexterity* is a construct that can be linked to specific behavioral data readily, *creativity* is far more abstract. Thus, when it comes to evaluating these traits, determining who has greater manual dexterity is much easier than determining who is more creative.
- *Introversion* is a simpler and more narrowly defined construct than *conscientiousness*. While the latter is potentially useful in predicting a broader range of behaviors, it is also more difficult to assess.

Synonyms: The terms *construct* and *latent variable* are often used interchangeably. A *latent variable* is a characteristic that presumably underlies some observed phenomenon but is not directly measurable or observable. All psychological traits are latent variables, or constructs, as are the labels given to factors that emerge from factor analytic research, such as verbal comprehension or neuroticism.

Perhaps the most significant consequence of the traditional definition of validity is that it became attached to tests and to what they purport to measure, rather than to test *scores* and the interpretations that could justifiably be based on them. By implication, then, any evidence labeled as *test validity* came to be seen as proof that the test was valid and worthy of use, regardless of the nature of the link between test score data and the inferences that were to be drawn from them. Consequently, innumerable studies in the psychological literature have used scores from a single instrument to classify research participants into experimental groups, many clinicians have relied exclusively on test scores for diagnosis and treatment planning, and an untold number of decisions in educational and employment settings have been based on cutoff scores from a single test. Too often, choices like these are made without considering their appropriateness in specific contexts or without reference to additional sources of data and justified simply on the basis that the test in question is supposed to be "a valid measure of. . . ." whatever its manual states.

An important signpost in the evolution of the concept of validity was the publication of the *Technical Recommendations for Psychological Tests and Diagnostic Techniques* (APA, 1954), the first in the series of testing standards that were retitled, revised, and updated in 1955, 1966, 1974, 1985, and most recently, in 1999 (AERA, APA, NCME). With each subsequent revision, the *Testing Standards*—previously discussed in Chapter 1—have attempted to promote sound practices for the construction and use of tests and to clarify the basis for evaluating the quality of tests and testing practices.

The *Technical Recommendations* published in 1954 introduced a classification of validity into four categories to be discussed later in this chapter: content, predictive, concurrent, and construct validity. Subsequently, the 1974 *Standards* reduced these categories to three, by subsuming predictive and concurrent validity under the rubric of criterion-related validity, and further specified that content, criterion-related, and construct validity are *aspects of,* as opposed to *types of,* validity. In the same year, the *Standards* also introduced the notion that validity "refers to the appropriateness of inferences from test scores or other forms of assessment" (APA, AERA, NCME, 1974, p. 25).

In spite of the specifications proposed by the 1974 *Standards* more than a quarter century ago, the division of validity into three types (which came to be known as the *tripartite view* of validity) became entrenched. It has survived up to the present in many test manuals and test reviews, as well as in much of the research that is conducted on psychometric instruments. Nevertheless, successive revisions of the *Standards*—especially the current one—have added stipulations that make it increasingly clear that whichever classification is used for validity concepts should be attached to the types of evidence that are adduced for test score interpretation rather than to the tests themselves. With this in mind, we turn now to a consideration of the prevailing view of validity as a unitary concept and to the various sources of evidence that may be used to evaluate possible interpretations of test scores for specific purposes. For further information on the evolution of validity and related concepts, see Anastasi (1986), Angoff (1988), and Landy (1986).

CURRENT PERSPECTIVES ON VALIDITY

Beginning in the 1970s and continuing up to the present, there has been a concerted effort within the testing profession to refine and revise the notion of validity and to provide a unifying theory that encompasses the many strands of evidence from which test scores derive their significance and meaning. One consistent theme of this effort has been the integration of almost all forms of validity evidence as aspects of construct validity (Guion, 1991; Messick, 1980, 1988, 1989; Tenopyr, 1986). This, in turn, has prompted a reexamination of the meaning of *construct*—defined in general terms in Rapid Reference 5.2—as it applies specifically in the context of validity in psychological testing and assessment (see, e.g., Braun, Jackson, & Wiley, 2002; Embretson, 1983).

The Integrative Function of Constructs in Test Validation

In psychological testing, the term *construct* has been used, often indistinctly, in two alternate ways:

1. To designate the *traits, processes, knowledge stores,* or *characteristics* whose presence and extent we wish to ascertain through the specific behavior samples collected by the tests. In this meaning of the word, a construct is simply what the test author sets out to measure—that is, any hypothetical entity derived from psychological theory, research, or observation of behavior, such as anxiety, assertiveness, logical reasoning ability, flexibility, and so forth.
2. To designate the *inferences* that may be made on the basis of test scores. When used in this way, the term *construct* refers to a specific interpretation of test data, or any other behavioral data—such as the presence of clinical depression or a high probability of success in some endeavor—that may be made based on a network of preestablished theoretical and empirical relationships between test scores and other variables.

Several theorists have tried to explain how these two meanings relate to the notion of test score validity. One of the earliest formulations was Cronbach's (1949) classification of validity into two types, namely, logical and empirical. Subsequently, in an influential paper he coauthored with Meehl in 1955, Cronbach suggested the use of the term *construct validity* to designate the *nomological net,* or network of interrelationships between and among theoretical and observable elements that support a construct. In an attempt to clarify how these two meanings could be distinguished in the process of test development, construction, and evaluation, Embretson (1983) proposed a separation between two aspects of construct validation research, namely, construct representation and nomothetic span. According to Embretson (p. 180), *construct representation* research "is concerned with identifying the theoretical mechanisms that underlie task performance." From an information-processing perspective, the goal of construct representation is *task decomposition*. The process of task decomposition can be applied to a variety of cognitive tasks, including interpersonal inferences and social judgments. It entails an examination of test responses from the point of view of the processes, strategies, and knowledge stores involved in their performance. *Nomothetic span,* on the other hand, concerns "the network of relationships of a test to other measures" (Embretson, p. 180); it refers to the strength, frequency, and pattern of significant relations between test scores and other measures of the same—or different—traits, between test scores and criterion measures, and so forth.

Embretson (1983) described additional features of the concepts of construct representation and nomothetic span that help to clarify the differences between these two aspects of construct validation research. Two of the points she made, concerning the distinction between the functions the two kinds of research can serve, are particularly useful in considering the role of sources of validity evidence:

1. *Construct representation research is concerned primarily with identifying differences in the test's tasks, whereas nomothetic span research is concerned with differences among test takers.* In construct representation research, a process, strategy, or knowledge store identified through task decomposition (e.g., phonetic coding, sequential reasoning, or ability to comprehend elementary-level texts) may be deemed essential to the performance of a test task, but yield no systematic differences across a test-taking population made up of readers. On the other hand, in order to investigate the nomothetic span of test scores (i.e., the network of relationships between them and other measures), it is necessary to have data on individual differences and variability across test takers. This reinforces the crucial importance that score variability has for deriving information that can be used to make determinations or decisions about people, which was discussed previously in Chapters 2 and 3. If the scores of a group of people on a test designed to assess the ability to comprehend elementary level texts, for instance, are to be correlated with anything else—or used to determine anything other than whether these people,

as a group, possess that ability—there must be some variability in the scores.

2. *Validation of the construct-representation aspect of test tasks is independent of the supporting evidence that may be gathered in terms of the nomothetic span of test scores, and vice versa.* In other words, while we may know precisely what processes are involved in the performance of test tasks, absent significant correlations with meaningful extratest behaviors or measures, test scores may be of limited use. By the same token, it is possible to obtain a strong network of relationships between test scores and other measures, without having a clear notion of the construct that those scores represent. The example Embretson (1983) uses is that of intelligence test scores, which have a strong nomothetic span (in that they consistently correlate more or less strongly with a variety of other measures) but still have relatively unclear theoretical bases.

The conceptual scheme outlined by Embretson (1983) retains the notion of construct validation as a unitary and comprehensive way of expressing the scien-

DON'T FORGET

People make inferences based on observations and behavior samples all the time. For example, if we hear someone speak using poor grammar we may infer that the person is uneducated. If a person is invariably on time for appointments, we may infer that she or he is punctual. Some of our inferences are correct and some are not. Some matter, and some do not.

If the inferences we make matter enough for us to wish to ascertain their correctness, and thereby validate them, we need to

1. define our terms unequivocally (e.g., What do we mean by "uneducated"? Does "being on time invariably" capture the entire concept of punctuality?);

2. investigate the reliability of our observations (e.g., Does the person always use poor grammar or only in some circumstances? Is our friend on time for all appointments or only for those we have had a chance to observe?); and

3. decide whether there is sufficient evidence to justify the inferences we wish to make, based on our definitions and on the available data (e.g., Being on time for all appointments *is* a sufficient basis on which to judge a person's punctuality) or whether we need to corroborate our inference with additional data (e.g., Does the person display other indexes of what we mean by "uneducated"?).

Psychological tests are tools designed to help refine and quantify behavioral observations for the purpose of drawing inferences about individuals, groups, or psychological constructs. Fundamentally, psychological test scores are valid to the extent that they can help us draw accurate inferences.

tific approach to the integration of any evidence bearing on the meaning or interpretation of test scores. At the same time, it provides a basis for distinguishing between (a) the sources of evidence for test score validity that bear primarily on knowing what we are measuring (i.e., construct representation) and (b) those that deal mainly with the inferences we can make based on what we are measuring (i.e., nomothetic span). It should be noted that these sources of evidence may be, and often are, interrelated and that both involve theoretical and observable elements, as well as models or postulates concerning the interrelationships among elements.

SOURCES OF VALIDITY EVIDENCE

In general, the essence of judgments about the validity of test scores centers on the relationship between what the scores represent and the questions test users need to answer with the use of tests. The questions we pose determine the type of evidence we need as well as the logical relationships—inductive and deductive—that have to be established to address the issues of (a) what we are measuring with tests and (b) what inferences we can draw from test scores. It should also be clear at this point that the greater the significance or potential impact of the answers we want, the more convincing the evidence needs to be. In the remainder of this chapter, we deal with the types of evidence required for validating test score inferences, with the understanding that the proposed interpretation of a test score determines the conceptual framework for its validation. Table 5.1 presents a list of the major categories under which aspects of validity may be classified, along with the principal sources of evidence for each, which are discussed in the remainder of this chapter. It is important to recognize at the outset that neither the aspects of validity nor the sources or types of evidence associated with them are mutually exclusive. Validation strategies should, in fact, incorporate as many sources of evidence as practicable or as appropriate to the purposes of a test.

Validity Evidence Based on Test Content and Response Processes

Some psychological tests are designed to sample behavior that can be linked more or less directly to the inferences we wish to make based on their scores. By and large, these instruments fall in the category of content- or criterion-referenced tests, already discussed at some length in Chapter 3. As noted there, most of these tests are used in educational and occupational settings, although they can also be applied in fields (e.g., neuropsychological assessment) where it is necessary to as-

Table 5.1 Aspects of Construct Validity and Related Sources of Evidence

Aspect of Construct Validity	Sources of Evidence[a]
Content-related	Relevance and representativeness of test content and task response processes
	— Face validity (i.e., superficial appearances)
Patterns of convergence and divergence	Internal consistency of test results and other measures of reliability
	Correlations among tests and subtests
	Multitrait-multimethod matrix
	Score differentiation consonant with expected differences based on age or other status variables
	Experimental results (i.e., correspondence between test scores and the predicted effects of experimental interventions or theory-based hypotheses)
	Exploratory factor analysis
	Structural equation modeling techniques
Criterion-related	Accuracy of decisions based on concurrent validation (i.e., correlations between test scores and existing criteria)
	Accuracy of decisions or predictions based on predictive validation (i.e., correlations between test scores and predicted criteria)

[a]See Chapter 5 text for explanations of terms

Handwritten annotations: r = weak; Relates to another test; 2 different test relates to same thing; high r = means whats the diff (mod); Correlation; Regression Analysis

certain whether a person is able or unable to perform tasks that may hold diagnostic significance. These tests are made up of items that either sample knowledge from a defined content domain or require test takers to demonstrate that they possess a given ability or competence in some skill. Validation procedures for tests of this type are in many ways the simplest and most agreed-upon aspect of test development because the evidence on which inferences are to be made can be defended on logical grounds as well as by demonstrable relationships between the content of the test and the construct that the test is designed to represent.

Evidence of test score validity that derives from the content of the test can be built into a new instrument at the outset, by the choice of items or tasks that are included in the test. The primary requirement for developing tests of this sort is a careful specification of the content domains, cognitive processes, skills, or types of performance to be sampled by the test and of their relative importance or weight.

- In the educational context, examples of such specifications can be found in school curricula, course syllabi, textbooks, and any other materials that outline, define, or prioritize the outcome objectives of educational or training experiences in terms of both content knowledge and performance capabilities. The process of delimiting knowledge domains and determining the desired outcomes of instruction is within the purview of teachers, trainers, and other subject matter experts who determine curricula or write the textbooks in various disciplines.

- In occupational settings, the specifications of the skill or knowledge domains to be sampled by the test are based on job analyses. *Job analysis* refers to any one of a variety of methods aimed at discovering the nature of a given job through the description of the elements, activities, tasks, and duties related to it (see, e.g., Brannick & Levine, 2002). Job analysis methodology has a variety of applications in the management of human resources, including performance appraisal and the determination of training needs among others. Within the context of occupational selection and classification, job analyses—based on input from employers, job supervisors, and/or current employees—are used to delineate the abilities, skills, and knowledge stores required for job performance.

- In neuropsychological assessment, the specifications of the processes and cognitive capabilities to be assessed are derived from theoretical and empirical knowledge of the linkages between the central nervous system and behavioral functions. The nature of the content of neuropsychological assessment tools is based on accumulated scientific and clinical evidence about brain-behavior relationships.

Rapid Reference 3.7, in Chapter 3, lists some simple examples of objectives and items typical of domain-referenced tests. More extensive examples, including tables of specifications for content-referenced tests and guidance in how they are prepared, are available in Gronlund (2003) and Linn and Gronlund (1995, pp. 119–125). Regardless of the setting in which a content-referenced test is applied, once the specifications for the knowledge, skills, or processes to be gauged through the test have been set, content validation procedures involve the critical review and examination of test content from two perspectives. The first is the *relevance* of the content sampled by the test to the specified domain; the second one is the *representativeness* of the content sampled by the test with regard to the specifications about the domain that it is designed to cover. Although the issue of relevance must rely on a consensus of subject matter experts, it can also be supported by empirical findings, such as differences in the scores of students in successive grades or individuals at various stages of a training process. The authors and developers of tests must support claims of the content-related validity of test scores in manuals, technical handbooks, and other such sources of supporting documentation for tests. When the primary basis of an instrument's validation evidence centers on the specific content, skills, or cognitive processes it assesses, a description of the systematic procedures used to ensure the relevance and representativeness of test content to the specified domains is required. Rapid Reference 4.3 presents an example of the role that inadequate representativeness of content coverage can play in undermining both the reliability and validity of content-referenced test scores.

Educational Testing

Scores that derive their validity from a direct and demonstrable connection between test content and the specifications used in developing the test abound at all levels of education and training in which the outcomes of instruction can be unambiguously defined. Almost all teacher-designed classroom tests fit into this category, as do many of the standardized tests published by ETS, the ACT, and similar organizations. The primary purpose of these instruments is to gauge educational achievement—that is, what students have learned through their schooling. Scores from these tests can answer most directly questions such as "How much of the specified domain has the learner mastered?" or "What degree of mastery or proficiency has the test taker attained in the skill in question?" Content- or domain-referenced instruments may be applied for a variety of decisions, including assigning grades in a course, providing course credits through examination, conferring a degree or diploma after a program of study, certifying or licensing individuals to practice in a given field, or even ascertaining readiness to undertake a more advanced level of training. Typically, the decisions based on these tests hinge on the levels of mastery displayed by test takers. These levels of mastery, in turn, may be gauged in terms of percentage grades, percentile ranks in comparison to appropriate normative groups, or simple pass-fail determinations based on preestablished criteria, as discussed in Chapter 3. Rapid Reference 5.3 lists some typical examples of standardized educational tests, along with the purposes for which they were developed (i.e., the knowledge and skills they are designed to evaluate) and their primary applications. Sample questions and more elaborate descriptions of those tests are available on the Internet sites listed in Rapid Reference 5.3.

Occupational Testing

Many instruments used to select or place job applicants consist of job samples or simulations that actually call for performing the tasks of which the job is com-

≡ Rapid Reference 5.3

Examples of Standardized Educational Tests Using Evidence Based on Content As a Principal Source of Validation

Test Title	Main Purpose of Test	Primary Applications	Web Site Location of Test Description and Samples
Test of English as a Foreign Language (TOEFL)	Evaluates the English proficiency of people whose native language is not English	Determining whether foreign students possess sufficient knowledge of English to be admitted into college	http://www.toefl.org
College-Level Examination Program (CLEP) Introductory Psychology Test	Measures knowledge of material usually taught in a one-semester undergraduate course in introductory psychology	Determining whether students have sufficient command of introductory psychology to be awarded college credit by examination	http://www.collegeboard.com/clep
ACT Assessment Science Reasoning Test	Measures interpretation, analysis, evaluation, reasoning, and problem-solving skills required in the natural sciences, including biology, chemistry, physics, and the earth and space sciences	Evaluating the knowledge and skills a student has acquired in order to determine readiness to undertake college-level work	http://www.act.org
National Assessment of Educational Progress (NAEP)	Measures subject matter knowledge and skills in reading, mathematics, science, writing, U.S. history, civics, geography, and the arts	Providing information about the performance of student populations and subgroups across the United States and participating states	http://nces.ed.gov

posed (e.g., typing tests) or sample behaviors that can be directly linked to job performance by means of job analyses. Some of these tests are developed in-house by employers themselves and use local norms or performance criteria. Others are standardized instruments that provide normative scores for individuals in various occupations and measure constructs of varying degrees of breadth. Numerous examples of these tests can be found in the Vocations section of the Classified Subject Index of *Tests in Print VI* (Murphy et al., 2002). Two that may be used to illustrate the diversity among tests of this type are described in Rapid Reference 5.4.

Partly due to the cost and difficulty involved in developing and validating skill assessment instruments at the local level, the ACT (formerly American College Testing Program) organization (www.act.org) has initiated a program known as the WorkKeys system that combines a number of components aimed at helping businesses recruit, select, hire, and train employees. The job-profiling component allows job incumbents or their supervisors, in consultation with ACT experts, to select the most important tasks for a given job and identify the skills and levels of skills necessary for successful performance of that job. The assessment aspect of WorkKeys provides standardized instruments to evaluate applicants' or employees' levels of skills in several critical areas, such as Applied Technology, Business Writing, Locating Information, Listening, and Teamwork, among others. The assessment of skills in Locating Information, for example, provides questions at four increasingly higher levels of complexity and is designed to measure skills ranging from finding information embedded in elementary workplace graphics—such as simple order forms, bar graphs, and floor plans—to drawing conclusions from information presented in very detailed charts, tables, blueprints, and so forth. Based on comparisons of the information provided through these skill assessment tools and the minimum skill levels required by the job profiles, employers can evaluate the qualifications of applicants or the training needs of current employees.

Evidence of Content Validity in Other Assessment Contexts

The extent to which test items are relevant to and representative of a construct can be an additional source of validity evidence for instruments in almost any field. For instance:

- *In neuropsychological assessment,* as mentioned earlier, specifications of the cognitive processes and behavior capabilities to be assessed are derived from well established theoretical and empirical knowledge of the relationships between cognitive or behavioral functions and the neurological foundations that presumably underlie those functions. Thus, to a

≣ *Rapid Reference 5.4*

Examples of Standardized Occupational Tests Using Evidence Based on Content As a Source of Validation

Test Title	Construct Assessed	Description	Primary Application
Crawford Small Parts Dexterity Test (CSPDT)[a]	Eye-hand coordination and fine motor dexterity.	The CSPDT consists of two tasks: (a) working with tweezers to insert small pins into the holes of a plate and then placing small collars over the protruding pins; (b) threading screws into the plate and then tightening them with a screwdriver. Speed of performance is the major factor in the scoring of this test.	Used to determine whether an individual has the manual dexterity required for any position that involves precise work with one's hands, such as engraving or watch repairing.
Clerical Abilities Battery (CAB)[a]	Several components of a broad range of clerical occupations identified through job analysis of general clerical behaviors.	The CAB has seven self-explanatory subtests: Filing, Comparing Information, Copying Information, Using Tables, Proofreading, Basic Math Skills, and Numerical Reasoning.	Used for recruitment and evaluation of clerical workers. In a *Mental Measurements Yearbook* review, Randhawa (1992) states that the sampling and range of tasks of the CAB's subtests is not sufficiently representative and suggests additional standardization, reliability, and predictive validity data are needed. However, he concedes that the development process and format of the battery are impressive and provide the bases for a potentially excellent tool.

[a]Published by Psychological Corporation (http://www.PsychCorp.com).

large extent, the process of neuropsychological assessment relies on the experts' knowledge of accumulated scientific evidence about brain-behavior relationships. A proper neuropsychological battery must include items that tap a range of behaviors that is sufficiently broad and representative as to elicit evidence of functional capability, or impairment, in the various systems it is designed to assess (see, e.g., Franzen, 2000; Lezak, 1995). The Boston Diagnostic Aphasia Examination (Goodglass, Kaplan, & Barresi, 2001), for example, provides a systematic sampling of several communication functions, such as auditory comprehension and oral expression, in order to help in the diagnosis of aphasic syndromes and disorders of language.

- *In personality assessment,* many self-report tools—such as checklists, inventories, and attitude or opinion surveys—rely to a large extent on the content of their items to help in generating hypotheses or drawing inferences about the particular constructs they aim to evaluate. Structured observation procedures, as well as various inventories used to collect data based on the reports of peers, parents, spouses, teachers, or other observers, also use item content as a basic source of validity evidence. Similarly, psychological tests designed to aid in the diagnosis of psychiatric disorders often include, or may even be entirely composed of, items that reflect critical symptomatic aspects of the syndromes they are designed to diagnose. Here again, the relevance and representativeness of the items sampled by these instruments is of crucial importance in determining their usefulness for diagnostic purposes. Examples of tests of this type include the Beck Depression Inventory (BDI), the State-Trait Anxiety Inventory (STAI), the Symptom Checklist-90-Revised (SCL-90-R), and the Attitudes Toward Women Scale (AWS; Spence & Helmreich, 1972).

Evidence of Validity From the Viewpoint of Test Takers

The relevance and representativeness of test content is also pertinent with regard to an issue that is less substantive than score validity, but is nevertheless quite important. *Face validity* refers to the superficial appearance of what a test measures from the perspective of a test taker or any other naive observer. All of the instruments discussed up to this point would have some face validity when used in the contexts we have been discussing. They would appear to test takers to be consonant with the stated educational, occupational, clinical, or investigative purposes of the assessment situations in which they are typically applied. Even though face validity is not necessarily an indication of validity from the psychometric perspective, it is nevertheless a desirable feature of tests because it promotes rapport and acceptance of testing and test results on the part of test takers. If the content of a test appears to be inappropriate or irrelevant to test takers, their willingness to cooperate with the testing process is likely to be undermined. Thus, test developers need to consider the appearance of validity from the perspective of all parties—including test takers and other nonprofessionals—and, whenever possible, incorporate test content that seems relevant and appropriate to the situations in which a test will be used.

Validity Evidence Based on Exploring Patterns of Convergence and Divergence

As test score interpretation moves beyond direct and fairly unequivocal relationships between test content and the knowledge stores, skills, and functional processes the tests are designed to evaluate, it begins to rely on increasingly indirect sources of validity evidence. This is especially true for tests in the area of personality, not only because the constructs they assess are usually more theoretical and abstract than those assessed by cognitive tests, but also because test takers' responses to personality assessment tools are influenced by many more stylistic and situational determinants than cognitive test responses.

There is a large and constantly expanding number of methods that can be used to augment the meaning of test scores beyond the relevance and representativeness of test content. The common denominator of all of these procedures is that they produce evidence in the form of patterns of convergence and divergence between test scores and other variables (see Table 5.1). Although a detailed explanation of these methods is well beyond the scope of this volume, a basic description of the most frequently encountered procedures is in order.

Test Score Reliability As a Source of Validity Evidence

Investigations of the reliability of test scores from the point of view of stability, interscorer differences, content sampling error, and content heterogeneity may provide evidence concerning the cohesiveness, or distinctiveness, of test content. As discussed in Chapter 4, score reliability can in itself be seen as preliminary evidence that a trustworthy measure of a sample of behavior has been attained and thus can contribute indirect evidence of test score validity. If, for example, a test is designed to assess a unidimensional construct such as spelling ability, high internal consistency coefficients would support the contention of unidimensionality. Similarly, if score consistency across different scorers can be achieved, one may suppose that they are all employing the same criteria and, thus, probably evaluating the same characteristics. If the construct being assessed is supposed to be stable—for instance, a personality trait or type—high test-retest score reliability would be an essential prerequisite for evidence of validity.

Correlations Among Tests and Subtests

A simple and frequently used way of gathering evidence that a particular test measures the construct it purports to measure is by establishing high correlations between its scores and those of other instruments that are meant to assess the same construct. One of the most basic examples of this type of procedure occurs when tests are revised and renormed. In such cases, test manuals almost invariably cite high correlations between the new and previous editions as evidence that both are measuring the same constructs. This is somewhat akin to computing correlations between alternate forms of a test to establish the reliability or consistency of scores across different forms of a test. It may be recalled from Chapter 3, however, that even if correlations between the old and the revised versions of tests are very high, the normative scores for restandardized versions tend to drift in one direction or another due to changes in the population at different time periods.

In a similar fashion, test developers typically present correlations between the scores of their tests and those of comparable instruments as evidence of score validity. For instance, all of the manuals of major individual intelligence scales cite correlations between their scores and those of the other well-established instruments of the same type. By examining these data one can learn—for example—that the correlation between WAIS-III Full Scale IQ and the global composite score of the Stanford-Binet-IV (SB-IV), computed for a sample of 26 individuals who took both tests, was .88 (Psychological Corporation, 1997, p. 84) or that the correlation obtained between the composite scores of the SB-IV and the Kaufman Adolescent & Adult Intelligence Test (KAIT), for a sample of 72 individuals tested with both instruments, was .87 (Kaufman & Kaufman, 1993, p. 100). Correlation coefficients of this size are typical for the major intelligence scales and serve to corroborate the fact that a good deal of the variance in the scores on these tests is shared.

Correlation coefficients can also be obtained across the scores of subtests from different scales. Typical examples of this would be the correlations between the scores of various depression scales, for instance, the Depression scale scores of the MMPI-2 and those of the Dysthymia scale ($r = .68$) of the Millon Clinical Multiaxial Inventory-III (MCMI-III), or the Beck Depression Inventory scores and those of the MCMI-III Major Depression scale ($r = .71$; Millon, Millon, & Davis, 1994, pp. 126, 129). As might be expected, correlation coefficients calculated across various types of tests and subtests abound in test manuals and in the psychological literature, even though these indexes often are not very cogent or informative.

Intertest correlations are as ubiquitous as they are because the data for correlational studies on small convenience samples are easy to gather, especially for paper-and-pencil tests that can be administered to groups readily. Correlations obtained in this fashion can, of course, range anywhere from zero to ±1.00, depending on the scores in question and nature of the samples used (cf. Chapter 2, especially the section on Range Restriction and Correlation). Although the meaning of any single obtained coefficient is open to interpretation, if sufficient data showing consistently high or consistently low correlations across measures are accumulated, some patterns of convergence and divergence may be discerned. These patterns inform test users about the approximate amounts of shared or common variance across sets of scores and, indirectly, about the meaning of the scores themselves. Consistently high correlations between measures designed to assess a given construct—such as the correlations cited in the previous paragraph for depression scales—may be taken as evidence of *convergent validity*, that is, evidence regarding the similarity, or identity, of the constructs they are evaluating. By the same token, *discriminant validity* evidence, based on consistently low correlations between measures that are supposed to differ, also may be used to substantiate the identities of the constructs they tap. An example of this kind of divergent pattern can be gleaned from the correlations between scores on the Bipolar, Manic scale of the MCMI-III and the Depression scale of the MMPI-2 ($r = .06$), as well as between scores on the Major Depression scale of the MCMI-III and the Hypomania scale of the MMPI-2 ($r = .08$), both computed on a sample of 132 individuals (Millon, Millon, & Davis, 1994, pp. 129–130).

The Multitrait-Multimethod Matrix

In an effort to organize the collection and presentation of convergent and discriminant validation data, D. T. Campbell and Fiske (1959) proposed a design they called the *multitrait-multimethod matrix* (*MTMMM*). This approach refers to a validation strategy that requires the collection of data on two or more distinct traits (e.g., anxiety, affiliation, and dominance) by two or more different methods (e.g., self-report questionnaires, behavioral observations, and projective techniques). Once these data are collected and all their intercorrelations are computed, they can be presented in the form of a matrix, such as the one in Table 5.2. Multitrait-multimethod matrices display (a) reliability coefficients for each measure, (b) correlations between scores on the same trait assessed by different methods (i.e., convergent validity data), and (c) correlations between scores on different traits measured by the same methods, as well as (d) between scores on

Table 5.2 A Hypothetical Multitrait-Multimethod Matrix (MTMMM)

Method	Trait	Self-Report			Observation			Projective		
		Anx	Aff	Dom	Anx	Aff	Dom	Anx	Aff	Dom
	Anx	(.90)								
Self-report	Aff	*.45*	(.88)							
	Dom	*.35*	*.38*	(.80)						
	Anx	**.60**	.23	.10	(.92)					
Observation	Aff	.25	**.58**	−.08	*.47*	(.93)				
	Dom	.12	−.12	**.55**	*.30*	*.32*	(.86)			
	Anx	**.56**	.22	.11	**.65**	.40	.31	(.94)		
Projective	Aff	.23	**.57**	.05	.38	**.70**	.29	*.44*	(.89)	
	Dom	.13	−.10	**.53**	.19	.26	**.68**	*.40*	*.44*	(.86)

Note: Anx = Anxiety; Aff = Affiliation; Dom = Dominance. Reliability coefficients are in parentheses, along the principal diagonal. Validity coefficients (same trait assessed by different methods) are in boldface. All other coefficients are indexes of the discriminant validity of scores of different traits assessed by a single method (representing common method variance and set in italics) and different traits assessed by different methods (in plain type).

different traits assessed by different methods (both of which constitute discriminant validity data). Table 5.2 is a hypothetical MTMMM with a pattern of results that would be considered exemplary for this type of validation design. The matrix in this table shows:

- the highest coefficients, which are indicative of adequate score reliability (in parentheses), in the principal diagonal;
- the next highest coefficients—in **bold** print—between measures of the **same** trait across **different** methods, indicating convergence among their scores;
- the next highest coefficients—in *italics*—between measures of *different* traits assessed by the *same* method, indicating that a fair amount of the variance in the scores is due to the methods employed; and
- the smallest coefficients—in plain type—between measures of different traits assessed by different methods, indicating that the measures do discriminate fairly well among distinct traits.

The MTMMM design is ideally suited to investigate patterns of convergence and divergence among test scores and data gathered from other types of assessment instruments. It does, however, constitute a rather stringent validation standard that is often difficult to meet, especially for personality assessment instruments, whose scores are prone to exhibit a good deal of *method variance* (i.e., variability that is related to characteristics inherent in their methodologies). In addition, the MTMMM design is not applied in its full-fledged form very frequently because collecting information through multiple methods is quite laborious (see, e.g., Terrill, Friedman, Gottschalk, & Haaga, 2002). Nevertheless, simpler variations of the MTMMM scheme, based on the scores of tests that measure both similar and dissimilar constructs, albeit through similar methods, are being increasingly employed in the process of test validation. Furthermore, some instruments have features that facilitate the collection of data from different sources which can then be used to study patterns of convergence and discrimination. For example, the Revised NEO Personality Inventory (NEO PI-R) provides parallel versions of the same item sets—Form S, for self-reports, and Form R, for ratings by observers such as peers or spouses—that can be used to correlate and compare scores derived from both sources (Costa & McCrae, 1992, pp. 48–50).

Age Differentiation

Test results that are consonant with well-established developmental trends across age groups are often seen as evidence of score validity. In fact, the criterion of age differentiation is one of the oldest sources of evidence for validating ability tests. It may be recalled from Chapter 1 that the success of the original Binet-Simon scales was gauged primarily through studies that proved that their sampling of cognitive functions produced results that could be used to describe children's levels of ability quantitatively, in terms of the age levels to which their performance corresponded. In most ability tests, the performance of children and adolescents in the normative samples typically shows an upward trend at successive chronological ages. At the other end of the age spectrum, declining performance is observed among samples of older adults on instruments that measure abilities that tend to diminish with age, such as memory tests and tests that assess speed of performance. Age differentiation is also evident in carefully designed studies of long-term trends in the performance of individuals at various ages on mental ability tests, such as the Seattle Longitudinal Study (Schaie, 1994). Increases or declines in scores that are consonant with age-appropriate expectations provide evidence that is necessary, albeit not sufficient, to show that a test is measuring the ability constructs it was designed to measure.

Experimental Results

Another indirect source of evidence that can be useful in test score validation is provided by investigations that use psychological test scores as a dependent variable to gauge the effects of experimental interventions. In the area of ability testing, this evidence derives primarily from pre- and posttest score differences following interventions aimed at remediating deficiencies or upgrading performance in various cognitive and intellectual skills. For example, if the scores on a test of basic conceptual development in young children (e.g., the Bracken Basic Concept Scale-Revised) showed a significant increase for a group exposed to a short-term enrichment program—versus no change for a matched group who did not participate in the program—the change in scores could be viewed as evidence of their validity, as well as of the program's efficacy. Similar pre- and posttest contrasts are often used to document the validity of scores derived from personality assessment tools. An example of this type of validation study can be found in the manual of the Quality of Life Inventory (QOLI; Frisch, 1994, pp. 15–16), which is a tool for the assessment of levels of life satisfaction and subjective well-being that may be used—among other things—to gauge the effectiveness of counseling or psychotherapeutic interventions.

Factor Analysis

One way to deal with the huge number of constructs tapped by existing tests—and with the unwieldy number of correlations that can be obtained from their global scores, their subtest scores, and their item scores—is through a series of statistical procedures known collectively as *factor analysis* (*FA*). The principal goal of factor analysis is to reduce the number of dimensions needed to describe data derived from a large number of measures. It is accomplished by a series of mathematical calculations, based on matrix algebra, designed to extract patterns of intercorrelation among a set of variables.

There are two basic ways to conduct factor analyses. The original approach to the method is exploratory in nature and thus is known as *exploratory factor analysis,* or EFA; it sets out to discover which *factors* (i.e., latent variables or constructs) underlie the variables under analysis. A second, more recent, approach is called *confirmatory factor analysis* (*CFA*) because it sets out to test hypotheses, or to confirm theories, about factors that are already presumed to exist. Both approaches can be used in analyzing psychological test data, as well as many other kinds of data sets. Confirmatory analyses are more sophisticated from the methodological standpoint and will be discussed later in this chapter as a subset of the techniques for analyzing covariance structures known as structural equation modeling.

What are the steps involved in factor analyzing psychological test scores? Exploratory factor analyses start with a *correlation matrix,* a table that displays the intercorrelations among the scores obtained by a sample of individuals on a wide variety of tests (or subtests or items). The fact that this is the starting point of EFA is important in understanding the results of factor analytic research because it points out two crucial features of FA that are too often forgotten. Both of these features concern limitations in the applicability of results stemming from any single FA, namely, that the results depend largely on (a) the choice of measures included in the analysis and (b) the specific make-up of the sample whose scores provide the data for the analysis.

Table 5.3, Part A, shows an example of a simple correlation matrix. This matrix was derived from the scores obtained by 95 college students on the five subtests of the Beta III, which is a nonverbal test of intellectual ability descended from the Army Beta (see Chapter 1). The data are part of a study on sex differences in cognitive abilities (Urbina & Ringby, 2001).

Table 5.3

A. Correlation Matrix: Intercorrelations of Scores on Five Subtests of the Beta III for 95 College Students

Subtest	Coding	Picture Completion	Clerical Checking	Picture Absurdities	Matrix Reasoning
Coding	1.00	.13	.62**	.20	.05
Picture Completion		1.00	.09	.21*	.11
Clerical Checking			1.00	.18	.20
Picture Absurdities				1.00	.31**
Matrix Reasoning					1.00

Note: Data are from Urbina and Ringby (2001).

$*p \leq .05$ $**p \leq .01$

B. Factor Matrix for the Two Factors Extracted from the Exploratory Factor Analysis (EFA) of Five Beta III Subtests[a]

Subtest	Loadings on Factor 1	Loadings on Factor 2
Coding	**.90**	.06
Picture Completion	.07	**.54**
Clerical Checking	**.88**	.14
Picture Absurdities	.15	**.75**
Matrix Reasoning	.02	**.73**

Note: Boldface indicates the highest loadings on the two varimax-rotated factors.

[a]Factors 1 and 2 account for 61% of the variance in the subtest scores; the remaining 39% of the variance is accounted for by factors specific to each subtest, and by error variance.

The next steps in factor analysis depend on the specific choice of techniques employed by the investigator. Several different procedures may be used to conduct these analyses and to extract factors (see, e.g., Bryant & Yarnold, 1995; Comrey & Lee, 1992). A discussion of factor analytic procedures is beyond our purposes, as it would involve delving into technicalities, such as methods for extraction and rotation of factors, that are fairly complex. Nevertheless, the fact that various approaches to FA exist must be noted and kept in mind because one can arrive at different solutions depending on the assumptions and methods that are used. Differences in the solutions generally pertain to the number of factors extracted and to their relative independence from one another. For insight into these and other issues related to the methodology of FA, see Russell (2002).

The end product of factor analyses is a *factor matrix*, which is a table that lists the loadings of each one of the original variables on the factors extracted from the analyses. *Factor loadings* are correlations between the original measures in the correlation matrix and the factors that have been extracted. Part B of Table 5.3 displays the factor matrix for the two factors extracted from a factor analysis of the data in the correlation matrix in Part A of the same table. This factor matrix indicates that two subtests (Coding and Clerical Checking) have very high loadings on Factor 1 and negligible loadings on Factor 2, whereas the other three subtests (Picture Completion, Picture Absurdities, and Matrix Reasoning) show the reverse pattern in their factor loadings.

Interpreting the results of factor analyses. Once factor matrices are obtained, they can be examined to try to determine the nature of the factors that account for most of the variance in the original data set. The factors themselves are then labeled on the basis of inductive logic. In order to identify and label the factors, one examines the distinguishing features of the measures that load most and least heavily on each of the factors in the matrix. In our example, the factor matrix in Table 5.3 suggests that the first factor involves *speed of performance*, because the two subtests that load heavily on that factor involve extremely simple tasks and have very brief time limits. The second factor has high loadings on the remaining three subtests, all of which involve problems that require *reasoning* based on pictorial or graphic stimuli. This factor matrix pattern coincides with the ones derived from exploratory and confirmatory factor analyses of the Beta III standardization sample data, which are presented in the Beta III

DON'T FORGET

Factors are not "real" entities, although they are often discussed as though they were. They are simply constructs or latent variables that may be inferred from the patterns of covariance revealed by statistical analyses.

manual. Factors 1 and 2 are labeled "Processing Speed" and "Nonverbal Reasoning," respectively (Kellogg & Morton, 1999).

Factor analysis was developed by psychologists in an attempt to investigate the underlying bases for the interrelationships among test scores, and among the scores of various types of ability tests in particular. However, the techniques of FA were promptly applied to personality test data and personality trait descriptions as well. The history of FA, both in the area of abilities as well as personality, has been fraught with controversy about the appropriateness of its various methods and the extrapolations that can reasonably be made on the basis of factor analytic results (Cowles, 2001, chap. 11).

In the field of cognitive abilities, much of the controversy has centered on the general factor of mental ability, or g (originally postulated by Charles Spearman), especially on questions related to its significance and heritability (Jensen, 1998). Additional theorizing and basic research in this field have dealt mainly with issues concerning the nature, number, and organization of intellectual traits. An outstanding compilation of much of the factor analytic literature on human cognitive abilities, along with a widely accepted hierarchical theory of cognitive trait organization, can be found in John Carroll's (1993) book on this subject.

In the field of personality assessment, factor analysis has been applied to the task of identifying and measuring the major dimensions required for a comprehensive description of personality, an issue about which there has also been a good deal of debate. Within this area, two separate traditions of factor analytic research arose independently. One of them centered from the outset on the use of personality questionnaire data. The other—known as the *lexical* tradition—started by reducing the myriad of words used to describe personality attributes to a manageable number by combining synonyms. This was followed by an attempt to identify the primary dimensions of personality through intercorrelations and factor analyses of ratings on various traits assigned to heterogeneous groups of individuals by their associates, as well as by self-report questionnaire data. More recently, research from both traditions has coalesced and achieved some degree of consensus. The prevailing model centers on the use of a hierarchical pattern of analysis to simplify the collection of data of varying degrees of generality pertinent to personality functioning, and has come to be known as the *five-factor model* (*FFM;* Carroll, 2002; Costa & McCrae, 1992; Digman, 1990; Wiggins & Pincus, 1992).

In spite of its problems and limitations, the factor analytic tradition has been extraordinarily fruitful for psychological testing and, more generally, for psychological theorizing. The longevity of these methods, as well as their continuing refinements and extensions, have created a rich archive of tools and data from which to proceed to extend our understanding of psychological traits and tests. Rapid Reference 5.5 outlines some of the benefits that can be derived from FA, as well as its major limitations.

Structural Equation Modeling Techniques

Exploratory factor analysis is just one of several types of multivariate statistical techniques that allow investigators to examine the relations among multiple measures to try to determine the underlying constructs that account for observed variability. The increased availability of powerful computers and computer software in recent decades has greatly enhanced the ease with which factor analytic

Rapid Reference 5.5

Part I: Benefits of Factor Analysis

Construct validation: By pooling together large numbers of measures and examining the factors that seem to account for the variance those measures share, we can learn more about the composition of tasks sampled by psychological tests and about the organization of traits, in terms of their generality and specificity.

Practical application: When a test battery is made up of a large number of tests, factor analytic results provide a way to simplify the interpretation and reporting of subtest scores. This is accomplished by means of factor scores, which are essentially indexes that aggregate subtest scores into a smaller number of cohesive construct categories derived from factor analyses.

Part II: Limitations of Factor Analysis

Interpretation of the results of any single factor analytic study cannot extend beyond the data used in the analysis, in terms either of what is being measured or of their generalizability across populations.

What is being measured? Both the manual of the Beta III (a test that purports to measure nonverbal intellectual ability) and the analysis displayed in Table 5.3 suggest that the five subtests of the Beta III can be configured into two clusters that have a good deal of variance in common. Examination of the tasks involved in the five subtests confirms that the two factors are nonverbal. However, these data cannot reveal whether or to what extent these factors capture the essential aspects of nonverbal intellectual ability.

Generalizability of factor analytic results: The correlational data derived from 95 college students (Urbina & Ringby, 2001) and presented in Table 5.3 yield results similar to those obtained with the Beta III standardization group, a much larger ($N = 1,260$), and far more representative, sample of the U.S. population. Although this convergence of results supports the factor structure obtained in both investigations, it leaves open the question of whether this structure would generalize to other populations, such as people of different cultures, individuals with uncorrected hearing or visual impairments, or any other group whose experiential history differs significantly from that of the samples used in the two analyses at hand.

techniques—and other sophisticated methods of analysis of multivariate correlational data, such as multiple regression analyses—can be used to investigate latent variables (i.e., constructs) and the possible direct and indirect causal links or paths of influence among them.

One rapidly evolving set of procedures that can be used to test the plausibility of hypothesized interrelationships among constructs as well as the relationships between constructs and the measures used to assess them is known as *structural equation modeling (SEM)*. The essential idea of all SEM is to create one or more models—based on theories, previous findings, or prior exploratory analyses—of the relations among a set of constructs or latent variables and to compare the covariance structures or matrices implied by the models with the covariance matrices actually obtained with a new data set. In other words, the relationships obtained with empirical data on variables that assess the various constructs (factors or latent variables) are compared with those predicted by the models. The correspondence between the data and the models is evaluated with statistics, appropriately named *goodness-of-fit* statistics. SEM provides several advantages over traditional regression analyses. Its advantages derive primarily from two characteristics of this methodology: (a) SEM is based on analyses of *covariance structures* (i.e., patterns of covariation among latent variables or constructs) that can represent the direct and indirect influences of variables on one another, and (b) SEM typically uses multiple indicators for both the dependent and independent variables in models and thus provides a way to account for measurement error in all the observed variables. Readers who wish to pursue the topic of SEM, and related techniques such as path analysis, in more detail might consult one or more of the sources suggested in Rapid Reference 5.6.

As far as psychological test validation is concerned, SEM techniques are used for the systematic exploration of psychological constructs and theories through research that employs psychological testing as a method of data collection for one or more of the indicators in a model. SEM can provide supporting evidence for the reliability of test scores as well as for their utility as measures of one or more constructs in a model. However, at present, the most extensive application of SEM techniques in test score validation is through confirmatory factor analyses.

Confirmatory factor analysis (CFA), mentioned briefly in a preceding section, involves the a priori specification of one or more models of the relationships between test scores and the factors or constructs they are designed to assess. In CFA, as in all other SEM techniques, the direction and strength of interrelationships estimated by various models are tested against results obtained with actual data for goodness of fit. These analyses have been facilitated by the development of computer programs—such as LISREL (Jöreskog & Sörbom, 1993)—de-

≡ Rapid Reference 5.6

Sources of Information on Structural Equation Modeling (SEM)

- For a good introduction to SEM that does not presuppose knowledge of statistical methods beyond regression analysis, see the following:

  Raykov, T., & Marcoulides, G. A. (2000). *A first course in structural equation modeling.* Mahwah, NJ: Erlbaum.

- A more advanced presentation of SEM that includes contributions from many of the leading authorities on this methodology can be found in the following:

  Bollen, K. A., & Long, J. S. (Eds.). (1993). *Testing structural equation models.* Newbury Park, CA: Sage.

- The Internet is an excellent source of information about many topics, including SEM techniques that are being used in a number of fields. One of the best starting points is a site created and maintained by Ed Rigdon, a professor in the Marketing Department of Georgia State University. The address for this site is as follows:

  http://www.gsu.edu/~mkteer/sem.html.

signed to generate values for the hypothesized models that can then be tested against the actual data.

Examples of this kind of work are becoming increasingly abundant both in the psychological literature and in the validity sections of test manuals. The confirmatory factor analyses conducted with the standardization sample data of the WAIS-III (Psychological Corporation, 1997, pp. 106–110) are typical of the studies designed to provide validity evidence for the psychological test scores. In those analyses, four possible structural models—a two-factor, a three-factor, a four-factor, and a five-factor model—were successively evaluated and compared to a general, one-factor model to determine which of them provided the best fit for the data in the total sample and in most of the age bands of the WAIS-III normative group. The results of the CFA indicated that the four-factor model provided the best overall solution and confirmed the patterning previously obtained with EFAs of the same data. These results, in turn, were used as the bases for determining the composition of the four index scores (Verbal Comprehension, Perceptual Organization, Working Memory, and Processing Speed) that can serve to organize the results of 11 of the 14 WAIS-III subtests into separate domains of cognitive functioning.

In contrast to the kind of CFA conducted with the WAIS-III data, other CFA studies involve more basic work aimed at clarifying the organization of cognitive and personality traits. An example of this type of study can be found in Gustafsson's (2002) description of his reanalyses of data gathered by Holzinger and Swineford in the 1930s from a group of seventh- and eighth-grade students ($N = 301$) who were tested with a battery of 24 tests designed to tap abilities in five broad ability areas (verbal, spatial, memory, speed, and mathematical deduction). Using two different models of CFA, Gustafsson found support for the hypothesized overlap between the G (general intelligence) and Gf (fluid intelligence or reasoning ability) factors that had been suggested by the analyses done in the 1930s. Gustafsson also used contrasts in the patterns of results from the original factor analysis done in the 1930s and his own contemporary CFAs to illustrate significant implications that various measurement approaches, as well as sample composition, have for the construct validation of ability test scores.

Confirmatory factor analysis and other structural modeling techniques are still evolving and are far from providing any definitive conclusions. However, the blending of theoretical models, empirical observations, and sophisticated statistical analyses that characterizes these techniques offers great promise in terms of advancing our understanding of the measures we use and of the relationships between test scores and the constructs they are designed to assess.

Validity Evidence Based on Relationships Between Test Scores and Criteria

If the goals of psychological testing were limited simply to describing test takers' performance in terms of the frames of reference discussed in Chapter 3 or to increasing our understanding of psychological constructs and their interrelationships, the sources of evidence already discussed might suffice. However, the valid interpretation of test scores often entails applying whatever meaning is inherent in scores—whether it is based on norms, test content, response processes, established patterns of convergence and divergence, or any combination of these sources of evidence—to the pragmatic inferences necessary for making decisions about people. When this is the case, validity evidence needs to address the significance test scores may have in matters that go beyond those scores or in realms that lie outside the direct purview of the test. In other words, test scores must be shown to correlate with the various criteria used in making decisions and predictions.

Some Essential Facts About Criteria

Merriam-Webster's Collegiate Dictionary (1995) defines *criterion* as "a standard on which a judgment or decision may be based" or "a characteristic mark or trait."

Although the plural form, criteria, is often used as a singular, in the present context it is necessary to apply both forms of the word appropriately because they are both central to our purposes. A criterion may also be defined, more loosely, as that which we *really* want to know. This last definition, though less formal than the dictionary's, highlights the contrast between what test scores tell us and the practical reasons why we use tests.

For psychological tests that are used in making judgments or decisions about people, evidence of a relationship between test scores and criterion measures is an indispensable, but not necessarily sufficient, basis for evaluating validity. *Criterion measures* are indexes of the criteria that tests are designed to assess or predict and that are gathered independently of the test in question. Rapid Reference 5.7 provides a list of the kinds of criteria typically used in validating test scores. Since the nature of criteria depends on the questions one wishes to answer with the help of tests, it follows that validation procedures based partly or entirely on relationships between test scores and criterion measures must produce evidence of a link between the *predictors* (test scores) and the criteria.

Criterion measures or estimates may be naturally *dichotomous* (e.g., graduating vs. dropping out) or artificially *dichotomized* (e.g., success vs. failure); *polytomous*

≡Rapid Reference 5.7

Typical Criteria Used in Validating Test Scores

Although there is an almost infinite number of criterion measures that can be employed in validating test scores, depending on what the purposes of testing are, the most frequent categories are the following:

- *Indexes of academic achievement or performance in specialized training,* such as school grades, graduation records, honors, awards, or demonstrations of competence in the area of training through successful performance (e.g., in piano playing, mechanical work, flying, computer programming, bar exams, or board certification tests).
- *Indexes of job performance,* such as sales records, production records, promotions, salary increases, longevity in jobs that demand competence, accident-free job performance, or ratings by supervisors, peers, students, employees, customers, and so forth.
- *Membership in contrasted groups* based on psychiatric diagnoses, occupational status, educational achievement, or any other relevant variable.
- *Ratings* of behavior or personality traits by independent observers, relatives, peers, or any other associates who have sufficient bases to provide them.
- *Scores on other relevant tests.*

(e.g., diagnoses of anxiety vs. mood vs. dissociative disorders, or membership in artistic vs. scientific vs. literary occupations); or *continuous* (e.g., grade point average, number of units sold, scores on a depression inventory, etc.). Whereas the nature of criteria depends on the decisions or predictions to be made with the help of test scores, the methods used to establish the relationships between test scores and criteria vary depending on the formal characteristics of both test scores and criterion measures. In general, when the criterion measure is expressed in a dichotomous fashion (e.g., success vs. failure) or in terms of a categorical system (e.g., membership in contrasted groups), the validity of test scores is evaluated in terms of *hit rates*. Hit rates typically indicate the percent of correct decisions or classifications made with the use of test scores, although mean differences and suitable correlation indexes may also be used. When criterion measures are continuous (e.g., scores on achievement tests, grades, ratings, etc.) the principal tools used to indicate the extent of the relationship between test scores and the criterion measure are correlation coefficients. However, if a certain value on a continuous criterion, such as a 2.0 grade point average, is used as a cutoff to determine a specific outcome, such as graduation from college, scores on the predictor test can also be evaluated in terms of whether they differentiate between those who meet or exceed the criterion cutoff and those who do not.

The history of psychological testing in recent decades reflects not only an evolution in understanding the nature and limitations of tests and test scores but also an increased appreciation of the significance and complexity of criterion measures (see, e.g., James, 1973; Tenopyr, 1986; Wallace, 1965). As a result, with rare exceptions, the notion that there is such a thing as "a criterion" against which a test may be validated is no longer any more tenable than the proposition that the validity of a test can be determined on an all-or-none basis. Instead, the following facts about criteria are now generally understood:

1. In most validation studies, there are many possible indexes (both quantitative and qualitative) that can qualify as criterion measures, including scores from tests other than those undergoing validation. Therefore, careful attention must be given to the selection of criteria and criterion measures.
2. Some criterion measures are more reliable and valid than others. Thus, the reliability and validity of criterion measures need to be evaluated, just as the reliability and validity of test scores do.
3. Some criteria are more complex than others. As a result, there may or may not be a correlation among criterion measures, especially when criteria are multifaceted.

4. Some criteria can be gauged at the time of testing; others evolve over time. This implies that there may or may not be substantial correlations between criterion measures that are available shortly after testing and more distant criteria that may be assessed only over a longer period of time.

5. Relationships between test scores and criterion measures may or may not generalize across groups, settings, or time periods. Therefore, criterion-related validity evidence needs to be demonstrated anew for populations that differ from the original validation samples in ways that may affect the relationship between test scores and criteria, as well as across various settings and times.

6. The strength or quality of validity evidence with regard to the assessment or prediction of a criterion is a function of the characteristics of both the test and the criterion measures employed. If the criterion measures are unreliable or arbitrary, indexes of test score validity will be weakened, regardless of the quality of the test used to assess or predict the criteria.

Criterion-Related Validation Procedures

The criterion-related decisions for which test scores may be of help can be classified into two basic types: (a) those that involve determining a person's current status and (b) those that involve predicting future performance or behavior. In a sense, this dichotomy is artificial because regardless of whether we need to know something about a person's current status or future performance, the only information test scores can convey derives from current behavior—that is, from the way test takers perform at the time of testing. Nevertheless, criterion-related validation procedures are frequently categorized as either concurrent or predictive, depending on the measures employed as well as their primary goals.

Concurrent and Predictive Validation

Concurrent validation evidence is gathered when indexes of the criteria that test scores are meant to assess are available at the time the validation studies are conducted. Strictly speaking, concurrent validation is appropriate for test scores that will be employed in determining a person's current status with regard to some classificatory scheme, such as diagnostic categories or levels of performance. *Predictive validation* evidence, on the other hand, is relevant for test scores that are meant to be used to make decisions based on estimating future levels of performance or behavioral outcomes. Ideally, predictive validation procedures require collecting data on the predictor variable (test scores) and waiting for criterion data to become available so that the two sets of data can be correlated. This process is often impractical because of the time element involved in waiting for criteria to mature and also because of the difficulty of finding suitable samples to use in such studies. As a result, concurrent validation is often used as a substitute for predictive validation, even for tests that will be used for estimating future performance, such as college admissions or preemployment tests. In these cases, the test under development is administered to a group of people, such as college sophomores or employees, for whom criterion data are already available.

Often the distinction between the two kinds of validation procedures hinges on the way test users pose the questions they want to answer with the help of a test. Rapid Reference 5.8 contains examples of some typical questions and decision-making situations that may call for either concurrent or predictive validation evidence, depending on how the question is posed and on the time horizon that is chosen. To illustrate the distinction between concurrent and predictive validation strategies, a relatively simple example of each type of study will be presented, followed by a discussion of the major issues pertinent to criterion-related validation.

Concurrent Validation Example: The Whitaker Index of Schizophrenic Thinking

Tests that are used to screen for psychiatric disorders, such as schizophrenia or depression, usually undergo concurrent validation. Typically, these studies employ two or more samples of individuals who differ with respect to their independently established diagnostic status. One of the many instruments whose scores are validated in this fashion is the Whitaker Index of Schizophrenic Thinking (WIST; Whitaker, 1980). The WIST was designed to identify the kind of thinking impairment that often accompanies schizophrenic syndromes. Each of its two forms (A and B) consists of 25 multiple choice items.

In standardizing the WIST, Whitaker used samples of acute and chronic schizophrenic patients (S), as well as three groups of nonschizophrenics (NS), to derive cutoff scores that would optimally differentiate S from NS individuals. The cutoff scores established with the standardization groups discriminated between S and NS groups with 80% efficiency for Form A and 76% efficiency for Form B. Thus, depending on the form, the cutoff index resulted in 20% to 24% incorrect decisions. With Form A, incorrect decisions of the *false negative* type—those in which S subjects were classified as NS by the index—were much higher (33%) than *false positive* decisions, wherein NS subjects were classified as S (10%). The same pattern (38% false negatives vs. 13% false positives) was obtained with

⟱ Rapid Reference 5.8

The Relationship Among Questions, Decisions, and Predictions Requiring Criterion-Related Validation

Questions About Current Status	Immediate Goal: Decisions	Implicit Questions: Predictions
Is John X suffering from Schizophrenia, Panic Disorder, Clinical Depression, Attention Deficit, or some other mental disorder?	Should John X receive the treatment (medication, psychotherapy, etc.) that is recommended for the disorder in question?	Will John X profit (a little, a lot, or not at all) from the recommended treatment?
Is Mary Y subject to suicidal (or homicidal) impulses she may not be able to overcome if left to her own devices?	Should Mary Y continue to be hospitalized (or incarcerated)?	Will Mary Y attempt to kill herself (or someone else) if left at liberty?
Is Joe Z gifted (or suffering from severe mental retardation)?	Should Joe Z be admitted to a special education program for gifted (or mentally retarded) individuals?	Will Joe Z benefit (a little, a lot, or not at all) from a special education program?
Is Tom P honest and trustworthy (or motivated for sales work)?	Should Tom P be hired for work as a cashier (or salesperson)?	Will Tom P be a conscientious cashier (or a successful salesperson), or will he steal money (or make few sales)?
Is Jane Q capable of doing college-level work (or flying an airplane)?	Should Jane Q be admitted into college (or granted an airplane pilot's license)?	Will Jane Q be able to finish college with a grade-point average high enough to graduate (or be able to fly a plane without causing accidents)?

Form B. See Chapter 7 for further explanation of the terminology used to designate incorrect decisions (e.g., false positive and false negative decisions).

Additional validation evidence for the WIST includes studies done in Mexico and Spain with Spanish translations of the instrument. These studies show some support for the WIST's ability to detect the thought impairment associated with schizophrenia, albeit with different rates of efficiency and different cutoff scores.

The hit rate obtained when the WIST cutoff scores are used to discriminate S from NS subjects is fairly typical for tests of this kind. Because of the relatively high error rates that the WIST cutoff scores can yield, they should never be used as the sole vehicle for establishing a diagnosis of schizophrenia, any more than any other single indicator should. However, depending on the setting and context of testing, the WIST may prove useful as part of a screening battery or as one index of change in the symptomatology of patients diagnosed with schizophrenia. Although the discriminations made

> # CAUTION
>
> • Psychological test results, as well as medical test results and those in many other fields, are not expected to achieve 100% accuracy.
> • Because of the less-than-perfect nature of all diagnostic indicators, psychologists engaged in clinical assessment—as well as diagnosticians in other fields—should never rely on a single indicator.

with the use of WIST cutoff scores are far from perfect, they may still be useful in investigating the possibility that a person suffers from thought impairment. For a review of the WIST, see Flanagan (1992).

Predictive Validation: A Hypothetical Example

Tests that are used to predict performance in occupational and educational settings require validation strategies geared toward prediction. The ideal design for a predictive validation study in either one of those fields would involve the following steps: (a) testing an unselected group of applicants with an ability test or test battery, (b) hiring or admitting them without regard to their test scores, (c) waiting until criterion measures of job or academic performance became available, (d) obtaining correlations between the preemployment or admission test scores and criterion measures, and (e) using the correlational data to derive a regression equation to estimate or predict the criterion performance of future applicants. For obvious reasons, most employers and school administrators are not willing to hire or accept all applicants—especially when their numbers exceed the number of positions available—in order to conduct a validation study. Nevertheless, for the sake of simplicity and to illustrate the way in which predictions can be made on the basis of test scores, a simple hypothetical example of this type of study will be described.

To provide some context for this example, let us say that—in order to ensure a profitable level of production—the owner of a small factory wants to hire people who are able to process at least 50 widgets per hour on the assembly line. Since there are no other requirements for this job, besides showing up for work on time, the criterion to be predicted is simply the number of widgets produced per hour on the assembly line. Output on the assembly line is primarily a function of the workers' speed and accuracy in manual tasks. Therefore, a test of manual

Table 5.4   Data for Predictive Validation Example

Applicant	Test Score (X)	Output (Y)	$X - M_x$ (x)	$Y - M_y$ (y)	x^2	y^2	xy
1	18	56	5	6	25	36	30
2	12	50	−1	0	1	0	0
3	8	47	−5	−3	25	9	15
4	20	52	7	2	49	4	14
5	14	52	1	2	1	4	2
6	5	42	−8	−8	64	64	64
7	10	48	−3	−2	9	4	6
8	12	49	−1	−1	1	1	1
9	16	50	3	0	9	0	0
10	15	54	2	4	4	16	8
Sum	130	500	0	0	188	138	140
Mean	13	50					

dexterity is selected as the predictor. Table 5.4 shows the *bivariate data* for 10 hypothetical applicants for the assembly line job who take the *manual dexterity test,* are hired and trained, and have their *assembly line output per hour* gauged on repeated occasions and averaged so as to produce a viable criterion measure.

As discussed in Chapter 2, when two variables exhibit a linear relationship and a strong correlation with each other, it is possible to predict one based on knowledge of the other by applying the linear regression model. Figure 5.1 shows the scatter diagram for the bivariate data in Table 5.4, and indicates that the relationship between the manual dexterity test scores and assembly-line output per hour is strong, positive, and linear.

In this case, it is necessary to solve a linear regression equation to predict the criterion of assembly-line output (the Y variable) from scores on the manual dexterity test (the X variable). This equation expresses the relationship between X and Y, and contains the two major components needed to draw the *regression line,* portrayed in Figure 5.1. The regression line is the line that best fits the bivariate data, in that it minimizes errors in predicting Y from X. The two pivotal components of the linear regression equation are (a) the Y intercept, which is the point at which the line meets the vertical axis representing the Y variable, and (b) the slope of the line, which is the ratio of change in the Y variable for every unit of change in the X variable. These values, as well as the correlation coefficient for X and Y, are computed from the bivariate data. The necessary analyses have been

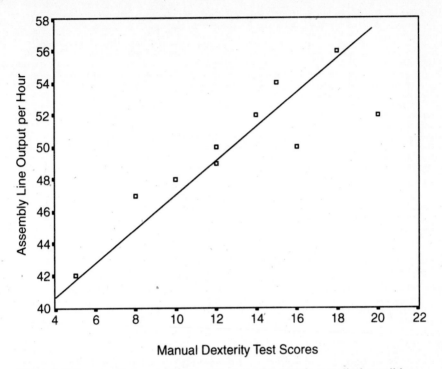

Figure 5.1 Scatter diagram of data and regression line for predictive valida-tion example

performed in Table 5.5. This table shows that the Pearson $r(r_{xy})$ is .87 (significant at the .001 level). The *coefficient of determination,* obtained by squaring r_{xy}, is .755. It indicates that 75.5% of the variance in Y (assembly line output) is associated with the variance in X (scores on the dexterity test). Both of these coefficients confirm that there is a strong relationship between X and Y, making it possible to predict the criterion measure based on the test scores with substantial accuracy. The factory owner in our example may apply this information to estimate the assembly line output of subsequent applicants by administering the manual dexterity test and inserting their scores in the regression equation, as follows.

Suppose that the 11th person to apply for a job (after the 10 who were used in the hypothetical validation study) obtains a manual dexterity test score of 17. Using the coefficients shown in Table 5.5 to solve the regression equation $Y' = 40.32 + .745 (17)$, the factory owner would learn that the estimated assembly line output per hour for the 11th applicant is 53 widgets, or three more than the desired minimum number.

Correlations between test scores and criterion measures (r_{xy}) are usually called

Table 5.5 Analysis of Predictive Validation Data

Descriptive Statistic	Number of Observations (N)	Mean	Standard Deviation (SD)
X = predictor (test scores)	10	13	4.57
Y = criterion (output)	10	50	3.91

Pearson r $\qquad r_{xy} = \dfrac{\Sigma\, xy}{(N-1)(SD_x)(SD_y)} = \dfrac{140}{(9)(4.57)(3.91)} = .87$

Coefficient of determination $\qquad\qquad r_{xy}^2 = .755$

Linear regression equation[a] $\qquad\qquad Y' = a_{yx} + b_{yx}(X)$

Example data $\qquad\qquad\qquad a_{yx} = 40.32$

$\qquad\qquad\qquad\qquad\qquad\qquad b_{yx} = .745$

Regression equation for predicting assembly-line output based on dexterity test scores

$$\text{Predicted output} = Y' = 40.32 + .745\,(X)$$

[a]Where Y' = predicted criterion score; $a_{yx} = M_y - b_{yx}(M_x)$ = intercept of the regression line; $b_{yx} = (\Sigma\, xy)/(\Sigma\, x^2)$ = slope of the regression line; and X = score on the predictor (manual dexterity test score).

validity coefficients. If r_{xy} were 1.00, indicating a perfect correlation between test scores and the criterion, perfect prediction would be possible. Although the r_{xy} of .87 obtained with the data in our example is extremely high—much higher than the typical predictive validity coefficients obtained with real data—it is not perfect. Thus, there is bound to be some error in the estimates of the criterion made by using the test scores. This error is gauged by the *standard error of estimate* (SE_{est}), a statistic that expresses, in the scale used for the criterion measure, the error in predictions that are based on imperfect correlations.

Formulas for the SE_{est} and for a correction term applied to the SE_{est} due to the small sample size are presented in Rapid Reference 5.9, along with the results for the data in our example. Interpretation of the SE_{est} assumes (a) that the predicted criterion score, or Y', is the average value in a hypothetical normal distribution of all possible criterion scores for the applicant in question, and (b) that the SE_{est} is the standard deviation of that distribution. These assumptions allow us to attach a level of probability to the predictions made from test scores, based on the normal curve areas in Appendix C. To do this, one calculates the range encompassed within Y' ± SE_{est} (z), where z is the value that corresponds to the desired probability level. For the 11th applicant, in our example, the dexterity test score of 17 resulted in a predicted Y' of 53. The SE_{est} for the test scores, calculated in Rapid Reference 5.9, is 2.05 (or 2). Therefore, we can predict that the chances that this applicant will produce between 51 and 55 widgets per hour (i.e., 53±2) on the as-

DON'T FORGET

Evaluating the adequacy of validity coefficients of various magnitudes is a relative matter that depends on the purpose for which test scores will be used. In general, there are two major ways to approach this matter:

1. When validity is expressed in the form of a correlation coefficient (r_{xy}), the proportion of variance shared by the predictor (X) and the criterion (Y) is often estimated by squaring r_{xy} and obtaining the *coefficient of determination,* or r_{xy}^2. A coefficient of determination, discussed in Chapter 2, expresses the proportion of the variance in Y that is associated with the variance in X. For example, the predictive validity coefficient of .87 obtained in the example presented in Table 5.5 indicates that the scores on the manual dexterity test used as a predictor can explain approximately 76% of the variance ($.87 \times .87 = .76$) in the criterion of assembly line output.

2. Validity coefficients can also be evaluated in terms of the *incremental validity* contributed by a test—that is, by the extent to which use of a test (or any other instrument) brings about an increase in the efficiency of decisions made in a given situation compared to the validity of other methods. This aspect of validity concerns the utility of a test and is discussed further in Chapter 7.

Coefficients in the .20s and .30s are not uncommon in predictive validity studies. As a general rule, coefficients of .40 or higher are considered acceptable. Although some of these figures may seem low, they must be viewed in the context of the multidetermined nature of performance in most endeavors *and* they must be weighed in light of the predictive efficiency of alternative methods of making selection decisions.

≡ Rapid Reference 5.9

Standard error of estimate (SE_{est})

$$SE_{est} = SD_y \sqrt{1 - r_{xy}^2}$$

SE_{est} for predictive validation example:

$$SE_{est} = 3.91 \sqrt{1 - .755} = 3.91(.495) = 1.935$$

SE_{est} corrected for sample size:

$$SE_{est} \text{ corrected} = SE_{est} \sqrt{\frac{N-1}{N-2}} = 1.935 \sqrt{\frac{10-1}{10-2}} = 1.935(1.06) = 2.05$$

sembly line are 68/100. To make a prediction at the 95% (instead of 68%) confidence level we would use a z value of 1.96, which demarcates the .05 level of significance for a two-tailed test. Solving the equation $Y' \pm SE_{est} (1.96)$, we could predict that chances are 95/100 that the applicant in question would produce between 49 and 57 widgets per hour (53 ± 4).

Issues Concerning Criterion-Related Validation Studies

Some of the difficulties inherent in criterion-related validation studies were mentioned earlier in this chapter in connection with the discussion of the notion of criteria. Additional considerations that deserve thorough examination by potential users of instruments buttressed by this kind of validity evidence are discussed next, using some of the features of the examples just described as a starting point. Although our scope does not allow extensive exploration of these issues—or of the various methods that can be used to deal with them—some of the more salient ones need to be briefly described.

Characteristics of Criterion Measures

As mentioned earlier, the criteria upon which test scores are validated can differ greatly in terms of their own reliability and validity. In the case of the WIST, the criterion used in establishing the validity of scores was the diagnostic status (S vs. NS) of the individuals in the validation samples. If the initial classification of subjects in these studies included some incorrect diagnoses (some S's who were NS's, or viceversa), validity data would obviously be weakened. A similar caution applies to all validation procedures that rely on subjective criteria, such as ratings or other qualitative judgments that are used to categorize people into criterion groups. In addition, the validity of criterion measures can be eroded when those who are charged with determining the criterion standing of individuals in the validation samples have access to scores on the test that is used as a predictor. This type of error, known as *criterion contamination,* is easily prevented by making sure that teachers, supervisors, diagnosticians, and others who assign ratings or make judgments related to criterion measures remain unaware of and are not influenced by the knowledge of test scores. With regard to the ratings themselves, as well as other criterion measures that depend on subjective judgment, test developers need to provide evidence that the instruments and methods used to rate or to classify the criterion groups employed in validation studies are reliable and valid. When the criterion consists of membership in a group such as a certain diagnostic category, its reliability and validity can be improved by careful subject selection that is based on evidence from multiple and preferably independent sources. As far as ratings criteria are concerned, their reliability and validity should also be ascertained. To this end, there is an extensive literature devoted to ways of training raters so as to minimize biases and to exploring the best rating formats and methodologies (see, e.g., Guion, 1998, chap. 12).

Our hypothetical study of the validity of manual dexterity test scores—meant to illustrate predictive validation procedures as simply as possible—contains several unrealistic features. For instance, in that example, the criterion of assembly line output could be assessed reliably and accurately by counting the number of widgets produced by the workers. Not all criteria are that simple or easy to assess. Success in many occupational endeavors, such as management, medical practice, teaching, and so forth, may be judged on the bases of criteria that differ in terms of how reliably they can be assessed, how much control a worker has with respect to them, and the value the organization places on them. For example, the success of a manager may be gauged in terms of (a) worker productivity and (b) worker satisfaction, among other things. The skills and personal characteristics that make managers successful with regard to (a) are not necessarily the same as those leading to success in (b), and in some situations these two criteria may even conflict with one another. Moreover, each of these criteria can be assessed by various methods. Productivity may be gauged by the quantity or the quality of production, or both; workers' satisfaction may be measured through ratings of supervisors, by the amount of personnel turnover in a unit, and so forth. Test scores that can predict one facet of the criterion may have no correlation or may even be negatively correlated with those that predict another.

Using Multiple Predictors

The traditional way of dealing with the prediction of complex criteria, such as job performance, has been to use a test battery. In this context, the term *battery* refers to a combination of predictors especially selected to predict one or more criteria. This meaning contrasts with the use of the term in clinical or counseling settings, where a battery usually refers to any group of tests that are administered to an individual in the process of psychological assessment. The scores on the separate predictors in a test battery can be combined in a variety of ways, depending on the requirements of the selection or classification problem. *Multiple regression techniques,* for instance, combine the scores on each test in the battery by inserting them into a linear regression equation that includes a numerical weight for each test score in the battery. *Multiple regression equations* are extensions of the simple linear regression method presented in Table 5.5, but they involve multiple predictors instead of a single one. The weight for each predictor is directly proportional to its correlation with the criterion and inversely proportional to its correlation with the other predictors in the battery, so that test scores with the highest validity and least amount of overlap with other scores are weighted most heavily. A multiple correlation coefficient (R) can then be computed to represent the correlation between the optimally weighted combination of test scores and the criterion. An alternative procedure for combining the scores in a test battery is through *profile analysis.* This method involves establishing a cutoff score for each predictor—based on its relation to the criterion—and results in the rejection of all applicants whose scores fall below the minimum on any of the tests or, possibly, on only those that assess skills that are considered critical for performing successfully on the criterion.

Each of the two methods just described has some disadvantages. Multiple regression equations allow deficiencies in one or more predictors to be compensated for by superior performance in other predictors. The particular weighting of predictors in these equations must also be checked on samples that are independent from the ones used to derive the equations, to see if the multiple correlation (R) holds up. Replication of predictor-criterion relationships on separate samples—which is a process known as *cross-validation*—is needed because any correlation coefficient, regardless of its magnitude, is to some extent dependent on sample-specific error. Some reduction in the magnitude of the original R, or *shrinkage*, is expected upon cross-validation. To the extent that shrinkage is negligible, the original weights may be considered stable enough to be applied without further work.

One of the major disadvantages of using the method of profile analysis, along with cutoff scores, is that this method typically fails to take into account the possible unreliability of scores (see Quantifying Error in Test Scores: The Standard Error of Measurement, in Chapter 4). Another difficulty stems from the fact that having multiple cutoff scores may result in rejecting too many candidates, especially those candidates from disadvantaged backgrounds who may score below the cutoff on one or more of the ability tests but might be able to overcome those deficiencies by virtue of training or a strong motivation to succeed. In general, the use of cutoff scores is justified only in situations when a deficit in a specific skill would have serious and deleterious consequences for job performance. One possible solution, when this is the case, is to select on the basis of cutoff scores only for tests that assess the skills that are critical to the job and to use a regression equation for the other predictors in the battery.

The Problem of Restricted Range in the Validation Samples

As mentioned earlier, another unrealistic feature of the hypothetical validation study involving manual dexterity test scores presented earlier in this chapter is that it involved a heterogeneous sample of ten applicants for whom criterion measures did not yet exist at the time of testing. Most predictive validity studies do not proceed in this manner. Instead, they use samples of individuals for whom criterion data are already available, such as employees or students who have already entered the jobs or educational pursuits for which the test under validation will be used. In other words, most of these studies use concurrent validation strategies to develop evidence of predictive validity. The kind of individuals for whom criterion measures are already available differ from those on whom the test will eventually be used in that they have already been selected for employment or admission into a program of study *and* have remained on the job or in school without being fired or dropping out. Because of this, we can almost always assume that their scores on the predictor tests undergoing validation, and on the criterion measures as well, will have a narrower range than would be the case with an unselected sample of applicants. It may be recalled from Chapter 2 that the effect of a restriction in the range of either one of the variables is to reduce the size of the correlation coefficients. Thus, as a consequence of range restriction, the correlations between test scores and criteria (i.e., the validity coefficients) resulting from these retrospective validation studies are usually smaller than would be the case if the samples were drawn from a more heterogeneous population, such as *all* those who apply for the jobs or academic programs in question.

Validity Generalization

The magnitude of the predictive validity indexes obtained for test scores depends on four basic elements: (a) the composition of the validation samples in terms of size and variability; (b) the nature and complexity of the criterion to be predicted; (c) the characteristics of the test itself; and (d) the interactions among all of these. Since each of these four factors can alter the results of validation studies, test users need to consider them carefully before assuming that the published evidence of test score validity derived from a single study will be applicable for their purposes and for their populations of test takers.

With regard to the composition of validation samples, we have already discussed the problems attendant to criterion measures and range restriction. Small sample size frequently is also a problem. Most employers do not have large numbers of employees in the same job category, and validation research findings based on small samples are more prone to sample-specific error than those based on large samples. The bivariate data set for ten job applicants in our hypothetical example of predictive validity yielded an unrealistically large validity coefficient of .87. Although it is possible to obtain sizable correlations when individuals who participate in validation studies are not screened and criteria are narrowly construed, as in the example, the fact remains that local validation studies conducted using small samples, with a restricted range of scores and unreliable criteria, typically yield low and unstable estimates of the correlation between the predictor and criterion.

Moderator Variables

An additional issue related to the make-up of samples in predictive validation studies concerns the possible role of moderator variables. A *moderator variable* is any characteristic of a subgroup of persons in a sample that influences the degree of correlation between two other variables. In theory, almost any demographic characteristic (e.g., sex, ethnicity, level of education, social class, geographic location, etc.) or psychological trait (interests, motivation, anxiety level, etc.) can act as a moderator variable in predictive validity studies and produce an interaction effect that either lowers or raises the predictor-criterion correlation. In order to pursue this possibility it is necessary to conduct separate validation studies or divide the validation samples into subgroups that differ on the variable that is presumed to moderate validity coefficients.

Considerable differences, in favor of Whites and Asians compared to Blacks or Hispanics, have consistently been found in the average scores on tests of academic abilities obtained by people from different racial or ethnic groups. These differences have engendered the suspicion that race or ethnicity may moderate the predictive validity of selection tests. As a result, many studies have conducted separate analyses of the magnitude of the predictor-criterion correlation and regression coefficients for Whites, Blacks, Hispanics, and members of other racial or ethnic minorities. The purpose of such studies is to ascertain whether test scores have comparable validity for different groups and predict equally well for all, or whether test scores have different validities for different groups and are therefore biased. In this context, the term *bias* is used to indicate any systematic difference in the relationship between predictors and criteria for people belonging to different groups. Systematic differences can manifest themselves in two ways, namely, differential validity and differential prediction.

Differential validity, in the context of test bias, refers to differences in the size of the correlations obtained between predictors and criteria for members of different groups. Differences in the magnitude of validity coefficients suggest that the test scores predict more accurately for members of the group with the larger coefficient. Graphic evidence of differential validity is seen when the slopes of the regression lines for the two groups in question are different; the slope of the regression line is steeper for the group with the higher validity coefficient. Because of this, the problem of differential validity is also referred to as *slope bias* (see Table 5.5 and Fig. 5.1).

Differential prediction, on the other hand, occurs when test scores underpredict or overpredict the criterion performance of one group compared to the other. This problem is labeled *intercept bias,* because when a predictor overpredicts or underpredicts criterion performance for a group, the Y intercept, or point of origin of that group's regression line on the Y axis, is different than for the other groups. With regard to the problems of differential validity and differential prediction for test scores, several outcomes are possible, though not equally likely. Test scores may show (a) no bias with respect to different groups, (b) both differential validity and differential prediction, (c) differential validity without differential prediction, or (d) differential prediction without differential validity. In general, the search for evidence that race acts as a moderator variable resulting in differential validity and differential prediction for members of racial minorities based on ability test scores has not been very fruitful. In fact, studies that have investigated differences across ethnic groups in the accuracy of predictions of criterion performance indicate that tests often tend to *overpredict* the performance of Blacks and Hispanics, compared to Whites and Asians. On the other hand, some tests—especially those used in educational admission decisions—sometimes underpredict the performance of women, albeit to a smaller extent than they overpredict the performance of some racial or ethnic minority groups (see, e.g., Young, 2001; Zwick, 2002, chaps. 5 & 6).

Naturally, the reasons why some test scores generally overpredict criterion performance—typically in the form of grade point averages—for members of certain racial or ethnic minority groups and often underpredict the performance of women have been the subject of much conjecture and debate. The unreliability, and possible bias, of the criterion of grades is frequently cited as a possible explanation for the overprediction of the academic performance of racial or ethnic minorities, as are disparities in their upbringing or in the quality of their prior educational experiences. A novel explanation revolves around the notion of *stereotype threat,* which refers to the deleterious effects that fear of confirming negative racial stereotypes seems to have on the test performance of some minority group members (Steele, 1997). As far as the underprediction of the college performance of women, the most frequently cited conjectures center on the fact that, as opposed to men, women as a group (a) tend to choose courses that are less stringently graded or (b) are more serious about their studies. Although it may be true that these and other variables related to ethnic and gender status influence the test scores and criterion performance of different groups, as well as the correlations between them, it is not always possible to establish precisely what these factors are. Moreover, it appears that the extent of differential prediction of the college performance for racial or ethnic minority groups and women has been decreasing over the past quarter century (Young, 2001). Furthermore, whatever these variables are, they obviously do not apply to all members of those groups—which are themselves quite heterogeneous—in the same fashion. Nevertheless, the possibility of differential validity for members of different ethnic groups, sex groups, non-native English speakers, and other traditionally disadvantaged categories of individuals always needs to be investigated to ascertain that test scores used in high-stakes decisions are fair to all.

One possible solution to the problem of differential prediction of test scores would be to use different regression equations, and different cutoff scores, for selection of individuals from different ethnic groups and genders. In the case of test scores that overpredict the performance of Blacks and Hispanics, for instance, this would mean requiring higher cutoff scores for members of those minorities than for Whites and Asians. However, this obviously runs counter to the goals of extending opportunity to groups through affirmative action and of increasing diversity in higher education and in the workplace. Another proposed solution, implemented in the 1980s with the General Aptitude Test Battery (GATB) developed by the United States Employment Service (USES), is to use subgroup norms to ensure comparable rates of employment referrals for Blacks, Hispanics, and Whites. This practice generated so much opposition that it led to the passage of the Civil Rights Act of 1991 (P.L. 101-336), which banned any kind of score adjustment based on race, color, sex, religion, or national origin. In light of these obstacles, most of the work in the area of fairness in testing is now concentrated on (a) identifying factors that may be contributing to differential prediction across gender and ethnic groups (see, e.g., Steele, 1997; Willingham, Pollack, & Lewis, 2000) and (b) analyzing how tests items function for different subgroups, while tests are under construction, to make sure that those which function differently for different subgroups are not included (see Chapter 6).

Meta-analyses

Since the late 1970s, a good deal of clarity and renewed enthusiasm has been brought to bear on the somewhat pessimistic outlook stemming from earlier research on the validity of selection test scores. This change is largely due to the use of meta-analyses that allow investigators to collate data from many different studies—especially in areas where conflicting findings abound—and reach conclusions that are more definitive than those resulting from the traditional ways of conducting literature reviews. In contrast to the qualitative nature of traditional literature reviews, *meta-analyses*

> **DON'T FORGET**
> ....
> - Validity generalization (VG) studies have now been in use for over a quarter century. They are bound to increase in number and in the impact they have on psychometric theory and practice.
> - Readers who want to pursue the topic of VG in greater depth might wish to consult *Validity Generalization: A Critical Review*, a volume edited by Murphy, Fleishman, and Cleveland (2003).

rely on a series of quantitative procedures that provide for the synthesis and integration of the results obtained from the research literature on a given subject. These techniques, which had been used in other scientific fields for some time, were introduced into psychometric research by Schmidt and Hunter (1977) as a way to approach the problem of validity generalization. In the past couple of decades, meta-analytic techniques have actually demonstrated that the predictive validity of test scores is not as situationally specific as previously thought and have become an important method for clarifying conflicting findings in other portions of the psychological literature (Hunter & Schmidt, 1990, 1996).

Widespread interest in, and use of, meta-analyses has been stimulated by the realization that many conflicting findings in psychological research—including those of validation studies—are attributable to the imperfections of individual studies. When the influence of artifacts such as sampling error, measurement error, range restriction, and unjustified dichotomization of variables are removed through statistical corrections, a much clearer picture emerges. Concomitantly, there has been a growing recognition that hypothesis testing in psychological studies has overemphasized *statistical significance levels* that stress the avoidance of *Type I errors* (i.e., incorrectly rejecting the null hypothesis of no difference when it is true) while neglecting the possibility of *Type II errors* (i.e., incorrectly accepting the null hypothesis when it is false). Since the relation between Type I and Type II errors is inverse, the emphasis on avoiding Type I increases the likelihood of Type II errors. As a consequence, an enormous number of research results that do not reach the desired levels of statistical significance (e.g., .05 or .01), but nevertheless can contribute valuable information, have been either ignored or left out of the literature. Rapid Reference 5.10 lists some references that provide additional information on the disadvantages and advantages of null hypothesis significance tests. At any rate, these discussions have led to what most investigators see as a salutary change in the way that research findings are reported. Instead of merely stating the significance levels or probability of results, it is now considered necessary to include indexes of the *effect sizes,* or the strength of the relationships found by a research study, along with confidence intervals for the effect sizes and for all estimates of parameters resulting from an investigation (APA, 2001).

Although the methodology of meta-analyses is still evolving, it has already made substantial contributions to the evidence of the predictive validity of test scores and non-test procedures—such as employment interviews and biographical data inventories—that are used in personnel selection (Hartigan & Wigdor, 1989; Schmidt & Hunter, 1998; Schmidt et al., 1993). In addition, meta-analyses have helped to clarify the research literature and to further the development of theories in several areas of industrial-organizational psychology—such as the re-

≡ Rapid Reference 5.10

Sources of Information on the Pros and Cons of Significance Tests

A debate about the merits and drawbacks inherent in the use of null hypothesis tests of statistical significance for making inferences in social science research has been going on for decades among statisticians and methodologists. Some of them have been so convinced that these tests have a detrimental effect on the scientific enterprise that they have suggested a ban of significance testing in research reports. Although no such ban has been instituted, it is now common for psychological journals, as well as journals in most other related disciplines, to require effect-size estimates whenever probability (p) values are reported, along with confidence intervals for effect sizes, correlation coefficients, and other estimates of population parameters. Additional information about the issues involved in this debate can be found in the following sources:

- Abelson, R. P. (1997). On the surprising longevity of flogged horses: Why there is a case for the significance test. *Psychological Science, 8,* 12–15.
- Cohen, J. (1994). The earth is round (p < .05). *American Psychologist, 49,* 997–1003.
- Thompson, B. (2002). What future quantitative social science research could look like: Confidence intervals for effect sizes. *Educational Researcher, 31,* 25–32.
- Wilkinson, L., & APA Task Force on Statistical Inference. (1999). Statistical methods in psychology journals: Guidelines and explanations. *American Psychologist, 54,* 594–604.

lation between job satisfaction and job performance—as well as in various other fields (see, e.g., Hunter & Schmidt, 1996; Kirsch & Sapirstein, 1998; Rosenthal & DiMatteo, 2001). An example from the area of admissions testing in higher education will illustrate the potential inherent in meta-analytic research.

An educational case in point. Studies of the validity of Graduate Record Examination (GRE) scores as predictors of performance in graduate school programs have a long history—dating back to the 1940s—that has been plagued by inconsistent findings. Whereas some investigations (e.g., Briel, O'Neill, & Scheuneman, 1993; Broadus & Elmore, 1983) found the GRE General and Subject tests to be fairly valid predictors of graduate school performance, many others—including some limited meta-analytic studies—concluded that the relationship between GRE scores and various indexes of success in graduate school was less than adequate (e.g., Goldberg & Alliger, 1992; Marston, 1971; Morrison & Morrison, 1995; Sternberg & Williams, 1997). Many GRE validity studies yielded coefficients ranging from small negative correlations to positive correlations in the low .20s for the Verbal and Quantitative scores of the GRE, and somewhat higher coefficients for the GRE Subject test scores. Although some of these findings were criticized on the basis of methodological artifacts such as highly restricted ranges in both GRE scores and criterion measures, as well as unreliability of criteria, the general tenor of the literature on the validity of GRE scores did not seem to provide substantial evidence to support their use in graduate school admission decisions (see, e.g., Kuncel, Campbell, & Ones, 1998).

Against this background, Kuncel, Hezlett, and Ones (2001) recently conducted a meticulous and comprehensive meta-analysis of the GRE data from 1,753 independent samples comprising a total of 82,659 graduate students. This study systematically addressed theoretical, statistical, and methodological aspects of the literature on the predictive validity of GRE scores. Kuncel and his colleagues examined the relationships between five predictors—GRE Verbal (GRE-V), Quantitative (GRE-Q), Analytical (GRE-A), and Subject test scores as well as undergraduate grade point average (UGPA)—and eight different criteria of graduate school success, including first-year GPA and graduate GPA (GGPA), comprehensive examination scores, faculty ratings, degree attainment, and numerical indexes related to research productivity. They conducted separate analyses for the total sample and for subsamples representing students in the areas of humanities, social sciences, life sciences, and math-physical sciences, as well as for non-native English speakers and for students older than the traditional graduate school age. Among the many methodological refinements Kuncel and colleagues employed in their analyses were corrections for range restriction and for changes in the variability of distributions of both predictor and criterion variables as well as for the unreliability of criterion measures. In addition, these investigators addressed a number of potential pitfalls inherent in meta-analyses.

Kuncel and his colleagues (2001) report their major results in terms of average observed correlations, along with their standard deviations, weighted for sample size. They also report estimated operational validities with their standard deviations and 90% confidence intervals. Those findings indicate that the four GRE measures (GRE-V, GRE-Q, GRE-A, and GRE Subject tests) are reasonably good predictors of most of the criteria employed for the total sample as well as for the subsamples. In fact, in most cases GRE scores seem to be better predictors than UGPA. The GRE Subject test scores turned out to be the best single predictors of graduate GPA across all disciplines, with estimated operational validities ranging from .40 to .49. In contrast, the scores on the general tests (GRE-V, GRE-Q, and GRE-A)—while correlating substantially with those of the Subject tests—had operational validity coefficients ranging between .27 and .48. Kuncel and colleagues conclude that although the GRE general test scores contribute only a small increment in validity when added to the Subject test scores, they can still be of value, especially for students whose undergraduate degrees are in areas other than the ones in which they are applying for admission.

In short, Kuncel and colleagues' (2001) meta-analysis clearly suggests (a) that much of the inconsistency in previous GRE validation studies was the result of range restriction and sampling error in those studies and (b) that GRE scores deserve a role in the process of graduate school admissions. However, these authors did not investigate the issue of differential prediction for women and members of racial or ethnic minorities, and they do concede that there is still much room for improving the validity of the graduate school admissions process. With regard to the latter point, the following notions should be kept in mind:

- The purpose of GRE scores and most other predictors used in selection decisions is not to estimate the *exact* criterion standing of applicants but rather to determine whether applicants can achieve the necessary level of success. If criterion scores had to be predicted exactly, the margin of error (SE_{est}) for coefficients in the .30s and .40s would indeed be considerable.

- Performance on most criteria, including graduate school success, is determined by multiple factors, including attitudinal and emotional characteristics and behavioral habits, as well as creative and practical talents that are not measured by the GRE or by other cognitive tests ordinarily used as predictors.

- Most other selection decisions, including graduate school admissions, are rarely, if ever, made solely on the basis of a single predictor. Therefore, the crucial issue with regard to selection tests concerns their utility. This means that the question that has to be asked is whether the use of test scores as part of a decision-making process increases the number of valid decisions over and above what it would be with the use of the non-test predictors, such as GPAs. In most situations, including admissions decisions in higher education, the data suggest that test scores do contribute to predictive

DON'T FORGET

An abundance of information regarding the predictive validity of tests used in higher education, including many of the issues related to differential prediction for various subgroups, can be found on the Internet. See, especially, the following sites:

- ACT (http://www.act.org)
- The College Board (http://www.college.board.com)
- Educational Testing Service (ETS; http://www.ets.org)

efficiency in decision-making (see, e.g., Hartigan & Wigdor, 1989; Ko-brin, Camara, & Milewski, 2002; Kuncel, Hezlett, & Ones, 2001).

Beyond Selection: Using Test Scores for Other Types of Decisions

Up to this point the discussion of criterion-related validation procedures has cen-tered primarily on the use of tests for selection or screening made on the bases of either concurrent or predictive test score validity. *Selection* decisions are those that require a choice between two alternatives. In employment and educational set-tings, the usual alternatives are whether to accept or reject an applicant; in clini-cal and forensic settings, selection decisions usually involve a determination of whether a particular syndrome or condition is present or absent. The term *screen-ing* refers to a preliminary step of a selection process usually undertaken to sepa-rate individuals who merit or require more extensive evaluation from those who do not. For example, many clinics periodically use a simple and short question-naire to screen for disorders such as depression or anxiety in the general popula-tion; employers may screen applicants with a brief instrument in order to limit the pool of applicants to those who meet the minimal requirements for a job.

Psychological test scores are also used for making placement and classification decisions, both of which involve more than two options. Of these two, *placement* decisions are simpler. They involve assigning individuals to separate categories or treatments on the basis of a single score, or of a composite score computed from a single regression equation, with reference to a single criterion. Although place-ment decisions do not involve the option of rejecting individuals who do not meet a certain level of performance on a test or predictor, they are not substan-tially different from selection decisions in terms of the evidence they require, which is a demonstrable relationship between one or more predictors and a cri-terion. Scores on a reading test, for instance, may be used to place students in in-structional groups suitable to their levels of reading skills. Similarly, scores on a depression scale might be used to classify psychiatric patients in terms of the severity of their depressive symptoms to help determine appropriate types and levels of therapeutic intervention.

Classification decisions, on the other hand, are a good deal more complicated. In classification—as in placement—nobody is rejected, but individuals must be *differentially* assigned to distinct categories or treatments on the bases of multiple criteria. This means that multiple predictors are required and their relationships with each criterion have to be determined independently, through separate re-gression equations. The most appropriate tool for classification decisions is a bat-tery of tests or predictors whose results are validated against the various criteria to be predicted and then combined in equations that reflect their relative weights for the prediction of each criterion.

Classification decisions are required in employment, educational, counseling, and clinical settings. In the realm of employment, including military or industrial settings, these decisions are necessary when the aptitudes of an available personnel pool have to be evaluated in order to assign individuals to the jobs or training programs in which they are most likely to function effectively. Vocational counseling of individuals wanting to decide on a program of study or career choice also calls for classifications decisions. In clinical settings, classification decisions must be made in cases that require differential diagnosis. A typical example would be the need to establish whether an older patient who shows symptoms of depression and memory problems may be suffering from a depressive disorder that affects memory and concentration, from an incipient dementing process that is causing the depression, or from a combination of the two.

Batteries of tests that are used for classification decisions must be evaluated on evidence of differential validity. Within this context, the term *differential validity* means that a battery should be able to predict, or establish, differences among two or more criteria. In a two-criterion classification problem an ideal battery would consist of predictors that correlate highly with one criterion and not at all, or negatively, with the other. In the problem of differential diagnosis of depression versus dementia, for instance, one might look for differences in the temporal sequencing of symptoms of depression and cognitive impairment or for differences in relative levels of performance on various types of memory tests.

When the classification situation involves predictions against more than two criteria, such as assigning personnel to any one of several possible jobs or training programs, the problem of establishing validity evidence becomes even more complex. In this kind of condition, a predictor that correlates equally well with all of the criteria involved in the decision—such as a test of general intelligence with respect to most job performance criteria—is of relatively little use. One possible way of handling classification problems of this type is through the use of multiple discriminant function analyses. *Discriminant functions* involve the application of weighted combinations of scores on the predictors—derived by means of regression analyses—to determine how closely an individual's profile of scores matches the profiles of individuals in different occupational groups, different specialties, or different psychiatric categories. Although discriminant functions are useful in certain instances (e.g., when criteria consist simply of membership in one group versus another or when there is a nonlinear relationship between a criterion and one or more of the predictors), they fall short in terms of the requirements of many situations because they do not allow for the prediction of level of success in a specific field. For an example of the application of discriminant function analysis in the differentiation of WAIS-R profiles of nonlitigating head-injured patients from those of subjects instructed to feign head trauma, see Mittenberg, Theroux-Fichera, Zielinski, and Heilbronner (1995).

Another traditional strategy that can be used for both selection and classification problems is *synthetic validation* (Balma, 1959). This technique essentially relies on detailed job analyses that identify specific job components and their relative weights in different jobs. Based on such analyses, previously established regression coefficients for test scores that predict those separate job elements can be combined into a new, synthetic battery that will predict performance on the jobs in question. Statistical procedures associated with this method were developed by Primoff (1959; Primoff & Eyde, 1988) and have been expanded by others since then. However, in order to be useful in classification decisions, synthetic validation strategies must involve predictors that show good discriminant validity, unless the criterion components themselves are correlated substantially (Guion, 1998, pp. 354–355).

Additional Perspectives on Criterion-Related Validation

Several of the methodological advances discussed earlier in this chapter, such as structural equation modeling and meta-analytic validity generalization studies, have been brought to bear on recent research on the problems of criterion-related validation. At the same time, the availability of these increasingly sophisticated statistical tools has focused attention on the conceptualization of both predictors and performance criteria, as well as their interrelationships (see, e.g., J. P. Campbell, 1990). One of the most significant recent developments, in terms of predictors, is the recognition that the inclusion of factors related to personality dimensions—in addition to those related to abilities—can increase the validity of instruments used to predict performance in a number of arenas (see, e.g., Lubinski & Dawis, 1992). With regard to the criterion problem, the multifaceted nature of performance in most jobs and educational endeavors is now widely acknowledged and increasingly scrutinized. This requires analyzing the various elements that make for success, assessing their relative value, recognizing which ones are under the control of the individual, developing methods to evaluate each element separately, and then combining them into a total measure of performance that takes into account all of these factors and their relative weights.

A Model Program of Criterion-Related Validation

An outstanding example of the application of many innovations in validation research methods can be found in the work that John P. Campbell and his colleagues (J. P. Campbell, 1990, 1994; J. P. Campbell & Knapp, 2001) have conducted over the past two decades, in conjunction with a comprehensive effort to evaluate and improve the U.S. Army's procedures for personnel selection and classification, known as Project A. A complete account of this work, which may possibly be the largest single project in the history of personnel research, is not feasible in this context. However, some of its highlights are presented here to give readers an idea of its scope and significance.

Project A

Using an extensive database of more than 50,000 people, the Project A investigators selected 21 military occupational specialties (MOSs), out of a total of more than 200 Army entry-level jobs, on which to conduct both concurrent and longitudinal predictive validation studies. The predictors studied included the ten subtests of the Armed Services Vocational Aptitude Battery (ASVAB) listed in Rapid Reference 5.11. Various composite scores consisting of different subtest combi-

≡ Rapid Reference 5.11

....

Armed Services Vocational Aptitude Battery (ASVAB)

The ASVAB is administered as a computerized adaptive test (CAT-ASVAB) at military entrance processing stations and as a paper-and-pencil test at mobile test sites. Individuals who take the ASVAB have already been pretested with shorter screening instruments administered by recruiters. The ten subtests that make up the ASVAB, used by all the U.S. Armed Forces for selection and classification of personnel, are the following:

- Arithmetic Reasoning
- Numerical Operations
- Paragraph Comprehension
- Word Knowledge
- Coding Speed
- General Science
- Mathematics Knowledge
- Electronics Information
- Mechanical Comprehension
- Automotive-Shop Information

The first four of these subtests make up the Armed Forces Qualification Test (AFQT) composite, which, along with high school graduation status, is used to determine eligibility for enlistment. The ASVAB subtests are also combined into ten different aptitude composite scores that are used as predictors of success at the Army school training programs (J. P. Campbell & Knapp, 2001, pp. 14–18).

nations from the ASVAB have traditionally been used for selection and classification of individuals who apply for service in the Armed Forces. In addition, several new instruments—including tests of psychomotor and spatial abilities as well as personality and interest measures—were also included in the validation work.

Project A investigators carried out extensive job analyses and paid special attention to the standardization of measures of job proficiency for each of the MOSs. Exploratory and confirmatory factor analyses, as well as other statistical techniques, were employed in performance modeling studies that led to the specification of the factor scores that were used as criteria at three different career stages: end of training performance, first-tour job performance, and second-tour job performance. Exploration of validity evidence at various career stages was a significant aspect of this research because, in addition to developing a test battery capable of differential prediction, another important goal of the personnel management task in the All Volunteer Armed Forces is to minimize attrition.

The actual validation analyses performed through the duration of Project A included (a) correlations between each predictor and performance criteria; (b) comparisons of the incremental validity provided by the experimental measures with respect to each criterion, over and above the predictive power of the previously available ASVAB scores; (c) development and comparison of various optimal equations for maximum validity in the longitudinal prediction of first-tour performance; and (d) analyses of the validity of alternative equations using different combinations of test data and previous performance for the prediction of second-tour performance. Validity generalization and synthetic validation methods were used to investigate the efficiency of various combinations of predictors for the 21 MOSs originally selected for analysis as well as for many other MOSs and clusters of occupations. Additional studies included an evaluation of the utility and gains achieved through alternative classification strategies and conditions.

Among the many useful findings of Project A, one of the most significant has been the corroboration of the potential value of several of the new measures that were studied, including those related to personality dimensions, as well as some new tests of psychomotor and spatial abilities. These additional predictors are now at various preliminary stages of implementation and are being explored further. According to the principal Project A investigators, these measures are not yet fully operational due to obstacles posed by the many parties involved in the Army selection and classification system as well as by organizational inertia (J. P. Campbell & Knapp, 2001, pp. 570–574). Nevertheless, Project A and the subsequent investigations it has spawned have already contributed a number of substantive and methodological advances that are sure to improve the caliber of val-

DON'T FORGET

The judgment concerning the validity of test scores is relative. When the evidence that has accumulated concerning the validity of scores produced by a test is considered in the abstract, it may or may not be deemed sufficient for the test's intended purpose.

However, when any specific score or set of scores from an individual or group is considered, it must be understood that the scores may have been affected by factors uniquely pertinent to the test takers, the examiner, the context in which testing takes place, and the interaction between these factors. Thus, the testing situation must always be taken into account when test scores are interpreted.

In addition, making inferences on the bases of test scores requires information about their frames of reference and their reliability, as well as validity evidence from all pertinent sources.

idation research for selection and classification, both in the military and in many other contexts, and thus will help in the overarching goal of maximizing the utilization of human talents.

ADDITIONAL ASPECTS OF VALIDITY:
UTILITY AND CONSEQUENCES

There are two significant aspects concerning the use of test scores that are closely connected to their validity but are not necessarily of its essence, namely, their utility and the consequences attendant to their uses. The complexity of these topics prevents an extended discussion of them within the scope of this volume. However, their crucial importance to the psychological testing enterprise warrants their introduction at this point, to be followed by a more extensive treatment in Chapter 7.

Evaluating the Utility of Testing

The *utility* of tests, and test scores, refers to the benefits they bring to decision-making. Utility is contingent on the extent to which the use of tests can increase the rate of accuracy of the inferences and decisions we wish to make—over and above what it would be if we used other available tools. Typically, utility is assessed in economic terms, such as the cost-benefit ratios involved in using tests versus non-test data. Given that test use always takes place within a context, the analysis of its costs and benefits necessarily must take into account additional data pertinent to each particular situation in which the use of tests is contemplated. Depending on the context, these data include matters such as the probabilities and risks involved in making false positive and false negative determinations, the availability of alternative tools—and their relative efficiency compared to the tests—as well as the relative ease or difficulty of the determinations that need to be made. This aspect of test use is part of the much larger topic of decision theory, which applies not only to psychometrics, in particular, and psychology, in general, but also to such diverse fields as medicine, economics, jurisprudence, military science, and gaming, as well as any other human endeavor in which strategic planning is required. For a sample of the numerous contributions psychometric experts have made to decision theory over the past few decades, see Boudreau (1991), Brogden (1946), Brown and Ghiselli (1953), Buchwald (1965), Cronbach and Gleser (1965), Hunter and Schmidt (1981), Schmidt, Hunter, McKenzie, & Muldrow (1979) and Taylor and Russell (1939). An excellent discussion of the statistical aspects of decision theory within the context of enhancing the accuracy and utility of diagnostic decisions is available in a recent report by Swets, Dawes, and Monahan (2000).

Assessing the Consequences of Test Use

The individual and social consequences of test use, which can be either positive or negative, have to be assessed in terms of their value implications. Some theorists, notably Messick (1989, 1995), have argued that validity judgments are actually value judgments. Messick has proposed the inclusion of *consequential* aspects of the use and interpretation of test scores—that is, the evaluation of their intended and unintended social consequences—within the notion of validity in its most comprehensive sense. In criticizing Messick's proposal some have labeled it "consequential validity," a term that Messick himself never used. Be that as it may, this particular aspect of Messick's immense contributions to psychometric theory and practice has not been widely adopted by the testing profession. Most would argue that while the consequential aspects of test use are of paramount importance, and should be investigated prior to implementation and documented afterward, they lie within the realms of professional ethics, moral values, and political considerations rather than of validity determination as such (Cole & Moss, 1989; Lees-Haley, 1996; Linn, 1998).

The *Ethical Principles of Psychologists and Code of Conduct* (APA, 2002), for instance, enjoins all psychologists—including those who use tests and other assessment tools—to take into account the possible ramifications of their work in order to maximize benefits and prevent or minimize harm to others. Users of tests and assessment tools, specifically, are bound to guard against misinterpretations and misuses and to obtain the consent of test takers, prior to testing, as to the purposes of testing, the manner in which scores will be used, the persons to whom scores will be released, and other such matters. Similar constraints apply to the work of test authors and developers, test publishers, and test reviewers, as well as other professionals involved in the testing enterprise (e.g., Society for Industrial and Organizational Psychology [SIOP], 2003). To add to the already complex notion of test score validation the additional facet of evaluating the ramifications of test use in terms of broader social concerns—such as balancing moral principles like justice and fairness—would place an undue burden, which belongs to society as a whole, on the testing profession.

An example of how the ethical principles and practices in testing may be applied to the realm of education can be found in a resource guide for educators and policymakers that presents both the professional standards and the legal principles pertinent to the use of tests in making high-stakes educational decisions for students (U.S. Department of Education, Office for Civil Rights, 2000). Similar sets of guidelines for the use of tests in other specialty fields will be discussed in Chapter 7 (e.g., SIOP, 2003).

CONCLUDING COMMENTS

Rapid Reference 5.12 outlines how various sources of evidence and validation strategies can be brought to bear in the interpretation of scores from a single test, depending on the purposes for which the test is used. In most cases, to the extent that the proposed interpretation of the scores on a test moves away from the original purpose for which the test was developed, the lines of evidence for alternative uses and interpretations will become less direct. For instance, the test used as an example in Rapid Reference 5.12 was a final exam in a Calculus I course; thus, we can infer that its original purpose was to determine whether test takers had mastered enough of the content in that course to achieve a passing grade. As the interpretation of the scores on this test is extended to determining readiness for Calculus II, predicting success as a mathematics major, or using test scores as a proxy for mathematical ability in an investigation of correlates of personality type, the link between the validation evidence and the intended interpretation becomes more and more tenuous. This does not mean that the final exam in Calculus I should not be used for purposes other than the original one, but it does suggest that additional evidence will be required for those other purposes.

In the present chapter we have discussed the evidence for validity of test scores from the point of view of the test as whole. In the next, we turn to a more minute analysis of test data from the perspective of the behavior sample units that make up test scores, namely, test items.

☰ Rapid Reference 5.12

Validation Strategies in Relation to Test Score Interpretation

Test From Which Scores Are To Be Interpreted	Proposed Purpose of Test Score Interpretation	Type of Validation Strategy Desired	Possible Sources of Evidence
Final exam in a Calculus I course	Determine whether students pass course in Calculus I	Content	Relevance and representativeness of test content in relation to the subject matter covered in Calculus I course
	Determine whether students are ready for Calculus II	Criterion-related, concurrent type	High positive correlation between Calculus I test scores and grades in Calculus II course
	Predict whether students can successfully complete a major in mathematics	Criterion-related, predictive type	High positive correlation between Calculus I test scores and completion of math major
	Investigate the relationship between mathematical ability and personality type	Convergence	Support for the hypothesis that introverted students will score higher than extroverted students on the Calculus I test

TEST YOURSELF

1. **Validity is the degree to which**
   (a) a test measures what it purports to measure.
   (b) evidence supports inferences from test scores.
   (c) test scores are consistent across situations.

2. **In recent decades the various forms of validity evidence have been subsumed within the notion of _____ validity.**
   (a) content
   (b) concurrent
   (c) predictive
   (d) construct

3. **Nomothetic span refers to**
   (a) a network of relationships between measures.
   (b) the decomposition of tasks.
   (c) identifying differences among test takers.
   (d) the scope of the construct being measured.

4. **Evidence of validity that is based on test content and response processes is particularly applicable to**
   (a) interest inventories.
   (b) educational tests.
   (c) personality tests.

5. **Face validity refers primarily to**
   (a) the representativeness of test content.
   (b) evidence of validity from the psychometric perspective.
   (c) the superficial characteristics of a test.
   (d) the amount of empirical validation data accumulated for a test.

6. **In order to gather discriminant validity evidence, one would correlate the scores of tests that purport to assess _____ constructs.**
   (a) the same
   (b) similar, but not the same
   (c) different

7. **One of the most useful aspects of factor analysis, as applied to test validation research, is that the results of applying this technique can**
   (a) simplify the interpretation and reporting of test scores.
   (b) reveal the essential aspects of the constructs that tests are assessing.
   (c) readily be generalized across populations.

8. **Which of the following statements about criterion measures is *not* true?**
   - (a) Criterion measures can differ in terms of their reliability and validity.
   - (b) Different criterion measures do not always correlate with each other.
   - (c) Criterion measures may or may not generalize across different groups.
   - (d) The best criterion measures are usually available at the time of testing.

9. **Standard errors of estimate are used in order to gauge the**
   - (a) reliability of criteria.
   - (b) reliability of predictors.
   - (c) accuracy of obtained scores.
   - (d) accuracy with which criteria are predicted.

10. **From the standpoint of criterion-related validation procedures, which of the following types of decisions is the most complex?**
    - (a) Selection
    - (b) Placement
    - (c) Classification

Answers: 1. b; 2. d; 3. a; 4. b; 5. c; 6. c; 7. a; 8. d; 9. d; 10. c.

Six

ESSENTIAL TEST ITEM CONSIDERATIONS

Test items are the units that make up a test and the means through which samples of test takers' behavior are gathered. It follows that the overall quality of a test depends primarily on the quality of the items that make it up, although the number of items in a test, and their sequencing or position within the test, are also matters of fundamental importance. Just as tests are evaluated with regard to the extent to which they meet their intended purposes, individual items must be evaluated based on the extent to which they meet the purposes of the test as a whole. *Item analysis* is a general term that refers to all the techniques used to assess the characteristics of test items and evaluate their quality during the process of test development and test construction.

Item analysis involves both qualitative and quantitative procedures. *Qualitative item analysis* procedures rely on the judgments of reviewers concerning the substantive and stylistic characteristics of items as well as their accuracy and fairness. The major criteria used to evaluate items qualitatively are (a) appropriateness of item content and format to the purpose of the test and the populations for whom the test is designed, (b) clarity of expression, (c) grammatical correctness, and (d) adherence to some basic rules for writing items that have evolved over time. As discussed later in this chapter, item content is also carefully examined to identify and eliminate possible sources of bias or offensive portrayals of any specific subgroup of the population. Rapid Reference 6.1 lists books that provide information about the process of item development and practical guidelines for writing test items. *Quantitative item analysis* involves a variety of statistical procedures designed to ascertain the psychometric characteristics of items based on the responses obtained from the samples used in the process of test development. Most of the remainder of this chapter deals with the quantitative analysis of test items.

≡ *Rapid Reference 6.1*

Writing Test Items

For insight into the process of preparing items for ability tests, as well as explicit guidance on how to write them, readers may wish to consult one of the following sources:

- Bennett, R. E., & Ward, W. C. (Eds.). (1993). *Construction versus choice: Issues in constructed response, performance testing, and portfolio assessment.* Hillsdale, NJ: Erlbaum.
- Haladyna, T. M. (1997). *Writing test items to evaluate higher order thinking.* Boston: Allyn & Bacon.
- Haladyna, T. M. (1999). *Developing and validating multiple-choice test items* (2nd ed.). Mahwah, NJ: Erlbaum.

Although no comparable guidebooks exist for all of the vast range of approaches to the development of personality assessment instruments, some basic principles for preparing objective items can be gleaned from the following books:

- Aiken, L. R. (1996). *Rating scales and checklists: Evaluating behavior, personality and attitudes.* New York: Wiley.
- Aiken, L. R. (1997). *Questionnaires and inventories: Surveying opinions and assessing personality.* New York: Wiley.
- Fink, A. (2002). *How to ask survey questions* (2nd ed., Vol. 2). Thousand Oaks, CA: Sage. [This is one of the ten volumes in the *Survey Kit*, edited by Arlene Fink and published by Sage.]

THE CONTEXT OF ITEM ANALYSIS: TEST DEVELOPMENT

Fundamentally, the procedures involved in item generation, item selection, and item analysis pertain to the topic of test theory and design. As such, they are of critical importance to test authors and test developers. Test users need to be familiar with these procedures in order to understand the nature of the tasks involved in a test and evaluate the instruments they select. However, by the time a test is made available to test users, it is already a finished product. From the point of view of test users, once a test has been selected, its items are of interest—especially in the context of individual assessment—primarily as a means of observing and inspecting test takers' responses from the unique perspective of the specific situation and circumstances in which a test is administered. In individual assessment, the ways in which examinees respond to test tasks and their particular response patterns can provide additional information to supplement the process of test score interpretation. Test users, naturally, are also concerned with the practical features of test items. Chief among these features are the appropriateness of items for specific types of settings and examinees, the ease with which items can be administered and scored, the time involved in administering the items, and the amount of training required to master the procedures involved in the administration and scoring of items.

Item analysis procedures are implemented at various points during the process of test development, a process that includes several other steps. In order to provide a context for the discussion of item analysis, the steps involved in developing a test are described briefly in the next few paragraphs. More extensive treatments of the test development process are available in many sources (e.g., AERA, APA, & NCME, 1999, chap. 3; DeVellis, 2003; Ramsay & Reynolds, 2000; Robertson, 1992).

As Robertson (1992) makes clear, developing a standardized test entails a considerable investment of time and money and requires specialized professional expertise in psychometrics as well as in the particular area with which the test deals. Because of this, the development of tests intended for commercial distribution—as opposed to experimental measures to be used primarily for research purposes, classroom tests, or tests developed by employers for in-house use—is typically undertaken by test publishing firms that have the necessary financial resources and technical expertise. The impetus for new tests may stem either from the test publishers' own staffs or from independent test authors and investigators who submit their ideas to publishers.

The decision to develop a test usually is made when the prospective test developer realizes either that no test exists for a particular purpose or that the existing tests for a certain purpose are not adequate for one reason or another. Marketing considerations are also central to the decision-making process in commercial test publishing. At any rate, as the decision to develop a test is made, and its purpose and rationale are carefully articulated in terms of the sorts of inferences to be drawn from test scores, the test developer must also make a plan for the test.

Planning a test entails specifying (a) the constructs or knowledge domains that the test will assess, (b) the type of population with which the test will be used, (c) the objectives of the items to be developed, within the framework of the test's purpose, and (d) the concrete means through which the behavior samples will be gathered and scored. This last point includes decisions about the method of administration, the format of test item stimuli and responses, and the scoring procedures to be used. After these issues are decided and a preliminary plan for the test is made, the process of test development usually involves the following steps:

1. Generating the item pool by writing or otherwise creating the test items, as well as the administration and scoring procedures to be used;

2. Submitting the item pool to reviewers for qualitative item analysis, and revising or replacing items as needed;

3. Trying out the items that have been generated and reviewed on samples that are representative of the population for whom the test is intended;

4. Evaluating the results of trial administrations of the item pool through quantitative item analysis and additional qualitative analysis;

5. Adding, deleting, and/or modifying items as needed, on the basis of both qualitative and quantitative item analyses;

6. Conducting additional trial administrations for the purpose of checking whether item statistics remain stable across different groups—a process known as *cross-validation*—until a satisfactory set of items is obtained;

7. Standardizing, or fixing, the length of the test and the sequencing of items, as well as the administration and scoring procedures to be used in the final form of the test, on the basis of the foregoing analyses;

8. Administering the test to a new sample of individuals—carefully selected to represent the population of test takers for whom the test is intended—in order to develop normative data or performance criteria, indexes of test score reliability and validity, as well as item-level statistics for the final version of the test;

9. Publishing the test in its final form, along with an administration and scoring manual, accompanying documentation of standardization data, reliability and validity studies, and the materials needed for test administration and scoring (see AERA, APA, & NCME, 1999, chap. 6).

For a test that is to be published commercially, these steps may take years and may have to be repeated several times if the initial results are less than adequate. In addition, most standardized tests are revised from time to time due to the gradual obso-

DON'T FORGET

It is standard practice to categorize tests broadly into the areas of "ability" and "personality." This traditional distinction—repeatedly used in this chapter and elsewhere for the sake of convenience—rests on the notion that some tests are designed primarily to assess aspects of cognitive behavior whereas others are designed to assess aspects of behavior related to emotional functioning. However, when considering the topic of test items, and tests in their entirety, it is important to remember that cognitive and emotional factors are inseparable and that behavior samples reflect all aspects of a person's functioning.

lescence of norms, performance criteria, and test content. Some standardized instruments used in large-scale testing, such as the SAT (formerly known as the Scholastic Aptitude Test), are almost continuously revised and refined. Obviously, tests that are used on a limited basis, such as in classroom settings or in specific research studies, do not undergo such a rigorous process. Nevertheless, they still need to be designed with care according to preestablished specifications, and their results must be psychometrically defensible—in terms of item characteristics, validity, and reliability—if they are to accomplish their purposes successfully.

TEST ITEM TYPES

The variety of items that make up psychological tests is immense. Such a variety defies easy categorization. Test items, like tests as a whole, can differ in terms of content and format, as well as in the medium through which they are administered, the manner in which they are scored, and the kind of processing that they call forth in test takers. One of the most basic distinctions among test items concerns the type of responses they require from test takers. From this standpoint, all test items can be classified into two broad categories, namely, selected-response items and constructed-response items. Tests designed to evaluate abilities as well as those intended for the assessment of personality use either one or both of these item types, depending on the nature of the behavior samples needed for the purpose of the test. Similarly, items of both types may be used either in group or in individual testing. Rapid Reference 6.2 provides information on where to obtain samples of various kinds of test items.

Selected-Response Items

Selected-response items, also known as *objective* or *fixed-response items,* are close-ended in nature; they present a limited number of alternatives from which the test taker must choose. In ability tests, items of this type include multiple-choice, true-false, ranking, and matching, as well as items that call for a rearrangement of the options provided. Typically, objective items in tests of ability are scored simply as pass-fail, although it is also possible to assign partial credit for certain response options. Examples of various kinds of selected-response ability items, both from standardized and teacher-made tests, will be recalled by anyone who has been schooled in the United States within the past few decades. Selected-response items were not always used as frequently in the United States as they are at present, nor are they used as frequently in all nations. In fact, much of the criticism

≡ Rapid Reference 6.2

How To Locate Examples of Various Types of Test Items

- The Educational Testing Service Web site (http://www.ets.org) provides links to several of its major testing programs. Sample items are available in the test preparation sections of the Web site for these programs. For instance:
  - The College Board Web site (http://www.collegeboard.com) provides SAT Verbal and Math mini-tests—with the kinds of items used in the real SAT—that prospective test users can take for free.
  - The Graduate Record Examinations (GRE) site (http://www.gre.org) offers a practice version of the GRE General Test.
  - Questions from the various sections of the Test of English as a Foreign Language (TOEFL) can be downloaded from the TOEFL site (http://www .toefl.org).
- Samples of items from a variety of ability and personality tests are available at http://www.schuhfried.co.at, which is the Web site for the Schuhfried Company, an Austrian organization that markets software products for computerized test administration.
- Pictures of the instruments used in many sensitivity and performance tests can be found in the *Evaluation and Assessment* catalog of the Lafayette Instrument Company, available at http://www.licmef.com/downloads.htm#cat
- Test publishers' printed catalogs provide descriptions of test content and often include sample items. Catalogs posted on the Internet tend to list and describe tests but usually do not include sample items. Prospective test users can obtain printed catalogs by contacting the test publishers (see Appendix B).

aimed at standardized testing in education within the United States revolves around the pervasive use of selected-response test items—especially multiple-choice items—and their perceived weaknesses from the pedagogical point of view. Many critics of "standardized testing" use this term loosely, and incorrectly, as a synonym for tests that employ the multiple-choice item format (see, e.g., Mitchell, 1992; Sacks, 1999).

In personality tests, objective items may be either dichotomous or polytomous. *Dichotomous* items require a choice between two alternatives (e.g., true-false, yes-no, like-dislike, etc.), whereas *polytomous* items present the test taker with three or more (usually an odd number such as 3, 5, or 7) alternative responses to a statement. These alternatives are typically scaled in terms of degree of acceptance (e.g., *like, indifferent,* or *dislike*), intensity of agreement (e.g., from *strongly agree* to *strongly disagree*), frequency (e.g., from *never* to *very often*), and so forth—with the midpoint usually signifying a neutral, uncertain, or middle-of-the-road position.

Forced-Choice

Objective items that require test takers to choose which one of two or more alternatives is most or least characteristic of them are called *forced-choice items*. Each of the alternatives in a forced-choice set represents a different construct, but they are matched in terms of social desirability so that they appear equally attractive or equally unattractive to test takers. This kind of item is used mainly in multidimensional personality inventories (i.e., inventories designed to assess several personality constructs) in order to control for the tendency of test takers to respond in the direction they perceive as more socially desirable. However, forced-choice alternatives are often paired in such a way that each choice test takers make limits the possible range of their scores on another one of the constructs or traits assessed by the multidimensional test. When this is the case, the resulting scores are ipsative in nature and cannot be interpreted in a normative fashion. *Ipsative* scores are essentially ordinal numbers that reflect test takers' rankings of the constructs assessed by the scales within a forced-choice format test. This means that the relative magnitude of the scores on each of the scales in such a test can be gauged only in comparison to the other scores obtained by the same individual on the other scales of the test, rather than to scores obtained by the normative groups. Moreover, the forced-choice format cannot eliminate the influence of social desirability altogether and may even interfere with test-taking rapport (see Chapter 7 for a definition of *rapport*). In spite of these problems, forced-choice items are still used, especially in interest inventories and in tests—such as the Myers-Briggs Type Indicator (MBTI)—whose primary aim is to classify individuals into mutually exclusive categories. Some forced-choice format tests (e.g., the Jackson Vocational Interest Survey) avoid the problem of ipsativeness by pairing alternatives that are drawn from two different sets of parallel scales so that the range of scores in each scale is not constricted.

Advantages of Selected-Response Items

Objective items are by far the most popular and frequently used type of test item. Their advantages derive from the ease and objectivity with which they can be scored, which result in significant time savings and enhance test score reliability; the issue of scoring error is virtually inapplicable to items of this type, except through clerical mistakes. Moreover, selected-response items make efficient use of testing time because more of them can be administered within any given time period than is the case with constructed-response items. Although they can also be administered individually, most tests that use selected-response items are intended for group testing.

All the responses to objective items can easily and reliably be transformed into a numerical scale for scoring purposes, a fact that greatly simplifies the quantitative analysis of these items. In ability tests, correct and incorrect answers are usually assigned values of 1 or 0, respectively; occasionally, variations, such as 2, 1, or 0, are available for partial credit. In personality tests, dichotomous items are also scored 1 or 0, depending on whether the test taker's response is or is not in the direction of the construct that the test is designed to assess. The alternatives presented in polytomous or multiple-response items may be translated into various numerical scales, such as 5, 4, 3, 2, 1 or +2, +1, 0, −1, or −2, or reduced to a binary (1 or 0) scoring format by collapsing categories.

Disadvantages of Selected-Response Items

In spite of their advantages, selected-response items are more susceptible than constructed-response items to certain problems. In tests of ability the major problem connected to objective items revolves around the issue of guessing. The possibility of correct guessing is ever-present when responses simply have to be selected. In dichotomous items, such as true-false, the probability of guessing correctly is a substantial 50%. When test takers guess the correct answers to objective items, the amount of error introduced into their scores varies depending on what factors (e.g., pure chance, partial knowledge, the wording of items, etc.) were responsible for the correct guesses. Similarly, incorrect answers to objective items can easily occur as a result of haste, inattention, carelessness, malingering, or other chance factors unrelated to the test taker's level of knowledge or ability in the area covered by the item.

In personality testing, the intended goals of selected-response items can be easily subverted for an even greater number of reasons. These include not only random or careless responding, but also test-taking response sets that are either intentionally or unintentionally misleading. Depending on the context in which the testing takes place and the particular mental set of the test taker, personality test responses can mislead in either a positive or a negative direction. For example, individuals taking a personality inventory in the context of applying for a job would naturally choose to present themselves in a much more favorable light than would persons being tested to determine whether psychiatric illness may be used as a mitigating factor in determining culpability in a criminal trial. Clearly, responses to objective personality test items can be more easily manipulated by test takers than responses to ability test items, which cannot be faked in a positive direction, except by cheating (for a thorough treatment of many aspects of cheating on tests, see Cizek, 1999). Because of their vulnerability to distortion, many personality inventories use special sets of items, validity scales, or other devices specifically designed to detect misleading or careless responding.

All of the possibilities just outlined can diminish the reliability and validity of test scores. Whereas constructed-response items are also susceptible to some of these problems, guessing on constructed-response ability tests is more difficult and, therefore, less likely. Responding in misleading ways on projective techniques and other constructed-response personality assessment tools presents a greater challenge for test takers. Moreover, the relatively unstructured nature of those instruments is such that even when test takers consciously attempt to deceive they may be providing some useful information.

Preparing selected-response items is a difficult and time-consuming task that requires specialized test development and item writing skills, in addition to great familiarity with the construct or subject matter with which the test deals. Poorly prepared objective items can inadvertently provide clues to test takers or be phrased in terms that work to the benefit or detriment of a subset of test takers. Carelessly written multiple-choice items, in particular, often include alternatives that are (a) grammatically incompatible with the stem of the item, (b) susceptible to various interpretations due to imprecise wording, or (c) so ludicrous that they can be easily dismissed.

Finally, selected-response items are clearly less flexible than constructed-response items with regard to the possible range of responses. Therefore, they offer no opportunity for assessing characteristics that may be special or unique to an individual test taker or that lie outside the range of alternatives provided.

Constructed-Response Items

The essential characteristic of *constructed-response items,* also known as *free-response items,* is that they are open-ended. Their variety is limitless, because constructed responses may involve writing samples, free oral responses, performances of any kind, and products of all sorts.

In ability tests, the most common type of constructed-response items are essay questions and fill-in-the-blanks. The only constraints pertinent to free-response items in psychological tests are the conditions imposed by the test instructions. Thorough instructions and procedural rules are indispensable for the standardized administration and scoring of all tests, including free-response tests. Directions for administering constructed-response tests should include stipulations on matters such as (a) time limits; (b) medium, manner, or length of the required response; and (c) whether access to materials or instruments pertinent to the test (e.g., textbooks, calculators, computers, etc.) is permitted.

Interviews, biographical data questionnaires, and behavioral observations are tools for the assessment of personality that often rely on open-ended responses.

In personality testing proper, the use of constructed responses is limited mainly to *projective techniques*. These methods usually require test takers to respond to ambiguous stimuli in the form of pictures (including inkblots) or verbal materials, such as words or incomplete sentences. Some projective techniques call for self-expression through drawings or other kinds of performances. The basic idea in all of these methods—which originated and are used mainly in clinical settings—is to present test takers with tasks that have a minimal amount of structure so they may respond as freely as possible and, in the process, reveal significant aspects of their personalities. In contrast to inventories, surveys, and other such objective instruments designed to evaluate specific constructs or trait constellations related to personality, projective techniques provide a less focused, more global approach to assessment.

By and large, the advantages and disadvantages of constructed-response items are the opposites of those presented by selected-response items. They nevertheless deserve mention.

Advantages of Constructed-Response Items

Even when they are not individually administered, constructed-response items provide richer samples of the behavior of examinees and allow for their unique characteristics to emerge. Open-ended items offer a wider range of possibilities and more creative approaches to testing and assessment than selected-response items. Moreover, constructed-response tasks elicit authentic samples of test takers' behavior in specific domains, as opposed to mere choices among prepackaged alternatives. If one wishes to evaluate writing skills, memory, mathematical knowledge, mechanical skills, leadership ability, or any other type of performance, actual samples of what an individual can do are the only unassailable standard.

Disadvantages of Constructed-Response Items

The major disadvantages of constructed-response items are related to score reliability and, as a consequence, to validity as well (see the section on the relationship between reliability and validity in Chapter 4). These disadvantages stem from the way in which constructed responses are scored and from the practical limitations that responses of this type impose on the length of a test.

Scoring constructed responses, both in ability and personality tests, is always a more time consuming and complex matter than scoring selected responses because some degree of subjectivity is invariably necessary. Even when *scoring rubrics* (instructions that specify the criteria, principles, and rules to be used in scoring and that provide illustrative examples) are carefully prepared and applied, there is always the possibility that a response will be evaluated differently by different scorers due to its uniqueness or to some other factor. Checking the reliability of scores assigned by different raters is an indispensable and costly aspect of using tests with constructed-response items. Although interscorer differences cannot be eliminated completely, they can certainly be minimized by means of thorough, explicit, and pilot-tested scoring procedures as well as by the proper training of scorers.

Scoring constructed responses gathered from the projective tools used in personality assessment poses a special challenge in that the subjectivity of the scorer can enter into play in more ways than it does in the scoring of constructed responses in ability tests. In addition, projective techniques lend themselves more readily to the use of informal, and often idiosyncratic, methods of administration and scoring that can further weaken their psychometric integrity (see, e.g., Lanyon & Goodstein, 1997, chap. 4).

Test length is another factor that affects the reliability of scores from tests that use constructed responses. Because these responses require more time for administration and scoring, the number of items that can be included in constructed-response tests is usually much smaller than it is in selected-response tests. As discussed in Chapter 4, all other things being equal, shorter tests are more prone to content sampling errors and produce scores that are less consistent than those of longer tests. Thus, from the point of view of internal consistency as well, the scores of constructed-response tests tend to be less reliable than those of selected-response tests.

An additional complication pertinent to constructed-response items concerns the matter of *response length*. Since longer responses contain more material than shorter ones, variations in the length of constructed responses can affect scores considerably. This is especially pertinent for projective techniques, because longer—or more elaborate—projective responses are likely to contain more scorable (i.e., psychologically significant) elements than shorter ones. Moreover, projective devices that allow for variability in the number, as well as the length, of responses pose yet another complicating factor in the investigation of their psychometric properties due to lack of uniformity across test takers. The Rorschach test is the preeminent example of this problem, as evidenced by the long-standing controversy regarding the impact of response productivity on Rorschach scoring and interpretation (see, e.g., Groth-Marnat, 1997, p. 399; Meyer, 1992).

ITEM ANALYSIS

In the past few decades, the field of test development and test design, as well as the techniques of item analysis, have been undergoing a transition that is taking hold gradually but is fundamentally altering the nature of psychological tests. This transition is partly due to the ease and efficiency with which test data can be collected, stored, analyzed, retrieved, and disseminated with the use of computers. In addition, since the 1960s, the methodology provided by the new approaches to psychological test construction collectively known as item response theory (IRT) or latent trait theory has been steadily supplementing—and in some cases replacing—traditional methods of test construction and design. Though IRT methods can be, and are, used in developing paper-and-pencil as well as computer-based tests of fixed length, their most salient advantage over traditional methodology is that they allow a more flexible and efficient test format through *computerized adaptive testing* (CAT). In CAT, item sequences can be individually tailored to the test takers' ability levels, or to the test takers' positions on whatever trait the test is designed to assess, on the bases of prior responses. In the next sections of this chapter, traditional item analysis procedures are presented first, followed by a discussion of IRT methodology.

Quantitative Methods of Item Analysis

For psychological tests, in general, the most important aspect of quantitative item analysis centers on statistics that address *item validity*. The question that item validity indexes attempt to answer is whether a specific item carries its own weight within a test by eliciting information that advances the purpose of the test. Psychometricians usually refer to item validity statistics as indexes of *item discrimination,* because their role is to reveal the extent to which an item accurately differentiates among test takers with regard to the traits or behaviors that the test is designed to assess. For tests of ability, in particular, item analysis includes procedures designed to gauge two additional characteristics of items that have a bearing on their validity, namely, *item difficulty* and *item fairness*. All of these item characteristics can be evaluated qualitatively as well as quantitatively. Qualitative evaluation usually is carried out by subject matter experts who inspect the content of items with regard to their appropriateness

CAUTION

The term *discrimination* has acquired a negative connotation in everyday usage due to its frequent association with the unfair treatment of women and racial minority groups.

In contrast, within the field of psychometrics, *discrimination* is considered a desirable feature for test items. It refers to the extent to which items elicit responses that accurately differentiate test takers along the dimensions that tests are designed to evaluate.

and difficulty level as well as to whether they reflect the objectives that were specified for the test. Item content is also examined from the point of view of its possible unfairness or offensiveness to any group of potential test takers. Quantitative evaluation of item difficulty and discrimination is carried out through statistics that assess whether items perform the way they were intended to perform when they are administered to the kinds of test takers for whom the test is designed.

Item Difficulty

The Role of Item Difficulty in Ability Testing

Given the self-evident proposition that the difficulty level of a test as a whole is a function of the difficulty levels of the individual items that make up the test, it follows that an easy test is one that is made up of easy items and a difficult test is one made up of hard items. This apparently simple premise becomes a bit more complicated as soon as we consider that difficulty is a relative matter. How difficult a test item is depends not only on its intrinsic simplicity or accessibility, but also on the ability level of the test taker. For example, the proper use of the verb *être* (to be)—which is the most common verb in the French language—is a far easier test task for a student in an Advanced French class than for one who is beginning to study that language. Thus, in order to properly calibrate the difficulty level of a test, indexes of the *relative* difficulty of items for one or more relevant groups of test takers are needed. Test developers use these indexes to determine the appropriateness of the items for the population and purpose for which a test is designed, as well as to decide where items are placed within a test.

DON'T FORGET

In much the same way that the frames of reference for test score interpretation, discussed in Chapter 3, may be either normative or criterion-referenced, so can the difficulty of test items be determined on either an absolute or a relative basis. Both aspects need to be considered in the process of test construction and test development with specific reference to the intended population of test takers and purpose of the test.

How Is Item Difficulty Gauged?

During the initial stages of test development, when the pool of items is generated, test authors can gauge the difficulty of the items they create based on more or less objective standards delineated in the specifications that have been drawn up for the test or based on criteria that are agreed upon by experts in the subject matter or cognitive skills covered in a test. For instance, one standard that may be applied to calibrate the difficulty of words is the frequency with which they are used within a language. Thus, in a vocabulary test, easy items are words that are employed frequently by the users of the language in question whereas the most difficult items consist of words that occur rarely and would be unfamiliar to most test takers. Similarly, in a test of arithmetic, individual items can be aligned in terms of difficulty based on the evident complexity of the operations they require, such as multiplication of whole numbers versus multiplication of fractions, and so forth.

Once a set of items is administered to one or more groups, quantitative indexes of item difficulty, which addresses this issue from a normative perspective, can also be obtained. In analyzing test items from the normative viewpoint, the essential piece of information used to determine item difficulty is the percentage of test takers who answer an item correctly, also known as *proportion* (or *percentage*) *passing*, or *p*, for short. The higher the percentage passing, the easier the item is. Since the *p* values of items hinge entirely on the ability level of the groups to whom they are administered, the make-up of such groups is quite important and should reflect the make-up of the population for whom the test is intended.

Percentage passing or *p* values are ordinal numbers that, like percentile ranks, do not represent equal units. For this reason, provided that the trait an item measures can be assumed to be normally distributed, *p* values are often transformed into *z* values, using the Table of Areas of the Normal Curve (see Appendix C). Once *p* values are converted into *z* values, the relative difficulty levels of items can be compared across various groups by administering a common set of items—called *anchor* items—to two or more groups. Formulas to estimate the difficulty levels of additional items across the groups in question can then be derived based on the established relationships among the anchor items. This procedure, known as *absolute scaling*, was developed by Thurstone (1925). It allows for the difficulty of items to be placed on a uniform numerical scale for samples of test takers at different ability levels, such as students in various school grades. Rapid Reference 6.3 presents a simple numerical example of how this is accomplished using the results of five items that were administered to two groups. Since all of the five items in the example have higher *p* values (and lower *z* values) for Group B than for Group A, we may surmise that Group B is functioning at a more advanced level than Group A in the ability or content area tapped by these items. Figure 6.1 portrays the relative difficulty of the five items for the two groups and graphically demonstrates that the difficulty levels of the five items for the two groups correlate strongly and positively. The kind of data presented in Rapid Reference 6.3 and

≡*Rapid Reference 6.3*

Conversion of Item Difficulty From Proportion Passing (*p*) to Normal Curve Units (**z**)

Item difficulty can be represented in normal curve units (*z* values), provided that the trait measured by an item is assumed to be normally distributed.

The *z* value for an item is derived by locating the proportion who passed (i.e., its *p* value) in the Table of Areas of the Normal Curve (see Appendix C): *p values above .50* are found in column 3 of the table and assigned the corresponding *z* values with a *negative* sign; *p values below .50* are located in column 4 of the table and the corresponding *z* values are assigned a *positive* sign. If *p* = .50, the *z* value for the item is zero.

Numerical example for five items administered to two groups:

Item Number	Group A p Value[a]	Group A z Value[b]	Group B p Value[a]	Group B z Value[b]
1	.841	−1.00	.894	−1.25
2	.50	0.00	.691	−0.50
3	.067	+1.50	.159	+1.00
4	.023	+2.00	.067	+1.50
5	.977	−2.00	.994	−2.51

[a]The *p* values represent the proportion of individuals in Group A and Group B who passed each item.

[b]The *z* values for the easiest items are large and negative whereas those for the most difficult items are large and positive.

Figure 6.1 can be used to estimate the difficulty levels of additional items for one group, based on their difficulty values for the other, by means of regression analysis (see Chapter 5). These types of procedures are applied in equating tests and test scores via anchor tests and fixed reference groups (see Chapter 3).

Item Difficulty Levels, Test Difficulty Levels, and Test Purpose

For any given group of test takers, the average score on a test is the same as the average difficulty of its items. Thus, if the *average* percentage passing (p) for the items in a test is 80%, the average score on the test will be 80% as well. The significance of the relationship among item difficulty, test purpose, and the ability level of the population of test takers for whom the test is designed may be clarified by a few examples.

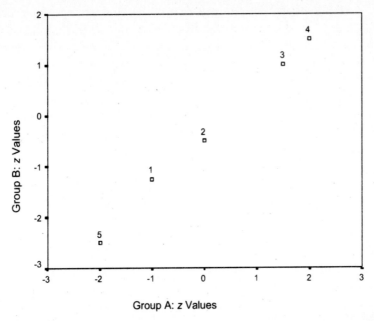

Figure 6.1 Scatterplot of relative difficulty of five items for Groups A and B (see Rapid Reference 6.3)

- Classroom achievement tests are designed to evaluate the extent to which the students in a class have mastered the content of a course. In most academic settings a grade within the 70 to 79% range is considered to be average. In order to achieve this average, most of the items in classroom tests should be within the reach of the majority of students, provided they have mastered course content at a level that the instructor considers to be average. Such tests may include some items—involving concepts that have been emphasized in the course—that the whole class answers correctly ($p = 1.00$), even though such items do not differentiate among the test takers (see Table 6.1 later in this chapter). However, an item that no one answers correctly ($p = 0$) is not desirable in a classroom test because it indicates that even the best students failed to grasp it.

- On the other hand, a test designed to screen a large applicant pool in order to select the top 10% of individuals might have items that cluster around a p value of .10, or 10%. Such a test would be considered too difficult for all except the most highly qualified applicants who possess an extensive amount of the knowledge or skills that the test is designed to assess.

- Many tests of ability are designed to maximally differentiate individuals within a given population in terms of a cognitive trait that is assumed to be normally distributed, such as general intelligence or verbal skills. In such tests the range of difficulty of items has to be sufficiently broad to accommodate both the most and least capable individuals in the potential population of test takers, and the p value of items should cluster around .50 (or 50%) to provide maximum differentiation among test takers. Items with extreme p values (i.e., close to 0 or 1.00) should be avoided in such tests because they fail to differentiate among test takers and are therefore excess baggage. Furthermore, if individuals who belong to the population for whom a test of this nature is designed are able to pass either all of the items or none of the items, their scores are indeterminate. As discussed in Chapter 3, when test items are too easy for a certain group, the test is said to have *insufficient ceiling* and its score distribution will be negatively skewed; when the items are too difficult for a group, the test has an *inadequate floor* and its score distribution is positively skewed. Figure 2.4 displays examples of skewed distributions.

Distractors and Difficulty

In tests that use multiple-choice items, the incorrect alternatives, or *distractors,* can have a great deal of influence on item difficulty in two major respects. In the first place, the number of distractors directly affects indexes of item difficulty because the probability of guessing correctly is higher when the number of choices is smaller. In addition, item difficulty is also affected by the caliber of distractors. An ideal multiple-choice item is one in which (a) the correct alternative is obvious to the test takers who know the answer and (b) the distractors appear equally plausible to those who do not know it. Such items are hard to construct. To the extent that the distractors seem obviously wrong, are poorly worded, or are much shorter or longer than the correct alternative, they provide clues that savvy examinees who do not know the answer may use to narrow their choices and select the correct answer. In order to avoid these and other problems in devising multiple-choice items, test authors should follow the guidelines for item writing provided in textbooks such as Haladyna's (1999). After a test is administered, an analysis of the distractors also ought to be conducted. Such analyses tally the number of test takers who choose each distractor. Careful examination of the frequencies with which various distractors are chosen by test takers of different ability levels serves to detect possible flaws in the items. If a test is still under development, distractors that are not functioning adequately (e.g., those that are not chosen by anyone or those that are more often chosen by test takers of high ability levels) should be discarded and replaced.

Is Item Difficulty a Relevant Concept in Personality Testing?

The tasks that make up personality tests may not be designed to evaluate cognitive functioning, but they do involve cognitive processes. In selected-response instruments, such as personality inventories and questionnaires, the relevant cognitive processes are related to the inventory taker's ability to understand the items. Therefore, the vocabulary levels and reading skills of potential test takers need to be considered in devising those items. Projective tasks, on the other hand, involve a certain amount of proficiency in whatever mode the responses are to be expressed. Most projective instruments require a modicum of skill in verbal expression, drawing, or some other kind of performance. Thus, the relative difficulty or ease of projective tasks for various kinds of examinees must also be considered in the development, administration, and interpretation of these instruments.

Item Discrimination

Item discrimination refers to the extent to which items elicit responses that accurately differentiate test takers in terms of the behaviors, knowledge, or other characteristics that a test—or subtest—is designed to evaluate. For the vast majority of tests, discriminating power is the most basic quality that items must have in order to be included in a test. In the process of test development, item discrimination indexes—also known as indexes of item validity—are obtained using some criterion or indicator of the test takers' standing on the construct that the test assesses. Criteria employed for this purpose may be (a) internal criteria with respect to the test that is under development (i.e., total score on the test), (b) external criteria of the same kinds as those used to validate tests as a whole and described in Chapter 5 (e.g., age, education, membership in contrasted diagnostic or occupational groups, etc.), or (c) combinations of both internal and external criteria.

Item Validation Criteria

The choice of criteria against which test items are validated depends on the purpose of the test. Ability tests require criteria related to the content areas or skills they assess; personality tests require criteria pertinent to traits or aspects of behavior with which they deal. The quality and appropriateness of criteria used in validating test items have important consequences with respect to the selection of items that will be retained in a test and, consequently, on the reliability and validity of the test scores.

When criteria external to the test are used in validating items, the validity of scores on the test as a whole is enhanced; when the internal criterion of total test score is used to validate items, the homogeneity of the test increases and, hence, reliability indexes based on interitem consistency are enhanced. In the development of tests that assess a single unidimensional trait such as vocabulary or depression, total score may be used to validate items. This practice is based on the assumption that all the items within such tests ought to correlate highly with the total score on the test and with each other. On the other hand, in the development of tests that assess complex and multifaceted constructs such as intelligence, items are validated against external criteria that are also more global. Since the items of those tests may be assessing different aspects of a complex construct, they do not necessarily have to correlate highly with one another and their degree of correlation with the total score may vary. Most intelligence scales, for instance, include a mixture of items tapping the various types of skills associated with that construct—such as verbal, numerical, spatial, and logical reasoning abilities—and provide composite scores that incorporate performance on all the item types and are validated against external criteria, such as educational achievement. In instruments of this kind, items are usually grouped into subtests with homogeneous content which are scored separately (see Table 4.1 and Fig. 4.1 in Chapter 4).

As we have just seen, even though both external validity and internal consistency are desirable goals in test construction, the nature of the constructs assessed by a test may not allow both goals to be realized concomitantly. In addition to the limitations imposed by the purpose of the test, external validation of test items may also be impractical due to the unavailability or inaccessibility of external criterion data. A typical example of this kind of situation is provided by items from teacher-prepared classroom tests, such as those presented in Table 6.1. When conducting item analyses of these tests, teachers cannot use any criterion other than total test score because to do so would be unfair. Classroom tests are designed to evaluate mastery of the skills and content covered within a course and their scores are not supposed to be tied to any factor other than students' mastery of the specified objectives.

Item Discrimination Statistics

All statistical procedures used to gauge the degree to which items discriminate in terms of a criterion require information on (a) item performance and (b) criterion standing for individuals in the samples from which the item discrimination statistics are extracted. The traditional statistics used for this purpose are of two types: the index of discrimination statistic (or D) and a variety of correlational indexes.

The *index of discrimination* (D) is used primarily for items in tests of ability that are scored as pass or fail, but it can also be applied for analyzing the items of other tests that use binary scoring. In order to compute D, test takers must be classified into distinct criterion groups based either on their total scores on the test or on some external indicator of their standings on the construct assessed by the test. It

Table 6.1 Sample Item Analysis Data From a Classroom Test

Item Number	Percentage Passing (p value)			D index (Upper – Lower)	Point Biserial Correlation (r_{pb})[b]
	Total Group	Upper[a] Group	Lower[a] Group		
1	100%	100%	100%	0	0.00
2	88%	100%	50%	50	0.67
3	38%	100%	0%	100	0.63
4	75%	50%	50%	0	0.13
5	75%	50%	100%	–50	–0.32
6	13%	50%	0%	50	0.43

[a]The upper and lower criterion groups are made up of students whose scores on the whole test were in the top and bottom 27%, respectively, of the score distribution.

[b]Point biserial is an index of the correlation between the performance of each one of the test takers on the dichotomously scored item (pass-fail) and their total scores on the test.

is customary to create criterion groups by separating the test takers used for item validity analyses into two extreme groups, for example, those who are in the top and bottom thirds on the criterion measure. Once the upper and lower criterion groups are created, the percentage of individuals (p) within each group who passed the item—or responded to it in whatever direction is keyed as indicative of the construct assessed by the test—is calculated. The *index of discrimination* is simply the difference in the percentage or proportion of test takers in the upper and lower criterion groups who pass a given item or answer it in the keyed direction; D can range from +100 to –100 (or from +1.00 to –1.00). For ability tests, positive discrimination indexes indicate that more individuals in the upper criterion group than in the lower criterion group passed the item and the most desirable values of D are those closest to +100. Negative D values indicate that the items in question discriminate in the opposite direction and need to be either fixed or discarded.

Table 6.1 displays the item discrimination indexes for six items from a test administered to a psychological testing class. Item 1, the easiest one of the six, was passed by all the students ($p = 100$%) and Item 6, the most difficult one, was passed by only 13%. Item 3, passed by 38% of the students, was relatively difficult and was the most discriminating item among them, with a D value of 100. Items 4 and 5 were relatively easy ($p = 75$%) but of questionable value. Item 4 did not discriminate between the two extreme criterion groups at all and Item 5 actually had to be discarded because its D index of –50 indicated that the item discriminated in the wrong direction.

DON'T FORGET

....

Most indexes of item discrimination are biased in favor of items of intermediate difficulty. For instance, if the percentage passing (*p* value) of an item for the total sample is extreme (100% and 0%), there can be no difference in the *p* values of the upper and lower criterion groups for that item and its *D* index is 0. On the other hand, when the *p* value for the total group is 50%, it is possible for the *D* index to reach its maximum value of +100 if everyone in the upper criterion group and no one in the lower criterion group passes it. Thus, for all tests whose goal is to ascertain differences among individuals in terms of some ability, items that center around a 50% difficulty level are preferred.

Correlation coefficients of various kinds can also express the relationship between performance on an item and criterion standing, and thus provide indexes of item discrimination. The type of correlation coefficient chosen to calculate these indexes depends on the nature of the two variables that are to be correlated, which are the item scores and the criterion measures. For instance, when item scores are dichotomous (e.g., pass-fail) and the criterion measure is continuous (e.g., total test score) the point biserial (r_{pb}) correlation coefficient is most often used. On the other hand, when the item scores and the criterion measure are both dichotomous, the phi (ϕ) coefficient is used. Both the point biserial and phi coefficients of correlation can range from -1.00 to $+1.00$ and are interpreted in the same way as the Pearson *r*. Formulas for computing point biserial and phi coefficients, and several other types of correlation coefficients used in the analysis of item discrimination, are available in most basic statistics textbooks. In any case, high positive correlations indicate a direct and strong relationship between item and criterion, high negative correlations indicate an inverse and strong relationship between item and criterion, and low correlations indicate a weak relationship between the two. Table 6.1 also lists the point biserial correlations between items and test scores for each of the six items discussed earlier.

A Note About Speed

Whenever tests of ability have time limits, speed of performance affects test scores to some extent. This topic was discussed in Chapter 4, in connection with the problems speeded tests pose in the computation of split-half reliability coefficients, and it needs to be considered in relation to item statistics as well. With regard to speed, tests can be classified into three types: pure speed tests, pure power tests, and tests that blend speed and power.

- *Pure speed tests* simply measure the speed with which test takers can perform a task. In a pure speed test, difficulty is manipulated mainly through timing. These tests have items whose difficulty levels are uniform and well within the capabilities of individuals who are likely to take the test, but time limits are so short that most test takers cannot complete all the items. Thus, in most cases, the total score on a pure speed test is simply the number of items completed by the test taker. If test takers finish all of the items in a pure speed test, their actual capacity has not been determined because there is no way of knowing how many more items they might have completed if more items were available.

- *Pure power tests,* on the other hand, have no time limits. In these tests, difficulty is manipulated by increasing or decreasing the complexity of items. Their difficulty range needs to be sufficiently wide to accommodate the ability levels of all potential test takers. In power tests, items are arranged in ascending order of difficulty so that all test takers are able to complete at least some items, but the most difficult items are usually beyond the reach of the majority of test takers. A perfect score in a pure power test suggests that the test taker's ability level exceeds the difficulty level of the most difficult items. In such cases, the test taker's actual level of ability is indeterminate due to the test's insufficient ceiling.
- Most ability tests fall somewhere between the extremes of the pure-speed/pure-power continuum. Their time limits typically allow test takers to reach and attempt all or most of the items. As discussed previously, the specific range and average of difficulty levels of ability test items depend on the purposes for which the tests are employed.

In any test that is closely timed, the p values and discrimination indexes of items are a function of their *position* within the test rather than of their intrinsic difficulty or discriminant validity. This is so because items in the latter part of a test in which speed plays a significant role are attempted by fewer test takers, and those who attempt such items tend to be either the most capable test takers or those who rush through a test by responding randomly. As a result, the difficulty and discrimination indexes for items that occur late in speeded tests are likely to be misleading and special strategies need to be implemented in order to gain insight into the specific roles of speed and difficulty in such tests.

Combining Item Difficulty and Item Discrimination

In light of the interrelationship between item difficulty and item discrimination, the development of most tests of ability requires analyses that combine both of these item characteristics. There are two approaches to achieving this end. The older methods consist of analyzing item-test regression and the more recent ones involve the use of item response theory (IRT).

Item-Test Regression

To perform item-test regression analyses it is necessary to calculate the proportion of individuals at each total score level who passed a given item. Table 6.2 presents sample data of this kind for two items of a hypothetical ten-item ability test on which the total scores range from 1 to 10. Figure 6.2 displays the item-test regressions for both items, plotted from the data in Table 6.2. Item-test regression graphs combine information on item difficulty and item discrimination and allow us to visualize how each item functions within the group that was tested. If we assumed that the item statistics presented in Table 6.2 were based on a large and representative sample of test takers, these data would make it possible to evaluate the two items and draw certain conclusions about them, as described in the following paragraphs.

- *Item 1 is easier than Item 2, because its 50% threshold is lower.* The 50% thresholds are represented in Figure 6.2 by perpendicular broken lines that have been drawn from the points where the regression graphs for each item meet the horizontal line at $p = .50$ down to the baseline that displays total scores on the test. For Item 1, the 50% threshold is at the point where total score equals 4, whereas for Item 2, it is where total

Table 6.2 Item-Test Regression Data for Two Items

Total Score	Proportion of Examinees Who Answered Each Item Correctly	
	Item 1	Item 2
10	1.00	1.00
9	.60	.85
8	.75	.70
7	.65	.50
6	.70	.45
5	.80	.30
4	.50	.00
3	.40	.00
2	.30	.00
1	.35	.00

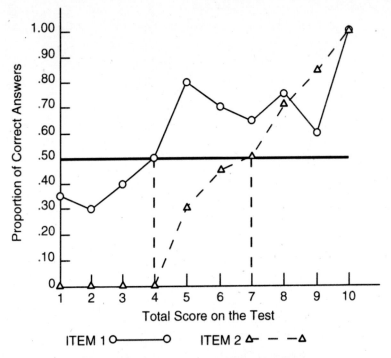

Figure 6.2 Item-test regression for Items 1 and 2 (see Table 6.2)

score equals 7. These data suggest that the level of ability needed to have a 50-50 chance of passing Item 1 is lower than the level of ability needed to have an equal chance of succeeding on Item 2.

- *Item 2 discriminates better than Item 1.* The item-test regression is steeper for Item 2 than for Item 1 and shows no reversals of direction in the proportion passing the item at each total score point. In contrast, Item 1 shows a more gradual item-test regression and four reversals in its direction (at the total score points of 2, 6, 7, and 9). Since total score on the test is assumed to reflect a test taker's level of ability, the item-test regressions in Figure 6.2 suggest that the relationship between ability and item performance is more direct and stable for Item 2 than it is for Item 1.
- *Item 1 is more likely than Item 2 to be answered correctly by guessing.* This inference is based on the fact that the proportion of correct answers to Item 1 is fairly high (.35) even for those individuals who obtained a total score of 1, which was the lowest score on the test. In contrast, no one with a test score below 5 was able to answer (or guess) Item 2 correctly.

- *Conclusion.* Altogether, examination of the item-test regression data presented in Table 6.2 and Figure 6.2 suggests that (a) Item 2 is more difficult than Item 1, (b) Item 2 appears to function better than Item 1 in terms of its power to discriminate among individuals with low and high scores on the hypothetical set of ten ability items, and (c) Item 2 is more impervious to guessing than Item 1.

Although these analyses of item-test regression are informative, they are fairly crude and quite dependent on the samples and item sets from which the data are obtained. Item response theory uses the same kinds of empirical data involved in item-test regression analyses as a point of departure for far more sophisticated forms of item analyses and more ambitious test development strategies.

ITEM RESPONSE THEORY

The label *item response theory (IRT)* refers to a wide, and growing, variety of models that may be used to design or develop new tests and to evaluate existing tests. IRT models differ in the mathematical formulas they employ, in the number of item characteristics that they may account for, and in the number of trait or ability dimensions they specify as the objectives of measurement. In addition, different methods are used depending on whether item data are dichotomous (pass-fail, true-false, etc.) or polytomous (i.e., consisting of multiple response categories). The procedures encompassed within IRT are extensive and complex. Until fairly recently, published presentations of these methods were too difficult to understand without a solid grasp of mathematics and statistics. Fortunately, in the past few years a number of excellent and more accessible materials on IRT techniques have been published. Rapid Reference 6.4 lists a selection of some of the most useful resources available.

Classical Test Theory Versus Item Response Theory

The label *classical test theory (CTT)* is used, in contradistinction to IRT, to refer to all of the traditional psychometric methods of developing and evaluating tests that predate IRT. The fundamental methods of CTT were developed in the early part of the 20th century and were well established by the middle of that century. They were perhaps best summarized in Gulliksen's (1950) classic volume on the theory of mental tests but have been described before and since then in countless other sources. The psychometric principles and procedures of CTT have been continuously refined and expanded; they are still widely used and will continue to

≡Rapid Reference 6.4

....

Sources of Information on Item Response Theory and Computer Adaptive Testing

Books

- Bond, T. G., & Fox, C. M. (2001). *Applying the Rasch model: Fundamental measurement in the human sciences.* Mahwah, NJ: Erlbaum.
- Embretson, S. E., & Reise, S. P. (2000). *Item response theory for psychologists.* Mahwah, NJ: Erlbaum.
- Hambleton, R. K., Swaminathan, H., & Rogers, H. J. (1991). *Fundamentals of item response theory.* Newbury Park, CA: Sage.
- Wainer, H. (2000). *Computer adaptive testing: A primer* (2nd ed.). Mahwah, NJ: Erlbaum.

Internet Resources

Many of the item response theory (IRT) resources previously available at the now-defunct online Educational Resource Information Center (ERIC) Clearinghouse on Assessment and Evaluation can be found at http://edres.org/irt, a Web page maintained by Lawrence Rudner, the former director of the ERIC Clearinghouse on Assessment and Evaluation. Through this Web site one can access many useful IRT-related materials, such as the following:

- An excellent tutorial on item response theory, made available by the University of Illinois at Urbana-Champaign's IRT Modeling Lab;
- The second edition of Frank Baker's classic book *The Basics of Item Response Theory* (2001);
- Links to free and commercially available IRT software, as well as to paper collections and books on IRT.

CAT Central is a Web site that has a variety of resources for research and applications of computerized adaptive testing (CAT), including basic information on CAT, an extensive bibliography, a listing of major testing programs that employ CAT, and links to other CAT-related resources. CAT Central can be found at the following address:

- http://www.psych.umn.edu/psylabs/CATCentral

be used for the foreseeable future. In fact, most books on psychological testing—including the present one—deal largely with CTT. Some of the major contrasts between CTT and IRT were mentioned briefly in Chapter 3 in connection with the topic of test equating. However, the range and significance of the changes entailed in the transition between the conventional procedures of CTT and the model-based approach to measurement that characterizes IRT extend well beyond that topic.

DON'T FORGET

The sections on item response theory (IRT) and computer adaptive testing (CAT) in Chapter 3 provide a basic introduction to some of the distinctive features of these relatively novel approaches to psychological measurement. Readers may find it useful to look back at those earlier sections as a prelude to the material on those topics presented in this chapter.

At present, IRT methods are employed in a more limited range of instruments than the traditional methods of CTT. This is due partly to the significant assumptions IRT requires—concerning item responses, latent traits, and their relationships—and partly to the more extensive data collection efforts needed in order to calibrate items using IRT models. Moreover, in contrast to the well-established, comparatively simple, and widely used techniques of CTT, IRT methods are still evolving, considerably more sophisticated from the mathematical standpoint, and unfamiliar even to many testing professionals. As Embretson (1996, 1999) has made abundantly clear, even though CTT and IRT share some conceptual foundations and there is a certain amount of reciprocity between the two approaches, many of the traditional rules of measurement implicit in CTT must be revised or abandoned when IRT models are applied to measurement tasks. Rapid Reference 6.5 presents one of the several contrasting features of the two approaches.

One of the most basic differences between CTT and IRT stems from the fact that in CTT, interest centers mainly on the examinee's total score on a test, which represents the sum of the item scores; whereas in IRT—as its name implies—the principal focus is on the examinee's performance on individual items. In IRT, the careful development and calibration of test items in terms of the information they provide about a specific psychological construct is a primary concern. To accomplish this calibration IRT relies on mathematical models of the relationships between abilities—or whatever other unobservable constructs (i.e., latent traits) a test is designed to assess—and responses to individual items.

Broadly speaking, the goals of IRT are (a) to generate items that provide the maximum amount of information possible concerning the ability or trait levels of examinees who respond to them in one fashion or another, (b) to give examinees items that are tailored to their ability or trait levels, and thus (c) to reduce the number of items needed to pinpoint any given test taker's standing on the ability or latent trait while minimizing measurement error. Reducing the number of items in a test by selecting those that are most appropriate to the test taker's level of ability—without a consequent loss of reliability—is an important goal in group testing. This is especially true for testing programs that are carried out on a massive scale, such as the SAT. A reduction in the number of items administered saves

≡ *Rapid Reference 6.5*

Classical Test Theory Versus Item Response Theory: A Contrast on the Matter of Test Length and Reliability

The new rules of measurement, described by Embretson (1996, 1999), highlight some crucial differences between classical test theory (CTT) and item response theory (IRT). Among these is the contrast between the old rule that "longer tests are more reliable than shorter tests" and the new rule that "shorter tests can be more reliable than longer tests" (p. 343). To wit:

- As discussed in connection with split-half reliability and the Spearman-Brown formula (Chapter 4), CTT holds that, all other things being equal, a larger number of observations will produce more reliable results than a smaller number of observations. If the length of a test increases, through the addition of parallel items, the proportion of true variance to error variance also increases and, hence, so does test score reliability. Thus, for two comparable tests of fixed lengths (e.g., 50 vs. 40 items), the scores on the longer test will be more reliable than those on the shorter test.

- In the computer adaptive testing (CAT) that IRT methods allow, item selection is optimally suited to test takers' levels on the trait being assessed. Inappropriate items (e.g., those that are too easy or too difficult for the test taker) are eliminated, resulting in a shorter test. Because IRT methods also calibrate the information that is obtained from each item response more precisely, measurement error can be reduced and reliable scores can be obtained from fewer, but more informative, item responses.

- For more detailed explanations of these notions, along with numerical and graphic illustrations, see Embretson (1996, 1999) and Embretson and Reise (2000).

time, saves money, and minimizes the frustration test takers experience when confronted with items that are not suited to their ability levels. Indeed, in large-scale testing programs, CATs developed through IRT methods are gradually replacing tests of fixed length in paper-and-pencil and computer-administered formats (Embretson & Reise, 2000).

Shortcomings of Classical Test Theory

Classical test theory and IRT differ in many other respects. Although a full discussion of these differences is beyond the scope of this volume, a few need to be mentioned because of their significance with regard to test development and the analysis of items. One way to contrast the two methodologies is by outlining the shortcomings of CTT that IRT attempts to overcome. Although some of these points have been mentioned earlier in this volume, they are reiterated here more fully and in specific reference to the comparison between CTT and IRT.

• CTT indexes of item difficulty and item discrimination are *group-dependent:* Their values may change when computed for samples of test takers who differ from the ones used for the initial item analyses in some aspect of the construct being measured. In contrast, the estimates of item characteristics obtained through IRT methods are assumed to be invariant and provide a uniform scale of measurement that can be used with different groups.

• For tests of fixed length developed using CTT methods, the trait or ability estimates (i.e., the scores) of test takers are *test–dependent.* In other words, scores are a function of the specific items selected for inclusion in a test. Therefore, comparisons of scores derived from different tests or different item sets are not possible unless test equating procedures, which are often not feasible, are used (see Chapter 3). Moreover, even when equating procedures are applied, the comparisons that can be made are limited to the tests that were equated. In the case of IRT—provided that the data fit the model and provided that certain assumptions are met—estimates of abilities or traits are independent of the particular item set administered to examinees. Instead, trait estimates are linked to the probabilities of examinees' item response patterns.

• In CTT methodology, the reliability of scores (i.e., trait or ability estimates) is gauged by means of the standard error of measurement (SEM), which is assumed to be of equal magnitude for all examinees (see chap. 4). In fact, since score reliability depends on how well suited test items are to examinees' trait or ability levels, and since trait levels are not equal across examinees, this assumption is not plausible for traditional tests. On the other hand, when IRT methodology is combined with adaptive testing procedures, the standard errors of trait or ability estimates resulting from a test administration depend on the particular set of items selected for each examinee (see Rapid Reference 6.5). As a consequence, these estimates vary appropriately at different levels of the trait dimensions and convey more precise information about the reliability of measurement.

Essential Features of Item Response Theory

Since most IRT models currently in use are unidimensional models, the present discussion is limited to those. *Unidimensional IRT models* assume (a) that the items comprising a test or test segment measure a single trait and (b) that the item responses of test takers depend only on their standing with regard to the trait being measured. As Rapid Reference 6.6 suggests, from a realistic viewpoint, neither

≡ Rapid Reference 6.6

....

What Makes the Behavior Samples Gathered Through Test Items So Complex?

- *Regardless of what construct test items are meant to assess, they always involve multiple dimensions.* To begin with, some ability to attend to test stimuli is required in order to respond to *any* test task, as is a modicum of short-term memory. In addition, all test items involve a specific content, format, and medium, and require a specific set of cognitive skills. For instance, depending on its mode of presentation and response, a simple vocabulary item may involve reading, writing, spelling, oral comprehension, verbal expression, logical reasoning ability or knowledge of etymology, not to mention attention, memory, and possibly speed as well.
- *Test takers are complex and unique beings.* They bring a combination of factors—such as genetic endowment, experiential histories, developed skills, traits, habits, and attitudes, as well as transitory physiological and emotional states—to bear on test tasks. Because responses to test items are a function of test takers' unique blend of all the elements they bring to the tasks, such responses are never equivalent in every respect. For example, test items that require a series of arithmetical computations present a bigger problem for a test taker who experiences math anxiety than for one who does not, even if both are equally capable of performing the computations in a non-test situation.

one of these assumptions can ever be fully met. However, when all the items in a test or test segment are designed to measure a single predominant trait, the assumptions of unidimensional models can be met adequately enough to make the models workable.

In the next few paragraphs, some of the features common to most of the IRT models currently in use are summarized to give readers a general idea of how IRT methodology is applied to the calibration of test item data. For the sake of brevity and simplicity, this presentation avoids the use of mathematical formulas and concepts that are not essential to a basic understanding of the fundamental ideas of IRT. Interested readers can find more extensive treatments of these methods, as well as explanations of their mathematical bases, in the sources listed in Rapid Reference 6.4.

- In IRT, models are based on the premise that a person's performance on any test item is a function of, and can be predicted by, one or more traits or abilities. The models seek to specify the expected relationships between examinees' (observable) responses to items and the (unobservable) traits that govern their responses. Because they entail predictions, IRT models can be evaluated (i.e., confirmed or rejected) depending on how well they fit the data derived from responses to test items.

• IRT methods employ test and item response data from large samples known to differ on the ability or personality trait that the test under development is designed to assess. Such samples need not be representative of a defined population, but they must include groups of individuals who are at different levels in the trait or ability continuum. In addition, the items in the initial pool need to be carefully constructed or selected for their potential as indicators of the trait to be assessed.

• After item and test score data are collected, they are used to derive estimates of item parameters that will place examinees and items along a common scale for the ability or trait dimension. *Item parameters* are the numerical values that specify the form of the relationships between the abilities or traits being measured and the probability of a certain item response. For instance, *item difficulty* parameters express the difficulty of an item in terms of the ability scale position where the probability of passing the item is .50. Table 6.3 displays a small, hypothetical set of raw data on ten dichotomously scored items administered to ten individuals (A through J). Although a realistic example would include a much larger and more varied sample of test takers—possibly grouped into categories based on their total scores, instead of individually—the data in Table 6.3 illustrate the kind of information that may be used to estimate item difficulty parameters in relation to ability levels. Item parameters are obtained through a variety of procedures that require the use of specialized computer programs (see, e.g., Embretson & Reise, 2000, chap. 13). These procedures employ *nonlinear* mathematical functions, such as logistic functions, which yield item characteristic curves (see below). Nonlinear mathematical models are necessary because the linear regression model, discussed in Chapters 2 and 5, is not suitable for describing how changes in trait levels relate to changes in the probability of responding to an item in a specific way.

• An *item characteristic curve* (*ICC*) is the graphic representation of a mathematical function that relates item response probabilities to trait levels, given the item parameters that have been specified. For instance, the ICC of a dichotomous ability test item visually expresses the expected relationship between ability level and probability of passing an item. In the case of personality test items, ICCs display the expected relationship between trait levels and probability of responding to an item in a specific manner. The hypothetical ICCs presented in Figure 6.3 exemplify the three most common unidimensional logistic models for dichotomous item response

Table 6.3 Hypothetical Example of Raw Item and Person Data Used in IRT Parameter Estimation

Person	Item										Total
	1	2	3	4	5	6	7	8	9	10	
A	1	1	1	1	0	0	1	1	1	1	8
B	0	0	1	1	1	1	0	0	0	0	4
C	0	0	1	1	1	1	0	0	0	0	4
D	1	1	0	0	1	0	0	0	1	1	5
E	1	1	1	1	1	1	1	1	1	1	10
F	1	1	1	1	0	0	0	0	1	1	6
G	1	1	0	1	0	1	0	1	1	1	7
H	0	1	1	1	0	0	0	0	0	0	3
I	0	0	1	0	0	0	0	1	1	1	4
J	0	1	1	1	0	0	0	0	1	1	5
Total	5	7	8	8	4	4	2	4	7	7	

Note: The 1's and 0's in each cell indicate whether Persons A to J passed or failed each of the 10 items. Test takers' total scores, in the last column, can be used to calculate ability estimates; item total scores, in the last row, can be used to calculate item difficulties.

data. Panel A of Figure 6.3 displays ICCs for the one-parameter logistic model, also known as the *Rasch model* in honor of the mathematician who developed it (Rasch, 1960/1980). Panels B and C of Figure 6.3 portray the two- and three-parameter logistic models, respectively.

- *Panel A of Figure 6.3* displays the ICCs for two items that differ only with respect to difficulty. Item 1 is easier than Item 2. The location of the difficulty parameter (i.e., the ability level associated with a .50, or 50%, probability of success) is lower for Item 1 (X_1) than for Item 2 (X_2). Since the slopes of the two curves are the same, we can infer that the two items function equally well in terms of the relationship between ability and probability of success throughout the ability scale.
- *Panel B of Figure 6.3* shows ICCs for two items that differ in two parameters, namely, difficulty and discrimination. In this instance, the ability level associated with a 50% probability of success is somewhat higher for Item 1 (X_1) than for Item 2 (X_2). Furthermore, the slopes of the two curves—which show the ratio of change in ability to change in probability of success for each item—are different and cross over at a certain

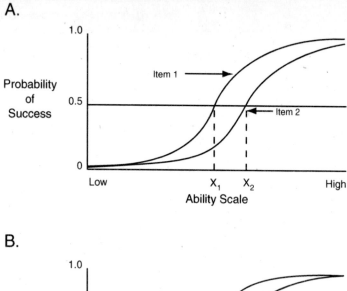

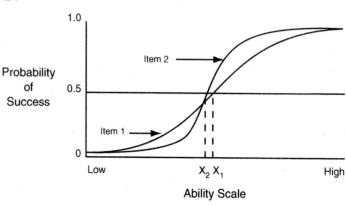

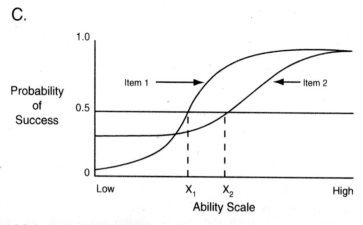

Figure 6.3 Item characteristic curves: A, one-parameter; B, two-parameter; and C, three-parameter models

point. This configuration suggests that the two items function differently in terms of their relation to the ability trait and do not discriminate equally well at all points in the ability scale. In a truly unidimensional test, items with ICCs that intersect—such as those in Panel B—are undesirable.

- *Panel C of Figure 6.3* displays the ICCs for two items that differ along three parameters, namely, difficulty, discrimination, and probability of chance success (or guessing). The ICC for Item 1 has a steeper slope than the curve for Item 2, and shows a steady rise in the probability of success as ability levels increase up to a certain point. In contrast, Item 2 clearly does not discriminate among individuals at different ability levels as well as Item 1: Its ICC shows a less pronounced relationship between ability level and probability of success. Note also that the ICC for Item 2 shows a fairly high probability of success even at the lowest end of the ability spectrum. This suggests that test takers at low levels of ability are able to correctly guess the answer to Item 2. Moreover, the 50% success probability is associated with a higher level of ability (X_2) for Item 2. Clearly, an item with an ICC like that of Item 2 in Panel C would be less efficient than Item 1 from a measurement perspective.

- As is the case with any theoretical model, the extent to which the assumptions of IRT models are met can be gauged by comparing their predictions against empirical data and evaluating the magnitude and significance of any discrepancies that are found between the observed data and the predictions of the models. If the fit between the ICC model-based expectations and the performance of examinees on a test item is sufficiently close, IRT parameters are used to derive the item's information function.

- An *item information function* reflects the contribution an item makes to trait or ability estimation at different points in the trait or ability continuum. Item information functions help to decide whether and where to incorporate items into a test, in light of the test's objectives. Trait-level estimates that locate test takers on the trait dimension are derived from their specific patterns of successes or failures on a series of items. In

DON'T FORGET

In item response theory (IRT), item parameters are assumed to be *invariant* for the population, meaning that they should be stable even when they are computed on groups differing in the ability or trait being measured. Thus, unlike the item analysis statistics described earlier in the chapter, IRT parameters are not linked to the performance of any given reference group.

IRT, the *test information function*, which is the sum of item information functions, corresponds to the CTT notion of score reliability (see Chapter 4). Test information functions are calculated and used to obtain standard errors of estimation at each level in the trait or ability scale. These standard errors, in turn, create confidence bands for the ability estimates in a fashion similar to the way standard errors of measurement in CTT are used to create confidence bands for obtained scores.

As may be gathered from the discussion of the ICCs presented in Figure 6.3, even the unidimensional IRT models exemplified in that figure can become quite complex, as the number of parameters encompassed in the models increases. Applying IRT models to the development of instruments aimed at assessing broader and more contentious intellectual and personality constructs is a much more difficult proposition (see, e.g., Reise & Henson, 2003). Multidimensional IRT models—which assume that two or more traits contribute to item responses—are now being used to explore and explain more complex and multifaceted constructs. Some of these newer, and more complicated, models are described by Embretson and Reise (2000).

Item Fairness

Generally speaking, there are many ways in which test items, as well as tests, can be biased or unfair to individual test takers or groups of test takers. As far as tests are concerned, the possibility of bias can be investigated by ascertaining whether test scores have the same meaning for members of different subgroups of the population (see Chapter 5). The question of test *fairness,* on the other hand, is a more complex and controversial issue. Whereas there is general agreement that unfair uses of tests must be avoided, exactly what constitutes fairness in testing is a matter of considerable debate (AERA, APA, NCME, 1999, pp. 74–76). Nevertheless, test users have a major responsibility in implementing fair testing practices through a thoughtful consideration of the appropriateness of instruments for their intended purposes and for potential test takers (Chapter 7).

At the level of test items, questions concerning bias and unfairness are more circumscribed and are usually taken up while a test is under development. To this end, test items are analyzed qualitatively and quantitatively throughout the process of test construction. Naturally, the extent to which test items undergo these reviews is related to the intended purpose of a test. Special care is taken to eliminate any possible bias or unfairness in the items of ability tests that are to be used in making decisions that have significant consequences for test takers.

Qualitative Analysis of Item Bias

The qualitative evaluation of test items from the point of view of fairness is based on judgmental procedures conducted by panels of demographically heterogeneous individuals who are qualified by virtue of their sensitivity to such matters and, preferably, by their expertise in the areas covered by a test as well. Typically these reviews occur at two stages. During the initial phase of test construction, when items are written or generated, they are examined in order to (a) screen out any stereotypical depictions of any identifiable subgroup of the population, (b) eliminate items whose content may be offensive to members of minority groups, and (c) ensure that diverse subgroups are appropriately represented in the materials contained in an item pool. In this initial review, individuals who are familiar with the linguistic and cultural habits of the specific subgroups likely to be encountered among potential test takers should also identify item content that may work to the benefit or detriment of any specific group, so that it may be revised. The second stage of qualitative item review occurs later in the process of test construction, after the items have been administered and item performance data have been analyzed separately for different subgroups. At this stage, items that show subgroup differences in indexes of difficulty, discrimination, or both are examined to identify the reasons for such differences and are either revised or discarded as warranted.

Quantitative Analysis of Item Bias

The quantitative assessment of item bias has sometimes been linked simply to the differences in the relative difficulty of test items for individuals from diverse demographic groups. However, this interpretation of item bias is viewed as naive by testing professionals who do not consider differences in the relative difficulty of an item for different groups to be sufficient evidence that the item is biased (see, e.g., Dragow, 1987). Instead, from a psychometric standpoint, an item is considered to be biased only if individuals from different groups who have the same standing on a trait differ in the probability of responding to the item in a specified manner. In tests of ability, for instance, bias may be inferred when persons who possess equal levels of ability, but belong to different demographic groups, have different probabilities of success on an item. Thus, in the testing literature, item bias is more properly described as *differential item functioning (DIF)*, a label that more pointedly denotes instances in which the relationship between item performance and the construct assessed by a test differs across two or more groups.

Classical procedures for the quantitative analysis of DIF involve comparisons of the item difficulty and item discrimination statistics for different groups. For example, if a test item has a low correlation with total test score (i.e., poor discrimination) and is more difficult for females than for males, it would obviously be suspect and should be discarded. However, the analysis of DIF by means of simple comparisons of the item-test correlations and p values for different groups is complicated by the fact that groups of various kinds (e.g., sex groups, ethnic groups, socioeconomic groups, etc.) often differ in terms of their average performance and variability, especially on ability tests. When group differences of this kind are found in the distributions of test scores, (a) item difficulty statistics become confounded by valid differences between groups in the ability that a test measures and (b) correlational indexes of item discrimination are affected by the differences in variability within the groups being compared. Because of these complicating factors, traditional item analysis statistics have not proved very helpful in detecting differential item functioning.

Differential Item Functioning

The proper assessment and study of DIF requires specialized methods and a number of them have been proposed. One of the most commonly used is the Mantel-Haenszel technique (Holland & Thayer, 1988) which expands on traditional item analytic procedures. In this type of analysis each of the groups in question (e.g., majority and minority groups) is divided into subgroups based on total test score, and item performance is assessed across comparable subgroups. Although this method is more refined than the simple comparison of item analysis statistics across groups, the Mantel-Haenszel procedure still relies on an internal criterion (total score) that may be insensitive to differences in item functioning across groups, and its ability to detect DIF is substantially dependent on the use of very large groups (Mazor, Clauser, & Hambleton, 1992).

Item response theory provides a much better foundation for investigating DIF than classical test theory methods. In order to establish whether individuals from different groups with equal levels of a latent trait perform differently on an item, it is necessary to locate persons from two or more groups on a common scale of ability. The IRT procedures for accomplishing this goal start by identifying a set of anchor items that show no DIF across the groups of interest. Once this is done, additional items can be evaluated for DIF by comparing the estimates of item parameters and the ICCs obtained separately for each group. If the parameters and ICCs derived from two groups for a given item are substantially the same, it may be safely inferred that the item functions equally well for both groups. Not surprisingly, IRT procedures are becoming the methods of choice for detecting DIF (see Embretson & Reise, 2000, chap. 10, for additional details).

Applications of Item Response Theory

As noted in Chapter 3, the use of IRT methods in test development and item calibration does not preclude the normative or criterion-referenced interpretation of test scores. In fact, because of its more refined methods for calibrating test items and for assessing measurement error, IRT can enhance the interpretation of test scores. Although IRT cannot provide solutions to all psychological measurement problems, it has already helped to bring about a more disciplined and objective approach to test development in the areas in which it has been applied.

At present, IRT methods are being applied most extensively in developing computerized adaptive tests used in large-scale testing programs, such as the SAT and the ASVAB. Development of tests of this type requires input from individuals with considerable technical expertise in mathematics and computer programming in addition to knowledge of the content area covered by the tests. More limited applications of IRT methods have been in use for some time. For instance, the assessment of item difficulty parameters through IRT methods has become fairly common in the development of ability and achievement batteries, such as the Differential Ability Scales, the Wechsler scales, the Wide Range Achievement tests, and the Woodcock tests. Item-response-theory models are also being used increasingly in the assessment of DIF in cognitive tests. Although IRT methods hold promise in the field of personality testing, their application in this area has been much more limited than in ability testing (Embretson & Reise, 2000, chap. 12).

Explorations in Item Development and Scoring

The revolution in computer technology, along with the rapid pace of developments in the theory and methodology of psychological science, permit an almost boundless exploration of innovative techniques that can be applied to measurement problems. In concluding this chapter, two promising applications of computer technology to the realm of test items are presented.

Recent Developments in Item Generation

The task decomposition and test protocol analysis methods ushered in by cognitive psychology have led to significant advances in exploring and clarifying the processes, strategies, and knowledge stores involved in the performance of test items (see Chapter 5). In fact, since the 1980s, these advances—along with concomitant strides in IRT and technology—have been applied in computerized test item generation for the development of ability and achievement tests. This methodology is still in its infancy, comparatively speaking, because the specifications needed to create rules whereby computer programs can generate test items must be considerably more detailed than they are for traditional methods of generating items and require a higher level of theoretical grounding. Nevertheless, computerized item generation has already been implemented in developing tools for areas—such as mathematics assessment and aptitude testing in aviation—in which (a) cognitive models of performance exist, (b) constructs to be examined can be represented in terms of a logical syntax, and (c) item difficulty can be gauged through objective referents. Undoubtedly, techniques for item generation will continue to be actively pursued by researchers because of the many advantages they present in terms of efficiency and economy, as well as for their potential in pedagogical applications (Irvine & Kyllonen, 2002).

Automated Essay Scoring

A significant innovation in the effort to standardize the scoring of essays is the development of computer technology for *automated essay scoring* (*AES*). The endeavor to evaluate written prose by means of computer software has been in progress for the past few decades and, like computerized item generation, has also been facilitated by advances in cognitive psychology and computational science. Though still in its early stages, AES shows great promise not only as a means of increasing the reliability and validity of scores but also as an instructional tool (Shermis & Burstein, 2003).

TEST YOURSELF

1. **The procedures involved in item analysis pertain primarily to test**
   (a) developers.
   (b) users.
   (c) takers.
   (d) administrators.

2. **Qualitative item analysis typically takes place**
   (a) after a test is standardized.
   (b) at the same that a test is cross-validated.
   (c) after the item pool is generated.
   (d) just before a test is published.

3. **Forced-choice items belong to the category of**
   (a) constructed-response items.
   (b) selected-response items.
   (c) neither a nor b.

4. **Which of the following is *not* one of the advantages of selected-response over constructed-response items? Selected-response items**
   (a) are less prone to scoring errors.
   (b) make more efficient use of testing time.
   (c) are easier to quantify.
   (d) are easier to prepare.

5. **Item discrimination indexes are statistics primarily used to assess item**

   (a) validity.
   (b) fairness.
   (c) reliability.
   (d) difficulty.

6. **If one wished to produce a test that would result in maximum differentiation among test takers, one would aim for an average difficulty level (p value) of**

   (a) 1.00.
   (b) 0.75.
   (c) 0.50.
   (d) 0.

7. **The Pearson r is the correlation coefficient most commonly used to calculate indexes of the relationship between item performance and criterion standing.** True or False?

8. **For a pure speed test, the customary indexes of item difficulty and discrimination are _____ they are for a pure power test.**

   (a) less appropriate than
   (b) more appropriate than
   (c) just as appropriate as

9. **Which of the following is *not* one of the basic objectives toward which item response theory (IRT) is geared?**

   (a) To provide maximum information about the trait levels of examinees
   (b) To give examinees items that are tailored to their trait levels
   (c) To increase the number of items included in a test
   (d) To minimize measurement error

10. **Item response theory, so far, has been applied least extensively in the area of _____ testing.**

    (a) achievement
    (b) aptitude
    (c) cognitive
    (d) personality

Answers: 1. a; 2. c; 3. b; 4. d; 5. a; 6. c; 7. False; 8. a; 9. c; 10. d.

Seven

ESSENTIALS OF TEST USE

Prior to their use, tests can be evaluated only from a scientific and technical standpoint by people who have the necessary expertise in test development, in psychometric principles, and in the aspects of behavior that the tests attempt to evaluate. After testing is implemented—through the processes of selection, administration, and scoring—test results have to be evaluated, interpreted, and communicated in a manner appropriate to the purpose for which they are to be employed by professionals who have knowledge of the context in which the testing takes place as well as of the technical aspects and psychological issues involved in a given situation. At a minimum, evaluating the applications of psychological and educational tests involves considerations pertaining to the skill with which the test user employs these instruments and to their suitability for the test takers with whom they are used. In a larger sense, to the extent that testing acquires practical significance in the lives of individuals, test use also needs to be evaluated in light of societal values and political priorities. In this wider context, testing can become highly controversial and test users must rely on their personal and professional codes of ethics to determine whether they are willing to lend their expertise to a particular use of tests.

Proper testing practices are regulated by the ethical principles and standards promulgated by each of the professions that make use of psychological and educational tests (e.g., American Counseling Association, 1995; AERA, APA, NCME, 1999; APA, 2002; National Association of School Psychologists, 2000). In the past few decades, increasing concerns about the possibility of test misuse have led these professions and the organizations involved with testing to become engaged in preparing and disseminating information on test user qualifications. One of the major efforts in this direction was spearheaded by the APA and resulted in the publication of an explicit set of guidelines to inform all concerned parties of the qualifications that the APA considers important for the competent and responsible use of tests (Turner, DeMers, Fox, & Reed, 2001). Rapid Reference 7.1 provides a brief summary of these guidelines. In addition, the *Testing Stan-*

≡Rapid Reference 7.1

Qualifications for Users of Psychological Tests

As discussed in Chapter 1, no formal set of credentials, whether by education, licensure, or certification, can ensure competence in the use of a particular test in a given situation.

Rather, the qualifications of users of psychological tests are based on two main factors:

1. Their knowledge and skills in
   - psychometric principles and statistics;
   - selection of tests in light of their technical qualities, the purpose for which they will be used, and the characteristics of examinees;
   - procedures for administering and scoring tests, as well as for interpreting, reporting, and safeguarding their results; and
   - all matters relevant to the context and purpose of the test use.

2. The extent to which test users have received appropriate supervised experience in all aspects of the knowledge and skills pertinent to the intended use of a specific test.

For further information, see Turner, S. M., DeMers, S. T., Fox, H. R., & Reed, G. M. (2001). APA's guidelines for test user qualifications: An executive summary. *American Psychologist, 56,* 1099–1113.

---

dards (AERA, APA, NCME, 1999) include a chapter that outlines the responsibilities of test users, as well as separate chapters devoted to issues related to (a) fairness in testing and test use, (b) testing individuals of diverse linguistic backgrounds, (c) testing individuals with disabilities, (d) psychological testing and assessment, (e) educational testing and assessment, (f) testing in employment and credentialing, and (g) testing in program evaluation and public policy.

Documents that provide additional guidance in the use of tests as part of high-stakes decision making for students (U.S. Department of Education, Office for Civil Rights, 2000) and principles for the validation and use of personnel selection procedures (Society for Industrial and Organizational Psychology [SIOP], 2003) are also available and worth consulting prior to undertaking endeavors in those areas. A particularly helpful feature of the U.S. Department of Education document is that, besides summarizing the basic principles of sound testing practice in the field of educational measurement, it also discusses federal legal requirements that apply to the nondiscriminatory use of tests for high-stakes purposes. The SIOP document, while not intended to interpret statutes, regulations, or case law regarding employment decisions, provides principles for the application and use of selection procedures that can inform and guide the parties responsible for authorizing and implementing such procedures in evaluating their adequacy and appropriateness.

In recent years, the professions most closely associated with psychological testing—which are represented in the Joint Committee on Testing Practices (JCTP)—have increasingly come to recognize that test takers also need to be informed of their rights and responsibilities in the testing process. To that end, they have published a document whose sole purpose is to provide such information (JCTP, 1998). Rapid Reference 7.2 lists some of the most important rights and responsibilities that are outlined and described in this document, which is available in its entirety in the Testing and Assessment section of the APA's Web site (http://www.apa.org/science/ttrr.html).

The application of tests for inappropriate purposes or in inappropriate ways by users who lack the proper training and qualifications invariably results in test

≡ *Rapid Reference 7.2*

Rights and Responsibilities of Test Takers

The document on *Rights and Responsibilities of Test Takers: Guidelines and Expectations* (JCTP, 1998) can be freely reproduced and disseminated. Although it does not have the force of law—and state and federal laws supercede the rights and responsibilities stated therein—professionals involved in the testing process have the responsibility to ensure that test takers are made aware of the information contained in the document.

Some of the important *rights of test takers* include the following:

- The right to receive an explanation prior to testing about (a) the purposes for testing, (b) the tests to be used, (c) whether the test results will be reported to them or to others, and (d) the planned uses of the results. If test takers have a disability or difficulty comprehending the language of the test, they have the right to inquire and learn about possible testing accommodations.
- The right to know if a test is optional and to learn of the consequences of taking or not taking the test, fully completing the test, or canceling the scores.
- The right to receive an explanation of test results within a reasonable time and in commonly understood terms.
- The right to have test results kept confidential to the extent allowed by law.

Some of the important *responsibilities of test takers* include the following:

- The responsibility to read and/or listen to their rights and responsibilities.
- The responsibility to ask questions prior to testing about why the test is being given, how it will be given, what they will be asked to do, and what will be done with the results.

DON'T FORGET

....

- Even the most carefully developed and psychometrically sound instrument is subject to misuse.
- According to the *Testing Standards* (AERA, APA, NCME, 1999, chap. 11), the responsibility for appropriate test use and sound interpretation of test scores rests primarily on the test user.
- Test misuse can occur at every step of the testing process, starting with the inappropriate selection of instruments either for the purposes to which they are applied or for the individuals to whom they are administered. Errors in administration or scoring and in the interpretation or reporting of test results may compound the problem of test misuse.
- Whenever the possibility of using tests is contemplated, the best way to prevent their misuse is to ensure at the outset that the individuals involved in every facet of test use have the qualifications and competence necessary to fulfill their roles in the testing process.

misuse. This chapter deals with some of the essential considerations that must be taken into account in using psychological tests, including issues related to test selection, administration, and scoring, as well as to the interpretation and reporting of test scores. Since much of the information in former chapters is relevant to the fundamental issues involved in responsible test use, readers may want to refer to earlier parts of this volume when topics discussed previously are alluded to in the present chapter. To the extent that test users and test takers are aware of what constitutes sound testing practice, the possibility of test misuse diminishes and the potential benefits inherent in the use of tests are more likely to be realized.

ESSENTIALS OF TEST SELECTION

As discussed in Chapter 1, psychological tests are used primarily to help in making decisions about people in educational, employment, clinical, forensic, and vocational counseling settings. In addition, tests are also frequently used in psychological research and have recently begun to be applied in the process of psychotherapy for purposes of personal development, increased self-understanding, or both (Finn & Tonsager, 1997). The consequences of test misuse in these various applications differ widely in terms of their potential impact on individual test takers. Naturally, the amount of care devoted to each step of the testing process—from test selection on—must take into account and be proportional to the impact that testing is likely to have. Although most of the ensuing material is also applicable to the use of tests for research or therapeutic pur-

CAUTION

Of all the arenas in which psychological tests are used, perhaps none is more contentious than forensic applications. Due to the adversarial nature of most legal proceedings, professionals who agree to appear as experts in trials that involve evidence derived from psychological testing can expect to have the bases of their testimony questioned and challenged at every opportunity. It stands to reason that in such situations, so-called experts who are ill prepared to defend their test-based testimony can easily be humiliated and embarrassed by lawyers who are well prepared to attack it.

An instructive way to become acquainted with the potential pitfalls of misusing tests in the legal arena, as well as in other contexts, is by consulting the multivolume work on *Coping With Psychiatric and Psychological Testimony*, prepared by Jay Ziskin in collaboration with others and addressed primarily to lawyers. The fifth and latest edition of this work was published in 1995 by Law and Psychology Press of Los Angeles, CA. It has since been augmented by supplements issued in 1997 and in 2000. Of the three volumes in the main work, volume 2—which is devoted mainly to challenging testimony derived from psychological tests of various kinds—is the most pertinent to the topics considered in this chapter.

poses, the point of departure for the discussion of most topics in this chapter is the assumption that tests are used primarily for making decisions about people.

To Use or Not to Use (Tests), That Is the (First) Question

Regardless of the purposes for which psychological testing is intended, the first issue to be decided is whether testing is needed. In order to resolve this issue, prospective test users should engage in a cost-benefit analysis—similar to the one suggested by Goldman (1971)—and explicitly consider the following questions:

1. What kind of information do I seek to gain from testing?
2. How will this information be used?
3. How much, if any, of the information I seek is already available from other sources?
4. What other tools might be used to gather the information I seek?
5. What are the advantages of using tests instead of, or in addition to, other sources of information?
6. What are the disadvantages or the costs in time, effort, and money of using tests instead of, or in addition to, other sources of information?

If the rationale for test use and the expected application of test results are not explicit at the outset, test scores are not likely to be of much use or, worse still, they are likely to be misused. If the information that is needed is already available from other sources or can be obtained through other means, testing will probably be superfluous, unless its purpose is to confirm what is already known or to gather additional support for it. Finally, if the advantages or benefits to be gained from test use do not outweigh its cost or disadvantages, including any potential harm that might accrue from test use, testing is obviously not advisable. Rapid Reference 7.3 lists some of the main reasons why and circumstances in which testing may be inadvisable.

Two Important Reasons for Using Tests

Because testing occurs in so many different settings and is used for so many different purposes, it is difficult to discuss its impact in the abstract. However, in whatever context psychological tests are employed—provided that they have been carefully developed and that adequate documentation of their psychometric value for a given purpose is available—when they are used judiciously, they have distinct advantages over other methods of gathering information about people. The most significant advantages that psychological tests offer pertain to their characteristic efficiency and objectivity.

 *Rapid Reference 7.3*

Top 10 Reasons for *Not* Using Tests

There are many reasons why, and many situations in which, the use of psychological tests is not advisable; the following list merely presents the most salient ones. With few exceptions, psychological tests should not be used when any of these circumstances apply:

1. The purpose of testing is unknown or unclear to the test user.
2. The test user is not completely familiar with all of the necessary test documentation and trained on the procedures related to the test.
3. The test user does not know where the test results will go, or how they will be used, or cannot safeguard their use.
4. The information that is sought from testing is already available, or can be gathered more efficiently, through other sources.
5. The test taker is not willing or able to cooperate with the testing.
6. The test taker is likely to incur some harm due to the testing process itself.
7. The environmental setting and conditions for the testing are inadequate.
8. The test format or materials are inappropriate in light of the test taker's age, sex, cultural or linguistic background, disability status, or any other condition that might invalidate test data.
9. The test norms are outdated, inadequate, or inapplicable for the test taker.
10. The documentation on the reliability or validity of test scores is inadequate.

- *Efficiency.* Many of the questions that are addressed through psychological testing could be answered by other methods, provided that the individuals who seek the required information have the time and resources necessary to gather it. For instance, most people do not require the use of tests to sketch a psychological profile of those with whom they have had extensive and continuous personal contact. By observing the behavior of individuals and interacting with them in a variety of situations over a long period of time, ample data can be gathered from which to draw conclusions about their skills and personal attributes and even about how they are likely to behave in the future. Psychological testing affords those who are in a position to evaluate and make decisions about people—but do not have the opportunity for prolonged observation and interaction with them—the tools for gathering the information they require in a timely and cost-effective manner.

- *Objectivity.* Even when there is extensive opportunity for observing and interacting with people, the data we can gather through informal observations and interactions may be of questionable or limited value. Observational data obtained in an unsystematic fashion can easily lead to judgments that are inaccurate on account of the subjectivity of observers, including variations in *what* they observe and remember, as well as *how well* they observe, report, and evaluate their observations. Needless to say, this subjectivity comes into play most particularly when observers are not impartial, as is the case when they are friends, relatives, or associates of the person who is observed. Even when observers are keen and able to maintain detachment with regard to the subjects of their observation, the raw data gathered from naturalistic observations and interactions cannot be appropriately evaluated and interpreted without some standardized frame of reference against which to compare it. As discussed in earlier chapters, the meaning and value that can be derived from the behavior samples obtained through standardized tests depend almost entirely on the normative or criterion-based frames of reference that are available for comparisons and on the accumulated data on test score reliability and validity.

Test Utility

Whenever the use of tests for making decisions about people is contemplated, the potential utility of their use should be considered and analyzed. The concept of *utility*, introduced briefly in Chapter 5 as a consideration that is closely related to validity, refers to an appraisal of the subjective desirability of an outcome or event. Utility is an aspect of the much larger topic of decision theory, a widely used approach to gathering and analyzing information, usually in mathematical form, in order to devise rational strategies for making decisions (see, e.g., Bell, Raiffa, & Tversky, 1988). Estimating the value of correct decisions versus the cost of incorrect decisions is invariably a complicated matter, especially when the decisions to be made will affect the lives of human beings in significant ways. Decision theory concerns itself with the development and analysis of possible strategies for decision-making, using available information to estimate their utility by calculating the costs and benefits of various alternative outcomes in quantitative—usually monetary—terms. Naturally, in order to estimate the utility of an outcome, a subjective point of view has to be adopted and that point of view typically stems from the values and priorities of the decision makers.

For example, in the field of employment selection there are two possible decisions (hiring vs. not hiring) that can be made. Assuming that the criterion of job performance can be dichotomized into the categories of success or failure, these decisions have four possible outcomes: (a) valid acceptances, (b) valid rejections, (c) false acceptances, and (d) false rejections. Valid acceptances are the most desirable of all outcomes; not only do they not pose any hazards for either the employer or the applicant who is hired, but they in fact provide benefits to both. False acceptances, on the other hand, pose some risks to the employer (e.g., lost revenue or liability incurred due to the employees' incompetence, wasted time and effort in hiring and training activities, increased turnover, etc.) but usually not to the employee. Valid rejections are for the most part advantageous to the employer but most likely not so to the applicants who are rejected. False rejections typically do not present significant risks to the employer, unless the decisions are contested, but they may harm the applicants who are falsely rejected, possibly in significant ways.

Clearly, the utility of outcomes differs for the various parties affected by a decision. Furthermore, the potential consequences of decisions to all parties involved can never be fully anticipated, let alone quantified. Still, the notion of explicitly trying to anticipate and assess the probable benefits and risks inherent in using tests—as opposed to other tools—is at the heart of responsible test use. To that end, decision theory provides some basic concepts that may be used in considering whether and to what extent tests can contribute to improved outcomes by increasing the number of correct decisions and minimizing the number of incorrect decisions. These concepts are especially suitable for organizations seeking to determine possible gains in the accuracy of selection decisions that may be achieved by implementing a decision strategy that includes the use of test scores (see, e.g., Kobrin, Camara, & Milewski, 2002). The following are the essential items of information needed in order to estimate such gains:

- *Validity data:* Test scores can improve decision making only to the extent that they have demonstrable validity for assessing test takers' standing, or predicting their performance, on a criterion; all other things being equal, the higher the validity coefficient of test scores is, the greater the accuracy of criterion estimates and predictions will be (see Chapter 5).

- *Base rate data:* The concept of a *base rate* refers to the starting point from which potential gains in accuracy can be calculated, that is to say, the established probability of events in a population prior to the introduction of any novel procedure, such as testing. For example, if the proportion of students who graduate from a program of study is .60, or 60%, of those who were admitted into the program, the base rate is .60. In employment selection decisions, the base rate is the proportion of hired applicants for a given position who turn out to be successful at their jobs. For the purpose of calculating the *incremental validity* or improvement contributed by a test in selection decisions, the base rate refers to the proportion of correct decisions that are made without the use of test scores. All other things being equal, the potential gains in accuracy of selection decisions are greatest when the base rates are close to .50. Base rates close to the extremes (e.g., .10 or .90) indicate that accurate selection is either very difficult or very easy under existing circumstances. In such cases, using test scores as the basis for selection—even if they have a relatively high degree of validity—may not increase the accuracy of decisions and might even lower it.

- *Selection ratios:* Another constraint on the potential contribution test scores might make to the improvement of selection decisions stems from the *selection ratio,* which is the ratio that results when the number of positions available is divided by the number of applicants for those positions. If 5 positions are available and 500 people apply for them, the selection ratio is 5 ÷ 500 or 1%, whereas if only 25 people apply, the selection ratio is 5 ÷ 25 or 20%. Naturally, smaller selection ratios afford decision makers the opportunity to be more selective than do larger selection ratios. As an extreme example, if three positions are open and three people apply, the selection ratio is 100% and the employer has no latitude for choice if the organization needs to have those workers. In such a situation, the incremental validity that test scores can contribute—regardless of how predictively valid they may be—is nil. On the other hand, when the selection ratio is very small, even a test whose scores have only a moderate degree of predictive validity may help to increase the rate of accurate decisions.

As the foregoing discussion makes clear, the degree of improvement in the accuracy of selection decisions that can be gained through the use of test scores in employment and education settings depends on a combination of the base rates and selection ratios in a given situation, as well as on the validity of test scores. The interactive effects of these three variables on selection accuracy has been appreciated for a long time; in fact, as far back as 1939, Taylor and Russell published a set of tables that display the expected proportion of successes (valid acceptances) that can be expected for various combinations of base rates, selection ratios, and validity coefficients. The Taylor-Russell tables, which predate the advent of decision theory, provide a basic amount of information that can be used in evaluating the possibility of using a given test within a certain context, but they do not evaluate all possible outcomes of a decision nor do they address all of the factors pertinent to selection decisions.

Since the Taylor-Russell tables were published, industrial-organizational psychologists have advanced well beyond them and developed additional ways to evaluate the effects of test use, incorporating decision theory concepts and models. Refinements include the estimation of the effects of test use on outcomes other than valid acceptances, such as false rejections, and on outcomes gauged through continuous or graduated criteria that may be more realistic for decision-making applications than the simple dichotomy of success or failure embodied in the Taylor-Russell tables. Additional aspects of decision making, such as the use of multiple predictors in various combinations and the evaluation of strategies for selection, classification, and placement of personnel in terms of their utility from various points of view (e.g., increasing productivity, decreasing turnover, minimizing training costs, etc.) have also been investigated in relation to test use in human resource management (see, e.g., Boudreau, 1991; Schmidt & Hunter, 1998). For a detailed description of one of the most thorough applications of many decision theory concepts to the development and evaluation of a battery of tests and other tools for personnel selection and classification, interested readers are referred to J. P. Campbell and Knapp's (2001) account of the U.S. Army Project A (see Chapter 5 for more information on this topic).

Test Utility in Clinical Decision Making

Some decision theory concepts may be applied to maximize the efficiency of testing and assessment in areas other than personnel selection. In clinical psychology, for instance, *base rates* refer to the frequencies with which pathological conditions, such as depression, occur in a given population. Provided that the required information is available, knowledge of base rates can help in evaluating the possible utility of test use for diagnostic or predictive purposes within a given population. As is the case in selection decisions, the contribution that tests can make to improving predictive or diagnostic accuracy is greatest when base rates are close to .50. When a condition to be diagnosed is either pervasive or very rare within a population, that is, if the base rates are either very high or very low, the improvement in diagnostic accuracy that can be achieved through the use of diagnostic tests is lower than when the condition occurs with moderate frequency. The reason for this is the same as in selection decisions, namely, that base rates have a limiting effect on the accuracy of decisions. With regard to diagnoses, if the base rate of a condition within a population is very high (e.g., .80), the probability of a *false positive finding*—that is, of diagnosing the condition when it is not present—is low (.20) even if diagnostic decisions are made on a random basis. Similarly, if the base rate is extremely small, the probability of a *false negative finding*—that is, of not detecting the condition when it is present—is also low. In such situations, the cost of using test scores to identify the presence of a condition within an entire group or population may not be justified by the relatively modest gains in accuracy that the test scores could contribute. For an excellent discussion of the implications of base rates in clinical practice, the reader is referred to Finn and Kamphuis's (1995) chapter on that topic.

It should be noted that in clinical settings, as in other fields of assessment practice, decisions are usually made on an individual basis using data from a variety of tools, including the specialized knowledge and judgment of the assessor. A thorough review of medical records, including laboratory test results and findings from the various imaging techniques currently available, in order to explore or rule out physiological factors (e.g., drug use or abuse, neurological or endocrine disorders, etc.) that may be causing or contributing to psychiatric symptoms is an indispensable part of psychiatric and neuropsychological evaluations in clinical settings. Therefore, the contribution made by psychological test results in such settings cannot be evaluated in isolation. In addition, the potential utility of individual diagnostic decisions based only on test results is mitigated by the low base rates of most mental disorders in the general population (O'Leary & Norcross, 1998); by the relatively small validity coefficients of many of the tests used for such purposes; and by the evolving nature of psychiatric nosology and diagnostic criteria, especially with regard to personality disorders (see, e.g., Livesley, 2001). Furthermore, contextual issues related to the reasons why diagnostic assessment is undertaken can significantly alter the relative ease or difficulty of achieving accurate results from testing and other assessment tools. In view of all these factors, it is not surprising that the utility of tests in clinical decision-making is a subject of frequent debate within the field of psychology. Rapid Reference 7.4 lists a few noteworthy contributions to the various sides of this debate.

Other Assessment Tools

There are, of course, many avenues that can be used instead of or in addition to tests in order to gather information for evaluating and making decisions about people. Case history or biographical data, interviewing, systematic and naturalistic observation, academic and employment records, as well as references from teachers and supervisors, are among the most frequently used tools in the assessment of individuals. Each of these sources of information, singly or in combination, can provide valuable data and contribute to successful decision-making. In fact, several of these assessment tools (e.g., interviewing, ratings) can be standardized and evaluated in terms of their reliability and validity, as well as with re-

☰ *Rapid Reference 7.4*

....

Are Psychological Tests Useful in Clinical Decision-Making?

This question is a subject of almost as much debate as the question of whether psychotherapy is effective in treating mental disorders. Few would answer either one with an unqualified yes or no. Most practitioners who use tests in clinical, counseling, and forensic settings believe fervently in their value, whereas often the opposite is true for nonpractitioners. For an assortment of opinions on this topic, readers might consult the following sources:

- Eisman, E. J., Dies, R. R., Finn, S. E., Eyde, L. D., Kay, G. G., Kubiszyn, T. W., Meyer, G. J., & Moreland, K. (2000). Problems and limitations in the use of psychological assessment in the contemporary health care delivery system. *Professional Psychology: Research and Practice, 31,* 131–140.
- Hummel, T. J. (1999). The usefulness of tests in clinical decisions. In J. W. Lichtenberg & R. K. Goodyear (Eds.), *Scientist-practitioner perspectives on test interpretation* (pp. 59–112). Boston: Allyn & Bacon.
- Kubiszyn, T. W., Meyer, G. J., Finn, S. E., Eyde, L. D., Kay, G. G., Moreland, K. L., Dies, R. R., & Eisman, E. J. (2000). Empirical support for psychological assessment in clinical health care settings. *Professional Psychology: Research and Practice, 31,* 119–130.
- Meyer, G. J., Finn, S. E., Eyde, L. D., Kay, G. G., Moreland, K. L., Dies, R. R., Eisman, E. J., Kubiszyn, T. W., & Reed, G. M. (2001). Psychological testing and psychological assessment: A review of evidence and issues. *American Psychologist, 56,* 128–165. (See the Comment section of the February 2002 issue of *American Psychologist* for responses to Meyer et al.).

gard to their utility in decision-making. When claims concerning the validity of such tools for a specific purpose are made, their use falls under the purview and guidelines of the *Testing Standards* (AERA, APA, NCME, 1999, pp. 3–4). If the data these methods provide are demonstrably reliable and valid, they may suffice as a basis for making decisions, either singly or in combination.

Biodata

Life-history information, also known as *biodata,* can be obtained through a number of methods, including interviewing, questionnaires, and examination of existing records of past behavior, such as academic transcripts, police reports, and so on. As stated earlier, examination of medical records is an indispensable aspect of any clinical evaluation of symptoms that may be rooted in or affected by neurological or metabolic disorders, drug intake, or other possible physical conditions. Moreover, in almost any type of assessment, well-documented data about a person's past behavior and achievements are among the most valid and reliable sources of evaluative information because they are factual evidence of what an individual is capable of doing or accomplishing. For example, with regard to the difficult question of predicting violent behavior, the actuarial approach to risk assessment provides the fundamental anchor point for predictions. This approach—which can be supplemented by an assessment of current status, as well as by clinical information and testing—is based on a systematic examination of historical data that have demonstrated empirical relationships to dangerousness, such as previous violence, substance abuse, employment stability, mental disorder, and early maladjustment (Borum, 1996; Monahan & Steadman, 2001). A similar example of the value of historical data can be drawn from the realm of employment, where it is generally understood that a proven record of past success in an occupation is one of the best possible determinants of future success. Thus, if the information about a potential employee's past job performance is current, reliable, and highly favorable, most employers would not hesitate to hire the individual on that basis. A more structured and formal approach to the utilization of information on a person's life history is through biometric data derived from standardized biographical inventories, which can be validated as predictors of future performance in a variety of contexts. For a comprehensive account of the use of biographical information in selection decisions, interested readers should consult the *Biodata Handbook* edited by Stokes, Mumford, and Owens (1994).

Interview Data

Interviewing can provide a wealth of information in almost any assessment context; it affords the opportunity to observe the interviewee's behavior and to gather pertinent life-history data as well as information about the individual's attitudes, opinions, and values. A face-to-face interview is a very flexible tool and, when properly conducted, may prove to be of critical value in making decisions about people. In many clinical, forensic, and employment settings, interviewing the individuals who are being assessed as well as those who can provide collateral data is considered an essential aspect of the assessment process (see, e.g., Hersen & Van Hasselt, 1998). However, the reliability and validity of interview data are highly dependent on the interviewer's skill and objectivity in gathering, recording, and interpreting information. To combat the potential weaknesses inherent in interview data, current practices in most fields that use interviewing techniques stress either the intensive training of interviewers or the use of structured interviews—which are really standardized instruments akin to tests in many ways—or both.

Observation

Another ubiquitous source of assessment data consists of ratings, checklists, and coding systems based on various types of direct behavioral observation or on previous relevant contact with the person to be assessed. As with interviewing, the reliability and validity of ratings and other data derived from observation can vary greatly depending on the rater and on the system that is used for rating or recording observations. Training that provides raters with a uniform standard by which to evaluate performance can improve the quality of observational data. The use of standardized rating scales to gather data from informants, such as parents or teachers, is a common procedure in the assessment of children and adolescents (see, e.g., Kamphaus & Frick, 2002, chaps. 7 and 8).

Additional Sources of Information

Many of the alternative sources of information used in the evaluation and assessment of individuals cannot be properly evaluated for reliability and validity. For instance, the value of letters of recommendation and similar references depends on the extent to which the persons providing them are willing and able to disclose pertinent information in a conscientious and thorough manner. Those who receive the references are most often unaware of factors that may impinge on their trustworthiness. Similarly, over the past few decades, grade inflation at all levels of schooling has eroded the meaning of many academic credentials to the point that grade point averages, and even some degrees and diplomas, can no longer be taken at face value with regard to the competencies they signify.

Searching for and Evaluating Tests

When the use of psychological tests for a specific purpose is contemplated, prospective test users are confronted with two major tasks, namely, (a) finding available instruments for the purposes they have in mind and (b) evaluating them from that perspective as well as from the point of view of prospective test takers. With regard to the first one of these tasks, readers are referred to the section on Sources of Information about Tests in Chapter 1 of this book and, particularly, to the document on *FAQ/Finding Information About Psychological Tests* (APA, 2003), created and maintained by the Testing and Assessment staff of the APA and available on the APA Web site. As mentioned in Chapter 1, this resource is an excellent point of departure for the person who seeks information about published or unpublished psychological tests. The FAQ document lists and summarizes the contents of all the major reference works on tests of both types, and provides information on how to locate tests and test publishers, how to purchase tests, available software and scoring services, as well as additional information on the proper use of tests.

Evaluating instruments that have been identified as being of possible use for a specific purpose is a more complex matter. To be sure, the reviews and the literature on the tests in question typically provide basic information about the types of scores and coverage provided by a test, the purpose and population for which it was designed, how it was developed, its standardization procedures, the types of items it uses, possible sources of test bias, and findings related to the reliability and validity of its scores, as well as practical features of test content and design that have a bearing on the ease with which it can be administered and scored. This

DON'T FORGET

Lawrence Rudner's (1994) article on "Questions to Ask When Evaluating Tests," available on the Internet at http://edres.org/pare, provides a good starting point for test evaluation.

Most of the earlier chapters in this book contain material relevant to the evaluation of tests. A brief overview of some of the key aspects to consider in the process of test selection can be found in the following items:

- *Rapid Reference 3.2:* Information Needed to Evaluate the Applicability of a Normative Sample
- *Rapid Reference 4.7:* Reliability Considerations in Test Selection
- *Rapid Reference 5.8:* The Relationship Among Questions, Decisions, and Predictions Requiring Criterion-Related Validation
- *Rapid Reference 5.12:* Validation Strategies in Relation to Test Score Interpretation
- *Table 5.1:* Aspects of Construct Validity and Related Sources of Evidence
- *Rapid Reference 6.6:* What Makes the Behavior Samples Gathered Through Test Items So Complex?

information can help the test user decide if the instrument, such as it is, appears to be appropriate for the purpose and the persons for which it is intended or whether local norms or additional data on reliability and validity need to be collected. However, even when a test is deemed to be appropriate from a psychometric standpoint, the test user is faced with many other practical issues that are uniquely pertinent to the test taker's specific context and situation, to the level of qualifications and experience the use of a test requires, to time and financial constraints, and so on. Rapid Reference 7.5 lists some of the variables that need to be considered in relation to the specific individuals or groups to whom a test will be administered.

If the investment of time, effort, and financial resources that will be required in order to implement the use of a test within a given context seems likely to be justified by the information test scores can provide, the next step for prospective

≡ Rapid Reference 7.5

Some Variables to Consider in Selecting Tests in Relation to Prospective Test Takers

- *Variables related to test medium:* The choice of a specific medium of presentation for tests items, such as paper-and-pencil versus computer administration or oral versus visual presentation, will pose some advantages or disadvantages for examinees, depending on their familiarity with the medium, sensory acuity in the auditory and visual modes, motor skills, and so forth. Even when a test includes some practice items to familiarize test takers with a chosen medium, their varying amounts of prior experience with that medium will probably continue to affect their test performance.

- *Variables related to test format:* Regardless of their content, selected-response items tend to require more receptive skills than constructed-response items, which involve the use of expressive skills. Since test takers differ in terms of those skills, the choice of item format will also affect their performance. Additional variables, such as the use of time limits or individual versus group administration, will also affect test takers differentially based on their cultural and experiential backgrounds.

- *Variables related to the language of test items:* Whenever language is part of a test but not of its essence, the receptive and expressive linguistic skills of the test takers may unduly affect scores. Thus, depending on the requirements of a specific test, examiners should consider and ascertain whether test takers have sufficient levels of vocabulary, reading skills, and writing skills, to be able to understand and attempt to perform the tasks required of them. To this end, for instance, test manuals should and often do include information concerning the reading level required to understand test items.

test users is to actually obtain the test and try it out on themselves or on one or more individuals who are willing to submit to a practice administration. For this purpose, many publishers make available *specimen sets* of their instruments that include the test manual and samples of the materials needed for administration and scoring. Careful study of these materials, especially the test manual, is considered by the *Testing Standards* as a prerequisite to sound test use because they provide the documentation needed for test users to evaluate the extent to which test results will serve the purposes for which test use is intended. Moreover, test documents provided by the publishers of tests must specify the qualifications required for administering and interpreting test scores accurately and, whenever possible, alert readers about possible misuses of a test (AERA, APA, NCME, 1999, chap. 5). Such documents may include technical manuals, user's guides, and other similar materials intended to supplement the test manual.

ESSENTIALS OF TEST ADMINISTRATION AND SCORING

Unlike many other aspects of test use considered in the present chapter, the essentials of test administration can easily be summed up in two words: adequate preparation. The proper administration of psychological tests requires careful preparation of the testing environment, the test taker, and the person who administers the test.

Preparing the Testing Environment

The most important principle to follow in preparing the environment in which testing will occur is to anticipate and remove any potential sources of distraction. Rooms in which testing is conducted should be adequately lit and ventilated, should provide appropriate seating and space for test takers, and should be free from noises or other stimuli (e.g., food or drink) that might disrupt the test takers' ability to attend to their tasks. To prevent possible interruptions, it is customary to post a sign—which many test publishers freely provide—on the door of the examination room to alert passers-by that testing is in progress.

Beyond securing a suitable testing room, adequate preparation of the testing environment involves following the test manual's instructions for administration, which are geared toward replicating the conditions under which the test was standardized as closely as possible. For group testing, these instructions might include providing materials necessary for taking the test (e.g., pencils with erasers) and making sure that test takers are seated in such a way that they are prevented from conversing or looking into each others' response booklets, enlisting test proctors, and so forth. For individual tests, special seating arrangements need to be made so that the examiner can present test materials in the proper orientation, record responses unobtrusively, and fully observe the test taker's behavior.

As a general rule, the presence of anyone other than the examiner and the test taker in the room where an individual test administration takes place should not be allowed (see, e.g., National Academy of Neuropsychology, 1999). The presence of third parties poses the possibility of distracting from or even influencing the testing process and introduces an element that is inconsistent with standardized test administration and an additional, unnecessary risk to test security. There may be special circumstances that require the observation of a test administration by others—for example, students who are receiving formal training in test administration. Ideally, such observations should be made from a room adjacent to the testing room, through a one-way mirror. For test takers who may have difficulties communicating with the examiner because of their young age or linguistic background, or because of a disability, the presence of a parent or an interpreter may be required in the testing room. In such situations, as well as in any other case in which special accommodations that may have a bearing on the interpretation of scores are made, the report of test results should note them.

Preparing the Test Taker

There are two distinct aspects of testing that relate to the preparation of test takers. The first one is largely within the purview of the examiner and concerns the establishment of rapport as well as the proper orientation of the test taker prior to administering the test. The second aspect, which is not within the examiner's control, pertains to all the antecedent life experiences that test takers might have had that would affect their performance on a particular test.

Establishing Rapport

In the context of testing, the term *rapport* refers to the harmonious relationship that should exist between test takers and examiners. In order to maximize the reliability and validity of test results, a friendly atmosphere needs to be established from the beginning of the testing session and rapport ideally should range from good to excellent. Absence of rapport can, of course, be attributable to either party in the test situation and may stem from inexperience or ineptness on the part of the examiner, an unfavorable disposition on the part of the test taker, or both. Needless to say, to the extent that rapport is lacking, test performance is likely to be deleteriously affected, even to the point where test scores are invalidated. In order to build rapport, the examiner should attempt to engage the interest and cooperation of test takers in the testing process so that they may react to test tasks in an appropriate fashion, by putting forth their best efforts in tests of ability and by responding as openly and honestly as possible on instruments designed to assess personality.

The process of rapport-building is more extensive in individual than in group testing because individual testing allows examiners to observe the test taker's behavior closely and continuously and to extend their efforts to maintain rapport throughout the testing process. Nevertheless, even in group testing, examiners must try to explain the purpose of the test, the testing procedures, and so on (see Rapid Reference 7.2) in a friendly manner within the constraints of the directions for test administration provided in the test manual, which must be followed in order to keep conditions uniform.

Test Preparation From the Test Taker's Perspective

It goes without saying that the purpose for which testing takes place, and the contextual aspects of the situation and circumstances in which testing takes place, have a significant bearing on test takers' attitudes and motivation. Among the many other cognitive and emotional factors that have a bearing on examinees' predispositions toward testing and on the extent to which they are prepared for a test-taking experience, test anxiety and test sophistication are probably the two most frequently discussed and investigated in the psychological testing literature. A brief overview of each follows.

Test anxiety. The prospect of being evaluated tends to elicit some degree of apprehension in most test takers, especially when the test scores are to be used as a basis for making decisions that will have important consequences for them. For some test takers this apprehension is easily dissipated and dealt with—and may even improve their levels of performance by heightening their physiological arousal. For others, test anxiety becomes a debilitating or even incapacitating factor that may have a significant deleterious effect on test performance or prevent them from taking tests altogether. Moreover, the reasons why test takers experience anxiety before and during the testing process can vary widely as well. Some of these reasons may be related to the type of test to be taken (e.g., speed tests, math tests, etc.), some may be related to test takers themselves (e.g., expectations of failure based on antecedent experiences), and still others may be a function of the context in which testing takes place (e.g., preemployment testing) or of a combination of variables. Although examiners should be alert to try to reduce the level of test takers' anxiety as part of the process of building rapport, there are also measures that test takers themselves can take toward the same end. Rapid Reference 7.6 lists resources that may be helpful to test takers and others interested in current approaches to the assessment and treatment of test anxiety.

Test sophistication. Strictly speaking, the variable known as *test sophistication* (a.k.a. test-taking skills or test wiseness) refers to the extent to which test takers have had experience or practice in taking tests. As a general rule, on most types of ability tests, having had the experience of taking a particular test or type of test tends to be advantageous for the test taker in that it provides practice and may reduce anxiety and bolster confidence. In fact, when individuals are retested with either the same or an alternate form of a test of ability, their second scores are almost in-

≡ Rapid Reference 7.6

Sources of Information on Test Anxiety

Test takers who want help in coping with test anxiety will find a wealth of materials available in bookstores and on the Internet. Examples include the following:

- *Taking the anxiety out of taking tests: A step-by-step guide,* by S. Johnson. New York: Barnes & Noble Books, 2000.
- *No more test anxiety: Effective steps for taking tests and achieving better grades,* by E. Newman (available with audio CD). Los Angeles: Learning Skills Publications, 1996.
- The Test Anxiety Scale (Saranson, 1980), which provides a quick way to gauge the extent to which one may be prone to experience test anxiety and is available free of charge from Learning Skills Publications (at http://www.learning skills.com/test.html) and several other Internet sites.
- Many Web sites sponsored by university counseling centers are accessible by searching for "test anxiety" on the Internet; these sites provide tips on study habits and other information on coping with test anxiety.

For those who wish to delve further into the current theories and research on test anxiety, the following works are recommended:

- Sapp, M. (1999). *Test anxiety: Applied research, assessment, and treatment* (2nd ed.). Latham, MD: University Press of America.
- Spielberger, C. D., & Vagg, P. R. (Eds.). (1995). *Test anxiety: Theory, assessment, and treatment.* Washington, DC: Taylor & Francis.
- Zeidner, M. (1998). *Test anxiety: The state of the art.* New York: Plenum.

variably higher than the first, a phenomenon that is known as the *practice effect*. Naturally, given the enormous range in the kinds of tests and test items that exist, a test taker may be very sophisticated and practiced in taking tests of one type in a given medium (e.g., multiple-choice paper-and-pencil achievement tests) but not at all familiar with tests of other types in other media (e.g., individually administered general ability tests or computer-administered performance tests). By the same token, test takers differ greatly in terms of the spectrum of experiences they have had that may have made them less or more prepared for a test-taking experience.

Within the testing process itself, the traditional way of coping with variability in test sophistication has been to provide explicit instructions and practice items prior to the test as part of the standardized administration procedures, in order to ascertain that test takers are able to appropriately handle the mechanics of responding to test items. Although these practice orientation sessions cannot by any means obliterate the differences among test takers, they can at least ensure that examinees will be able to manage the test-taking procedures competently. In addition, it is always good testing practice for examiners to inquire about the test takers' prior experiences with the actual test or type of test they are about to take and to note this information for use in the interpretation of test scores.

Of course, there are many other avenues that test takers can use to acquire skills and practice in test taking. One of the simplest and most efficient methods for prospective takers of college and graduate school admission tests is to familiarize themselves with the items and procedures of such tests by taking the sample tests provided by the publishers of these instruments (see, e.g., Rapid Reference 6.2). Teachers and counselors can also be of help in providing students and clients with information and guidance in test-taking skills (see, e.g., Scruggs & Mastropieri, 1992). The importance that many people place on test preparation is underscored by the fact that coaching for tests has become a major industry that provides test takers with a multiplicity of manuals, software, courses, and tutoring services geared to a variety of testing programs. Whether and to what extent test takers are able to achieve significant score gains through various methods of coaching and test preparation is a subject of much debate. An interesting account of some of the issues and findings on this topic is provided in the chapter on "Gaming the Tests: How Do Coaching and Cheating Affect Test Performance?" in Zwick's (2002) book *Fair Game? The Use of Standardized Admissions Tests in Higher Education.*

Another aspect of the debate about test preparation pertains to the distinction between intensive drilling aimed solely or primarily at raising test scores, on one hand, and teaching that addresses the broader objectives of the curriculum, on the other hand. This issue has been highlighted by the rather controversial practice of mandated testing that many states and localities are increasingly instituting for the purpose of making public schools accountable for student learning. In this case, as in many others, economic and political considerations create conditions in which the very purpose of testing may be subverted and the responsibilities of various parties in the educational process deflected from the test users to the tests.

The Problem of Test-Taker Dissimulation

An entirely different perspective on test takers' predispositions is presented in situations in which the type of decision-making for which a test is used promotes dissimulation. Attempts on the part of test takers to present themselves in either an unrealistically favorable or unfavorable fashion are not at all uncommon and may or may not be conscious. Validity scales designed to detect various types of attempts at impression management or response sets such as defensiveness are embedded in a number of personality inventories (e.g., the MMPI-2 and the MCMI-III) and have a long history. In recent years, instruments designed especially to evaluate the possibility of malingering on cognitive tests administered in the context of forensic and neuropsychological assessment—such as the Validity Indicator Profile—have been added to the repertoire of tools available for that purpose (see, e.g., R. Rogers, 1997). Undoubtedly, obtaining the full cooperation of test takers in the testing process is a crucial matter upon which depends the reliability and accuracy of test results (see Rapid Reference 7.3).

For a survey of the research on many additional topics that have a bearing on the test taker's outlook on educational and psychological testing, readers might wish to consult Nevo and Jäger's (1993) edited volume on this topic. The studies presented in this work were conducted by investigators in Germany, Israel, and the United States who were seeking to gather feedback on examinees opinions, attitudes, and reactions to various aspects of their test-taking experiences with the ultimate goal of improving specific tests and testing in general.

Preparation of the Examiner

Obtaining Informed Consent

According to the *Ethical Principles of Psychologists and Code of Conduct* (APA, 2002), prior to the administration of a psychological test or assessment procedure, psychologists must obtain and document the *informed consent* of test takers either orally or in writing. In order to be considered *informed*, the consent obtained from test takers has to be preceded by a suitable explanation of the nature and purpose of the evaluation, as well as information concerning confidentiality limits and how the security of test results will be maintained. Other practical matters that might affect test takers in a specific situation (e.g., fees, ability to refuse or discontinue testing, involvement of third parties, etc.) should also be discussed. Test takers should be given the opportunity to ask questions they might have about the testing process and have them answered. The code of ethics of psychologists (APA, 2002) lists a few exceptional circumstances in which the informed consent is not required either because it is implied or because the assessment is mandated. Special provisions that pertain to such cases, as well as to persons who do not have the capacity to consent, are also outlined in the code. Other professions engaged in the use of psychological testing and assessment instruments have similar guidelines for the attainment of informed consent (see, e.g., American Counseling Association, 1995).

Importance of Examiner Preparation

The key role that proper administration and scoring of tests plays in gathering interpretable data cannot be overemphasized. Standardized procedures for the administration and scoring of a test as specified in its manual provide the foundation that allows for the application of a normative or criterion-based frame of reference to the interpretation of test scores. To be sure, deviations from or modifications of standardized procedures are sometimes inevitable or necessary, as, for instance, when the administration of a test is disrupted by some event or when special accommodations need to be made for test takers with disabilities. In such cases, examiners need to document the modifications that were made. Moreover, to the extent that there is reason to believe that test score meaning may be affected by disruptions or modifications of standardized procedures, the nature of the disruptions or modifications should be reported to those who will be interpreting or making decisions on the basis of the test scores (AERA, APA, NCME, 1999).

As far as the actual preparation of examiners is concerned, the person who administers a test has to be thoroughly familiar with the purpose and procedures of the test, able to establish rapport, and ready to answer test takers' questions or cope with any foreseeable emergency that might arise during testing. In general, group test administration does not require any additional training beyond the aforementioned. Individual testing, on the other hand, inevitably involves a great deal more preparation and usually requires supervised experience. For instance, when test questions are presented orally they must be stated verbatim. In order for the administration to go smoothly, proceed at a good pace, and allow examiners the opportunity to attend to and record responses (also verbatim), examiners need to have committed to memory not only the items and their sequence, but also a number of additional rules for such things as timing the presentation of and responses to items and the starting and stopping points, as well as for scoring the responses as they are produced. When materials such as puzzle pieces, blocks, pictures, and other objects are used in individual testing, they must be presented and removed in the exact manner that is called for in the manual. Unless examiners memorize and practice all test procedures beforehand until they are thoroughly adept at them, the test administration and possibly the test taker's performance, as well, will be affected in ways that could easily jeopardize the validity of the test data.

Computer-Based Test Administration   *Benefits?*

One sure way to bypass the possibility of errors in test administration, as well as the likelihood that test performance might be unduly influenced by variables related to the examiner's sex, race, age, appearance, interpersonal style, and other such variables, is through computer-based test administration. The advantages of this testing medium, with regard to the relative uniformity in the presentation of test materials and the precision with which responses can be timed, recorded, and scored, are self-evident. In fact, the trend to replace paper-and-pencil testing with computerized test administration is well underway, especially in large-scale testing programs, and is likely to continue to expand as computerization becomes more cost effective. Moreover, the development and use of tests—such as the Test of Variables of Attention—that by their nature can exist only in computer versions, is also progressing rapidly. On the other hand, the administration of individual tests of general ability, projective techniques, and many neuropsychological tests (provided administration is performed by a skilled examiner) has some definite advantages in terms of the qualitative data that can be gathered, especially in the context of clinical, neuropsychological, and forensic assessments. In addition, prior to instituting a change from traditional methods of administering tests to computerized administration, the comparability of results under the two sets of conditions—which varies depending on the type of instrument in question—needs to be thoroughly investigated (Mead & Drasgow, 1993). For more information regarding computerized psychological assessment, including the issue of the equivalence of standard versus computerized test administration, see Butcher (2003).

Test Scoring

It may be recalled that interscorer differences and the associated topic of scorer reliability—discussed in Chapter 4, among the possible sources of measurement error—were considered as pertinent only to the scoring of open-ended responses in which the subjectivity of the scorer plays a part. When this is the case, test users need to ascertain empirically that those who will be scoring such responses—from individual or group testing—are trained well enough to achieve results virtually identical to those produced by an independent and experienced scorer. As a general rule, when interscorer reliability coefficients can be computed, they should approach +1.00 and should not be much below .90. When scores are expressed in some other fashion, the goal should be to get as close as possible to 100% agreement in the scores assigned by independent, trained scorers. It should be noted that the ease with which such high standards of accuracy can be met when the scoring requires subjective judgment differs greatly across different types of tests. This is so because guidelines for scoring some open-ended responses (e.g., essay answers on achievement tests) tend to be clearer and easier to master than those for others (e.g., responses to projective techniques such as the Rorschach). For a discussion of issues related to scorer reliability for the Rorschach Comprehensive System, see Acklin, McDowell, Verschell, and Chan (2000).

In tests that are scored objectively—simply by counting responses in various categories and performing the computations required to transform raw scores into some other numerical form, such as standard scores of various types—scoring errors need not occur. One way to avoid them is through computer-based test administration and scoring. Another is through the use of optical scanners and appropriate software, although this requires the careful examination of answer sheets for incomplete erasures and other such problems prior to scanning. If objective scoring is done by hand, especially when templates that are superimposed on answer sheets are involved, the possibility of clerical errors has to be forestalled by impressing upon scorers the absolute importance of accuracy and by instituting procedures to double-check all of the required calculations and score transformations.

The transformation of the raw scores of individually administered tests, such as the Wechsler scales, into standard scores typically involves a series of arithmetical computations as well as looking up the scaled-score equivalents of raw scores in various tables provided in the manuals. To prevent errors from entering into scores as a result of carelessness in carrying out these procedures, test publishers also offer software that can perform all the required calculations and transformations once the raw scores obtained by the examiner are (carefully) entered into the computer. If test users are not able to avail themselves of this kind of scoring aid, good testing practice requires double-checking the accuracy of all computations and equivalent scores obtained from tables.

ESSENTIALS OF TEST SCORE INTERPRETATION AND REPORTING

Most of the preceding material in this book has been aimed at communicating to readers the complexities involved in the proper use and application of psycho-

logical test data. Test score interpretation and the communication of the inferences obtained from psychological testing are the culminating points of test use.
They are also the components of psychological testing through which test takers
can either derive the greatest benefit, or incur the greatest harm, that can flow
from test use. Since all the various principles involved in the interpretation and
reporting of test results cannot be conveyed in a single book—let alone in one
portion of a chapter—this section presents a general perspective on these aspects
of testing and selected references on related topics.

A Particular Perspective on Test Interpretation

Psychological test scores supply more or less reliable quantitative data that concisely *describe* the behavior elicited from individuals in response to test stimuli. To
the extent that tests are carefully selected, administered, and scored, they provide
information that can be used in a variety of ways, the most basic of which is
simply to place test takers' performance within the descriptive normative or
criterion-based categories provided by the frame of reference a test employs (see
Chapter 3). If they are sufficiently reliable and appropriately interpreted, test
score data can also be of help in explaining the psychological make-up of individuals and in making decisions about them based on the estimates that scores
provide concerning test takers' characteristics or their future behavior (see Chapter 5). However, to arrive at defensible answers to the complex questions that
psychologists, teachers, and other human services professionals are asked, or ask
themselves, data from multiple sources are often necessary and informed judgment must *always* be exercised.

Making informed judgments about people requires an appreciation of the
value and limitations inherent in the frame of reference, reliability, and validity of
test score data, as well as in the data from all the other sources that might be employed in a given case. In addition, it requires knowledge about the context and
specific areas of human behavior relevant to the issue in question. Furthermore,
making decisions about people invariably involves value judgments on the part of
the decision makers and places upon them an ethical responsibility for the consequences of the decisions that are made. Unfortunately, in actual practice, contextual issues are frequently ignored, value judgments are not acknowledged explicitly, and test scores often become the major or even the sole determining
factor in decision-making. As a result, for reasons of expediency, the weight of responsibility for many decisions is unjustifiably transferred from test users and decision makers to the tests themselves. One way to counteract this problem is to
understand and appreciate the implications of the difference between psycho-

logical testing and assessment, discussed in Chapter 1. This difference is akin to the distinction between conducting medical tests, on one hand, and integrating their results with the history and presenting symptoms of a patient to produce a diagnosis and treatment plan, on the other (Handler & Meyer, 1998).

The overview of strengths and limitations of testing and other assessment tools presented earlier in this chapter attempted to convey the desirability of integrating as many sources of evidence as possible whenever a significant question that calls for the assessment of individuals or groups is asked. With regard to the interpretation and use of tests, the particular perspective presented here is as follows:

1. Psychological tests can sometimes be the most efficient and objective tools available for gathering reliable and valid data about people.
2. Psychological testing can often be a valuable component in the process of assessment of individuals and groups.
3. Psychological test scores should never be the only source of information on which to base decisions that affect the lives of individuals.

The particular manner in which the interpretation and reporting of test scores should be conducted depends on two interrelated factors: (a) the purpose for which the testing was undertaken and (b) the party on whose behalf the testing was undertaken. With respect to the latter, three distinct possibilities determine how test data are interpreted and communicated.

- *When psychologists use tests on their own behalf* (e.g., as instruments in research), they can interpret and report the grouped test score data of research participants in whatever manner they deem appropriate to the purposes of their investigations. Legal requirements and ethical standards for research with human participants govern practices in this type of testing and include provisions for obtaining the informed consent of participants and debriefing them promptly (APA, 2002). With regard to the role of testing within the research project itself, issues such as the choice of instruments, the way scores are reported, and the meaning assigned to them must be evaluated in light of the goals of the investigation. Scientific research and publication are essentially self-policing enterprises that use the mechanism of peer review to evaluate the substantive and methodological merits of proposed, ongoing, or completed work. Thus, when research that entails the use of test data is submitted for review or is published, it will either be accepted or rejected, cited or ignored, based—among other things—on how well such data were employed.

- *When psychologists use tests on behalf of their own clients,* they are singularly responsible for interpreting test data, integrating them with other sources of information, and communicating their findings to their clients in an appropriate and helpful manner. Whether these assessments are aimed at diagnosis, treatment planning, monitoring progress, or facilitating change, the client is the ultimate consumer of the information and the ultimate judge of its benefits. In fact, in many of these situations, test score interpretation, as far as the implications of scores are concerned, can be a collaborative effort between the psychologist or counselor and the client (Fischer, 2000). Rapid Reference 7.7 lists resources that provide explicit guidance on the use of tests within the context of counseling and clinical assessment.

- *When psychologists use tests on behalf of a third party,* such as an organization or another professional, they are acting as consultants in an assessment process initiated by others for their own purposes. Hence, the lines of responsibility are not as clear-cut as in the previous instance because the test taker who is undergoing assessment is not necessarily the ultimate consumer of test data. Nevertheless, as mentioned elsewhere, both from an ethical standpoint as well as for protection from possible liability, it behooves consultants to find out what the purpose of the consultation is, not

≡ Rapid Reference 7.7

Resources on the Use of Tests in Counseling and Clinical Practice

Articles and books that provide guidance and examples on the interpretation and use of psychological tests in clinical practice abound and their number is constantly expanding. The works included in this brief list present just a few of the many possible ways to apply testing in counseling and clinical settings. Resources for more specialized applications and populations are included in Rapid Reference 7.8.

- Beutler, L. E., & Groth-Marnat, G. (Eds.). (2003). *Integrative assessment of adult personality* (2nd ed.). New York: Guilford.
- Fischer, C. T. (1994). *Individualizing psychological assessment.* Hillsdale, NJ: Erlbaum. (Original work published 1985)
- Lowman, R. L. (1991). *The clinical practice of career assessment: Interests, abilities, and personality.* Washington, DC: American Psychological Association.
- Maruish, M. E. (Ed.). (2004). *The use of psychological testing for treatment planning and outcome assessment* (3rd ed., Vols. 1–3). Mahwah, NJ: Erlbaum.

only in terms of what information the third party is seeking, but also how it will be used. Only with this knowledge can assessment professionals determine whether the use of tests is called for, how scores will be reported, what other tools may be needed to derive the information that is sought, and whether they are able and willing to participate in the consultation process.

The interpretation of test results involves a series of inferences that are made on the basis of the data gathered from (a) the actual behavior samples (responses to test items), (b) the aggregation of these samples into one or more scores, (c) the available evidence concerning the reliability of the obtained scores, (d) the comparison of scores against the normative or criterion-based frames of reference the test provides, (e) the evaluation of scores in light of the quality of internal and external validation data available, (f) the specific context and situation in which the testing takes place, and (g) the personal characteristics of the individual being assessed. When all of these sources of evidence are viewed in conjunction with each other, and added to the pertinent information collected through other methods, their implications and limitations with regard to a specific assessment question should be clear. Occasionally (e.g., when data from various reliable and presumably valid sources are mutually contradictory or when there is reason to believe that some of the key pieces of evidence—whether derived from tests or other sources—are unreliable), the inconclusive nature of findings must be reported. In such cases, appropriate recommendations might include referral to another professional or additional data collection. Rapid Reference 7.8 lists a few of the many resources currently available on test interpretation and related topics.

Communicating Test Results and Assessment Findings

The most basic guideline to follow in communicating test results is to provide the information derived from test scores, including its limitations, in language that the recipient can understand. However, the specific manner in which scores are reported can vary widely depending on the tests administered, the setting or context in which testing takes place, the purposes for which the testing was undertaken, and the intended recipients of the information. Thus, the appropriate way to report the results of psychological testing or the findings of an assessment cannot be condensed into a single set of rules suitable for all cases. Nevertheless, issues pertaining to some of the various modes of communicating test results are presented in the ensuing paragraphs.

═Rapid Reference 7.8

Further Information on Test Interpretation and Assessment

The primary sources of information on the use and interpretation of specific tests and assessment tools are the manuals, guidebooks, and other supporting documentation provided by test authors and publishers. In addition, guidelines on test interpretation can be found in a great number of books and publications. A few examples follow.

For a general overview of test interpretation:

- Lichtenberg, J. W., & Goodyear, R. K. (Eds.). (1999). *Scientist-practitioner perspectives on test interpretation.* Boston: Allyn & Bacon.

For issues related to the assessment of children and adolescents:

- Kamphaus, R. W. (2001). *Clinical assessment of child and adolescent intelligence* (2nd ed.). Boston: Allyn & Bacon.
- Kamphaus, R. W., & Frick, P. J. (2002). *Clinical assessment of child and adolescent personality and behavior* (2nd ed.). Boston: Allyn & Bacon.
- Sattler, J. M. (2001). *Assessment of children: Cognitive applications* (4th ed.). San Diego, CA: Author.
- Sattler, J. M. (2002). *Assessment of children: Behavioral and clinical applications* (4th ed.). San Diego, CA: Author.

For perspectives on test interpretation for diverse populations:

- Sandoval, J., Frisby, C. L., Geisinger, K. F., Scheuneman, J. D., & Grenier, J. R. (1998). *Test interpretation and diversity: Achieving equity in assessment.* Washington, DC: American Psychological Association.
- Ekstrom, R. B., & Smith, D. K. (Eds.). (2002). *Assessing individuals with disabilities in educational, employment, and counseling settings.* Washington, DC: American Psychological Association.

- *When test results are communicated directly to test takers in score report cards or profiles produced by computers,* the organization responsible for the testing program must provide adequate interpretive information. For instance, the College Board Web site (at http://www.collegeboard.com/student/testing/sat/scores/understanding.html) has some material pertinent to the interpretation of SAT scores under the heading "Understanding Your Scores." Similar aids are available for interpreting scores derived from other large-scale testing programs, such as the ACT (at http://www.act.org/aap/scores/under.html).

- *Interpretations of scores derived from computer programs* apply decision rules based on the clinical experience and judgment of experts, actuarial approaches based on statistical associations and correlations between scores and criteria, or both. How these computer-based test interpretations (CBTIs) are employed, and by whom, is a subject of continuing discussion and debate within the testing profession. Originally meant as aids to clinicians in the interpretation of personality inventories and other diagnostic instruments, CBTIs have proliferated rapidly and have been extended to different kinds of tests and test uses. One of the problems stemming from these developments is that CBTI services are often made commercially available to individuals who may have seemingly appropriate credentials—such as a license to practice psychology or a medical degree—but who are not sufficiently knowledgeable about the test in question. As a consequence, the reports generated through CBTI are too often viewed uncritically and used as substitutes for individualized assessment that is based on multiple data sources and informed by the judgment of a qualified professional. In addition, the proprietary nature of the specific rules used in generating such reports often prevents a proper evaluation of the validity of their interpretations by prospective users. Nevertheless, professionals who avail themselves of CBTI services are under the same ethical obligations with regard to competence in their use as in the use of any other assessment tool. The providers of CBTI services, in turn, have an ethical obligation to supply their users with information concerning the sources, bases of evidence, and limitations of the interpretations they provide (see, e.g., APA, 2002; Moreland, 1991).

- *The traditional means for communicating test results and assessment findings is the written psychological report.* This individualized approach affords a great deal of flexibility in tailoring the communication to the purpose of the assessment and to the needs of clients and consumers of psychological test data. It also helps the assessor organize, clarify, and synthesize information from all the available sources and creates a record of the findings of an assessment that can be consulted in the future. A comprehensive description of the various approaches to psychological report writing and their benefits and pitfalls, as well as numerous examples of how to and how not to write such reports, are provided by Norman Tallent (1993). A briefer, step-by-step guide to report writing prepared by Raymond Ownby (1997) is also worthy of the attention of readers interested in this topic. Rapid Reference 7.9 lists a few examples of do's and don'ts in test interpretation that are especially pertinent to psychological report writing.

Safeguarding Test Data

The security of test data, whether they consist of individually identifiable records, scores, and reports or of test materials themselves (e.g., booklets, forms, questions, scoring keys, manuals, etc.), is a primary responsibility of the test users and

≡Rapid Reference 7.9

Do's and Don'ts in Test Interpretation

Some Examples of What Test Interpretation Is *Not*

- *Reporting numerical scores:* Whether scores are expressed as percentile ranks, IQs, percentage scores, or in some other format, simply listing them fails to convey their meaning and implications.

- *Assigning labels:* Placing individuals within diagnostic categories (e.g., Mild Mental Retardation, or Borderline Personality) or typologies on the bases of their scores is not an adequate substitute for interpretation that enhances understanding.

- *Stating findings in terms of trivial generalities:* Many statements can apply equally well to almost all human beings or to most individuals in certain categories (e.g., psychiatric patients, young children, etc.) because of their high base rates in those populations. Meehl (1956) proposed the phrase "Barnum effect" to characterize the worthless nature of descriptions of this sort.

What Test Interpretation Should be

- *At a minimum,* the interpretation of test scores for consumers of test data should include a clear explanation of (a) what the test covers, (b) the meaning of scores, (c) the limitations on the precision of scores that derive from measurement error, (d) common misinterpretations to which particular scores— for example, IQs—may be subject, and (e) the way in which test results may or will be used (AERA, APA, NCME, 1999, chap. 5).

- *At its best,* test score interpretation adds value to the aggregated behavior samples collected with tests by integrating them with all other available data and using informed professional judgment to draw useful and ecologically valid inferences.

---

institutions who control access to such data. In certain cases, this responsibility can become difficult to discharge because (a) many different and evolving legal mandates, institutional requirements, professional standards, and ethical concerns govern the decision of when, how, and to whom test data may be disclosed, and (b) these various strictures can differ substantially depending on the setting and the purpose of testing and may even conflict with one another. Most recently, for instance, the federal Health Insurance Portability and Accountability Act (HIPAA) Privacy Rule, which became effective in the United States on April 14, 2003, has imposed requirements that are raising many questions and creating some confusion among testing and assessment professionals as well as other health care practitioners. Some answers to frequently asked questions, and further information on how HIPAA affects psychologists, can be found in the APA Insurance Trust Web site at http://www.apait.org/resources/hipaa/.

As a general rule, legal mandates that address the release of test data take precedence over the regulations and concerns of other parties. However, test users need to be aware of their duties to (a) protect the confidentiality of test results and the security of test materials in specific settings and situations, (b) inform the parties involved about these duties, and (c) try to resolve conflicts between various obligations in a manner consistent with the ethical principles and standards of their profession. In addition to the *Testing Standards* (AERA, APA, NCME, 1999) and the *Ethical Principles of Psychologists and Code of Conduct* (APA, 2002), organized psychology has promulgated a number of documents to help psychologists identify and deal with issues related to the security of tests and test data and to prevent their misuse. Some of the most pertinent documents of this type are listed in Rapid Reference 7.10.

A New Medium: Testing on the Internet

The advent and rapid expansion of the Internet in the last two decades is revolutionizing the field of psychological testing as much as it has affected almost every other aspect of contemporary society. Readers may have noticed, scattered throughout this book, a fair number of references to Internet sites that provide

≡ *Rapid Reference 7.10*

Information on Safeguarding Tests and Test Data

In addition to the *Testing Standards* (AERA, APA, NCME, 1999) and the *Ethical Principles of Psychologists and Code of Conduct* (APA, 2002), both of which deal with issues concerning the security of test materials and test data, the American Psychological Association (APA) has provided guidance for test users with regard to these issues in several other documents. Among the most pertinent of these are the following:

- American Psychological Association, Committee on Legal Issues. (1996). Strategies for private practitioners coping with subpoenas or compelled testimony for client records or test data. *Professional Psychology: Research and Practice, 27,* 245–251.

- American Psychological Association, Committee on Psychological Tests and Assessment. (1996). Statement on the disclosure of test data. *American Psychologist, 51,* 644–648.

- American Psychological Association, Committee on Psychological Tests and Assessment. (2003). *Statement on the use of secure psychological tests in the education of graduate and undergraduate psychology students.* Retrieved February 19, 2003, from http://www.apa.org/science/securetests.html

- Test security: Protecting the integrity of tests. (1999). *American Psychologist, 54,* 1078.

information on psychological tests and testing issues. In addition to these and to the many other sources of information about tests and testing currently available online, the delivery of psychological testing services on the Internet by a variety of providers—some legitimate and many not so—is also well underway. Yet the impact that the Internet is likely to have on testing promises to be much greater in the coming decades due primarily to the speed with which tests can be developed, normed, published, and revised using the capabilities of the World Wide Web, as well as to the efficiency and economy with which testing services can be delivered online.

In every aspect of Internet use, whether for commerce, entertainment, information, or communication purposes, the highly democratic and accessible nature of the medium poses at once both huge advantages and dangers. As the reader may have gathered, with regard to testing, the possibilities the Internet presents for harmful uses abound as does the potential for unparalleled advances. Thus, the professional examination of the difficulties and benefits inherent in current and foreseeable psychological testing practices on the Internet has already begun (see, e.g., Buchanan, 2002). One of the most thorough efforts in this regard, up to this point, is a report prepared by the APA Task Force on Psychological Test-

Putting It Into Practice

How to Test Your Ability to Evaluate Psychological Tests

A number of Web sites offer surveys, questionnaires, and other tools that purport to be psychological tests. Almost any search engine will lead you to these sites upon entering the terms "psychological tests" or "personality tests." Among the many offerings in these sites are a variety of instruments, such as "IQ tests," "EQ tests," and "career tests," that may look like psychological tests and appeal to the layperson but have very little or no legitimate scientific bases. Some of these so-called tests are offered free of charge; others involve payment of a (typically) modest fee of $5, $10, or $15. In many cases, the free instruments do not include the full results (or even any results), unless a fee is first paid. Often test takers are not informed about the required fee until after they have completed the test.

Having read this chapter carefully, you should by now be aware that the publishers of legitimate psychological tests are extremely concerned with the issue of test security and do not wish to see their products disseminated to the public at large or used inappropriately. With rare exceptions (e.g., instruments that are in the process of development), one is not likely to find serious test publishers or authors making their products freely available on the Internet.

One way to apply some of the knowledge you have gained by reading this book is to inspect some of the instruments offered in the Internet and evaluate them with regard to (a) whether they meet the criteria that would qualify them as legitimate psychological tests and (b) whether the information they provide is of any value.

ing on the Internet (Naglieri et al., 2004). This report focuses on a variety of aspects related to the influence of the Internet on psychological testing and assessment, including psychometric, ethical, and legal issues as well as practical considerations regarding test security and access, among other things. It also contains examples that illustrate current applications of Internet testing and offers glimpses into future possibilities afforded by the medium as well as recommendations for the future.

CONCLUSION

Consider the following typical questions and problems:

- Does my child have an attention-deficit disorder?
- How should we go about selecting the best applicants for our police department?
- Is this 65-year-old patient suffering from an incipient dementing disorder, or is he depressed due to the death of his wife?
- Which of these three equally experienced candidates for the position of chief financial officer in my company should I hire?
- What should I major in?
- Should this convicted sexual predator be released from prison?
- What kind of therapeutic intervention would be most effective for this client?
- Is this individual feigning disability in order to collect compensation, or is she really disabled?

Although all of these questions and assessment problems can be addressed with the aid of tests, none can be answered by a single test score or even a combination of scores. The determinations that need to be made in these situations, and similar ones, require data from multiple sources as well as information about the specific objectives of the people involved, the contexts in which the questions are raised, and the potential consequences of the decisions entailed in each case.

It should be clear at this point that the application of psychological tests is fraught with the possibility of error at every step. However, so are most other human endeavors. Once the essential question to consider (i.e., whether the use of tests can contribute to more rational, equitable, beneficial, and responsible decision-making in a given situation) is answered affirmatively, what is needed is to implement the plan for test use as conscientiously as possible through all of its phases. If this is done, the role of tests, especially compared to other tools, is likely to prove quite useful.

🦅 TEST YOURSELF 🦅

1. **The first question to consider when psychological testing is contemplated is**
   (a) whether testing is necessary.
   (b) what kind of test to use.
   (c) the costs associated with testing.

2. **Which of the following is *not* a primary advantage attendant to the use of psychological tests?**
   (a) Objectivity
   (b) Efficiency
   (c) Easy availability

3. **All other things being equal, the potential gain in the accuracy of a selection decision is greatest when the base rate is closest to**
   (a) 1.00.
   (b) 0.75.
   (c) 0.50.
   (d) 0.00.

4. **An ideal situation, for purposes of accuracy in selecting employees, would involve a _____ base rate, a _____ selection ratio, and a test with a _____ degree of validity.**
   (a) moderate/high/high
   (b) moderate/low/high
   (c) high/low/moderate
   (d) high/high/high

5. **Which one of the following assessment tools is most likely to provide valid and reliable evaluative information for individual assessment?**
   (a) Interviewing
   (b) References
   (c) Informal observation
   (d) Biodata

6. **As a general rule, the presence of third parties, other than the examiner and test taker, during the administration of individual tests is**
   (a) desirable.
   (b) undesirable.
   (c) neither a nor b.

(continued)

7. **Which of the following is *not* one of the areas in which computer-based test administration offers advantages over individual test administration?**

   (a) Uniformity of procedure

   (b) Cost effectiveness

   (c) Precision capabilities

   (d) Qualitative data gathering

8. **The perspective on testing presented by the author stresses the fact that psychological tests**

   (a) can be a valuable component in most cases when assessment is needed.

   (b) can often be the sole source of information on which to base decisions.

   (c) invariably constitute the most efficient tools available for assessment.

9. **In communicating test results to the consumers of test data, the most pertinent information to be conveyed to them is the**

   (a) numerical score obtained by examinees.

   (b) labels or diagnoses derived from test scores.

   (c) meaning of test scores.

10. **The legal and ethical responsibilities of test users with regard to appropriate interpretation of test results is**

   (a) obviated when they use tests on their own behalf.

   (c) obviated when they use tests on behalf of a third party.

   (b) obviated when they use tests on behalf of their own clients.

   (d) never obviated.

Answers: 1. a; 2. c; 3. c; 4. b; 5. d; 6. b; 7. d; 8. a; 9. c; 10. d.

Appendix A

Commercially Available Tests Mentioned in the Text

Test Name (Abbreviation of Current Version)	Publisher's Code
ACT Assessment	ACT
Beck Depression Inventory (BDI)	TPC
Beta III	TPC
Boston Diagnostic Aphasia Examination (BDAS)	LWW
Bracken Basic Concept Scale–Revised (BBCS-R)	TPC
California Psychological Inventory (CPI)	CPP
Clerical Abilities Battery (CAB)	TPC
College-Level Examination Program (CLEP)	TCB
Crawford Small Parts Dexterity Test (CSPDT)	TPC
Das-Naglieri Cognitive Assessment System (CAS)	RIV
Differential Ability Scales (DAS)	TPC
Graduate Record Exam (GRE)	ETS
Halstead-Reitan Neuropsychological Battery (HRNB)	RNL
Infant-Toddler Developmental Assessment (IDA)	RIV
Iowa Test of Basic Skills (ITBS)	RIV
Jackson Vocational Interest Survey (JVIS)	SIG
Kaufman Assessment Battery for Children (K-ABC-II)	AGS
Kaufman Adolescent and Adult Intelligence Test (KAIT)	AGS
Law School Admission Test (LSAT)	LSAC/LSAS
Medical College Admission Test (MCAT)	AAMC
Millon Clinical Multiaxial Inventory (MCMI-III)	PA
Mini-Mental State Examination (MMSE)	PAR
Minnesota Multiphasic Personality Inventory (MMPI-2 & MMPI-A)	UMP/PA
Myers-Briggs Type Indicator (MBTI)	CPP
Otis-Lennon School Ability Test (OLSAT 8)	HEM
Quality of Life Inventory (QOLI)	PA
Revised NEO Personality Inventory (NEO PI-R)	PAR

Appendix B contains the complete names and internet addresses of the test publishers listed in here, arranged in alphabetical order according to the Publishers' codes used in this Appendix.

Test Name (Abbreviation of Current Version)	Publisher's Code
Rorschach	H & H
SAT (formerly known as Scholastic Aptitude Test)	TCB
Stanford-Binet Intelligence Scale (S-B 5)	RIV
Stanford Diagnostic Mathematics Test (SDMT)	HEM
Stanford Diagnostic Reading Test (SDRT)	HEM
State-Trait Anxiety Inventory (STAI)	Mind
Strong Interest Inventory (SII)	CPP
Symptom Checklist-90–Revised (SCL-90-R)	PA
Test of English as a Foreign Language (TOEFL)	ETS
Test of Variables of Attention (TOVA)	UAD
Thematic Apperception Test (TAT)	HAR
Validity Indicator Profile (VIP)	PA
Wechsler Adult Intelligence Scale (WAIS-III)	TPC
Wechsler Intelligence Scale for Children (WISC-IV)	TPC
Whitaker Index of Schizophrenic Thinking (WIST)	WPS
Wide Range Achievement Test (WRAT)	WRI
Wonderlic Personnel Test	WON
Woodcock-Johnson batteries	RIV
WorkKeys Assessments	ACT

Appendix B

Addresses of Test Publishers and Distributors

Code	Publisher's Name	Address
AAMC	Association of American Medical Colleges	www.aamc.org
ACT	ACT, Inc.	www.act.org
AGS	American Guidance Service	www.agsnet.com
CPP	Consulting Psychologists Press	www.cpp.com
ETS	Educational Testing Service	www.ets.org
HAR	Harvard University Press	www.hup.harvard.edu
HEM	Harcourt Educational Measurement	www.HEMWEB.com
H & H	Hogrefe & Huber Publishers	www.hhpub.com
LSAC/ LSAS	Law School Admission Council/Law School Admission Service	www.lsac.org
LWW	Lippincott Williams & Wilkins	www.lww.com
Mind	Mind Garden, Inc.	www.mindgarden.com
PA	Pearson Assessments (formerly NCS)	www.pearsonassessments.com
PAR	Psychological Assessment Resources	www.parinc.com
RNL	Reitan Neuropsychological Laboratory	www.reitanlabs.com
RIV	Riverside Publishing	www.riversidepublishing.com
SIG	Sigma Assessment Systems, Inc.	www.sigmaassessmentsystems.com
TCB	The College Board	www.collegeboard.com
TPC	The Psychological Corporation	www.PsychCorp.Com
UAD	Universal Attention Disorders, Inc.	www.tovatest.com
UMP	University of Minnesota Press	www.upress.umn.edu/tests
WON	Wonderlic, Inc.	www.wonderlic.com
WPS	Western Psychological Services	www.wpspublish.com
WRI	Wide Range, Inc.	www.widerange.com

See Appendix A for publishers' codes.

Appendix C

Table of Areas and Ordinates of the Normal Curve

EXPLANATION OF THE TABLE

Column (1) lists standard scores (i.e., z scores) from 0.00 to 3.24 (at intervals of .01) and from 3.30 to 3.70 (at intervals of .10).

$$z \text{ score} = \frac{x}{\sigma} \tag{C.1}$$

where

x = the distance between any point on the baseline and the *mean* of the distribution

σ (sigma) = the *standard deviation* of the distribution

The mean of z scores is zero; the standard deviation of z scores is 1.

Column (2) lists the proportion of the area of the curve comprised in the segment between the mean and any of the z scores. Since the normal curve is perfectly symmetrical, when $z = 0$ (at the mean), one half of the curve (.5000, or 50%) is above z and one half is below z.

When the curve is divided at any point other than the mean, there will be a *larger* area, listed in Column (3) and a *smaller* area, listed in Column (4). If the point that divides the curve is to the *left* of the mean, the z score has a *negative* sign and the smaller area is to its left; if the point that divides the curve is to the *right* of the mean, the z score is *positive* and the smaller area is to its right.

Column (5) lists the y ordinate values, or the height of the curve, at every z score point.

HOW TO USE THE TABLE

Relationship Between z Scores and the Areas of the Curve

Figure C.1, Panel A, displays the distance between a z score of +1.50 and the mean. If the z score of 1.50 is found in Column (1) of the table, Column (2) shows that the area between it and the mean is .4332, or 43.32% of the curve. Since the

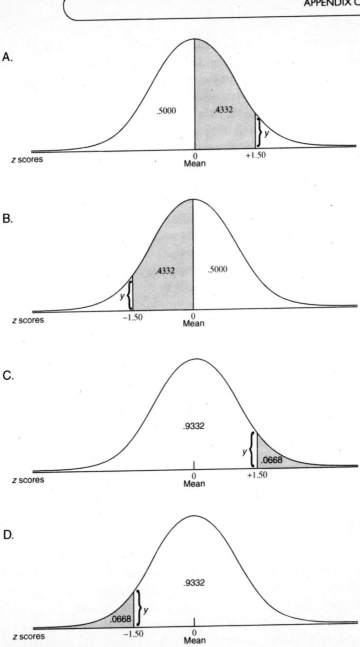

Figure C.1 Areas of the normal curve

curve is symmetrical, any given z score subtends the same area from the mean, whether it is positive (above the mean) or negative (below the mean). Therefore, in Figure C.1, Panel B, a z score of -1.50 again subtends an area of .4332 between the mean and z. To find the proportion, or percentage, of the area that falls *above* a z of $+1.50$, we subtract .4332 from .5000 and get .0668, or 6.68%. To find the area *below* a z of $+1.50$, we add .4332 to .5000 and get .9332, or 93.32%. These values are shown in Panel C of Figure C.1. Panel D of the figure shows the results with a z score of -1.50. Here, as is the case with all negative z scores in a normal curve, the larger portion is above the z and is thus found by adding the value in column (2) of the table to .5000 (.4332 + .5000 = .9332); the smaller portion falls below z and is found by subtracting .4332 from .5000, which results in .0668. Columns (3) and (4) of the table provide the results of these computations. To verify the results, find the entries for a z score of 1.50 in columns (3) and (4). For further practice, corroborate the areas of the curve shown in Figure 2.2 of Chapter 2 for σ values or z scores of ± 1, ± 2, and ± 3.

Using the Table for Hypothesis Testing

When the normal curve is applied to hypothesis testing, in inferential statistics, it is used to ascertain the likelihood that the critical value (z) obtained could have resulted by chance. Since z values give the proportion of the area in only one end of the curve, when hypotheses allow the possibility of variation in two directions, the proportion of the area that falls beyond the critical z value has to be doubled in order to find the probability level associated with the critical value obtained.

> *Example:* Suppose we are trying to find out whether a 10-point difference that has been obtained between the two IQ scores of an individual (e.g., a Verbal IQ of 115 and a Performance IQ of 105) is statistically significant, in a situation where neither IQ is expected to be higher than the other. To test the null hypothesis of no difference, we obtain the critical z value for the obtained difference of 10 points by dividing that difference by the standard error of the difference (SE_{diff}) between the scores, which is a statistic derived from the respective reliabilities of the Verbal and Performance scales (see Chapter 4). In this example, let us assume that the $SE_{diff} = 5$; thus, the critical z ratio is $10 \div 5 = 2.00$. The area beyond that critical z value, 0.0228, represents the probability (p) level for the obtained difference. However, because the score difference could have occurred in either direction, p is doubled ($0.0228 \times 2 = 0.0456$) to obtain the likelihood (4.56%) that a 10-point difference between the scores could have been obtained if there were no difference between the two IQ scores.

This example describes a *two-tailed test,* which is the typical way in which the significance of various findings is tested. If there is a specific directional hypothesis, as there might be in an experiment where one expects results to be in a certain direction, a *one-tailed test* is performed. In such cases, if the results do fall in the expected direction, the *p* level for the critical value does not have to be doubled.

Table C.1 Table of Areas and Ordinates of the Normal Curve in Terms of Standard Scores $z = x/\sigma_x$

Standard Score $z = x/\sigma_x$ (1)	Area from Mean to z (2)	Area in Larger Portion (3)	Area in Smaller Portion (4)	y at x/σ_x (5)
0.00	.0000	.5000	.5000	.3989
0.01	.0040	.5040	.4960	.3989
0.02	.0080	.5080	.4920	.3989
0.03	.0120	.5120	.4880	.3988
0.04	.0160	.5160	.4840	.3986
0.05	.0199	.5199	.4801	.3984
0.06	.0239	.5239	.4761	.3982
0.07	.0279	.5279	.4721	.3980
0.08	.0319	.5319	.4681	.3977
0.09	.0359	.5359	.4641	.3973
0.10	.0398	.5398	.4602	.3970
0.11	.0438	.5438	.4562	.3965
0.12	.0478	.5478	.4522	.3961
0.13	.0517	.5517	.4483	.3956
0.14	.0557	.5557	.4443	.3951
0.15	.0596	.5596	.4404	.3945
0.16	.0636	.5636	.4364	.3939
0.17	.0675	.5675	.4325	.3932
0.18	.0714	.5714	.4286	.3925
0.19	.0753	.5753	.4247	.3918
0.20	.0793	.5793	.4207	.3910
0.21	.0832	.5832	.4168	.3902
0.22	.0871	.5871	.4129	.3894
0.23	.0910	.5910	.4090	.3885
0.24	.0948	.5948	.4052	.3876
0.25	.0987	.5987	.4013	.3867

(continued)

Table C.I Continued

Standard Score $z = x/\sigma_X$ (1)	Area from Mean to z (2)	Area in Larger Portion (3)	Area in Smaller Portion (4)	y at x/σ_X (5)
0.26	.1026	.6026	.3974	.3857
0.27	.1064	.6064	.3936	.3847
0.28	.1103	.6103	.3897	.3836
0.29	.1141	.6141	.3859	.3825
0.30	.1179	.6179	.3821	.3814
0.31	.1217	.6217	.3783	.3802
0.32	.1255	.6255	.3745	.3790
0.33	.1293	.6293	.3707	.3778
0.34	.1331	.6331	.3669	.3765
0.35	.1368	.6368	.3632	.3752
0.36	.1406	.6406	.3594	.3739
0.37	.1443	.6443	.3557	.3725
0.38	.1480	.6480	.3520	.3712
0.39	.1517	.6517	.3483	.3697
0.40	.1554	.6554	.3446	.3683
0.41	.1591	.6591	.3409	.3668
0.42	.1628	.6628	.3372	.3653
0.43	.1664	.6664	.3336	.3637
0.44	.1700	.6700	.3300	.3621
0.45	.1736	.6736	.3264	.3605
0.46	.1772	.6772	.3228	.3589
0.47	.1808	.6808	.3192	.3572
0.48	.1844	.6844	.3156	.3555
0.49	.1879	.6879	.3121	.3538
0.50	.1915	.6915	.3085	.3521
0.51	.1950	.6950	.3050	.3503
0.52	.1985	.6985	.3015	.3485
0.53	.2019	.7019	.2981	.3467
0.54	.2054	.7054	.2946	.3448
0.55	.2088	.7088	.2912	.3429
0.56	.2123	.7123	.2877	.3410
0.57	.2157	.7157	.2843	.3391
0.58	.2190	.7190	.2810	.3372
0.59	.2224	.7224	.2776	.3352

Table C.1 Continued

Standard Score $z = x/\sigma_X$ (1)	Area from Mean to z. (2)	Area in Larger Portion (3)	Area in Smaller Portion (4)	y at x/σ_X (5)
0.60	.2257	.7257	.2743	.3332
0.61	.2291	.7291	.2709	.3312
0.62	.2324	.7324	.2676	.3292
0.63	.2357	.7357	.2643	.3271
0.64	.2389	.7389	.2611	.3251
0.65	.2422	.7422	.2578	.3230
0.66	.2454	.7454	.2546	.3209
0.67	.2486	.7486	.2514	.3187
0.68	.2517	.7517	.2483	.3166
0.69	.2549	.7549	.2451	.3144
0.70	.2580	.7580	.2420	.3123
0.71	.2611	.7611	.2389	.3101
0.72	.2642	.7642	.2358	.3079
0.73	.2673	.7673	.2327	.3056
0.74	.2704	.7704	.2296	.3034
0.75	.2734	.7734	.2266	.3011
0.76	.2764	.7764	.2236	.2989
0.77	.2794	.7794	.2206	.2966
0.78	.2823	.7823	.2177	.2943
0.79	.2852	.7852	.2148	.2920
0.80	.2881	.7881	.2119	.2897
0.81	.2910	.7910	.2090	.2874
0.82	.2939	.7939	.2061	.2850
0.83	.2967	.7967	.2033	.2827
0.84	.2995	.7995	.2005	.2803
0.85	.3023	.8023	.1977	.2780
0.86	.3051	.8051	.1949	.2756
0.87	.3078	.8078	.1922	.2732
0.88	.3106	.8106	.1894	.2709
0.89	.3133	.8133	.1867	.2685
0.90	.3159	.8159	.1841	.2661
0.91	.3186	.8186	.1814	.2637
0.92	.3212	.8212	.1788	.2613

(continued)

Table C.1 Continued

Standard Score $z = x/\sigma_X$ (1)	Area from Mean to z (2)	Area in Larger Portion (3)	Area in Smaller Portion (4)	y at x/σ_X (5)
0.93	.3238	.8238	.1762	.2589
0.94	.3264	.8264	.1736	.2565
0.95	.3289	.8289	.1711	.2541
0.96	.3315	.8315	.1685	.2516
0.97	.3340	.8340	.1660	.2492
0.98	.3365	.8365	.1635	.2468
0.99	.3389	.8389	.1611	.2444
1.00	.3413	.8413	.1587	.2420
1.01	.3438	.8438	.1562	.2396
1.02	.3461	.8461	.1539	.2371
1.03	.3485	.8485	.1515	.2347
1.04	.3508	.8508	.1492	.2323
1.05	.3531	.8531	.1469	.2299
1.06	.3554	.8554	.1446	.2275
1.07	.3577	.8577	.1423	.2251
1.08	.3599	.8599	.1401	.2227
1.09	.3621	.8621	.1379	.2203
1.10	.3643	.8643	.1357	.2179
1.11	.3665	.8665	.1335	.2155
1.12	.3686	.8686	.1314	.2131
1.13	.3708	.8708	.1292	.2107
1.14	.3729	.8729	.1271	.2083
1.15	.3749	.8749	.1251	.2059
1.16	.3770	.8770	.1230	.2036
1.17	.3790	.8790	.1210	.2012
1.18	.3810	.8810	.1190	.1989
1.19	.3830	.8830	.1170	.1965
1.20	.3849	.8849	.1151	.1942
1.21	.3869	.8869	.1131	.1919
1.22	.3888	.8888	.1112	.1895
1.23	.3907	.8907	.1093	.1872
1.24	.3925	.8925	.1075	.1849
1.25	.3944	.8944	.1056	.1826
1.26	.3962	.8962	.1038	.1804

Table C.I Continued

Standard Score $z = x/\sigma_x$ (1)	Area from Mean to z (2)	Area in Larger Portion (3)	Area in Smaller Portion (4)	y at x/σ_x (5)
1.27	.3980	.8980	.1020	.1781
1.28	.3997	.8997	.1003	.1758
1.29	.4015	.9015	.0985	.1736
1.30	.4032	.9032	.0968	.1714
1.31	.4049	.9049	.0951	.1691
1.32	.4066	.9066	.0934	.1669
1.33	.4082	.9082	.0918	.1647
1.34	.4099	.9099	.0901	.1626
1.35	.4115	.9115	.0885	.1604
1.36	.4131	.9131	.0869	.1582
1.37	.4147	.9147	.0853	.1561
1.38	.4162	.9162	.0838	.1539
1.39	.4177	.9177	.0823	.1518
1.40	.4192	.9192	.0808	.1497
1.41	.4207	.9207	.0793	.1476
1.42	.4222	.9222	.0778	.1456
1.43	.4236	.9236	.0764	.1435
1.44	.4251	.9251	.0749	.1415
1.45	.4265	.9265	.0735	.1394
1.46	.4279	.9279	.0721	.1374
1.47	.4292	.9292	.0708	.1354
1.48	.4306	.9306	.0694	.1334
1.49	.4319	.9319	.0681	.1315
1.50	.4332	.9332	.0668	.1295
1.51	.4345	.9345	.0655	.1276
1.52	.4357	.9357	.0643	.1257
1.53	.4370	.9370	.0630	.1238
1.54	.4382	.9382	.0618	.1219
1.55	.4394	.9394	.0606	.1200
1.56	.4406	.9406	.0594	.1182
1.57	.4418	.9418	.0582	.1163
1.58	.4429	.9429	.0571	.1145
1.59	.4441	.9441	.0559	.1127

(continued)

Table C.1 Continued

Standard Score $z = x/\sigma_X$ (1)	Area from Mean to z (2)	Area in Larger Portion (3)	Area in Smaller Portion (4)	y at x/σ_X (5)
1.60	.4452	.9452	.0548	.1109
1.61	.4463	.9463	.0537	.1092
1.62	.4474	.9474	.0526	.1074
1.63	.4484	.9484	.0516	.1057
1.64	.4495	.9495	.0505	.1040
1.65	.4505	.9505	.0495	.1023
1.66	.4515	.9515	.0485	.1006
1.67	.4525	.9525	.0475	.0989
1.68	.4535	.9535	.0465	.0973
1.69	.4545	.9545	.0455	.0957
1.70	.4554	.9554	.0446	.0940
1.71	.4564	.9564	.0436	.0925
1.72	.4573	.9573	.0427	.0909
1.73	.4582	.9582	.0418	.0893
1.74	.4591	.9591	.0409	.0878
1.75	.4599	.9599	.0401	.0863
1.76	.4608	.9608	.0392	.0848
1.77	.4616	.9616	.0384	.0833
1.78	.4625	.9625	.0375	.0818
1.79	.4633	.9633	.0367	.0804
1.80	.4641	.9641	.0359	.0790
1.81	.4649	.9649	.0351	.0775
1.82	.4656	.9656	.0344	.0761
1.83	.4664	.9664	.0336	.0748
1.84	.4671	.9671	.0329	.0734
1.85	.4678	.9678	.0322	.0721
1.86	.4686	.9686	.0314	.0707
1.87	.4693	.9693	.0307	.0694
1.88	.4699	.9699	.0301	.0681
1.89	.4706	.9706	.0294	.0669
1.90	.4713	.9713	.0287	.0656
1.91	.4719	.9719	.0281	.0644
1.92	.4726	.9726	.0274	.0632
1.93	.4732	.9732	.0268	.0620

Table C.1   Continued

Standard Score $z = x/\sigma_X$ (1)	Area from Mean to z (2)	Area in Larger Portion (3)	Area in Smaller Portion (4)	y at x/σ_X (5)
1.94	.4738	.9738	.0262	.0608
1.95	.4744	.9744	.0256	.0596
1.96	.4750	.9750	.0250	.0584
1.97	.4756	.9756	.0244	.0573
1.98	.4761	.9761	.0239	.0562
1.99	.4767	.9767	.0233	.0551
2.00	.4772	.9772	.0228	.0540
2.01	.4778	.9778	.0222	.0529
2.02	.4783	.9783	.0217	.0519
2.03	.4788	.9788	.0212	.0508
2.04	.4793	.9793	.0207	.0498
2.05	.4798	.9798	.0202	.0488
2.06	.4803	.9803	.0197	.0478
2.07	.4808	.9808	.0192	.0468
2.08	.4812	.9812	.0188	.0459
2.09	.4817	.9817	.0183	.0449
2.10	.4821	.9821	.0179	.0440
2.11	.4826	.9826	.0174	.0431
2.12	.4830	.9830	.0170	.0422
2.13	.4834	.9834	.0166	.0413
2.14	.4838	.9838	.0162	.0404
2.15	.4842	.9842	.0158	.0396
2.16	.4846	.9846	.0154	.0387
2.17	.4850	.9850	.0150	.0379
2.18	.4854	.9854	.0146	.0371
2.19	.4857	.9857	.0143	.0363
2.20	.4861	.9861	.0139	.0355
2.21	.4864	.9864	.0136	.0347
2.22	.4868	.9868	.0132	.0339
2.23	.4871	.9871	.0129	.0332
2.24	.4875	.9875	.0125	.0325
2.25	.4878	.9878	.0122	.0317
2.26	.4881	.9881	.0119	.0310

(continued)

Table C.1 Continued

Standard Score $z = x/\sigma_x$ (1)	Area from Mean to z (2)	Area in Larger Portion (3)	Area in Smaller Portion (4)	y at x/σ_x (5)
2.27	.4884	.9884	.0116	.0303
2.28	.4887	.9887	.0113	.0297
2.29	.4890	.9890	.0110	.0290
2.30	.4893	.9893	.0107	.0283
2.31	.4896	.9896	.0104	.0277
2.32	.4898	.9898	.0102	.0270
2.33	.4901	.9901	.0099	.0264
2.34	.4904	.9904	.0096	.0258
2.35	.4906	.9906	.0094	.0252
2.36	.4909	.9909	.0091	.0246
2.37	.4911	.9911	.0089	.0241
2.38	.4913	.9913	.0087	.0235
2.39	.4916	.9916	.0084	.0229
2.40	.4918	.9918	.0082	.0224
2.41	.4920	.9920	.0080	.0219
2.42	.4922	.9922	.0078	.0213
2.43	.4925	.9925	.0075	.0208
2.44	.4927	.9927	.0073	.0203
2.45	.4929	.9929	.0071	.0198
2.46	.4931	.9931	.0069	.0194
2.47	.4932	.9932	.0068	.0189
2.48	.4934	.9934	.0066	.0184
2.49	.4936	.9936	.0064	.0180
2.50	.4938	.9938	.0062	.0175
2.51	.4940	.9940	.0060	.0171
2.52	.4941	.9941	.0059	.0167
2.53	.4943	.9943	.0057	.0163
2.54	.4945	.9945	.0055	.0158
2.55	.4946	.9946	.0054	.0154
2.56	.4948	.9948	.0052	.0151
2.57	.4949	.9949	.0051	.0147
2.58	.4951	.9951	.0049	.0143
2.59	.4952	.9952	.0048	.0139
2.60	.4953	.9953	.0047	.0136
2.61	.4955	.9955	.0045	.0132

Table C.1   Continued

Standard Score $z = x/\sigma_x$ (1)	Area from Mean to z (2)	Area in Larger Portion (3)	Area in Smaller Portion (4)	y at x/σ_x (5)
2.62	.4956	.9956	.0044	.0129
2.63	.4957	.9957	.0043	.0126
2.64	.4959	.9959	.0041	.0122
2.65	.4960	.9960	.0040	.0119
2.66	.4961	.9961	.0039	.0116
2.67	.4962	.9962	.0038	.0113
2.68	.4963	.9963	.0037	.0110
2.69	.4964	.9964	.0036	.0107
2.70	.4965	.9965	.0035	.0104
2.71	.4966	.9966	.0034	.0101
2.72	.4967	.9967	.0033	.0099
2.73	.4968	.9968	.0032	.0096
2.74	.4969	.9969	.0031	.0093
2.75	.4970	.9970	.0030	.0091
2.76	.4971	.9971	.0029	.0088
2.77	.4972	.9972	.0028	.0086
2.78	.4973	.9973	.0027	.0084
2.79	.4974	.9974	.0026	.0081
2.80	.4974	.9974	.0026	.0079
2.81	.4975	.9975	.0025	.0077
2.82	.4976	.9976	.0024	.0075
2.83	.4977	.9977	.0023	.0073
2.84	.4977	.9977	.0023	.0071
2.85	.4978	.9978	.0022	.0069
2.86	.4979	.9979	.0021	.0067
2.87	.4979	.9979	.0021	.0065
2.88	.4980	.9980	.0020	.0063
2.89	.4981	.9981	.0019	.0061
2.90	.4981	.9981	.0019	.0060
2.91	.4982	.9982	.0018	.0058
2.92	.4982	.9982	.0018	.0056
2.93	.4983	.9983	.0017	.0055
2.94	.4984	.9984	.0016	.0053
2.95	.4984	.9984	.0016	.0051

(continued)

Table C.1 Continued

Standard Score $z = x/\sigma_x$ (1)	Area from Mean to z (2)	Area in Larger Portion (3)	Area in Smaller Portion (4)	y at x/σ_x (5)
2.96	.4985	.9985	.0015	.0050
2.97	.4985	.9985	.0015	.0048
2.98	.4986	.9986	.0014	.0047
2.99	.4986	.9986	.0014	.0046
3.00	.4987	.9987	.0013	.0044
3.01	.4987	.9987	.0013	.0043
3.02	.4987	.9987	.0013	.0042
3.03	.4988	.9988	.0012	.0040
3.04	.4988	.9988	.0012	.0039
3.05	.4989	.9989	.0011	.0038
3.06	.4989	.9989	.0011	.0037
3.07	.4989	.9989	.0011	.0036
3.08	.4990	.9990	.0010	.0035
3.09	.4990	.9990	.0010	.0034
3.10	.4990	.9990	.0010	.0033
3.11	.4991	.9991	.0009	.0032
3.12	.4991	.9991	.0009	.0031
3.13	.4991	.9991	.0009	.0030
3.14	.4992	.9992	.0008	.0029
3.15	.4992	.9992	.0008	.0028
3.16	.4992	.9992	.0008	.0027
3.17	.4992	.9992	.0008	.0026
3.18	.4993	.9993	.0007	.0025
3.19	.4993	.9993	.0007	.0025
3.20	.4993	.9993	.0007	.0024
3.21	.4993	.9993	.0007	.0023
3.22	.4994	.9994	.0006	.0022
3.23	.4994	.9994	.0006	.0022
3.24	.4994	.9994	.0006	.0021
3.30	.4995	.9995	.0005	.0017
3.40	.4997	.9997	.0003	.0012
3.50	.4998	.9998	.0002	.0009
3.60	.4998	.9998	.0002	.0006
3.70	.4999	.9999	.0001	.0004

Note: The entries in this table were generated using a computer program.

References

Abelson, R. P. (1997). On the surprising longevity of flogged horses: Why there is a case for the significance test. *Psychological Science, 8,* 12–15.

Acklin, M. W., McDowell, C. J., Verschell, M. S., & Chan, D. (2000). Interobserver agreement, intraobserver reliability, and the Rorschach Comprehensive System. *Journal of Personality Assessment, 74,* 15–47.

Aiken, L. R. (1996). *Rating scales and checklists: Evaluating behavior, personality and attitudes.* New York: Wiley.

Aiken, L. R. (1997). *Questionnaires and inventories: Surveying opinions and assessing personality.* New York: Wiley.

American Association for Counseling and Development. (1988). *Responsibilities of users of standardized tests.* Washington, DC: Author.

American Counseling Association. (1995). *Code of ethics and standards of practice.* Alexandria, VA: Author.

American Educational Research Association, American Psychological Association, & National Council on Measurement in Education. (1999). *Standards for educational and psychological testing.* Washington, DC: American Educational Research Association.

American Psychiatric Association. (1994). *Diagnostic and statistical manual of mental disorders* (4th ed.). Washington, DC: Author.

American Psychological Association. (1953). *Ethical standards of psychologists.* Washington, DC: Author.

American Psychological Association. (1954). *Technical recommendations for psychological tests and diagnostic techniques.* Washington, DC: Author.

American Psychological Association. (1966). *Standards for educational and psychological tests and manuals.* Washington, DC: Author.

American Psychological Association. (2000). *Report of the task force on test user qualifications.* Washington, DC: Author.

American Psychological Association. (2001). *Publication manual of the American Psychological Association* (5th ed.). Washington, DC: Author.

American Psychological Association. (2002). Ethical principles of psychologists and code of conduct. *American Psychologist, 57,* 1060–1073.

American Psychological Association. (2003). *FAQ/Finding information about psychological tests.* Washington, DC: Author. Retrieved July 5, 2003 from the World Wide Web: http://www .apa.org/science/faq-findtests.html

American Psychological Association, American Educational Research Association, & National Council on Measurement in Education. (1974). *Standards for educational & psychological tests.* Washington, DC: American Psychological Association.

American Psychological Association, Committee on Legal Issues. (1996). Strategies for private practitioners coping with subpoenas or compelled testimony for client records or test data. *Professional Psychology: Research and Practice, 27,* 245–251.

American Psychological Association, Committee on Psychological Tests and Assessment. (1996). Statement on the disclosure of test data. *American Psychologist, 51,* 644–648.

American Psychological Association, Committee on Psychological Tests and Assessment. (2003). *Statement on the use of secure psychological tests in the education of graduate and undergraduate psychology students.* Retrieved February 19, 2003, from http://www.apa.org./science/securetests.html

Ames, L. B. (1989). *Arnold Gesell: Themes of his work.* New York: Human Sciences Press.

Anastasi, A. (1954). *Psychological testing.* New York: Macmillan.

Anastasi, A. (1986). Evolving concepts of test validation. *Annual Review of Psychology, 37,* 1–15.

Anastasi, A. (1988). *Psychological testing* (6th ed.). New York: Macmillan.

Anastasi, A., & Urbina, S. (1997). *Psychological testing* (7th ed.). Upper Saddle River, NJ: Prentice Hall.

Angoff, W. H. (1984). *Scales, norms, and equivalent scores.* Princeton, NJ: Educational Testing Service.

Angoff, W. H. (1988). Validity: An evolving concept. In H. Wainer & H. Braun (Eds.), *Test validity* (pp. 19–32). Hillsdale, NJ: Erlbaum.

Archer, R. P. (1987). *Using the MMPI with adolescents.* Hillsdale, NJ: Erlbaum.

Baker, F. B. (2001). *The basics of item response theory* (2nd ed.). Retrieved May 10, 2003, from http://ericae.net/irt [currently available from http://edres.org/irt/baker/]

Balma, M. J. (1959). The concept of synthetic validity. *Personnel Psychology, 12,* 395–396.

Baugh, F. (2003). Correcting effect sizes for score reliability: A reminder that measurement and substantive issues are linked inextricably. In B. Thompson (Ed.), *Score reliability: Contemporary thinking on reliability issues* (pp. 31–41). Thousand Oaks, CA: Sage.

Bell, D. E., Raiffa, H., & Tversky, A. (Eds.). (1988). *Decision-making: Descriptive, normative, and prescriptive interactions.* New York: Cambridge University Press.

Bennett, R. E., & Ward, W. C. (Eds.). (1993). *Construction versus choice: Issues in constructed response, performance testing, and portfolio assessment.* Hillsdale, NJ: Erlbaum.

Beutler, L. E., & Groth-Marnat, G. (Eds.). (2003). *Integrative assessment of adult personality* (2nd ed.). New York: Guilford.

Blatt, J. (Producer/Writer/Director). (1989). *Against all odds: Inside statistics.* [VHS videocassette]. (Available from The Annenberg/CPB Project, 901 E St., NW, Washington, DC 20004-2006)

Bollen, K. A., & Long, J. S. (Eds.). (1993). *Testing structural equation models.* Newbury Park, CA: Sage.

Bond, T. G., & Fox, C. M. (2001). *Applying the Rasch model: Fundamental measurement in the human sciences.* Mahwah, NJ: Erlbaum.

Bondy, M. (1974). Psychiatric antecedents of psychological testing (before Binet). *Journal of the History of the Behavioral Sciences, 10,* 180–194.

Boring, E. G. (1950). *A history of experimental psychology* (2nd ed.). New York: Appleton-Century-Crofts.

Borum, R. (1996). Improving the clinical practice of violence risk assessment: Technology, guidelines, and training. *American Psychologist, 51,* 945–956.

Boudreau, J. W. (1991). Utility analysis for decisions in human resource management. In M. D. Dunnette & L. M. Hough (Eds.). *Handbook for industrial and organizational psychology* (2nd ed., Vol. 2, pp. 621–745). Palo Alto, CA: Consulting Psychologists Press.

Bowman, M. L. (1989). Testing individual differences in ancient China. *American Psychologist, 44,* 576–578.

Brannick, M. T., & Levine, E. L. (2002). *Job analysis: Methods, research, and applications for human resource management in the new millenium.* Thousand Oaks, CA: Sage.

Braun, H. L., Jackson, D. N., & Wiley, D. E. (2002). *The role of constructs in psychological and educational measurement.* Mahwah, NJ: Erlbaum.

Brennan, R. L. (2001). *Generalizability theory.* New York: Springer.

Briel, J. B., O'Neill, K., & Scheuneman, J. D. (Eds.). (1993). *GRE technical manual.* Princeton, NJ: Educational Testing Service.

Broadus, R. N., & Elmore, K. E. (1983). The comparative validities of undergraduate grade point average and of part scores on the Graduate Record Examinations in the prediction of two criterion measures in a graduate library school program. *Educational and Psychological Measurement, 43,* 543–546.

Brogden, H. E. (1946). On the interpretation of the correlation coefficient as a measure of predictive efficiency. *Journal of Educational Psychology, 37,* 65–76.

Brown, C. W., & Ghiselli, E. E. (1953). Percent increase in proficiency resulting from use of selective devices. *Journal of Applied Psychology, 37,* 341–345.

Bryant, F. B., & Yarnold, P. R. (1995). Principal components analysis and exploratory and confirmatory factor analysis. In L. G. Grimm & P. R. Yarnold, *Reading and understanding multivariate statistics* (pp. 99–136). Washington, DC: American Psychological Association.

Buchanan, T. (2002). Online assessment: Desirable or dangerous? *Professional Psychology: Research and Practice, 33,* 148–154.

Buchwald, A. M. (1965). Values and the use of tests. *Journal of Consulting Psychology, 29,* 49–54.

Butcher, J. N. (2003). Computerized psychological assessment. In J. R. Graham & J. A. Naglieri (Vol. Eds.), *Handbook of psychology: Vol. 10. Assessment psychology* (pp. 141–163). Hoboken, NJ: Wiley.

Butcher, J. N., Dahlstrom, W. G., Graham, J. R., Tellegen, A., & Kaemmer, B. (1989). *Minnesota Multiphasic Personality Inventory–2 (MMPI-2): Manual for administration and scoring.* Minneapolis: University of Minnesota Press.

Campbell, D. T., & Fiske, D. W. (1959). Convergent and discriminant validation by the multitrait-multimethod matrix. *Psychological Bulletin, 56,* 81–105.

Campbell, J. P. (1990). Modeling the performance prediction problem in industrial and organization psychology. In M. D. Dunnette & L. M. Hough (Eds.), *Handbook of industrial and organizational psychology* (2nd ed., Vol. 1, pp. 687–732). Palo Alto, CA: Consulting Psychologists Press.

Campbell, J. P. (1994). Alternative models of job performance and their implications for selection and classification. In M. G. Rumsey, C. B. Walker, & J. H. Harris (Eds.), *Personnel selection and classification* (pp. 33–51). Hillsdale, NJ: Erlbaum.

Campbell, J. P., & Knapp, D. J. (Eds.). (2001). *Exploring the limits of personnel selection and classification.* Mahwah, NJ: Erlbaum.

Carroll, J. B. (1993). *Human cognitive abilities: A survey of factor analytic studies.* New York: Cambridge University Press.

Carroll, J. B. (2002). The five-factor personality model: How complete and satisfactory is it? In H. I. Braun, D. N. Jackson, & D. E. Wiley (Eds.), *The role of constructs in psychological and educational measurement* (pp. 97–126). Mahwah, NJ: Erlbaum.

Cizek, G. J. (1999). *Cheating on tests: How to do it, detect it, and prevent it.* Mahwah, NJ: Erlbaum.

Cizek, G. J. (2001). *Setting performance standards: Concepts, methods, and perspectives.* Mahwah, NJ: Erlbaum.

Cohen, J. (1994). The earth is round ($p < .05$). *American Psychologist, 49,* 997–1003.

Cole, N. S., & Moss, P. A. (1989). Bias in test use. In R. L. Linn (Ed.), *Educational measurement* (3rd ed., pp. 201–219). New York: American Council on Education/Macmillan.

Comrey, A. L., & Lee, H. B. (1992). *A first course in factor analysis* (2nd ed.). Hillsdale, NJ: Erlbaum.

Constantinople, A. (1973). Masculinity-femininity: An exception to a famous dictum? *Psychological Bulletin, 80,* 389–407.

Cortina, J. M. (1993). What is coefficient alpha? An examination of theory and applications. *Journal of Applied Psychology, 78,* 98–104.

Costa, P. T., Jr., & McCrae, R. R. (1992). *Revised NEO Personality Inventory (NEO PI-R) and NEO Five-Factor Inventory (NEO-FFI): Professional manual.* Odessa, FL: Psychological Assessment Resources.

Cowles, M. (2001). *Statistics in psychology: An historical perspective* (2nd ed.). Mahwah, NJ: Erlbaum.

Cronbach, L. J. (1949). *Essentials of psychological testing.* New York: Harper & Row.

Cronbach, L. J. (1951). Coefficient alpha and the internal structure of tests. *Psychometrika, 16,* 297–334.

Cronbach, L. J. (1988). Five perspectives on validity argument. In H. Wainer & H. I. Braun (Eds.), *Test validity* (pp. 3–17). Hillsdale, NJ: Erlbaum.

Cronbach, L. J., & Gleser, G. C. (1965). *Psychological tests and personnel decisions* (2nd ed.). Champaign: University of Illinois Press.

Cronbach, L. J., Gleser, G. C., Nanda, H., & Rajaratnam, N. (1972). *The dependability of behavioral measurements: Theory of generalizability for scores and profiles.* New York: Wiley.

Cronbach, L. J., & Meehl, P. E. (1955). Construct validity in psychological tests. *Psychological Bulletin, 52,* 281–302.

DeVellis, R. F. (2003). *Scale development: Theory and application* (2nd ed.). Thousand Oaks, CA: Sage.

Digman, J. M. (1990). Personality structure: Emergence of the Five-Factor Model. *Annual Review of Psychology, 41,* 417–440.

Drasgow, F. (1987). Study of the measurement bias of two standardized psychological tests. *Journal of Applied Psychology, 72,* 19–29.

Drasgow, F., & Olson-Buchanan, J. B. (Eds.). (1999). *Innovations in computerized assessment.* Mahwah, NJ: Erlbaum.

DuBois, P. H. (1970). *A history of psychological testing.* Boston: Allyn & Bacon.

Dudek, F. J. (1979). The continuing misinterpretation of the standard error of measurement. *Psychological Bulletin, 86,* 335–337.

Eisman, E. J., Dies, R. R., Finn, S. E., Eyde, L. D., Kay, G. G., Kubiszyn, T. W., Meyer, G. J., & Moreland, K. (2000). Problems and limitations in the use of psychological assessment in the contemporary health care delivery system. *Professional Psychology: Research and Practice, 31,* 131–140.

Ekstrom, R. B., & Smith, D. K. (Eds.). (2002). *Assessing individuals with disabilities in educational, employment, and counseling settings.* Washington, DC: American Psychological Association.

Embretson, S. (1983). Construct validity: Construct representation versus nomothetic span. *Psychological Bulletin, 93,* 179–197.

Embretson, S. E. (1996). The new rules of measurement. *Psychological Assessment, 8,* 341–349.

Embretson, S. E. (1999). Issues in the measurement of cognitive abilities. In S. E. Embretson & S. L. Hershberger, (Eds.), *The new rules of measurement: What every psychologist and educator should know* (pp. 1–15). Mahwah, NJ: Erlbaum.

Embretson, S. E., & Reise, S. P. (2000). *Item response theory for psychologists.* Mahwah, NJ: Erlbaum.

Erikson, J., & Vater, S. (1995). *IDA administration manual: Procedures summary Provence Birth-to-Three Developmental Profile.* Itasca, IL: Riverside.

Eyde, L. E., Moreland, K. L., Robertson, G. J., Primoff, E. S., & Most, R. B. (1988). *Test user qualifications: A data-based approach to promoting good test use.* Washington, DC: American Psychological Association.

Fancher, R. E. (1985). *The intelligence men: Makers of the IQ controversy.* New York: Norton.

Fancher, R. E. (1996). *Pioneers of psychology* (3rd ed.). New York: Norton.

Fink, A. (2002). *How to ask survey questions* (2nd ed., Vol. 2). Thousand Oaks, CA: Sage.

Finn, S. E., & Kamphuis, J. H. (1995). What a clinician needs to know about base rates. In J. N. Butcher (Ed.), *Clinical personality assessment: Practical approaches* (pp. 224–235). New York: Oxford University Press.

Finn, S. E., & Tonsager, M. E. (1997). Information-gathering and therapeutic models of assessment: Complementary paradigms. *Psychological Assessment, 9,* 374–385.

Fischer, C. T. (1994). *Individualizing psychological assessment.* Hillsdale, NJ: Erlbaum. (Original work published 1985)

Fischer, C. T. (2000). Collaborative, individualized assessment. *Journal of Personality Assessment, 74,* 2–14.

Flanagan, S. G. (1992). Review of the Whitaker Index of Schizophrenic Thinking. *The Eleventh Mental Measurements Yearbook*, pp. 1033–1034.

Flynn, J. R. (1984). The mean IQ of Americans: Massive gains. *Psychological Bulletin, 95,* 29–51.

Flynn, J. R. (1987). Massive IQ gains in 14 nations: What IQ tests really measure. *Psychological Bulletin, 101,* 171–191.

Franzen, M. D. (2000). *Reliability and validity in neuropsychological assessment* (2nd ed.). New York: Kluwer Academic/Plenum.

Frederiksen, N., Mislevy, R. J., & Bejar, I. I. (Eds.). (1993). *Test theory for a new generation of tests.* Hillsdale, NJ: Erlbaum.

Frisch, M. B. (1994). *QOLI: Quality of Life Inventory.* Minneapolis, MN: National Computer Systems.

Glaser, R. (1963). Instructional technology and the measurement of learning outcomes: Some questions. *American Psychologist, 18,* 519–521.

Goldberg, E. L., & Alliger, G. M. (1992). Assessing the validity of the GRE for students in psychology: A validity generalization approach. *Educational and Psychological Measurement, 52,* 1019–1027.

Goldman, L. (1971). *Using tests in counseling* (2nd ed.). New York: Appleton-Century-Crofts.

Goldman, B. A., Mitchell, D. F., & Egelson, P. (Eds.). (1997). *Directory of unpublished experimental mental measures: Volume 7 (1990–1995).* Washington, DC: American Psychological Association.

Goodglass, H., Kaplan, E., & Barresi, B. (2001). *Assessment of aphasia and related disorders* (3rd ed.). Baltimore, MD: Lippincott, Williams & Wilkins.

Gronlund, N. E. (2003). *Assessment of student achievement* (7th ed.). Boston: Allyn & Bacon.

Groth-Marnat, G. (1997). *Handbook of psychological assessment* (3rd ed.). New York: Wiley.

Guion, R. M. (1991). Personnel assessment, selection, and placement. In M. D. Dunnette & L. M. Hough (Eds.), *Handbook of industrial and organizational psychology* (2nd ed., Vol. 2, pp. 327–397). Palo Alto, CA: Consulting Psychologists Press.

Guion, R. M. (1998). *Assessment, measurement, and prediction for personnel decisions.* Mahwah, NJ: Erlbaum.

Gulliksen, H. (1950). *Theory of mental tests.* New York: Wiley.

Gustafsson, J.-E. (2002). Measurement from a hierarchical point of view. In H. I. Braun, D. N. Jackson, & D. E. Wiley (Eds.), *The role of constructs in psychological and educational measurement* (pp. 73–95). Mahwah, NJ: Erlbaum.

Haladyna, T. M. (1997). *Writing test items to evaluate higher order thinking.* Boston: Allyn & Bacon.

Haladyna, T. M. (1999). *Developing and validating multiple-choice test items* (2nd ed.). Mahwah, NJ: Erlbaum.

Halpern, D. F. (1997). Sex differences in intelligence: Implications for education. *American Psychologist, 52,* 1091–1101.

Hambleton, R. K., & Rogers, H. J. (1991). Advances in criterion-referenced measurement. In R. K. Hambleton & J. N. Zaal (Eds.), *Advances in educational and psychological testing* (pp. 3–43). Boston: Kluwer.

Hambleton, R. K., Swaminathan, H., & Rogers, H. J. (1991). *Fundamentals of item response theory.* Newbury Park, CA: Sage.

Handler, L., & Meyer, G. J. (1998). The importance of teaching and learning personality assessment. In L. Handler & M. J. Hilsenroth (Eds.), *Teaching and learning personality assessment* (pp. 3–30). Mahwah, NJ: Erlbaum.

Hartigan, J. A., & Wigdor, A. K. (Eds.). (1989). *Fairness in employment testing: Validity generalization, minority issues, and the General Aptitude Test Battery.* Washington, DC: National Academy Press.

Hathaway, S. R., & McKinley, J. C. (1940). A Multiphasic Personality Schedule (Minnesota): I. Construction of the schedule. *Journal of Psychology, 10,* 249–254.

Hedges, L. V., & Nowell, A. (1995). Sex differences in mental test scores, variability, and numbers of high-scoring individuals. *Science, 269,* 41–45.

Hersen, M., & Van Hasselt, V. B. (Eds.). (1998). *Basic interviewing: A practical guide for counselors and clinicians.* Mahwah, NJ: Erlbaum.

Holland, P. W., & Thayer, D. T. (1988). Differential item performance and the Mantel-Haenszel procedure. In H. Wainer & H. I. Braun (Eds.), *Test validity* (pp. 129–145). Hillsdale, NJ: Erlbaum.

Howell, D. C. (2002). *Statistical methods for psychology* (5th ed.). Pacific Grove, CA: Duxbury.

Hummel, T. J. (1999). The usefulness of tests in clinical decisions. In J. W. Lichtenberg & R. K. Goodyear (Eds.), *Scientist-practitioner perspectives on test interpretation* (pp. 59–112). Boston: Allyn & Bacon.

Hunter, J. E., & Schmidt, F. L. (1981). Fitting people into jobs: The impact of personnel selection on national productivity. In M. A. Dunnette & E. A. Fleishman (Eds.), *Human performance and productivity: Vol. 1. Human capability assessment* (pp. 233–284). Hillsdale, NJ: Erlbaum.

Hunter, J. E., & Schmidt, F. L. (1990). *Methods of meta-analysis: Correcting error and bias in research findings.* Newbury Park, CA: Sage.

Hunter, J. E., & Schmidt, F. L. (1996). Cumulative research knowledge and social policy formulations: The critical role of meta-analysis. *Psychology, Public Policy, and Law, 2,* 324–347.

Impara, J. C., & Plake, B. S. (Eds.). (1998). *The Thirteenth Mental Measurements Yearbook.* Lincoln, NE: Buros Institute.

International Test Commission. (2000). *International guidelines for test use: Version 2000.* Retrieved June 8, 2002, from http://www.intestcom.org

Irvine, S. H., & Kyllonen, P. C. (Eds.). (2002). *Item generation for test development.* Mahwah, NJ: Erlbaum.

Ivnik, R. J., Malec, J. F., Smith, G. E., Tangalos, E. G., Petersen, R. C., Kormen, E., & Kurland, L. T. (1992). Mayo's older Americans normative studies: WAIS-R norms for ages 56 to 97. *Clinical Neuropsychologist, 6*(Suppl.), 1–30.

Jaeger, R. M. (1989). Certification of student competence. In R. L. Linn (Ed.), *Educational measurement* (3rd ed., pp. 485–514). New York: American Council on Education/Macmillan.

James, L. R. (1973). Criterion models and construct validity for criteria. *Psychological Bulletin, 80,* 75–83.

James, W. (1890). *The principles of psychology* (Vols. 1–2). New York: Henry Holt.

Janssen, R., Tuerlinckx, F., Meulders, M., & De Boeck, P. (2000). A hierarchical IRT model for criterion-referenced measurement. *Journal of Educational and Behavioral Statistics, 25,* 285–306.

Jensen, A. R. (1998). *The g factor: The science of mental ability.* Westport, CT: Praeger.

Johnson, S. (2000). *Taking the anxiety out of taking tests: A step-by-step guide.* New York: Barnes & Noble Books.

Joint Committee on Testing Practices. (1988). *Code of fair testing practices in education.* Washington, DC: Author.

Joint Committee on Testing Practices. (1998). *Rights and responsibilities of test takers: Guidelines and expectations.* Retrieved July 12, 2003, from http://www.apa.org/science/ttrr.html

Jöreskog, K. G., & Sörbom, D. (1993). *LISREL 8: User's reference guide.* Chicago: Scientific Software International.

Kamphaus, R. W. (2001). *Clinical assessment of child and adolescent intelligence* (2nd ed.). Boston: Allyn & Bacon.

Kamphaus, R. W., & Frick, P. J. (2002). *Clinical assessment of child and adolescent personality and behavior* (2nd ed.). Boston: Allyn & Bacon.

Kaufman, A. S. (2000). Tests of intelligence. In R. J. Sternberg (Ed.), *Handbook of intelligence* (pp. 445–476). New York: Cambridge University Press.

Kaufman, A. S., & Kaufman, N. L. (1993). *Kaufman Adolescent and Adult Intelligence Test: Manual.* Circle Pines, MN: American Guidance Service.

Kaufman, A. S., & Lichtenberger, E. O. (2002). *Assessing adolescent and adult intelligence* (2nd ed.). Boston: Allyn & Bacon.

Kellogg, C. E., & Morton, N. W. (1999). *Beta III: Manual*. San Antonio, TX: The Psychological Corporation.

Kirk, R. E. (1999). *Statistics: An introduction* (4th ed.). Fort Worth, TX: Harcourt Brace.

Kirsch, I., & Sapirstein, G. (1998, June 26). Listening to Prozac but hearing placebo: A meta-analysis of antidepressant medication. *Prevention & Treatment, 1,* Article 0002a. Retrieved July 2, 1998, from http://journals.apa.org/prevention/volume1/pre0010002a.html

Kobrin, J. L., Camara, W. J., & Milewski, G. B. (2002). *The utility of the SAT I and SAT II for admissions decisions in California and the nation.* (College Board Research Report No. 2002-6). New York: College Entrance Examination Board.

Kubiszyn, T. W., Meyer, G. J., Finn, S. E., Eyde, L. D., Kay, G. G., Moreland, K. L., Dies, R. R., & Eisman, E. J. (2000). Empirical support for psychological assessment in clinical health care settings. *Professional Psychology: Research and Practice, 31,* 119–130.

Kuncel, N. R., Campbell, J. P., & Ones, D. S. (1998). Validity of the Graduate Record Examination: Estimated or tacitly known? *American Psychologist, 53,* 567–568.

Kuncel, N. R., Hezlett, S. A., & Ones, D. S. (2001). A comprehensive meta-analysis of the predictive validity of the Graduate Record Examinations: Implications for graduate student selection and performance. *Psychological Bulletin, 127,* 162–181.

Landy, F. J. (1986). Stamp collecting versus science: Validation as hypothesis testing. *American Psychologist, 11,* 1183–1192.

Lanyon, R. I., & Goodstein, L. D. (1997). *Personality assessment* (3rd ed.). New York: Wiley.

Lees-Haley, P. R. (1996). Alice in Validityland, or the dangerous consequences of consequential validity. *American Psychologist, 51,* 981–983.

Lemann, N. (1999). *The big test: The secret history of the American meritocracy.* New York: Farrar, Straus & Giroux.

Lenney, E. (1991). Sex roles: The measurement of masculinity, femininity, and androgyny. In J. P. Robinson, P. R. Shaver, & L. S. Wrightsman (Eds.), *Measures of personality and social psychological attitudes* (pp. 573–660). San Diego, CA: Academic Press.

Lezak, M. D. (1995). *Neuropsychological assessment* (3rd ed.). New York: Oxford University Press.

Lichtenberg, J. W., & Goodyear, R. K. (Eds.). (1999). *Scientist-practitioner perspectives on test interpretation.* Boston: Allyn & Bacon.

Linn, R. L. (1994). Criterion-referenced measurement: A valuable perspective clouded by surplus meaning. *Educational Measurement: Issues and Practice, 13,* 12–14.

Linn, R. L. (1998). Partitioning responsibility for the evaluation of the consequences of assessment programs. *Educational Measurement: Issues & Practice, 17,* 28–30.

Linn, R. L., & Gronlund, N. E. (1995). *Measurement and assessment in teaching* (7th ed.). Upper Saddle River, NJ: Merrill.

Livesley, W. J. (Ed.). (2001). *Handbook of personality disorders: Theory, research, and treatment.* New York: Guilford.

Loevinger, J. (1957). Objective tests as instruments of psychological theory [Monograph Supplement]. *Psychological Reports, 3,* 635–694.

Lowman, R. L. (1991). *The clinical practice of career assessment: Interests, abilities, and personality.* Washington, DC: American Psychological Association.

Lubinski, D., & Dawis, R. V. (1992). Aptitudes, skills, and proficiencies. In M. D. Dunnette & L. M. Hough (Eds.), *Handbook of industrial and organization psychology* (2nd ed., Vol. 3, pp. 1–59).

Maloney, M. P., & Ward, M. P. (1976). *Psychological assessment: A conceptual approach.* New York: Oxford University Press.

Marston, A. R. (1971). It is time to reconsider the Graduate Record Examination. *American Psychologist, 26,* 653–655.

Maruish, M. E. (Ed.). (2004). *The use of psychological testing for treatment planning and outcome assessment* (3rd ed., Vols. 1–3). Mahwah, NJ: Erlbaum.

Masling, J. (1960). The influence of situational and interpersonal variables in projective testing. *Psychological Bulletin, 57,* 65–85.

Mazor, K. M., Clauser, B. E., & Hambleton, R. K. (1992). The effect of sample size on the functioning of the Mantel-Haenszel statistic. *Educational and Psychological Measurement, 52,* 443–451.

McClelland, D. C. (1958). Methods of measuring human motivation. In J. W. Atkinson (Ed.). *Motives in fantasy, action, and society* (pp. 7–45). Princeton, NJ: Van Nostrand.

McReynolds, P. (1986). History of assessment in clinical and educational settings. In R. O. Nelson & S. C. Hayes (Eds.), *Conceptual foundations of behavioral assessment* (pp. 42–80). New York: Guilford.

Mead, A. D., & Drasgow, F. (1993). Equivalence of computerized and paper-and-pencil tests: A meta-analysis. *Psychological Bulletin, 114,* 449–458.

Meehl, P. E. (1956). Wanted: A good cookbook. *American Psychologist, 11,* 263–272.

Mehrens, W. A. (1992). Using performance assessment for accountability purposes. *Educational Measurement: Issues and Practice, 11,* 3–9, 20.

Merriam-Webster's collegiate dictionary (10th ed.). (1995). Springfield, MA: Merriam-Webster.

Messick, S. (1980). Test validity and the ethics of assessment. *American Psychologist, 35,* 1012–1027.

Messick, S. (1988). The once and future issues of validity: Assessing the meaning and consequences of measurement. In H. Wainer & H. Braun (Eds.), *Test validity* (pp. 33–45). Hillsdale, NJ: Erlbaum.

Messick, S. (1989). Validity. In R. L. Linn (Ed.), *Educational measurement* (3rd ed., pp. 13–103). New York: American Council on Education/Macmillan.

Messick, S. (1995). Validity of psychological assessment: Validation of inferences from persons' responses and performances as scientific inquiry into score meaning. *American Psychologist, 50,* 741–749.

Meyer, G. J. (1992). Response frequency problems in the Rorschach: Clinical and research implications with suggestions for the future. *Journal of Personality Assessment, 58,* 231–244.

Meyer, G. J., Finn, S. E., Eyde, L. D., Kay, G. G., Moreland, K. L., Dies, R. R., Eisman, E. J., Kubiszyn, T. W., & Reed, G. M. (2001). Psychological testing and psychological assessment: A review of evidence and issues. *American Psychologist, 56,* 128–165.

Millon, T., Millon, C., & Davis, R. (1994). *MCMI-III manual: Millon Clinical Multiaxial Inventory–III.* Minneapolis, MN: National Computer Systems.

Mitchell, R. (1992). *Testing for learning.* New York: Free Press/Macmillan.

Mittenberg, W., Theroux-Fichera, S., Zielinski, R., & Heilbronner, R. L. (1995). Identification of malingered head injury on the Wechsler Adult Intelligence Scale–Revised. *Professional Psychology: Research & Practice, 26,* 491–498.

Monahan, J., & Steadman, H. J. (2001). Violence risk assessment: A quarter century of research. In L. E. Frost & R. J. Bonnie (Eds.), *The evolution of mental health law* (pp. 195–211). Washington, DC: American Psychological Association.

Moreland, K. L. (1991). Assessment of validity in computer-based test interpretations. In T. B. Gutkin & S. L. Wise (Eds.), *The computer and the decision-making process* (pp. 43–74). Hillsdale, NJ: Erlbaum.

Morrison, T., & Morrison, M. (1995). A meta-analytic assessment of the predictive validity of the quantitative and verbal components of the Graduate Record Examination with graduate grade point average representing the criterion of graduate success. *Educational and Psychological Measurement, 55,* 309–316.

Moss, P. A. (1994). Can there be validity without reliability? *Educational Researcher, 23,* 5–12.

Murphy, K. R., Fleishman, E. A., & Cleveland, J. N. (Eds.). (2003). *Validity generalization: A critical review.* Mahwah, NJ: Erlbaum.

Murphy, L. L., Plake, B. S., Impara, J. C., & Spies, R. A. (Eds.). (2002). *Tests in print VI: An index to tests, test reviews, and the literature on specific tests.* Lincoln, NE: Buros Institute.

Murray, H. A. (1938). *Explorations in personality.* New York: Oxford University Press.

Naglieri, J. A., Drasgow, F., Schmit, M., Handler, L., Prifitera, A., Margolis, A., & Velasquez, R. (2004). Psychological testing on the Internet: New problems, old issues. *American Psychologist, 59,* 150–162.

National Academy of Neuropsychology. (1999, May 15). *Policy statement: Presence of third party observers during neuropsychological testing.* Retrieved August 3, 2003, from http://nanonline.org/content/text/paio/thirdparty.shtm

National Association of School Psychologists. (2000). *Professional conduct manual: Principles for professional ethics guidelines for the provision of school psychological services.* Retrieved August 27, 2003, from http://www.nasponline.org/pdf/ProfessionalCond.pdf

Neisser, U. (Ed.). (1998). *The rising curve: Long-term gains in IQ and related measures.* Washington, DC: American Psychological Association.

Nevo, B., & Jäger, R. S. (Eds.). (1993). *Educational and psychological testing: The test taker's outlook.* Toronto: Hogrefe & Huber.

Newman, E. (1996). *No more test anxiety: Effective steps for taking tests and achieving better grades.* Los Angeles: Learning Skills Publications.

O'Leary, B. J., & Norcross, J. C. (1998). Lifetime prevalence of mental disorders in the general population. In G. P. Koocher, J. C. Norcross, & S. S. Hill III (Eds.), *Psychologists' desk reference* (pp. 3–6). New York: Oxford University Press.

Onwuegbuzie, A. J., & Daniel, L. G. (2002). A framework for reporting and interpreting internal consistency reliability estimates. *Measurement and Evaluation in Counseling and Development, 35,* 89–103.

Ownby, R. L. (1997). *Psychological reports: A guide to report writing in professional psychology* (3rd ed.). New York: Wiley.

Petersen, N. S., Kolen, M. J., & Hoover, H. D. (1989). Scaling, norming, and equating. In R. L. Linn (Ed.), *Educational measurement* (3rd ed., pp. 221–262). New York: American Council on Education/Macmillan.

Popham, W. J., & Husek, T. R. (1969). Implications of criterion-referenced measurement. *Journal of Educational Measurement, 6,* 1–9.

Primi, R. (2002, August). *Contribution to the development of a fluid intelligence scale.* Poster session presented at the annual meeting of the American Psychological Association, Chicago, IL.

Primoff, E. S. (1959). Empirical validations of the J-coefficient. *Personnel Psychology, 12,* 413–418.

Primoff, E. S., & Eyde, L. D. (1988). Job element analysis. In S. Gael (Ed.), *The job analysis handbook for business, industry, and government* (Vol. 2, pp. 807–824). New York: Wiley.

Provence, S., Erikson, J., Vater, S., & Palmeri, S. (1995). *Infant-Toddler Developmental Assessment (IDA).* Itasca, IL: Riverside.

Psychological Corporation. (1997). *WAIS-III/WMS-III technical manual.* San Antonio, TX: Author.

Ramsay, M. C., & Reynolds, C. R. (2000). Development of a scientific test: A practical guide. In G. Goldstein & M. Hersen (Eds.), *Handbook of psychological assessment* (3rd ed., pp. 21–42). Oxford, UK: Elsevier.

Randhawa, B. S. (1992). Review of the Clerical Abilities Battery. *The Eleventh Mental Measurements Yearbook,* pp. 187–189.

Rasch, G. (1980). *Probabilistic models for some intelligence and attainment tests* (Expanded ed.). Chicago: University of Chicago Press. (Original work published 1960)

Raykov, T., & Marcoulides, G. A. (2000). *A first course in structural equation modeling.* Mahwah, NJ: Erlbaum.

Reise, S. P., & Henson, J. M. (2003). A discussion of modern versus traditional psychometrics as applied to personality assessment scales. *Journal of Personality Assessment, 81*, 93–103.

Robertson, G. J. (1992). Psychological tests: Development, publication, and distribution. In M. Zeidner & R. Most (Eds.), *Psychological testing: An inside view* (pp. 169–214). Palo Alto, CA: Consulting Psychologists Press.

Robinson, J. P., Shaver, P. R., & Wrightsman, L. S. (Eds.). (1991). *Measures of personality and social psychological attitudes*. San Diego, CA: Academic Press.

Rogers, R. (1997). *Clinical assessment of malingering and deception* (2nd ed.). New York: Guilford Press.

Rogers, T. B. (1995). *The psychological testing enterprise: An introduction*. Pacific Grove, CA: Brooks/Cole.

Rosenthal, R., & DiMatteo, M. R. (2001). Meta-analysis: Recent developments in quantitative methods for literature reviews. *Annual Review of Psychology, 52*, 59–82.

Rotter, J. B. (1966). Generalized expectancies for internal versus external control of reinforcement. *Psychological Monographs, 80* (1, Whole No. 609).

Rudner, L. M. (1994). Questions to ask when evaluating tests. *Practical Assessment, Research, & Evaluation, 4*(2). Retrieved August 9, 2003, from http://edresearch.org/pare/getvn.asp?v=4&n=2

Russell, D. W. (2002). In search of underlying dimensions: The use (and abuse) of factor analysis in *Personality and Social Psychology Bulletin. Personality and Social Psychology Bulletin, 28*, 1629–1646.

Sacks, P. (1999). *Standardized minds: The high price of America's testing culture and what we can do to change it*. Cambridge, MA: Perseus Books.

Sapp, M. (1999). *Test anxiety: Applied research, assessment, and treatment* (2nd ed.). Latham, MD: University Press of America.

Sandoval, J., Frisby, C. L., Geisinger, K. F., Scheuneman, J. D., & Grenier, J. R. (1998). *Test interpretation and diversity: Achieving equity in assessment*. Washington, DC: American Psychological Association.

Sarason, I. G. (Ed.). (1980). *Test anxiety: Theory, research, and applications*. Hillsdale, NJ: Erlbaum.

Sattler, J. M. (2001). *Assessment of children: Cognitive applications* (4th ed.). San Diego, CA: Author.

Sattler, J. M. (2002). *Assessment of children: Behavioral and clinical applications* (4th ed.). San Diego, CA: Author.

Sawilowsky, S. S. (2003). Reliability: Rejoinder to Thompson and Vacha-Haase. In B. Thompson (Ed.), *Score reliability: Contemporary thinking on reliability issues* (pp. 149–154). Thousand Oaks, CA: Sage.

Schaie, K. W. (1994). The course of adult intellectual development. *American Psychologist, 49*, 304–313.

Schmidt, F. L., & Hunter, J. E. (1977). Development of a general solution to the problem of validity generalization. *Journal of Applied Psychology, 62*, 529–540.

Schmidt, F. L., & Hunter, J. E. (1998). The validity and utility of selection methods in personnel psychology: Practical and theoretical implications of 85 years of research findings. *Psychological Bulletin, 124*, 262–274.

Schmidt, F. L., Hunter, J. E., McKenzie, R. C., & Muldrow, T. W. (1979). Impact of valid selection procedures on work-force productivity. *Journal of Applied Psychology, 64*, 609–626.

Schmidt, F. L., Law, K., Hunter, J. E., Rothstein, H. R., Pearlman, K., & McDaniel, M. (1993). Refinements in validity generalization methods: Implications for the situational specificity hypothesis. *Journal of Applied Psychology, 78*, 3–12.

Scruggs, T. E., & Mastropieri, M. A. (1992). *Teaching test-taking skills: Helping students show what they know*. Cambridge, MA: Brookline Books.

Shavelson, R. J., & Webb, N. M. (1991). *Generalizability theory: A primer*. Newbury Park, CA: Sage.

Shermis, M. D., & Burstein, J. (Eds.). (2003). *Automated essay scoring: A cross-disciplinary perspective*. Mahwah, NJ: Erlbaum.

Silverlake, A. C. (1999). *Comprehending test manuals: A guide and workbook.* Los Angeles: Pyrczak.

Smith, C. P. (1992). Reliability issues. In C. P. Smith (Ed.) et al., *Motivation and personality: Handbook of thematic content analysis* (pp. 126–139). New York: Cambridge University Press.

Society for Industrial and Organizational Psychology. (2003). *Principles for the validation and use of personnel selection procedures* (4th ed.). Retrieved November 14, 2003, from http://www.siop.org/_Principles/principles.pdf

Spearman, C. (1904a). "General intelligence," objectively determined and measured. *American Journal of Psychology, 15,* 201–293.

Spearman, C. (1904b). The proof and measurement of association between two things. *American Journal of Psychology, 15,* 72–101.

Spence, J. T. (1993). Gender-related traits and gender ideology evidence for a multifactorial theory. *Journal of Personality and Social Psychology, 64,* 624–635.

Spence, J. T., & Helmreich, R. L. (1972). The Attitudes Toward Women Scale: An objective instrument to measure attitudes toward the rights and roles of women in contemporary society. *JSAS Catalog of Selected Documents in Psychology, 2,* 66–67.

Spielberger, C. D., & Vagg, P. R. (Eds.). (1995). *Test anxiety: Theory, assessment, and treatment.* Washington, DC: Taylor & Francis.

Steele, C. M. (1997). A threat in thin air: How stereotypes shape intellectual identity and performance. *American Psychologist, 52,* 613–629.

Sternberg, R. J. (1986). *Intelligence applied: Understanding and increasing your intellectual skills.* San Diego, CA: Harcourt Brace Jovanovich.

Sternberg, R. J., & Williams, W. M. (1997). Does the Graduate Record Examination predict meaningful success in the graduate training of psychologists? A case study. *American Psychologist, 52,* 630–641.

Stevens, S. S. (1946). On the theory of scales of measurement. *Science, 103,* 677–680.

Stokes, G. S., Mumford, M. D., & Owens, W. A. (Eds.). (1994). *Biodata handbook: Theory, research, and use of biographical information for selection and performance prediction.* Palo Alto, CA: Consulting Psychologists Press.

Swets, J. A., Dawes, R. M., & Monahan, J. (2000). Psychological science can improve diagnostic decisions. *Psychological Science in the Public Interest, 1,* 1–26.

Tallent, N. (1993). *Psychological report writing* (4th ed.). Englewood Cliffs, NJ: Prentice Hall.

Taylor, H. C., & Russell, J. T. (1939). The relationship of validity coefficients to the practical effectiveness of tests in selection. Discussion and tables. *Journal of Applied Psychology, 23,* 565–578.

Tenopyr, M. L. (1986). Needed directions for measurement in work settings. In B. S. Plake & J. C. Witt (Eds.), *The future of testing* (pp. 269–288). Hillsdale, NJ: Erlbaum.

Terrill, D. R., Friedman, D. G., Gottschalk, L. A., & Haaga, D. A. (2002). Construct validity of the Life Orientation Test. *Journal of Personality Assessment, 79,* 550–563.

Test security: Protecting the integrity of tests. (1999). *American Psychologist, 54,* 1078.

Thissen, D., & Wainer, H. (Eds.). (2001). *Test scoring.* Mahwah, NJ: Erlbaum.

Thompson, B. (2002). What future quantitative social science research could look like: Confidence intervals for effect sizes. *Educational Researcher, 31,* 25–32.

Thompson, B. (2003a). A brief introduction to generalizability theory. In B. Thompson (Ed.), *Score reliability: Contemporary thinking on reliability issues* (pp. 43–58). Thousand Oaks, CA: Sage.

Thompson, B. (Ed.). (2003b). *Score reliability: Contemporary thinking on reliability issues.* Thousand Oaks, CA: Sage.

Thurstone, L. L. (1925). A method of scaling psychological and educational tests. *Journal of Educational Psychology, 16,* 433–451.

Turner, S. M., DeMers, S. T., Fox, H. R., & Reed, G. M. (2001). APA's guidelines for test user qualifications: An executive summary. *American Psychologist, 56,* 1099–1113.

U.S. Department of Education, Office for Civil Rights. (2000). *The use of tests as part of high-stakes decision-making for students: A resource guide for educators and policy-makers.* Washington, DC: Author. Retrieved April 5, 2001 from http://www.ed.gov/offices/OCR/testing/index1.html

Urbina, S., & Ringby, K. C. (2001, August). *Sex differences in mechanical aptitude.* Poster session presented at the annual meeting of the American Psychological Association, San Francisco, CA.

Urdan, T. C. (2001). *Statistics in plain English.* Mahwah, NJ: Erlbaum.

Uzgiris, I. C., & Hunt, J. McV. (1975). *Assessment in infancy: Ordinal Scales of Psychological Development.* Urbana, IL: University of Illinois Press.

Viglione, D. J., & Rivera, B. (2003). Assessing personality and psychopathology with projective methods. In I. B. Weiner (Series Ed.). & J. R. Graham & J. A. Naglieri (Vol. Eds.), *Handbook of psychology: Vol. 10. Assessment psychology* (pp. 531–552). Hoboken, NJ: Wiley.

Vogt, W. P. (1998). *Dictionary of statistics and methodology: A nontechnical guide for the social sciences* (2nd ed.). Thousand Oaks, CA: Sage.

von Mayrhauser, R. T. (1992). The mental testing community and validity: A prehistory. *American Psychologist, 47,* 244–253.

Wainer, H. (2000). CATs: Whither and whence. *Psicologica, 21,* 121–133.

Wainer, H. (with Dorans, N. J., Eignor, D., Flaugher, R., Green, B. F., Mislevy, R. J., Steinberg, L., & Thissen, D.). (2000). *Computer adaptive testing: A primer* (2nd ed.). Mahwah, NJ: Erlbaum.

Wallace, S. R. (1965). Criteria for what? *American Psychologist, 20,* 411–417.

Wechsler, D. (1939). *Wechsler-Bellevue Intelligence Scale.* New York: The Psychological Corporation.

Wechsler, D. (1949). *Wechsler Intelligence Scale for Children (WISC): Manual.* New York: The Psychological Corporation.

Wechsler, D. (1991). *Wechsler Intelligence Scale for Children–Third Edition (WISC-III): Manual.* San Antonio, TX: The Psychological Corporation.

Wechsler, D. (1997). *Wechsler Adult Intelligence Scale–Third Edition (WAIS-III): Administration and scoring manual.* San Antonio, TX: The Psychological Corporation.

Whitaker, L. (1980). *Objective measurement of schizophrenic thinking: A practical and theoretical guide to the Whitaker Index of Schizophrenic Thinking.* Los Angeles: Western Psychological Services.

Wigdor, A. K., & Green, B. F., Jr. (1991). (Eds.), *Performance assessment for the workplace: Vol. 2. Technical issues.* Washington, DC: National Academy Press.

Wiggins, J. S., & Pincus, A. L. (1992). Personality: Structure and assessment. *Annual Review of Psychology, 43,* 493–504.

Wilkinson, L., & APA Task Force on Statistical Inference. (1999). Statistical methods in psychology journals: Guidelines and explanations. *American Psychologist, 54,* 594–604.

Willingham, W. W., Pollack, J. M., & Lewis, C. (2000). *Grades and test scores: Accounting for observed differences* (ETS RR-00-15). Princeton, NJ: Educational Testing Service.

Young, J. W. (2001). *Differential validity, differential prediction, and college admission testing: A comprehensive review.* (College Board Research Report No. 2001-6). New York: College Entrance Examination Board.

Zeidner, M. (1998). *Test anxiety: The state of the art.* New York: Plenum.

Ziskin, J. (1995). *Coping with psychiatric and psychological testimony* (5th ed., Vols. 1–3). Los Angeles: Law and Psychology Press.

Zwick, R. (2002). *Fair game? The use of standardized admissions tests in higher education.* New York: Routledge Falmer.

Index

Acknowledgments

The author is indebted to Dr. Joan Hill and Dr. Ping Sa, for proofreading and commenting on the manuscript, and to Dr. Bill Wilson for his help in developing the table in Appendix C. Special thanks are due to David Wilson of the Center for Instruction and Research Technology of the University of North Florida for preparing most of the figures in this work and to Tracey Belmont of John Wiley & Sons for her support in every phase of this work.

About the Author

Susana Urbina earned her doctorate in psychometrics from Fordham University and completed a postdoctoral fellowship in clinical neuropsychology at the University of Nebraska Medical Center. She is professor of psychology at the University of North Florida, where she has taught courses in psychological testing and psychological assessment, among others, since 1976. Dr. Urbina is a licensed psychologist in the state of Florida and practiced psychological assessment for over a decade. She is coauthor of the seventh edition of *Psychological Testing* with Anne Anastasi and author of the study guides that accompany the sixth and seventh editions of that text. In addition, Dr. Urbina has published numerous articles and reviews in the area of psychological testing, has conducted test validation research, and has consulted with test publishers on various test development and standardization projects. She is a fellow of Division 5 (Evaluation, Measurement, and Statistics) of the American Psychological Association (APA) and has chaired the Committee on Psychological Tests and Assessment and the Committee on Professional Practice and Standards of the APA. Her current interests center on the history of psychology, as well as testing and assessment theory and practice.

CPSIA information can be obtained at www.ICGtesting.com
Printed in the USA
BVOW00n0842230713

326645BV00003B/3/P